D0912892

Zellig Harris

Zellig Harris

From American Linguistics to Socialist Zionism

Robert F. Barsky

The MIT Press
Cambridge, Massachusetts
London, England

For information about special quantity discounts, please e-mail special_sales@mitpress .mit.edu

This book was set in Stone Sans and Stone Serif by Toppan Best-set Premedia Limited. Printed and bound in the United States of America.

Library of Congress Cataloging-in-Publication Data

Barsky, Robert F.
Zellig Harris : from American linguistics to socialist Zionism / Robert F. Barsky.
      p.   cm.
Includes bibliographical references and index.
ISBN 978-0-262-01526-4 (alk. paper)
1. Harris, Zellig S. (Zellig Sabbettai), 1909–1992. 2. Linguistics. 3. Language and languages—Political aspects. I. Title.

P85.H344B34   2011
410.92—dc22
[B]
                                                              2010030889

10 9 8 7 6 5 4 3 2 1

I dedicate this book to the many, many people who have spoken with me about Zellig Harris over the past fifteen years—in particular Noam Chomsky, Murray Eden, Nathan Glazer, John Goldsmith, Seymour Melman, Irene Schumer, and William Schumer—harbingers and sages

Contents

Thanks for your paper and review. I have just read them hastily, and will soon go over it point by point. Let me assure you that not only do I not consider it "unpleasant" but am glad of the controversy. No person, certainly not I, can be sure of his judgments as "always right"; the best way to get closer to the "truth"—after I have figured out whatever I could—is to get the divergent opinions which arise from a different scientific analysis. The only fun in science is finding out what was actually there.

—Zellig Harris to Albert Goetze, December 27, 1940

I get my main interest or pleasure out of consuming—in my case it's specialized not into food but into subject-matter and information. It is quite important for me to find out what gives—whether with linguistics, or with human language, or with politics, or with physics.

—Zellig Harris to Bernard Bloch, August 20, 1949

Preface

Fifteen years ago, I met with Noam Chomsky to discuss my interest in the early "milieus" that had contributed to his approach to both his language work and his politics, and that were to be the focus of my biographical study of him, which was eventually published in 1997 as *Noam Chomsky: A Life of Dissent*. Among the first things he suggested was that I turn my attention instead to Zellig Harris, someone who he (modestly) described as more interesting than himself. I pursued my work on Chomsky, but given my interest in the Chomsky-Harris milieus I also followed his suggestion, and it has turned out to be the most challenging project I've ever undertaken.

Harris and his approach have been elusive, complex—often opaque—in part because he himself was private, and in part because the work that he undertook comprised a whole other corpus that both overlapped but also differed significantly from that with which I've grown familiar through my work on Chomsky. Nevertheless, the enormous assistance I've received from Harris's friends, colleagues, and students has made this project rewarding, and I hope that I can make clear to a broad and diverse audience why Chomsky made this suggestion to me all those years ago. It's worth the effort.

I begin this book with a description of Zellig Harris himself, in the hope of providing some insight into his personality and the attitude he brought to his life's works. Given that he worked and circulated in quite different realms, sometimes simultaneously, there are competing interpretations of his actions and his legacy; but rather than trying to resolve these differences, I will present them in as much detail as possible, and allow the dialectical and dialogical processes to work their own magic. I am relying here on as much textual material as exists in the dozens of archives and personal collections I have consulted around the world. But given the dearth of personal materials like letters or early biographies, I have incorporated as well personal reflections from Harris's colleagues and friends, all recent, and therefore coming decades after the facts described. In order to validate some of the statements recorded here, I have asked the same questions of different interviewees, and I have tried to confirm statements with different people who knew him over the years. The result, I hope, is a sense of his overall approach and attitude, which is what I have found most compelling. I might also add that although I have met several of Harris's family members (including his brother, his sister-in-law, and his nephew), as well as many of his colleagues, friends, and students, I never met him in person, coming as I did to this work a few years after his death. I hope that the reminiscences of people who knew him intimately will nonetheless allow for a sense of Zellig Harris, the man.

When I move on to discussions of his work in linguistics in the second part, and his politics in the third part, some of this personal material will be recalled, but I make more direct reference to textual materials, including grant applications and correspondence between Harris and different individuals in his milieus. There are reasonably bountiful sources for the language and information studies, including Harris's own publications and the edited collection by Bruce Nevin,[1] so I focus on complementary work to that which is in the public record, including personal commentary from colleagues and information provided in declassified NSF grant applications. I should also add that most of the actual linguistic or scientific work Harris undertook was directed toward specialists, and they have sufficient sources to find the information required in the professional journals and monographs that make up their field. In the third chapter, I focus on crucial documents relating to his Zionism, his ideas about worker participation, and the general political attitudes reflected in the Frame of Reference (FoR) project, including both details and reactions to the posthumously published book on the transformation of capitalist society.

I have written this book for a general audience, and especially for people interested in the lives and works of universalist figures who have contributed directly and indirectly to both the sciences and the politics of the twentieth century. There have been ample studies, including biographical works, about people like Franz Boas, Louis Brandeis, Noam Chomsky, Albert Einstein, Eric Fromm, or Edmund Sapir, who each interacted with Zellig Harris's milieu, but to date Harris himself has remained in the background. Vitally aware of this lacuna, several of his friends, colleagues, family members, and students have generously urged me to complete this work, and I'm indebted to each of them. Regrettably, not all of those who have been critical interlocutors for me are still with us; but as the ink dries on this text, exactly 100 years after Harris's birth, I am grateful to have met so many amazing individuals, most in the autumn of their lives.

Because of overlapping interests and relationships, some of those cited in this book have been part of the milieus surrounding both Noam Chomsky and Zellig Harris. I would like to think that working on these projects, often simultaneously, has been valuable to both, because the nuances between their respective outlooks casts light on these remarkable individuals as well as on those who worked and befriended them along the way. Given the important differences between Harris and Chomsky, however, I have also suffered long periods of incomprehension, and I am deeply appreciative for reviews, sometimes scathing, of early drafts. With Chomsky, it has already taken me two books and many articles to cover the material I find most compelling, in part because I came to be fascinated by his relation to the milieus that inform his work, and to the impact he has had upon a huge number of interested communities. It will probably take me two books for me to document the elements of Harris's life and work that I find most compelling, if only because there has not to date been a full-length study of Avukah, the student Zionist organization with which Harris had significant involvement. In order to fill this void, I will be returning to the archive of Avukah material I've gathered over two decades to write a complete history of Avukah, over and above Harris's specific involvement therein.

Jewish Intellectuals and Semitic Studies

Many people who appear in this text are "Jewish intellectuals" of one sort or another, and most had strong views about Zionism, which means that this book is necessarily more than just an effort to revive a critical figure from Jewish America. As international pressure for a peaceful means of coexistence between Palestinians and Jews mounts in Israel and the occupied territories, there are important questions about what "peace in the Middle East" might look like. I'm not going to pretend that this historical overview of particular strains of Zionism offers clear-cut proposals, but I will recall avenues of debate that were ostensibly shut down in 1948, including a dream of establishing a (socialist) region in Palestine that would be a haven for not only persecuted Jews, but disenfranchised Arabs, stateless Palestinians, and other peoples who are in search of a sanctuary against oppression. This dream of a free and eventually expanding region in Palestine has been discussed over the years in a range of forums, including

Theodor Herzl's utopian novel *Alteneuland*, which describes aspects of Zellig Harris's own view quite succinctly:

Herzl insisted throughout the novel that the Old-New Land would rid itself of what he considered the worst invention of the nineteenth century, the fetish of nation-statehood: Zionism would not be realized through the establishment of a state but through the creation of a commonwealth, which Herzl defined as 'a large co-operative association composed of affili-ated co-operatives' with no true executive, a minimal legislature, no formal judiciary, no trappings whatsoever of a modern nation-state.[2]

Ideas of this nature come up in an array of curiously-neglected archival documents, and in some surprisingly unknown texts, to which I will refer in this book. The Harris milieu's interest in forming a vanguard of people whose mission would be to advocate socialist Zionism, cooperative Arab-Jewish relations, and a coherent worldview relating to such issues as worker/owner relations, may be one of the greatest political legacies of this remarkable group.

Accessing Information

Any sustained research project, especially one which touches on areas such as self-governed production, language studies, physics, Zionism, and the transformation of capitalist society, is bound to involve some intriguing anecdotes from the author concerning the amassing of information. On the personal side, I found it fascinating and challenging to undertake research on early and contemporary milieus surrounding both Noam Chomsky and Zellig Harris. In that spectrum, ostensibly from one generation to its prec-edent, considerable differences, and surprising similarities, emerge. Such discoveries help alleviate the dreams, fantasies, projections, assimilations and elisions which naturally emerge when working on the life and work of living influences. They also force us to confront ourselves, our own pasts, our own influences, our own intellectual development. This has happened to me in a range of ways, some coincidental, some forced, in part because my father's family came from Pavoloch, in the Ukraine. Pavoloch is in the region from which so many American Jews, including Harris and Chomsky, can trace their lineage (but not current ties; all of the Jews who remained in Pavoloch during the Nazi occupation in World War II were murdered).

I have come to be especially interested in how these Jewish families integrated into the United States (and Canada), while at the same time articulating their own resistance to some of the politics of their adopted homeland, and I've done so by traveling (by motorcycle!) to meet in person with many individuals mentioned in this book. Motorcycling across the United States in search of voices from my elders has helped me reconstitute past conceptions of appropriate approaches, and given me the sense that things could have been done quite differently; but observing up-close the urban sprawl, the infinite repetition of corporate outposts, the dilapidated environment and a decaying infrastructure has made me aware that although there's much to learn from the past, there's also a considerable distance traveled since the articulation of Harris's approach, to both language studies and politics. So although it's tempting to consider that all the answers are back in some forgotten past somewhere, it's also important to consider what kinds of challenges and possibilities haven't been grasped or anticipated by earlier generations.

I also have a range of anecdotes relating to the collection of information for this project. I suspected early on, partly on account of the funding agencies interested in research undertaken by linguists in the period during which Zellig Harris worked, and partly because of the radical nature of his political beliefs, that various US agencies would have interesting files dealing with Zellig Harris and his milieu. After years of efforts, it is has become obvious that this was true, but I must rely upon indirect evidence, such as Franz Boas's FBI file, to make the case. Even despite the sometimes considerable powers accorded to researchers under the Freedom of Information Act, some of the agencies I've contacted have turned-out to be less-than-forthcoming. In a letter from the CIA, for example, in which I requested whatever type of information that agency may have collected regarding Zellig Harris, I learned the following:

To the extent that your request seeks records that would reveal a covert connection between the CIA and the subject of your request, I must inform you that the CIA can neither confirm nor deny any confidential or covert relationship, or interest in developing such a relationship, with any particular individual, organization, or other entity. Records disclosing this type of information necessarily would be classified pursuant to Executive Order 12958. Further, the fact of the existence or nonexistence of such records would relate directly to information concerning intelligence sources and methods which, in accordance with Subsection 103c(5) of the National Security Act of 1947 and Section 6 of the CIA Act of 1949, the Director of Central Intelligence has the legal responsibility and obligation to protect from unauthorized disclosure. Therefore, to the extent your request might concern records containing such information, it is denied pursuant to FOIA exemptions (b) (1) and (b) (3). . . . By this action we are neither confirming nor denying that any such information exists.

I never did confirm (or deny) the existence of those files, but I do thank other agencies, notably the National Science Foundation, for doggedly pursuing files containing Harris's applications for funding; they have been most helpful.

The range of other organizations, and of the many persons who assisted in all sorts of ways over two decades is considerable, but rather than explaining each contribution, I'll restrict myself however to a thank you, and a mention of each name: Sam Abramovitch, Sumner Alpert, Stephen Anderson, Marc Angenot, Karl Brussel, Jill Brussel, Chelsea Davis, Zev Davis, Murray Eden, Norman Epstein, William Evan, Alice Gionetti, Lila Gleitman, Arthur Goren, John Goldsmith, Andrea V. Grimes, Jennifer Halliday, David Heap, Henry Hiz, Henry Hoenigswald, Michael Holquist, Seth Jerchower, Martin Jay, George Jochnowitz, Arthur Kiron, Richard Kittredge, Konrad Koerner, Ted Live, Irving London, Carlos Otero, Mark Pavlick, Michel Pierssens, Larry Portis, Martin Rapisarda, Daniel Ridge, Philip Rubin, Nicolas Ruwet, Willie Segal, Tiphaine Samoyault, Elise Snyder, Peter Steiner, Elmer Sweck, George Szanto, Jeff Tennant, Clive Thomson, Lisa Travis, Tyler Tokaryk, and Peter Tseng.

I'd also like to thank Maurice Herman of the Kibbutz Hazorea; the University of Pennsylvania, notably many members of the library staff as well as Lillian Gleitman, Henry Hoenigswald, Anthony Kroch, and Leigh Lisker; Columbia University, notably various reference librarians; the University of Western Ontario, notably Bill Bridger, Patrick Deane, Jim Good, Doug Kneale, Kathleen Okruhlik; Yale University, especially Peter Brooks, Michael Holquist, Gustav Ranis, Nancy Ruther and Elise Snyder, and, for funding, the Social Sciences and Humanities Research Council, the University of Western Ontario, the University of Quebec in Montreal, and, especially, Vanderbilt University. Vanderbilt has provided me with summer research assistance, material support and a major research grant to consult a host of people who are mentioned in this book, notably Sam Abramovitch, Noam Chomsky, Murray Eden, Norman Epstein, Nathan Glazer, Tami Harris, Tzvee Harris, Shoshanna Harris, Alfred Kahn, Lillian Kaplan, Harold Katz, Millie Katz, Ted Live, Seymour Melman, Howard Orlans, Elana & Meyer Rabban, Chava Rapkin, Irene and Zev Schumer, and Judith & Robert Wallerstein. I'd like to especially thank Carolyn Dever, Dennis Hall, Richard McCarty, Lynn Ramey, Elizabeth Shadbolt, and Nicholas Zeppos, of Vanderbilt University, for their continued support. This book would not exist were it not for the kindness and generosity of these people.

I have benefited enormously from assistance rendered by librarians in central collections, archives and rare book rooms at Berkeley, Brandeis, Columbia, the Hebrew Union College, McGill, MIT, Penn, Princeton, Stanford, UCLA, the University of Jerusalem, Yale, in addition to individuals at The Institute of Social History (Amsterdam), The American Philosophical Society Library in Philadelphia, The Jacob Rader Marcus Center of the American Jewish Archives Cincinnati Campus, Hebrew Union College, The San Francisco Public Library, The Jewish National and University Library in Jerusalem, The Albert Einstein Archives at the Hebrew University of Jerusalem and at Princeton University, as well as representatives from the Guggenheim Foundation, National Archives in Maryland, the National Science Foundation, the Jewish Historical Society, and the New York Public Library.

I owe special debts of gratitude to the Massachusetts Institute of Technology and especially the MIT Press, notably Amy Brand, who supported this project from its inception and Tom Stone, my former editor. I'd like to especially thank the inspiring Editorial Director, Gita Manaktala, who has worked with me on all three of my MIT Press books and, of course, my incredibly wise current editor, Philip Laughlin. Sandra H. Minkkinen has shepherded each of my MIT Press books through the editorial and production processes, and I've learned an enormous amount from her exceptional attention to both the details and the broader issues of these works.

Finally, thank you Marsha, for bringing magic to meaning, and, to my awesome sons, Ben and Tristan, and my stepson Kai, you all bring meaning to magic.

I The Man

1 Origins

Zellig Harris, born in Ukraine October 23, 1909, died in his sleep May 22, 1992, after a full day of work. Although he spent most of his life in the United States, his Jewish-Ukrainian origins played a key role in determining the type of work he undertook in his lifetime and the attitudes he brought to each of the many domains to which he eventually contributed. Harris was also very much an American, in that he both defined and followed values and approaches typical of certain American Jewish milieus, themselves best understood by a brief look back to the worlds from which they came.

Harris's family came to the United States when he was four years old, and he was naturalized in 1921, at the age of 12. He was one of the multitude of Jews who came to America from 1880 to 1929 and, like his younger brother Tzvi [or Tzvee], he became a leading American light, a central figure in a distinctly American school of academic research. It is fascinating to follow the narrative of how a boy like Zellig Harris, who grew up in a Jewish family from a small Ukrainian town, could become such a universalist figure with cosmopolitan, internationalist, and in many ways distinctly American values. This is owing to his family background, to the scholarly influences of the Jewish tradition within which he was raised, and also to an allegiance to the "scientific method" that was so celebrated in certain intellectual circles at that time. Thomas A. Ryckman, a historian of science, recalls that Zellig Harris did not consider himself a linguist but instead preferred to think of himself as a "methodologist,"[1] as though there were universal human values at stake, values that could only be understood with impartiality, rigor, and rationality. Zellig Harris was an original thinker who came to define, rather than follow, a version of what it meant to be a Jewish intellectual in America.

Sitting in a Corner in the Middle of the Room

Why should we be concerned about Zellig Harris? Because he exerted considerable influence upon crucial intellectual currents of the twentieth century and along the way came into contact with some of the leading intellectual figures of the Western world, most notably Louis D. Brandeis, Noam Chomsky, and Albert Einstein, while fostering a kind of inner circle of acolytes, friends, colleagues, and fellow travelers who have each contributed significantly to an array of fields and projects. And yet, strangely, he is little known, even among knowledgeable intellectuals in the fields to which he contributed, which inclines me to describe him in terms of the Israeli literary critic Dov Sadan's image of a person "sitting in a corner in the middle of the room." There is one well-known Zelig (a variation on the name Zellig), the scribe with chameleon-like tendencies who is featured in Woody Allen's film by the same name, but links between them, although provocative, are faint. Nonetheless, it is the case that most people did know him "in segments," as Eva (Chava) Rapkin (née Samuel), suggested to me in interviews in 2009 and 2010, the consequence of his not being a "fully rounded person," someone who "did not relate to people well at all." As such, she suggests, his identity was "fragmented," and therefore, "different people saw very different aspects of him." Rapkin, the daughter of Maurice Samuel (1895–1972), the renowned writer, translator, and lecturer, was married to Chester Rapkin (1919–2001), the influential theorist of urban planning, who she met through her affiliation with Avukah. Meyer Rabban, renowned psychologist and professor of child development, who also met his wife of sixty years, Elana Rabban, through involvement in Zionist organizations, suggested in an interview in 2009 that Harris did not necessarily manifest fragmented personalities, but he was an iconoclast, a polyglot, an expert in many fields, which may have fostered the impression that he dwelled in, and mastered, distinct realms. For Elana Rabban, who had been a member of Hashomer Hatzair, this made him quite difficult to be around: "There are people like him who are very brilliant, very interesting fellows, but they can be arrogant know it alls." Harris, in her opinion, was like this, both in terms of range and diversity of knowledge, but also in his presentation of this knowledge to others.

Some of these characteristics contributed to an aura, a sense of his being considered apart from others, even by his colleagues and friends. Even the name, Zellig, is unusual, a variant form of the Yiddish *selig*, from the German and Old English, meaning blessed, or holy. Each letter in the Jewish alphabet has special meanings, with Zellig—comprised of zayin,

ayin, lamed, yud, and gimel—signifying (zayin) sword, to ornament, to sustain, (ayin), eye or fountain, (lamed), to learn and to teach, (yud), emanation, the highest level in the Four World paradigm of Kabala, and (gimel) associated with loving kindness. W. C. Watt, who had been a student of Harris, adds to our understanding of the symbolism of Zellig Harris's name when he recalls in *Biographical Memoirs* 87 that Harris's middle name, Sabbatai, "set beside his brother's first name, 'Tzvee,' appears to identify the family as followers of Sabbatai Tzvee or Tsvee (1626–676), the 'False Messiah of the Caucasus'" (201). It is interesting to note that Tzvi himself was responsible for changing the spelling of his given name to the less common Tzvee to prevent mispronunciation. And finally the family name Harris, a somewhat common name even among Russian Jews, appears to be the Americanized form of a like-sounding Jewish name.

Ted Live, Harris's nephew, notes that "I have never been able to find out what Harris was, since Russian doesn't even have an 'h'. I never thought of asking anyone in my younger years what the real name was back in Russia. There is a lot of denial about things like that in the family. Even my own name, Live, should have been Suckaberg, because that was my father's name in Europe. When they came to the States they changed it to Live, and nobody else in the family knew this. I only found out when I was going through some of my father's papers after he died. I imagine that Live was more of an American name, without knowing anything else about it."

Part of Harris's legacy, including the Harris family aura, can therefore be traced to this interesting symbolic combination of meanings, but the concrete basis for it is to be found in his broad ambitions and accomplishments. He worked to revolutionize language studies, and, partly through his relationship with the renowned mathematician Bruria Kaufman, who was one of Einstein's principle assistants when he worked at Princeton, he came to be rather close to the physicist (and occasional social thinker) Albert Einstein. On the political front, he worked to update earlier versions of scientific socialism through careful study of industrial society, a passion he shared with the likes of Paul Mattick and the astronomer and social thinker Anton Pannekoek,[2] and which inspired students and colleagues, most notably Seymour Melman. And his work on Zionism, reflected in particular by his contributions to the Jewish Zionist student organization Avukah, retain a currency even today by the ambition and prescience of his approach.

Benjamin Harshov in *Language in Time of Revolution* describes the relationship between Jewish origins and the work undertaken by individuals, which is revealing for work on Zellig Harris. "For every individual, whether he was aware and proud of his Jewish origin . . . or whether he tried to deny it and ignore it . . . set out to be a secular, ethnically neutral, physicist in the general physical sciences, linguist, filmmaker, revolutionary, German or American writer, and so on, as an individual. Such Jews set out to adapt to the rules of the general cultural domain they embraced, whether it was science, modern fiction, or painting" (43). Harris, whose links to Judaism were through Jewish cultural affairs, Zionism, and his early studies of Semitic languages, had a complex relation to his "people," because most links were defined in terms of history rather than religion, but it is certainly the case that he followed Harshov's formula and gained recognition independent of his family's religion or origin. Nevertheless, the background, including the origins of his family, help us situate the work that Harris eventually undertook.

Zellig Harris's Balta Homeland

Zellig Harris was born in Balta, Odesskaya (Odessa oblast), Ukraine, 200 kilometers northwest of Odessa and 107 kilometers from Uman on the Kodyma River.[3] In the sixteenth century, Balta was part of the Kingdom of Poland, and from the beginning of the eighteenth century it became part of the Ottoman Empire. In 1791 it was annexed by Russia, possibly explaining why most Jews from this region describe themselves as Russian, even today. From 1924 until 1929, it was the capital of the Moldavian autonomous Soviet Socialist Republic within Ukraine, and it remained throughout the twentieth century the chief city of the district of the Odessa province. The earliest known Jewish community in Balta dates back to the beginning of the eighteenth century, and its Jewish inhabitants suffered persecution there beginning with attacks by Haidamacks (Russian brigand banks) from 1768 to 1782. A pattern of recurring violence prevailed throughout Ukraine; in Odessa, for example, pogroms occurred in 1821, 1859, 1871, 1881, 1882, and 1900, and there were critical upheavals in 1891–1892, 1903–1905, 1917, 1919, and 1933, leading up to the Second World War. Balta was significantly less important than Odessa, but it nevertheless saw its share of anti-Jewish violence, particularly with its growth as a commercial center subsequent to the construction of the Odessa-Kiev railroad in 1866.

Life for the roughly 9,000 Jews who lived in Balta at the time of the construction of the railroad was bearable, relatively speaking, with employment possibilities in wholesale and retail grain dealing, the processing of agricultural products, the production of tobacco and soap, tanning, flour milling, and liquor distilling. Things changed dramatically in 1881, however, when a pogrom led to the killing of forty Jews, the rape of several hundred women, the wounding of several hundred people, and the pillaging of over 1,200 Jewish houses and shops.

The year 1881 marks a turning point in the history of the Jews as decisive as that of 70 A.D., when Titus's legion burned the Temple at Jerusalem, or 1492, when Ferdinand and Isabella decreed the expulsion from Spain. On March 1, 1881, Alexander II, Czar of Russia, was assassinated by revolutionary terrorists; the modest liberalism of his regime came to an end; and within several weeks a wave of pogroms, inspired mostly by agents of the new government, spread across Russia. For the Jews packed into the Pale and overflowing its boundaries, the accession of Alexander III signified not only immediate disaster but also the need for a gradual reordering of both their inner life and their relationship to a country in which Jews had been living for hundreds of years. The question had now to be asked: should the east European Jews continue to regard themselves as permanent residents of the Russian empire or should they seriously consider the possibility of a new exodus?[4]

That same year Jews organized self-defense groups that were eventually suppressed by the police but nevertheless influenced later Zionist movements; indeed, the mindset of self-dependence and resisting state authority may explain why so many left-wing Jews in Zellig Harris's milieu remained nonaligned, despite pressures from the various "isms" and parties that sought to recruit them. An interesting example of this is provided by the American political sociologist Seymour Martin Lipset (1922–2006) in his academic memoir:[5]

My parents were both born in Czarist Russia in Minsk and Pinsk. My mother, Lena, came to America as a young child in 1907. Her parents, who died before I was born, in the 1918 flu epidemic, were religious Jews. She was a seamstress before she married, and she kept a kosher home afterwards. My father, Max, arrived as a young adult in 1911. He had apprenticed as a printer (compositor) in Russia. Shortly before he died in 1945, he told me of his experiences in Russia. The most noteworthy related to his membership in the printers' union in Kiev. Since the Russian printers, while supporting the Social Democratic party, refused to ally themselves with the Bolsheviks or Mensheviks, major leaders of both factions spent time at union meetings to win support. (112)

The harsh conditions of the region coupled with the increase in violence in this period produced an uptick of Jewish emigration; Chimen Abramsky, a Jewish Studies professor, commenting on Jonathan Frankel's *Prophecy and Politics: Socialism, Nationalism and the Russian Jews 1862–1917*,[6] described this period as "a watershed in Jewish life. Millions of Jews left for America,

Britain, Canada, Argentina, Palestine and South Africa, transporting with them their culture, institutions, and customs; these they adapted to the environment of their 'new' countries, as well as creating new institutions and absorbing ideas from the lands they had entered."[7]

It is nevertheless surprising that the 1881 pogrom in particular was so momentous, given the history of violence against the Jews in this region. Abramsky's explanation is that "the Jews were stunned not only by the pogroms and by the regime's passivity towards them, but also by the hostility of the new Czar, Alexander III, and the open declaration of his leading minister Ignatev, that 'the Western frontiers are wide open' for those Jews who wish to emigrate" (61). From that point on, it would appear that there was a high-level plan to target Jews.

In a word, with few exceptions, complete freedom to beat the Jews, to injure and mutilate them, to violate their wives and daughters, and to steal their property was granted [by the authorities]. Meanwhile, apart from a few rare exceptions, the rioters did not allow themselves any improper pranks against the authorities, or even against the lowest ranking officials. On the contrary, they often listened to the admonitions of private persons, . . . Christians not from the official ranks. Only thanks to this, several Jewish homes and shops with goods were left untouched. Many Christians themselves saved Jewish moveable property from destruction.[8]

The question of uprooting to move elsewhere became urgent, and the Harris family, living in one of the worst areas of violence, had to weigh the limited options.

Even in the wake of the worsening pogroms, the Harris family didn't leave immediately, and family members may have had a part in the widespread debate that raged after 1882 to determine whether some communal policy should be enacted in Russia. In his magnificent book titled *World of Our Fathers*, the historian, social critic, and literary figure Irving Howe offers some insight about the period that can help us understand the issues discussed at the time: "As early as 1882 a conference of 'Jewish notables' met in Saint Petersburg to discuss this question. The majority of the delegates feared that mass emigration, officially encouraged by the Jewish community, would appear unpatriotic and might undermine the struggle for emancipation" (Howe, 24–25). Citing *Russky Evrei*, a Russian-language weekly edited by Jews, Howe also notes that "pogroms are a result of rightlessness and when that has been obviated the attendant evils will vanish with it. By supporting mass emigration the Jews would be playing into the hands of their enemies, who hope they will flee from the field of battle" (25). As the inhabitants of the region waited to see the long-term effects of the violence upon their community, the number of Jews in the revolutionary movement grew steadily; between 1884 and 1889, Jews comprised around 13 percent of the movement, a figure that grew to 30 percent from 1900 to 1910, even though as a community Jews only represented 4 percent of the overall population (62–63). This increase came in response to fundamental changes that were occurring in Jewish communities throughout the world: "In this brief period there came into existence the largest free Jewish community in the world—in America—a development which led eventually to the creation of the State of Israel. It was the Holocaust which made Israel into a reality, but without the work of Russian-Polish Jews and their superhuman efforts in 1881–1923 there would have been no Israel. The period also witnessed the most remarkable and lively debate within East European Jewry in journalism, publicistic writings and Yiddish literature. This debate in turn gave rise to all the Jewish modern political movements which coalesced around the ideas of socialism and nationalism" (Howe, 63).

Benjamin Harshov goes even further in *Language in Time of Revolution*, describing a virtual revolution at every level of Jewish life.

We can date the beginning of this revolution in the year of the pogroms, 1881–1882, in Russia. What happened from then on completely changed the nature of the lives of Jews and their descendants in the world. It was the most radical change in the historical situation of the Jews in the last two thousand years, entirely transforming their geography, modes of living, languages, professions, consciousness, culture, politics, and place in general history. It was borne by a multifaceted, centrifugal movement with many directions and varying outcomes. Prominent failures, brutal disappointments, and dreadful sacrifices were part and parcel of these transformations. Individuals who experienced the change in their own bodies and souls paid an extraordinary emotional price for leaving their hometown, their parents' home, their childhood language, their beliefs, their ways of talking, and for the conquest of new modes of behavior, a new language, new traits, conventions, and beliefs. (8)[9]

To contemplate alternative approaches to life, within or beyond the Pale, involved confronting enormous obstacles, according to Howe. "Except for the religious and cultural movements, which by their nature were self-sufficient, all the new energies within the Jewish world of eastern Europe were doomed to failure. Neither communal growth nor political gradualism, neither socialist aggressiveness nor Zionist preparations could break, or break out of, the limits of the Pale. If nothing else, the cultural-political revival of these years made the Jews painfully aware of how intolerable their life remained" (23).

Jews occupied a precarious space in Russian society, and in the eyes of many younger Jewish radicals of the period even the Bund (the union of Jewish workers in Poland and Lithuania that engaged in revolutionary activity on a large scale) was locked in a kind of political impotence. Alternatives, such as the revolutionary movement, which at that time was gaining strength, were fraught with difficulties as well, on account of the populist aspirations of revolutionary groups such as Narodnaya Volya, which "defended pogroms against Jews on the grounds that such outbursts expressed the legitimate resentments of the peasants against their exploiters" (Howe, 23–24). In *Troubled Waters: The Origins of the 1881 Anti-Jewish Pogroms in Russia*, Michael Aronson reiterates this point in the context of a discussion on the rise of a broader revolutionary movement supported by leaders affiliated with groups like the Black Repartition, such as Georgii Plekhanov and Peter Lavrov. A Jewish leader of this organization, Lev Deich, made some revealing comments in response to Lavrov's April 1882 comment that revolutionaries had to walk a very fine line between condemning acts against the Jews and encouraging those who committed these acts to rise up against the ruling regime.

Realistically, in practice, the Jewish question is now almost insoluble for the revolutionaries. What, for example, are they to do now [1882] in Balta where they beat up the Jews? To intercede for them means, as Reclus says, "to call up the hatred of the peasants against the revolutionaries who not only killed the tsar but also defend the Jews." This is simply a dead-end avenue for Jews and revolutionaries alike. . . . Of course, it is our utmost obligation to seek equal rights for the Jews, . . . but that, so to speak, is activity in the higher spheres; and to conduct pacificatory agitation among the people is presently very, very difficult for the party. Do not think that this [situation] has not pained and confused me; . . . but all the same, I remain always a member of the Russian revolutionary party and do not intend to part from it even for a single day, for this contradiction, like some others, was of course not created by the party.[10]

These contradictions relate to a series of measures in effect during this period, ranging from the resettlement of Jews, to restrictions on Jewish trade and commerce, and culminating with the May 1881 laws that "prohibited new Jewish settlement outside towns and *shtetlekh* [little towns of the Pale] prohibited Jews from buying property in the countryside, and banned Jews from trading on Sunday mornings or Christian holidays," augmenting the arbitrary authority of local officials, while doing nothing to stem the pogroms, which culminated during that fateful Easter week of 1882. "This outbreak [in Balta] was notorious for the brutality and destructiveness of the *pogromshchiki* [pogroms], and the callousness of the provincial administration, who took the occasion to lecture the Jews on their own responsibility for the disorders. As one writer lamented soon afterwards, it was apparent that pogroms had now become an annual tradition in Russia."[11]

Jewish Self-Determination

These events in Ukraine are integral to Harris's background, in part because they may have promoted self-determination through the establishment of Jewish self-defense groups, which were "supported in certain towns (e.g., Odessa) even by cautious Zionist and national thinkers such as Ahad Ha-Am and Simon Dubnov" (Abramsky, 63). Taking matters into their own hands seemed essential to Jews because, Aronson points out, "the anti-Jewish, or pro-pogrom, or noncommittal positions taken by the various *narodnik* [Russian socialist movement] leaders and groupings made many Jews leave the revolutionary movement in disgust and rejoin their own people in its struggle for survival and a dignified existence"; nevertheless, "other Jewish socialists, perhaps the majority, remained loyal to their revolutionary comrades."[12] Whatever the reaction on the part of individuals in the community, there was certainly intense discussion about these pogroms, particularly the 1882 Balta violence. There was even stunned outrage in the Russian press about what had happened, including an article in *Golos* [*Voice*, a Russian newspaper] that cried out: "Everything pales before Balta!" The historian Stephen M. Berk notes that for weeks afterward, detailed analyses of the pogrom were widely reported. "Articles appeared which depicted the terrible suffering of the Balta Jews and their enormous losses of property. Coverage was given to the trials of people accused of raping Jewish women and girls. The paper dwelled upon the shortcomings of the military, police, and local civilian authorities who failed to prevent the pogroms and did not quickly suppress them." Most significantly, Berk recalls the conclusions that *Golos* drew from the Balta pogrom. "The Jews had to be made equal with other citizens so as to lessen their vulnerability and the government had to take the firmest possible measures to stop the pogroms. *Golos* speculated that, if the pogroms were not halted, the violence would spread from attacks on the Jews to other groups in society leading to a breakdown in order culminating in anarchy."[13]

I think that one must take this issue of Jews' self-sufficiency very seriously, particularly if we are to understand the mindset of those who came to America and resisted affiliating with Communist Party politics. Zellig Harris, and many of those who came to be associated with him, rejected not only Stalin and the Communist Party but also the Trotskyites, the Schachtmanites, and other anti–status quo groups that were active in the

United States. He was influenced by different individuals who were associated with Marxist thought and by *anti*-Bolshevik Marxists, such as Karl Korsch, Paul Mattick, and Anton Pannekoek. Although not of the generation that endured the pogroms firsthand, he seems to have considered that even in America one must remain wary of those who claimed to speak on behalf of larger groups. This is in part a consequence of an awareness within the Jewish community in the United States of events within Ukraine, including the pogroms in Balta. "The news, including the shocking and grisly, did eventually manage to reach other countries and crossed the ocean to America. When it finally came, the news unleashed a response on the part of Jews and Gentiles which in magnitude and vociferousness was unprecedented. . . . It heightened Jewish consciousness in the West and served to coalesce Ashkenazi Jews in the face of assimilation and dispersion."[14]

The image that is slowly coming into focus here is determined by the classic "push-pull" factors, according to which a population is pushed out of a country of origin by violence and horrid living conditions and pulled into a new world: America.

America was in everybody's mouth. Businessmen talked of it over their accounts; the market women made up their quarrels that they might discuss it from stall to stall; people who had relatives in the famous land went around reading letters for the enlightenment of less fortunate folk . . . children played at emigrating; old folks shook their sage heads over the evening fire, and prophesied no good for those who braved the terrors of the sea and the foreign goal beyond it; all talked of it, but scarcely anyone knew one true fact about this magic land.[15]

The force of this pull proved to so strong that "in the thirty-three years between the assassination of tsar Alexander II and the outbreak of the first world war, approximately one third of the east European Jews left their homelands—a migration comparable in modern Jewish history only to the flight from the Spanish Inquisition" (Howe, 26). Of the 2.4 million Jews who left the region between 1881 and 1914, 85 percent went to the United States (especially New York), and 12 percent went to Canada, Argentina, Europe, and South Africa. Even those who made up the proportion of the remaining 3 percent who did go to Palestine in this period often used it as a "temporary way station on the road westward"[16] (a phenomenon that would be repeated subsequent to the fall of the Soviet empire when thousands of Jews went to Israel under the Law of Return only to leave afterward for America and Europe).[17] The reasons for this were multiple, including the slender human and material resources available in Palestine to foster Jewish immigration during this period, the uncertain state of the region, and the sense that "next year in Jerusalem" was more a religious dream than a practical objective, something worth bearing in mind as we consider later on Zellig Harris's promoting Palestine as a homeland for the vanguard he was training. Zachary Lockman, in *Comrades and Enemies: Arab and Jewish Workers in Palestine 1906–1948,* offers valuable clarification on how a Jewish homeland was considered in a traditional Jewish framework.

[T]he idea of creating a sovereign Jewish state, in Palestine or anywhere else, was virtually unimaginable within the framework of traditional normative Judaism. For the few Jews who lived in Palestine, as for virtually all Jews before the modern era, only the end of history as manifested in the coming of the Messiah could bring about the termination of "exile" and its attendant sufferings, the redemption of the Jews, and their restoration to the land which God had promised to their ancestors but from which they had—also by divine decree—been uprooted. Despite its claims of ancient roots, unbroken continuities, and essential identities, then, Jewish nationalism—like Palestinian Arab and all other nationalisms—is a thoroughly modern phenomenon, a product of the nineteenth and twentieth centuries. Though it is possible to point to earlier precursors, modern Jewish nationalism, which came to be known as Zionism—a term which surfaced only in the 1890s, derived from the Hebrew *Tziyon,* a synonym for Jerusalem—emerged in a more or less recognizable form only in the last third of the nineteenth century. (23)

This obstacle to state-building in Palestine would be at the base of certain divisions that arose within the communities with which Zellig Harris had truck in his life. Nevertheless, even if Zion was not on the minds of all those in search of a new home, the urgency of finding an alternative to ever-present and mounting anti-Semitism certainly was. Harris's Balta was far smaller than Odessa or Kiev, but in the final years of the nineteenth century, community leaders made it into the center of the Zionist movement in Podolia, Volhynia, and Bessarabia by issuing statements aimed at sensitizing the world (especially the United States) to events in the region, and at pressuring the tsar.

Although American Jews needed no incentive after the first reports of the Easter atrocities drifted across the Baltic and the Atlantic, eye-witness accounts of refugees and Russian novelists served to heighten the prevailing attitude of horror and disgust. In April, 1903, Roosevelt received 363 addresses, 107 letters and 24 petitions, one of which was signed by 12,500 Americans of all faiths (including United States senators, governors, mayors, three archbishops and seven bishops), urging the Czar to cease and desist from religious persecution. Organized protest was initiated by Oscar Straus' "small committee," the Jewish Publication Society and the Independent Order of B'nai B'rith. Indeed, a June 1903 resolution made by the Jewish Publication Society, and acted upon a few years hence, requested that Congress denounce the 1832 commercial treaty with Russia, whose discriminatory policies violated the treaty's principle of equal rights to all American citizens. Such notables as Jane Addams, Carl Schurz, William G. Choate, August Belmont, John F. Dillon and Jacob Schiff played important roles in the protest movement. Between April and June, 1903, seventy-seven anti-Russian meetings were staged throughout the country. There were rallies in Atlanta, Baltimore, Boston, Chicago, New Orleans, San Francisco and St. Louis, and, most significantly, at Carnegie Hall in NYC, on May 27, 1903, where Mayor Seth Low introduced a most prominent speaker to address the gathering, ex-president Grover Cleveland.[18]

The situation worsened as the twentieth century followed its bloody path toward World War I and the Russian Revolution. During this period, the British government became committed to establishing a Jewish home in Palestine (Eretz Yisrael), an effort that culminated with a letter from Arthur James Lord Balfour to Lord Rothschild on November 2, 1917, a document that marked the first political recognition of Zionist aims by a great power.

Dear Lord Rothschild,

I have much pleasure in conveying to you, on behalf of his Majesty's Government, the following declaration of sympathy with Jewish Zionist aspirations which has been submitted to, and approved by, the Cabinet.

"His Majesty's Government view with favor the establishment in Palestine of a national home for the Jewish people, and will use their best endeavors to facilitate the achievement of this object, it being clearly understood that nothing shall be done which may prejudice the civil and religious rights of existing non-Jewish communities in Palestine, or the rights and political status enjoyed by Jews in any other country."

I should be grateful if you would bring this declaration to the knowledge of the Zionist Federation.

Yours sincerely,

Arthur James Balfour

Two years later, a special appeal to the countries of the West was organized by representatives of Jewish communities in Ukraine to help those who had suffered as a result of the pogroms.

ATTENTION! ATTENTION! ATTENTION! STOCKHOLM, COPENHAGEN, BRUSSELS, BERLIN, VIENNA, ROME, PARIS, BUENOS-AIRES. . . . It is for 4 years now and, especially, since 1918 that the Ukrainian Jewry has been suffering from a permanent pogrom. . . . Jewish settlements have been committed fire and sword, peaceful Jewish population, i.e. children, women, and the old have been brutally exterminated; even machine-gun shooting was used. . . . Each of the towns of Proskurov, Yelisavetgrad (Kirovograd now) lost up to 2,000 people at a time. Zhitomir, Balta, Fastov, Cherkassy, Felshtin, Trostinets, Zlatopol, Uman, Gaisin lost some hundreds people each.

The assistance of the Red Cross and the state cannot be sufficient. We appeal to Jewish communities and request that they should send in groups of assistance, medicines, food, and clothes immediately.[19]

In combination with worsening conditions in the old country and growing concerns about the future of Palestine as a Jewish homeland, a better system of transportation to the United States, as well as more complete information about what to do upon arrival there, encouraged families like the Harris's to make the journey. One such group was the Hebrew Immigrant Aid Society (HIAS), originally founded in 1881, dissolved 1883, and then revived, in New York, in 1892. In 1908, the HIAS had begun to issue a bilingual monthly, *The Jewish Immigrant*, which was circulated widely in Russia, providing reliable information (in Yiddish) on who could and could not be admitted into the United States. For example, Alexander Harkavy wrote a column for the paper, explaining immigration laws and giving advice on proper behavior at Ellis Island. Such bits of information proved extremely valuable, providing the immigrants not merely practical guidance but a sense that there were friends waiting for them in the host country. It is not clear whether the Harrises knew of the HIAS activities, but what is certain is that they arrived at a time when many people were informed about the possibilities of traveling to and settling in the United States.

The Harris Family in America

The Harrises came to America in 1913, at the tail end of a thirty-three-year period of heavy emigration from Russia, during which time an estimated two million Jews made the same trek. Irving Howe's *World of our Fathers* provides a vivid image of this flight.

No matter what the more Russified Jewish intelligentsia said by way of caution or how the handful of wealthy Jewish merchants hesitated, the masses made their own decision. Millions would soon tear themselves away from the land that held the dust of their ancestors; millions would leave the *shtetlakh* and cities in which they had built their life, their Houses of Study and burial societies, their wooden synagogues and paintless houses, their feeble economy and thriving culture. Obsolete artisans, socialist firebrands, bewildered wives, religious fanatics, virtuosos of the violin, illiterate butchers, scribblers of poetry, cobblers, students, *luftmenshn*—above all, the numberless ordinary Jews, the *folksmans* for whom being a Jew was not an idea or a problem but the vibrant substance of their lives—now began to ready themselves. And not merely because their life in common was weak, but because as Jews they knew themselves to be strong. (25)

Harris's nephew Ted Live told me in an interview (May 2009) that the "only thing I know about why the family left Balta was that there was increasing unease at that time about being Jewish. As far as the pathway, I know that there was some overland travel in Europe, which took a while, and then they boarded a boat to New York." From New York they chose to settle in Philadelphia, and once settled there, they came to be well known among a group of Jews who found both refuge and hospitality in the Harris home. Zellig Harris's father, H. H. (Hyman was the name he used for publishing) Harris, ran a drugstore, and his wife, Rachel, raised the four children. Shoshanna Harris (Tzvee's wife) spoke with great fondness of Rachel Harris, describing her as "a very bright, very well-read, up-to-date woman. She fit in to that scene in every way, and she was interested in Zionism and Jewish cultural affairs." Friends and family described her husband Hyman as a very pleasant man who worked on a range of fronts. He eventually became very important to a portion of the surrounding Jewish community, in part because his family, and eventually the children (in particular the two sons), all had very good connections with the left wing Zionist group in the United States, and because the Harris father used to run high holiday services in the vast basement in their house. "He would set up a couple of hundred folding chairs, and he would bring in other people to sing, and to do the services," recalls Ted Live. "These were non-official services, it was important for the members of the Jewish community who were not part of the established temples or synagogues, but who wanted to celebrate the holy days on a less official level." But even Hyman, who ran these services, was culturally Jewish but totally nonbelieving. "He did it out of Zionism, and he would collect money for the Zionist fund, not for himself, not for his house."

Murray Eden recalled meeting Hyman Harris when he was in his seventies (Zellig Harris was then in his mid-to-late thirties), and ended up developing "very close relations with the whole family." He also recalled Harris's involvement in Jewish cultural affairs, including scholarship on cantorial music (about which he wrote a book), and his work as a *mohel* (someone trained in the practice of circumcision), for which he (with his son Tzvee) invented a safer method. Their circumcision device required both a cutting motion and a compression component, and it was eventually used on a large number of the young males in this community, including Noam Chomsky. It is in all of these regards, according to Harold Orlans, that the Harris family was unmistakably Jewish; but the children's interests, outlook, and conversation—and even the socialist-Zionism espoused by the two boys in particular—was completely secular, according to Harshov's discussion earlier on, even if the father, Hyman Harris, did study Talmud and believed in the revival of the Hebrew language.

Faced with the decision of speaking Yiddish, Russian, Hebrew, or English in the home, the Harrises chose the Hebrew that was being created in the Yishuv in Palestine. English was used outside of the home, because, as Ted Live described, the Harris parents "didn't want to speak broken English, and thereby impact the kids' English. They wanted them to learn pure English, from native speakers. And they didn't want to speak Russian because of all the negative connotations they had of Russia." A generation later, the urgency of promoting Hebrew had abated, so the grandparents spoke Yiddish together, and the grandchildren spoke English among themselves. But Hebrew had left its mark, even in terms of the professional language work that was done in the milieu. Nathan Glazer indicated in an interview with me (May 2009) that "if you think of his own career, and that of Chomsky, you can consider his native use of Hebrew from the very beginning. It's true that it's a far cry from Hebrew, especially the Hebrew he spoke at home, to his early work in Near Eastern Semitic Dialects rooted in Cuneiform documents. But one reason he went into it was that he thought that he had a base in it from which to work. Interestingly, Noam Chomsky's father was also involved in advocating the new spoken Hebrew, and he wrote the first grammar of this modern Hebrew in the U.S., used when modern Hebrew was introduced as a language in some New York City high schools."

H. H. Harris was not particularly active politically, but he did add his signature to at least one of the editorials signed by his children, and by others who came to be part of their circle of friends and colleagues.[20] On the other hand, he was considered to hold "advanced views," which got him into trouble with the Philadelphia rabbinate, evidenced in his first accepting and then deciding to bow out of officiating for Murray Eden's 1945 wedding to a non-Jewish woman who had wanted a "religious" wedding. Eden, like so many others, recalled the cultural activities of the Harris household and the legendary hospitality of the Harris parents, who frequently hosted groups of friends, including himself, Harold Orlans, and Seymour Melman for weekend visits. The setting was gregarious, with lavish Friday night meals with all of the children, their spouses, and assortments of other folks including mathematicians, musicians, and medical scientists. Conversation was always vibrant, creating a cohesive and argumentative salon like atmosphere in which Jewish, scientific, and Zionist issues were discussed. Harold Orlans recalled his occasional stays in the family home, at 2222 N 53rd Street, a large white stucco house with brick trim, that comfortably accommodated the family and many visitors. He described the ambience as "pleasant comfort," with an emphasis on cultural discussions, notably about books and records. Eva Rapkin, born in 1921, also attended gatherings at the Harris household, and she remembers with great fondness the conversation and the hospitality. Ted Live was often a part of these dinners, but remembers more nonpolitical "very social gatherings with neighbors. Partly I may have been too young to remember the more political discussions. This applies as well to visits at Zellig's and Bruria's apartment. I recall people visiting them, but I probably wasn't completely aware of everything that was going on." Overall, though, "I remember Zellig Harris as an unassuming, friendly relative who seemed like all my other relatives, when he was around, but he was a lot less visible than my other relatives because he didn't live close by most of the time, as did his siblings and my grandparents. He was helpful, he certainly didn't strike me as being a particularly difficult person."

Irene Schumer, who had been an important member of Avukah right up to its dissolution in the early 1940s, recalled with great fondness the Harrises' generosity and the intellectual ambience of the period. She would visit the Harris household with Nathan Glazer, and she described the whole group of visitors as being very excited about being with the Harris family, who they considered a vanguard in the Jewish community—a crucial insight to understanding Zellig Harris's inner circle, as we'll see. Schumer recalled that these trips with Glazer from New York City to Zellig Harris's home were a "big thing" for them, and she remembers great discussions with all members of the family, and also the real challenges they faced in making the journey, given their meager resources. Glazer, who had met Harris through Melman, also recalls that the Harrises lived as an extended family, so Zellig and Tzvee lived in the family home even after they had appointments on the faculty of Penn. Everyone would gather for extended meals, "and the food choices reflected Tzvee's views on good nutrition, which he developed in the course of his studies."

The youngest child in the Harris household, Tzvee became a doctor and an immunologist. Everyone from the neighborhood described him with great fondness, including Al Katz who recalled to me in the course of an interview (March 2010) Tzvee's warmth, friendliness, and charisma. "You had to like him, and you believed, you had to believe, that when he said something he had thought through it, with intelligence, and not just for effect." Tzvee married Shoshanna (known as "Little Shush," in contrast to her sister-in-law, Zellig and Tzvee's sister, whom they called "Big Shush"). Shoshanna Harris, like her husband, worked in the field of immunology, to which Zellig also contributed later in his career through his efforts to normalize medical discourse for the purpose of advancing research possibilities. Tzvee's wife ["Little Shush"] had been a participant on a Hashomer Hatzair farm, intended to train American Jews for kibbutz life in Palestine. She left when she married Tzvee but maintained her devotion to the idea of Hashomer Hatzair, an organization she recalled with great fondness in my own discussions with her and Tzvee.

Tzvee and Zellig had two sisters, Enya and Shoshanna ["Big Shush"], who became elementary school teachers and eventually collaborated on a set of didactic history / ESL textbooks, designed for the grades they were teaching.[21] Their views on education were progressive, and they had difficulties in finding educational establishment approval for their nonstandard interpretations. Enya and Shoshanna were extremely close to one another, as is characteristic of the Harris family as a whole. They attended Penn at the same time, they both won the same scholarship, and then both of them taught English in high school. Enya (who went by the name Anna outside of the household) eventually married Israel Live, a veterinarian (Ted Live's parents), and Shoshanna married Yitzhak Sankowsky, a gifted and imaginative artist whose colorful and gleeful pictures usually depicted women, of different ages. In the late 1950s, Enya returned to Penn for an M.A. in romance languages, focusing on Provençal French. She then was awarded the PhD in linguistics in 1963, the same year her son Ted graduated Penn with a BA in biochemistry. Live recalls that "I attributed her studies in linguistics as being linked to her thinking of Zellig as a kind of mentor or paragon. That was why she worked in linguistics, it was an easy field for her to get into, but this doesn't do her justice. In fact, it never came up that Zellig was really paramount in his field, I never had a sense of that, even from him. I discounted that idea as silly old worship, a sisterly admiration that Enya had of Zellig."

Zellig Harris saw linguistics as a science, and indeed most of the family worked in some branch of the sciences, although Live thinks of it more as their being in academia. "Maybe they thought that science was more rigorous. But in most cases it wasn't to save the world, or to solve major issues. In my case it was to try to better understand life, and the environment around me, which is what drew me to biochemistry. This lasted until I figured out that biochemistry meant doing one tiny little thing in a lab, which meant that it would take forever to learn one tiny thing." There was a gender difference in Zellig's generation though, "so the two sisters weren't scientists. The boys were scientists, the girls were teachers, which was not atypical." Live recalls that "during that time Enya had begun teaching ESL courses at Penn, which she continued doing after completing her doctorate, and she ran a small ESL program when she stopped working as a high school teacher. She was interested in linguistics but not the structural work that Zellig was doing." The degree to which the community remained tightly-knit is remarkable, and, despite differences in gender and generation, came to participate in and contribute to a range of projects relating to the study of language, the promotion of Jewish cultural issues, and of course Zionism. And it is to Zionism that the far-reaching organization called Avukah was devoted, and Harris's involvement therein would dictate a general approach to society, with far-reaching implications.

2 Avukah

This sense of community within the household extended outward toward Zionist work through family engagement, and eventually through a small and little-known organization called Avukah, to which Zellig Harris belonged as an undergraduate. Avukah became a central locus that linked together a range of individuals who became central actors in Harris's linguistic, political, and Zionist interest groups. In "From Sociology to Socialism," a chapter from Bennett M. Berger's edited collection *Authors of their Own Lives*,[1] the renowned sociologist Nathan Glazer recalls his entrance into Harris's circle, through work with Avukah: "I entered City College in February 1940 (City in those days had two entering and graduating classes a year, keyed to the New York City public-school calendar) and majored in history. I liked history and had a good memory. But my academic life soon had to contend with another interest. I was persuaded by a fellow student to attend a meeting of Avukah, the student Zionist organization. I was not a Zionist but was willing to hear what there was to be said for Zionism. It was an accident that had a strong impact on the rest of my life. The speaker was Seymour Melman, a recent graduate of City College who had just spent a year in Palestine and was reporting on his experiences. Had Avukah been simply a Jewish organization, I doubt that it would have made much impact on me. But these were *socialist Zionists*. What is more, they were *intellectual* socialist Zionists and looked down on nonintellectual socialist Zionists." Attending this meeting led Glazer to seek out Seymour Melman: "Melman was a charismatic figure. What led me to speak to him after his lecture I do not know. But soon I was on the staff of *Avukah Student Action* (the organization's national newspaper) and had become a Zionist; indeed, before that was settled, I was named editor. No loyalty oaths were required to become a member of Avukah. We had a three-point program, presented in documents portentously titled theses and in theoretical pamphlets. The organization may have been Zionist but the culture was in most ways left sectarian. We were generally allied on campus issues with the anti-Stalinist Left—the socialists and the Trotskyites."

Many individuals who came to know Zellig Harris did so through Seymour Melman or through the Avukah Student Zionist Organization, to which both Harris and, later, Melman, belonged as undergraduates, and with which they remained affiliated until its demise in early 1943. It is hard to understand how Avukah, a small (and by now mostly forgotten) student organization formed in the 1920s, could generate such an attraction for such a remarkable group of people as those invoked in this narrative. For this reason it's important to describe some of its workings here, in order to help us understand why a small student Zionist organization with somewhere between six hundred and a few thousand members (depending upon whom you ask)[2] was so important to a host of individuals who came to play significant roles in shaping ideas and events of the twentieth century. When we speak of Harris's inner circle, it is primarily comprised of people who were part of Avukah, including Norman Epstein, Nathan Glazer, Tzvee Harris, Al Kahn, Seymour Martin Lipset, Seymour Melman, Myer D. Mendelson, Harry M. Orlinsky, Harold Orlans, Chava Rapkin, Meyer Rabban, Chester Rapkin, Ruth Slotkin (later Ruth Glazer, then Ruth Gay), Irene Schumer, William Schumer, Judith Wallerstein, and Robert Wallerstein. Begun as a kind of Jewish Zionist social club at Harvard in 1925, Avukah grew to be an important student organization on campuses throughout the Northeast, and as far north as McGill, as far south as Tulane, and into the midwest. Activities within each chapter varied depending on the interests of members, but there were common themes. A Chicago chapter described its activities as follows: "The Chicago Normal College Avukah, sponsored by Mr. Wise, is a chapter of the Avukah Organization of Chicago which has branches on other Chicago college campuses. The campus groups strive to promote interest in Jewish culture among the Jewish students and their friends. At the Normal meetings events, personalities, and literature are discussed by the members of the club, and outside speakers are also featured."[3]

Avukah membership and importance grew with the events of the 1930s, and it became decidedly antifascist and anti-Bolshevik, while serving through its discussion groups, publications, and summer meetings to bring together Jewish students from a broad geographical region, and from an array of left-socialist, labor Zionist, or social democrat perspectives. Nathan Glazer recalled in a 2009 discussion with me that

I was at that time a very ordinary social democrat, so I was somewhat surprised and even upset by their views and how dismissive they were of the ordinary socialist.

Not that I was a member of the party; I was an ordinary socialist, a Norman Thomas socialist.[4] But there were other radical types around Avukah at the time. Harold Orlans had gone to City College, probably at a very young age because when he was my age he had already graduated and was working as a reporter in San Francisco. I met him when he came back to New York. Chester Rapkin I met very fast, he had also just graduated.

Whatever the political orientation of its members, Avukah maintained a strong social component, leading up to the Second World War. Chava Rapkin, born in 1921, came into the Avukah organization to meet like-minded Zionists and Jews, at a time of rampant anti-Semitism in all levels of American life, including universities. She was born in the United States, but when her mother was separating from her father, in 1927, Chava was brought to live in Palestine, where she remained for ten years. In 1939, when she graduated from high school, she went on to Hunter College in New York City. Hunter's students were overwhelmingly first-generation Americans at this time, and only twenty-eight percent of students' fathers had been born in the United States. Furthermore, roughly 75 percent of the students at Hunter when Rapkin enrolled were Jewish, because of the cost of tuition, and because restrictive quotas at most private colleges and universities barred Jewish women from admission. Hunter absorbed all who qualified and became the largest college for women in the world; students found both comfort and strength in belonging to a community of their own. Jewish life flourished in the college, and the range of organizations grew to include the Menorah Society, Avukah, and Hillel. Hunter, like City College that Nathan Glazer had attended, was free, but its graduates went on to pursue important careers. The workforce did limit women's options to domains such as teaching, however, so as Jewish women graduated from Hunter in ever larger numbers, they came to dominate the ranks of New York's teaching force and the city's public schools.[5]

For Rapkin, it was important from the outset of her undergraduate years to seek out a Jewish organization, and she immediately gravitated toward Avukah. "It was a Zionist Jewish organization, and, having been raised in Palestine, Zionism was very close to my heart. My father [Maurice Samuel] was a famous lecturer on Zionism, as well as other subjects. It was in my bones, it was my whole life." There were other Zionist organizations that she briefly considered, including the American Student Union, and there were various factions of the Communist Party, "but none of them really attracted me, because none of them had any interest in Israel, and we were very simplistic in our vision: revolution or no revolution, I was focused upon Palestine as a home to the Jews. So I joined Avukah." Rapkin met a broad array of like-minded individuals within the organization. But, she recalled to me in an interview, "although I was on the editorial board for the Avukah newspaper, and although I wrote an article every now and again, I wasn't very politically active. I was more ornamental, in some ways. Social. We were a very social group. The Avukah office was where we'd come to flirt with the guys." She, like so many other members, attended the summer camp; but all in all, "the intellectual aspect of it all was, to me, on a level with the social. In fact the social for me took precedence, in a way."

A Sectlike Character

Avukah was not a monolithic organization; there were, as Rapkin described, "factions," with Zellig Harris and Seymour Melman "thinking about the Arabs, and how we were to work with them," on one side, and on the other, "you had a group of people who did not agree with him. So there were divisions, within Avukah. There is no question about that." Nathan Glazer concurs, and suggested to me that there was an inner circle, particularly with the involvement of Zellig Harris, centered primarily around New York and Philadelphia, close to Harris and to other Avukahites for whom Harris was a distant but "mythical figure." Glazer, a member of Avukah from 1940 to 1943, recalls that the inner circle developed a sectlike character that excluded the larger number of members from outside New York who were traditional Zionists, and who knew little about the radical orientation of the group around Harris. Avukah was important because it exposed its members and affiliates not only to a different analysis of the Jewish community, but also to a different approach to the organizations that were in it, and, by extension, to the wider world. One of the important members of Avukah in the early years of the war was Irene Schumer, who recalled in interview with me that Zellig Harris was particularly important in this regard, not only directly, "but also through his delegates, associates and friends. No matter what an individual's background was, there wasn't one person who knew him who wasn't influenced by him." She recalls great admiration for Harris on account of his intellectual prowess and, in her words, "when people are like that, especially to a group of strivers" like those associated with Avukah, "they get to wear a halo." She also noted that at that time, if you were "in any way bright," you were attracted to radical things. Avukah helped nourish those interests, and it broadened the worldview of its members, a process that was all the more marked for the inner circle of Avukah, especially those who had direct relations with the Harris household.

Despite the openness of the household, however, Zellig Harris kept his emotions to himself, and there were few personal reminiscences about him in the many hours of interviews I conducted. Robert Wallerstein, the renowned professor and practitioner in psychoanalysis, remembers the two brothers, Tzvee and Zellig, as the crucial consultants to this inner circle. He described Zellig as more philosophical than his younger brother, more policy setting, the one who would articulate big visions, and Tzvee as more practical—and approachable. Wallerstein would see Tzvee, and sometimes Zellig, either in Philadelphia or in the New York Avukah office, particularly on weekends when they weren't busy with college or other work. Wallerstein described Zellig as "the distant, respected guru, the great and more experienced" professor of linguistics at Penn. "Zellig was . . . someone who was distant, and who we knew as one of the original sponsors of the idea of Avukah. He was a far-off presence, who we knew to be in the background. He also made the final decision on who would go to make the annual trip to visit Louis Brandeis." Judith Wallerstein, also involved in psychology through her renowned research and writings on divorce, suggested that "in order to understand Zellig's psychology, you had to understand his background. And in order to understand the background, you have to understand that Zellig Harris in particular had very little contact with a wide range of people. He and his immediate circle developed their own ideas about the way the world should be, based on what would make life better for an immigrant kid. Their immigrant roots are very important." This insight applied to many of those in Avukah since, as Judith Wallerstein noted, "Seymour, and many others in that milieu including Al Kahn, came from poor families, and they were making their way up into American life. They did want to be assimilated, and they also wanted to hold on to however they interpreted their identity. For both Zellig and Seymour, there was an interest in being Jewish, but there was also an interest in changing the whole world. The motivation was very personally driven, it was a passion, especially for Seymour. Zellig was not a very passionate man, he was a one-track man, and, to me, really not a very interesting man."

For Irene Schumer, Zellig Harris's personality

was very alluring. We didn't come from comfortable houses. Nat [Nathan Glazer] came from a house that was not comfortable, and he and I would travel with a dime between us to go visit Harris. And the other kids didn't have money. The Harris household was very attractive, it was comfortable, a lot of people would come to eat.

. . . If you mentioned it to them they would say 'oh no', but it was! Who had books in their house to the extent that the Harris family had books? These were cultured people. Our parents were making it barely, my father had a sign manufacturing place, my mother shoveled coal to keep the house warm. They were very attractive, especially Tzvee and Shush. Tzvee was a father figure, and his wife too was very warm. We did think it was aspiration to have a lot of books, as the Harris family did. You really admired these people, who did graduate work, who pursued advanced degrees, this was impressive. Zellig was an extremely important guy, his work on linguistics was revolutionary, it has opened all sorts of things. And it's fine to be admired in that situation, we admired that; but in terms of Avukah, this little plaything that he had, for us it wasn't a plaything. People's hearts and souls were in this organization.

There was certainly a hierarchy of relations in this milieu, perhaps the consequence of Harris's belief, described to me by the remarkable social scientist, journalist, and biographer Harold Orlans (1921–2007), that "our respect for great people should increase over time." The example he recalled from Harris was that "an artist learns more as he ages, such that late Sibelius must contain secrets not present in early Sibelius." Orlans recalled that Zellig always treated him "with affectionate interest, and addressed his problems and questions seriously and directly, yet with this kind of elevated distance," a "certain emotional detachment." Orlans also suggested that this reserved behavior toward others, particularly people younger than himself, "may have been his way of limiting intimacy," even with people with whom he was quite close. Further, he indicated that Harris never expressed his feelings, to him or, so far as he knew, to other members of his inner circle. As Shoshanna Harris said, "Zellig was more of a detached person, that was his personality," but the family itself was warm and supportive. At the same time, though, it was "a close family of high achievers" who spent a lot of time in discussions that were on the one hand open to anyone who happened to be in the room at the time, but on the other hand "demanding, in that they required broad knowledge of burning issues." The Harrises were all humanistic, they were all left-wing kibbutz-oriented Zionists from early on, and they maintained these characteristics through their lives. But they did not suffer fools gladly, and some were less tactful than others. Zellig, from all reports, was the most respected but also the most dismissive of those whose arguments lacked the concision he demanded in his own work, and virtually everyone with whom I spoke maintained that he kept this attitude throughout his life.

Some of these impressions reaffirm this notion that Harris was a kind of "guru," something Meyer Rabban experienced firsthand. Rabban came to the Harris surroundings because as a young college student he had sought out kindred libertarian socialist spirits. He was at first disappointed, finding that "the Jewish circles were anemic and shallow and disgusting." Marion Care, who came from Philadelphia, told him about Avukah, and she suggested he invite some Avukah members from Philadelphia to tell him what they were about. Says Rabban, "They laid out the Avukah program of Socialist Zionism, and I found it to be the solution to the minority status of Jews, and it offered an expression of my socialist, libertarian, communitarian ideas." Shortly thereafter, there was a national convention in Cleveland, which Rabban attended. While there, he befriended members of Avukah, including Seymour Melman, "a loud and interesting character" with whom he became quite close. He then attended the Avukah summer program at Liberty, New York, where a group representing Hashomer Hatzair would meet. Hashomer Hatzair, a labor Zionist organization unaffiliated to universities, had close ties to Avukah with which it shared certain ideas. Meyer Rabban's wife, suggested, however, that members of Hashomer Hatzair considered themselves far more engaged with practical and important issues than those in the more "academic" Avukah. At the summer program, Meyer Rabban met this "guru," Zellig Harris, who "presented his ideas with such clarity, with such philosophical depth, such political astuteness," that Rabban described himself as being "captured: I remember thinking to myself that 'this is for me'."

Zellig Harris was a large part of what appealed to Rabban about Avukah, because, as he told me in a 2009 interview, Harris was a "person who came across as someone at a level beyond ordinary people, which is truly the aura that gurus of all colorations possess and exude. He literally set, for me, a series of beliefs to which I became committed." Rabban joined Avukah, and also Hashomer Hatzair, and became active in both. At the last summer school he attended, in 1939, he was asked to organize a group in Chicago, a plan that was changed when he was asked instead to join the central group in New York City. He agreed and was appointed the national administrative secretary in New York, where he ran the Avukah office for $25 a week, from September 1939 until he went into the army in January 1942. He traveled to take up his new duties in New York with friends of his from Hashomer Hatzair, and thus began a time that he described to me as the "happiest of my entire life. This was it, I'd found what I had to do."

Extended Family Relations

It is important to consider Noam Chomsky in this regard because although he was nineteen years younger than Zellig Harris, he had relations with the Harris family since childhood, and also (vaguely) recalled visiting the Harris household as a child, years before he would revisit Professor Zellig Harris at the University of Pennsylvania. And long before Zellig Harris and Noam Chomsky worked together, it is possible to find concordances between the work of William Chomsky, Noam's father, and the early Semitic research of Zellig Harris. This, along with the combination of marriages and working relationships that would eventually occur between individuals from the Jewish community in Philadelphia (and of course New York), point to how small this world was, and adds as well to the sense of amazement one feels for the impact that such a small number of people would eventually have upon American intellectual life through the twentieth century.

An example of how interconnected this group was is evident if we consider Bruria Kaufman, Zellig Harris's first cousin. Her father, Y. L. Kaufman, became an eminent mathematician, as did Bruria. He was also a philologist and scholar of Hebrew in Palestine, and Bruria also followed this path later on, with involvement in language studies at the University of Pennsylvania. This interest in the study of language is a fascinating thread that runs through this narrative, providing ties to the older generation, including William Chomsky, H. H. Harris, and Y. L. Kaufman, through scholarly work on (Hebrew) language research. Bruria was born in Manhattan, then lived for a year or two of her early childhood in Brooklyn, but she was taken to Palestine at age two, returning to the United States in 1940 to study music (she was a professional-level piano player). Upon her arrival, as a close relative she was welcomed into the Harris home. Soon thereafter, Meyer Rabban remembered learning that she wanted to leave the Harris house, and Zellig couldn't understand why. Zellig's mother turned to him and said "You're an idiot! You don't understand why she left? She's in love with you!" As Rabban recalled, "Zellig Harris was so aloof, he didn't know what the hell was going on!" Zellig and Bruria eventually married, and Bruria's remarkable career led her to become a professor at the Weizmann Institute, but after about a decade she chose instead to teach high school. She is best known, however, as Albert Einstein's principle assistant; she worked with him on the mathematics of his theories, an interesting twist in this story given the attraction that Harris had to Einstein's achievements. She was a scientist, having obtained a BS degree from Hebrew University of Jerusalem in 1938 and a PhD from Columbia University in 1948. She was an assistant to John von Neumann at the Institute for Advanced Study, Princeton (1947–1948), and she became a member of the

IAS in 1948, a post she held until 1950. She was then named as an assistant to Albert Einstein, also at the IAS (1950–1955), before becoming a member of the Courant Institute of Mathematical Sciences at NYU (1955–1956). Her research specialty for which she is best known, however, remains quantum mechanics, and she contributed to the general theory of relativity and to statistical physics. Given that Harris had originally dreamed of being a physicist and spent much of his professional life looking for mathematical, or at least mathematically inspired approaches to the world, his wife, as one of the leading mathematicians of the age, must have provided interesting input.

As regards how tightly knit and connected the Harris family was, Ted Live remarked, "I thought that all families were like that!" The family is still quite close, with Ted seeing two of his cousins in Boston from time-to-time, and he still kept in touch with Bruria in Israel. For him, the difficulty with family communication was that "we were all stymied by the lack of information; had we been more interested 30 or 40 years ago, we could have been more probing, but even back then there was a lot of closing off of information. It was unpolitic, or inappropriate." Irene Schumer, who had been so close to Avukah members and has remained in touch over the years with old friends from the organization, told me, "Even after all these years, everyone who was associated with the Harrises and with Avukah, no matter what their politics, cared a great deal about each other." Some family members changed political orientations along the way, which is hardly surprising given that the family relationships span more than sixty years.

Just as the events of the 1930s contributed toward making members of this group more radical, subsequent events modified the views of key Avukah members. Irene Schumer, in her words, "became less radical," Nathan Glazer became a key voice of the neoconservative movement and developed a certain distance from the group of surviving members. Seymour Melman remained true and faithful to the ideology that the group articulated early on, and he certainly exhibited disappointment that some of his close colleagues from that time (especially Nathan Glazer) did not share his continued enthusiasm. Along the way as well, given the close and sometimes intimate relations among members, there have been fallings-out, ruptures among friends, and divorces, which has affected the group in different ways. And there were strong feelings of love and attachment all along, evidenced in a letter from Irene Schumer on the occasion of Seymour Melman's passing, in 2004:

Our Seymour Melman was a fervent disciple of Zellig Harris, was a friend to Tzvee and Shush Harris, Meyer (Meir) Rabban, Murray Eden and Harold Orlansky (Orlans). Our Seymour was one of the CCNY cohort of 1939 that included Chester Rapkin, Al Kahn and other brash fellows who manned Alcove #1 and scorned the Stalinists. What a talented bunch of boys; they are the stuff of legend; awkward but oh so smart, so achieving, paradigms of CCNY's glory days. Al recalls, that in cap and gown, in the graduation processional, a voice called out "Melman, what, no counter-demonstration!"

This view of a close community hearkens back to Joseph Dorman's 1997 film titled "Arguing the World," which describes the City College scene as it was in the 1930s, when the different alcoves came to be associated with vastly different ideological orientations. On the film's website[6] there's lively reminiscence about these alcoves from the social and political critic Irving Kristol (1920–2009).

I would guess that, in all, there were more than a dozen alcoves, and just how rights of possession had been historically established was as obscure as the origins of the social contract itself. Once established, however; they endured, and in a manner typical of New York's "melting pot," each religious, ethnic, cultural, and political group had its own little alcove. There was a Catholic alcove, the "turf" of the Newman Society, a Zionist alcove, an Orthodox Jewish alcove; there was a black alcove for the handful of blacks then at CCNY, an alcove for members of the athletic teams, and so forth. But the only alcoves that mattered to me were No.1 and No. 2, the alcoves of the anti-Stalinist Left and pro-Stalinist Left respectively. It was between these two alcoves that the war of the worlds was fought, over the faceless bodies of the mass of students, whom we tried desperately to manipulate into "the right position" but about whom, to tell the truth, we knew little and cared less.

The film, featuring the perspectives of Daniel Bell, Nathan Glazer, Irving Howe, and Irving Kristol (with others interviewed or invoked as well, including memories of Seymour Melman recalled by Nathan Glazer), helps to portray not only the emergence of crucial voices in American life from CCNY but also the ways in which these voices came to diverge from one another and from the "New Left" that broke from it. As Schumer recalls, it is hard now to imagine the "hothouse" that was City College. One of the major things she recalls doing was presenting another point of view to the American Student Union (ASU),[7] the "enemy" of the anti-Stalinist alcove at CCNY and of the members of Avukah, who believed that the ASU was leading people down the "wrong paths" of Stalinism, of the Popular Front, of everything that Avukah members abhorred, because, said Schumer, they knew after the purges of 1936 and 1937 what the Soviet Union was about.

Zellig Harris's "Scientificity"

Another dominant theme that runs through the Harris family narrative is related to rationality, methodology, and the scientific method. Harold Orlans spoke about Harris's "cultivation and maintenance of a closely knit inner circle for work on language studies from a scientific perspective." In late 1943, Harris invited Orlans and others from his immediate circle of friends and students to serve as seeing-eye dogs to native speakers, the technique he used to teach elemental speech in a foreign language. This was also how Nathan Glazer got to pursue a master's degree in linguistics at the University of Pennsylvania, involving the study of Swahili. Glazer's recollection to me of this is fascinating for our understanding of Harris's approach and attitudes.

I graduated City College in January of 1944. For the last year or two I'd really been connected with the project that Harris had from the Defense Department during the war. He presented the project to me, in linguistics. And when he presented it to me he would come to New York, and stay at a hotel near Grand Central because he would take the train. He said that we would have to preserve an educated elite to serve the needs of society and the world, who can lead after the war. So first he asked me what I was doing at City College, and I was already on my third or fourth major. I had started in History, because I loved History, but then I got two 'B's, so I thought something is wrong. So I moved on to Economics, but only for a semester or two. By this time I moved to Public Administration, because I thought I'd get a job with the government. There was a Junior professional assistant exam which a lot of people were taking, and if you passed you got a job for $70/week, which at the time was sort of a job. I told him that I wasn't particularly interested in it. So Harris now gave me the double reason for me to work with him, first that I might find it interesting, and secondly it gives draft exemptions. At that time I hadn't even been called up. What interested me more was my interest in finding a field that I can work in, having been going around, than in the exemption. But fine, if the exemption comes, I will take it. So I said sure.

The projects with which Harris was involved, and for which he recruited the young Glazer, were twofold. The first was ideological, and in his words:

I was considered one of the good new recruits, and they could make good use of me. I remember Seymour giving me a pamphlet by Marx, one of the early important pamphlets. It was not so much theoretical, as laying out a schema of some sort. They felt that they could educate me, and Seymour told me that I must read *Partisan Review*, and I took to it. How deeply all of this went, I don't know. It was in the air. You might say a Marxist style of thought was very popular amongst certain circles, and you accepted it, how much you believed it, how much it activated you and so on, that's a rough question. I mentioned a number of times something that indicates how ideology can distort anything, that important article by Macdonald and Greenberg, "Theses on the War," that this was an imperialist war. How could you believe such a thing?

The second project that Harris had in mind for Glazer involved "teaching strange languages, or just languages, they didn't have to be that strange, to soldiers. And this was the approach that was to come out of the Bloomfield Sapir tradition. While they'd been trained as philologists in Indo Aryan written materials, they knew or knew about Indo-American languages, and they knew the way that you study languages without any written history, and this in a way was influencing them in many important ways."

The program itself responded to defense department requests to train people they had selected and, as Glazer suggests, "it was a wonderful opportunity for soldiers, because rather than being sent to the front, they were sent to universities to study language." It may seem surprising that Harris would invite a young student who was at that time completely untrained in linguistics to join such a project, but as Glazer says (and Chomsky has often said), "Harris took a somewhat dismissive attitude towards linguistics; if you weren't a theoretical physicist, then you weren't serious. So I said, 'what do I need to know about it?' He said 'You don't need to know anything, here are two books, this is it,' and one was Bloomfield, the other was Sapir. I know too that he gave me at least one article, which was by the Chinese linguist Y. R. Chao, about alternative solutions in phonemics." At that time, Glazer recalls that the armed forces were looking for ways to train soldiers to learn enough about a language to be useful, and for that task there were two alternative traditions available.

One came out of more classic materialism, and one came out of the tradition of American Indian anthropology, in which you would work with an informant (which is not to say that with the others you didn't too), and basically Harris's position was that that is the way you learn a language. I have never read Saussure, but I think that the significance of the difference between speech and written language and spoken language comes from Saussure. I don't recall hearing Saussure's name from Harris, although I'm sure he was aware of it.

Harris's approach was structuralist, erected on the idea that a language is built out of basic building blocks. "We didn't read Saussure, but we got Harris's point of view, and we knew that his view of language—and I think that this is why his research and Chomsky's early research was supported by the Defense Department—was the notion of automatic translation. If you could reduce a language to a structure, then you could find a way of translating that structure into another structure." The first informant with whom Glazer was involved for this Harris project was Moroccan Arabic.

My job, and I was living in NY, was to recruit informants. There was a candy shop and newspaper store on about 7th and 130th where various riffraff, people who jumped ship, were. My Arabs had been working on ships. I wasn't the only recruiter, but I was one. We had these programs, some underway, some getting started. One of us specialized in language, producing the materials and writing the scholarly work. The others were ringmasters; we had these materials, we had these five soldiers, we had the informant, and our job was to bring them together. The interesting thing was how committed the soldiers were, and that they soon surpassed us.

The project involved a whole range of languages, and the work required that he himself become proficient in the languages he worked on. "I had to recruit my own informant because Harris wanted me to work on Swahili, and I recruited a guy named Abdullah from the Grand Comore Islands. There were written materials on these languages, and there were books on Swahili, including a dictionary, but basically I was learning the language from Abdullah, and recording it, and having sessions with Harris on doing this."

In time, Glazer's work with Harris was compiled into a master's thesis on Swahili phonemics, which was eventually adopted by Harris as an appendix in the 1951 book *Methods in Structural Linguistics*,[8] and Glazer recalls that Harris sent him a copy, long after they had lost touch with each other: "And so my last note from Harris was an appreciative one saying, 'I know that you don't plan to continue in linguistics, but I appreciate all of the hard work that you've done, in this phonemic analysis.'"

Irene Schumer cited Glazer's case as an example of Zellig Harris's efforts to keep people out of the army after WWII had broken out, which was part of his broader effort to cultivate and maintain a vanguard of people around him. According to Schumer, "Harris promoted his work by recruiting students to some of the projects in which he was engaged, including learning and teaching foreign languages." She suggested that "the language work was important politically, as well as linguistically, because Harris was anxious to keep a core group of Avukahites with him in order to foster the interests and approach he favored." Harris didn't enlist in the army, and he discouraged those around him from doing so, in part because he expected that the course of WWII would resemble the course of WWI, so it was better to remain in the States and to oversee research and activities. This effort led people in his immediate circle into the study of linguistics, and propelled a number of them toward a mastery of different languages that was often characteristic of the anthropological linguistic work of the time (for example, that of Boas, Harris, Sapir, and others). The effort to keep the vanguard Avukah members out of the war was not limited to language studies, recalls Schumer. Milton Shapiro, "little Shush's" brother, was active in Avukah before going on to become a prominent attorney, and "Tzvee put him on a diet so that he would be underweight, and therefore not qualified for service." Irene Schumer recalls that he was already thin, but with the dieting he became "really thin, so thin that it was unbelievable!"

Unlike Glazer, Orlans declined to be part of the linguistics work because he did not "consider himself to be good at it," and he didn't like the idea of dodging the draft. As it turned out, though, he was drafted as a conscientious objector, and served in work camps and mental hospitals, while Glazer was excluded from serving not because of his language work but rather his poor eyesight. For Orlans, Harris was "impressive intellectually and personally, but he "had two big failings." He "thoughtlessly assumed that a 'scientific' approach was fruitful in political, social, and historical matters"—and he "never bothered to question or justify it"—and he believed that "putting a number with decimal places before each didactic statement, as in his posthumous book [*The Transformation of Capitalist Society*[9]], made it scientific." Meyer Rabban remembers visiting the Harris house, at 2222 North 53rd Street ("which seemed like a palace to me"), and in the course of the visit, Zellig received a phone call. Harris told Rabban that "the government wanted him to do something with Chinese, for the army, a big thing," which involved him having to learn Chinese. Harris responded that he would be interested, but told them "You'll have to give me six months!"

A Cold Man

Few people in the milieu claimed to know Zellig Harris intimately, as we have seen. Harold Katz, part of the founding Harvard Avukah group, remembered him to me in a telephone interview as "distant" and "what he stood for I didn't particularly understand even though I shared everybody else's conventional thinking, that the British Empire was dead, that there had been for a long time a phony war, and that Russia had gone to the wrong side. But my concern wasn't world revolution, or change of ideology, or conversion of the American capitalist system to anything else, not even socialism—unlike Zellig. I was perfectly happy with the American system, and I never questioned it ideologically. My concern was with Zionism." For Harold Orlans, one reason for the distance that people felt from Harris was that the ideology took precedence over everything else. "The longer and better you knew Zellig Harris, the more you were likely to perceive and be offended by his coldness, his inability to recognize or establish genuine friendship based on genuine emotions. He didn't recognize the role of emotion in history, art, politics, or personal relations, and that is, or was, a very big blind spot." In some ways, E. F. Konrad Koerner's biography,[10] which accompanies his comprehensive bibliography of Zellig Harris's writings, notes the unanimity of this view, concluding that Harris "would have thought any tribute to him inappropriate," which may explain why "many linguists around the world were surprised that he had been alive for so many years following the 'Chomskyan Revolution' and, still more surprised, to discover that he had remained scholarly active right to the end" (527).

Zellig Harris's seriousness and introverted nature was also manifested by the fact that he was more likely to show his displeasure through silence rather than invective. He was also brilliant, well-read in many languages, and knowledgeable in particular in the kinds of anthropology, sociology, and economics that were pertinent to his approach. Murray Eden, an important member of Avukah and the Harris circle who became a leading biophysicist and a professor of electrical engineering at MIT, recalls that while Harris was a very good talker, he was not quite so good as a listener if he "had no vested interest in the particular position being elucidated" because he was "much more likely to be engaged if the topic was one in which he was looking for fresh ideas." But if someone raised an objection to his stated position, he listened, "mostly to be polite, but would disregard the opposing opinion." Leigh Lisker, a colleague and former student of Harris's (beginning in 1938, with time out for military service, returning in 1945) confirmed that "it is true that Harris, while he had a ready laugh and could hardly ever be said to be 'in the dumps,' was never given to idle chitchat. Conversation with him, whatever the subject, was always serious; he couldn't abide the cocktail party situation. Thus the annual 25 Year Club dinner, at which I would regularly meet his brother Tzvee, was something he never attended. I don't think it was arrogance. Rather I suspect it was more like stage-fright, light conversation for the sake of social solidarity was something I suspect he simply felt incapable of."[11]

Another personality trait that bothered but also attracted certain members of Harris's circle was his propensity to build small, elite groups of like-minded individuals who excluded opposing viewpoints and stuck to the line he developed. Both Irene and William Schumer recall that Harris not only cultivated an inner circle (in Avukah centered around work on the *Avukah Student News*), but he also attempted to radicalize the quite diverse population of Avukah, who in many cases had just joined Avukah in order to have Jewish or Zionist contacts. The core group around Harris was decidedly more radical than the mainstream Avukah members, particularly those who were living outside of the New York area where much of the Avukah policy was created and the Avukah pamphlets, newspapers, and books were disseminated. A number of Avukahites considered that the radical core in New York was eager to convert the more mainstream members of Avukah to their side. William Schumer, one of a hundred or so Avukah members at the University of Michigan at the time, discussed the idea of small activist cells on the phone with Zellig Harris, who tried to recruit him to the more radical inner circle. Avukah was the "furthest thing" from Schumer's mind at that time, however, because as a Jew, he was, in his words, just "struggling to stay alive," and "worrying a lot about the German concentration camps, and the sinking of refugee ships," topics he considered to be "the issues of the day." For this reason, Schumer suggested in a rather tongue-in-cheek fashion that after his resistance to Harris in this conversation he was "scratched off of Zellig's list" of those who could serve as "revolutionary leaders." He was not alone; a number of Avukahites begrudged Harris's tendency to unceremoniously drop individuals, professionally and personally, when he felt that they were no longer part of the vanguard he was trying to develop.

Many former members noted the extent of the tensions within and beyond the Avukah organization on the basis of the strong ideological stance it promoted. In Michigan, the majority of Avukah members considered that the enemies on the left were the Jews in the American Student Union (ASU), and on the right, the Jewish fraternities. Schumer recalls that even the rabbi of Hillel had to be reckoned with because he was deemed a "secret Communist," which was frustrating because Avukah operated under the auspices of Hillel and the rabbi challenged Avukah activities "at every turn." And the former director of the New England Avukah chapter, Millie Kravetz, described the New England Avukah as being peripheral to the central Avukah activities, rendering it more of an outpost than an integrated participant in activities. Chava Rapkin does recall, though, that members of the Hunter University chapter or other New York Avukah chapters would sometimes go to Boston, and one trip there was particularly memorable: "I was a counselor at a summer camp, in upstate New York, and the man who was courting me came up and said 'come on, we are getting married.' And I agreed with him, because I had that in mind too. It was Chester Rapkin. So my boss gave me three days off, and we went to Boston. Why Boston? Because we thought we could get married there, past the three-mile limit. At the same time, I was told that a young man had come to the camp looking for me. It was Murray Eden. And he said, 'What happened to her?' The people in the camp said, 'Well, she went off to get married.' And Murray Eden laughed and said, 'Oh, she would say such a thing!' Chester and Chava Rapkin went to Boston, where Millie Katz (Kravetz) was, she introduced us to a Jewish Church, and signed, as though we had the proper testing or injections for whatever diseases they were testing for, and we were able to get married by a Justice of the Peace." Neither of them had any money for a hotel, though, so, recalled Chava, "I called my father, and I told him that I had just gotten married in Boston and I didn't have any money. And he said 'you didn't have to run off! I love Chester!'. I was 20 years old, it was so romantic to run off and get married!" But other than the outings to Philadelphia and Boston, Chava Rapkin didn't recall contact with other Avukahs and, except for during summer camp, with other Avukahites.

Many Avukah members who were close to Harris described a sense of feeling part of this vanguard, a sense that was reinforced by the summer educational camps that also served as the national convention. Some of the work undertaken in this framework was related to the study of attitude formation and modification, itself part of a broader interest that Harris shared with certain figures in the field of psychoanalysis, notably Erich Fromm and David Rapaport. Harris suggested to several students in his inner circle that they should read in this realm, and in the late 1940s he introduced Chomsky to some well-known figures in the field of psychoanalysis. Chomsky recalls that Harris "took me to visit Rapaport, one of the very few people in his circle I ever met (maybe Erikson was there too it was at their clinic in Connecticut, I think)." A passionate interest in psychoanalysis had also led Harris to the Frankfurt school, notably to the work of Erich Fromm, which he recommended to his colleagues. Fromm loomed large for Avukah members, in particular on account of the implications of his great work *Escape from Freedom*,[12] a text that is often mentioned in articles and discussions from that period. Murray Eden recalls that Harris was certainly moved by the notion of psychiatry, particularly in the idea that there exists a general principle that "what moves people is some kind of a program, in the sense of a computer program, something in people that makes initial decisions in a situation [that] establishes a frame of reference according which people pursue their lives." For Eden, this was in accord with Harris's general attitude, and it was based on the assumption that, among other things, you learn by studying the output recorded in, say, a conversation, and how it reflects the "program" of participant individuals. Then generalizing, on the basis of that program, we can say something about the framework that underwrites behavior in a community of people. From that perspective, Zellig Harris's interest in this realm was more in what might be called a sociology, or a study of social construction.

Chava Rapkin was accustomed through her family to being close to the Jewish cultural and Zionist vanguard, before even meeting Harris. She recalled that "David Ben-Gurion was a frequent visitor to our home. My father was a big, big name, in those days. I was in the same organization with Ben-Gurion's son, and I used to go to their home. Ben-Gurion and my father had great discussions, and they disagreed, very basically, on the issue of immigration. Ben-Gurion said bring in everybody and anybody, the more Jews we have the better. This was in the very early '30s before the Hitler period, and my father said, 'you have to be more selective on who you bring in, as to the kind of country you want to build'." In retrospect, Harris undoubtedly was of the same opinion as Chava Rapkin's father, Maurice Samuels, but unlike people like Irene Schumer, Harris kept to this idea of focusing upon a vanguard rather than mass movements through his life.

Linguistics and Politics

Zellig Harris's early studies and teaching focused on linguistics at the University of Pennsylvania, beginning with work on Semitic languages, which led him to a faculty position in 1931, one year after he completed his BA.[13] In 1932 he completed *Origin of the Alphabet*,[14] an unpublished master's thesis that is described in his 1933 article "Acrophony and Vowellessness in the Creation of the Alphabet," for the *Journal of the American Oriental Society*.[15] He continued his research and completed his doctorate while working as a faculty member at University of Pennsylvania. His doctoral thesis, completed in 1934, and first book, which offered a grammar and glossary of Phoenician, was described by the linguist Peter Matthews as "by all accounts excellent and still cited for points of detail." He had already contributed much to the analysis of the then new material in Ugaritic. The linguist Henry Hiz, in his tribute to Harris,[16] recalled that "partly in association with his teacher, James A. Montgomery, but soon very much on his own, he became a prominent contributor to the decipherment and reading of the Ugaritic texts. His 1934 book on Phoenician grammar made a great impression and, incidentally, attracted the methodological (and philological) attention of Edward Sapir. In 1939, the systematic and original study on the development of Canaanite dialects followed. Already manifest in all these works is the peculiarly precise, yet flexible, scholarly style that was to remain his for the rest of his life."

Harris was motivated in his professional studies by Edward Sapir's work, and he was deeply influenced by Leonard Bloomfield's monumental book *Language*,[17] which set out in a range of ways the program for Harris's linguistics explorations in the coming decades. Numerous passages could be cited, but in terms of the ideology-linguistics overlap that was already apparent in Harris's work, the final sentence of Bloomfield's book is particularly relevant: "The methods and results of linguistics, in spite of their modest scope, resemble those of natural science, the domain in which science has been most successful. It is only a prospect, but not hopelessly remote, that the study of language may help us toward the understanding and control of human events" (509). This points to Harris's eventual interest in discourse analysis, and some of the work he oversaw on such projects as propaganda and media analysis, as we will see in section II. Bloomfield's work is also cautionary, though; two paragraphs before the ambitious statement above, Bloomfield writes that "we cannot pretend to any sound knowledge of communal forms of human behavior" until we have "accurate and complete information abut the languages of the world" (508). The Harris-Bloomfield overlap is important, according to Hiz's tribute to Harris, since Bloomfield

strove to understand the phenomenon of meaning in language, just as Harris always did. However, they knew that at present there are no scientific ways to examine meaning in all of its social manifestations. But, as Harris repeated after Bloomfield: 'It frequently happens that when we do not rest with the explanation that something is due to meaning, we discover that it has a formal regularity or 'explanation'. It may still be 'due to meaning' in one sense, but it accords with a distributional regularity'. For Bloomfield, Sapir, and Harris, the primary datum for the scientific study of language is the relative position of the segments of speech utterances. (519)

Harris's next book (1939) was a study of the early history of the Canaanite branch of West Semitic languages, to which the Phoenician dialects including Hebrew, Moabite, and others belong. This too is an exemplary philological study, of a kind that he would not publish again. There seems little doubt that, "had he continued in the Semitic field, he would have been a leader in it."[18] Instead, beginning in 1940 or so, when he was in his early thirties, he and a group of associates began to meet to discuss a general program of what they regarded as an ideology, and this combination of linguistics and politics came to be central to Zellig Harris's life. The early group was composed of Murray Eden, Fred Karush, Harold Orlans, Chester Rapkin, and Murray Wax, and it later expanded to include, most notably, Nathan Glazer and Seymour Melman, and others who came to be associated in different ways with Avukah.

The overlap between linguistics and politics emerges from time to time in this narrative, as for example in the suggestion, from Seymour Melman, that "Harris invented transformational grammar for essentially political reasons, as a tool to show that the very sentential structure in the writings of Sidney Hook, with whom he disagreed profoundly, would show their falsehood." Or in the fact that much of the "discourse analysis" that he undertook, in ways considered novel for the time period, were applied to political speeches or other kinds of propagandistic literatures, to establish ideological threads in certain kinds of discourse. But overall, Zellig Harris's linguistics and politics were kept quite separate, such that colleagues knew him for his technical linguistic work, while political allies worked with him to advance his work on the transformation of capitalist society. Nathan Glazer suggested that "if there was a connection between the politics and the linguistics, I don't know what it was; they were two separate worlds that were combined in him, but he didn't bring characteristics of one to bear upon the other. Maybe in his mind. I don't recall similar efforts to take views taken from linguistics to understanding of society. For him, if you weren't in theoretical physics, if you're not at the highest level of abstract understanding, then anyone can learn it, it's minor, it's not such a big thing."

On this politics-linguistics overlap, there was a group of young people who joined Harris in the late 1930s and early 1940s to discuss political questions and to undertake analyses thereof based on studies of discourse. Leigh Lisker was a member of this group; in his sophomore year at Penn, he enrolled in a linguistics course with Harris (at that time under the sponsorship of the Department of Anthropology), where he became interested in Harris's methodology. After graduation he joined the war effort, and when he returned from his military service, he enrolled in Penn's graduate school, switching from German to the newly-minted Department of Linguistic Analysis, which Harris founded just after the end of the war. It was at that time that he joined a group of young people who would meet in his home to discuss political questions, with considerable emphasis placed on the findings of "mass observation" in determining the state of "public opinion" and how these related to more official views of that elusive creature. Particular attention was given to reaction (in the United States) to the death of Franklin D. Roosevelt, and in France, to attitudes toward the German occupation and certain events in the immediate post-liberation period.

Studies of this sort were of great interest to Harris's milieu, and indeed this whole period was peopled with some critical figures, like Lukoff and Glazer, who would remain marked by the work they did in this framework. Leigh Lisker recalls Lukoff's Master's thesis on discourse analysis which examined, using linguistic techniques, "how certain very influential US magazines slanted discussions of the new Labor government in Great Britain." Lisker himself had taken his first course in linguistics in around 1939 (under the sponsorship of the anthropology department), and, as he recalls, "in the next year I took his [Harris's] course in modern Hebrew, a 'practical' course that sold me on linguistics. I was then a major in German." Lisker eventually became one of Harris's colleagues, and they worked together on some common projects that were "a kind of forerunner to the Chomsky-Herman idea of 'managed public opinion', in the period just prior to Chomsky's arriving on the scene at Penn." Chomsky "didn't come onto the scene until long after I had dropped out," which he did "not for lack of sympathy, but because, as a beginning faculty person with a new family, I was too busy with teaching and research."[19] Lisker never did work alongside of either Murray Eden or Chomsky, Harris's most famous student of the period, because once named to the faculty at Penn, and was therefore busy teaching, researching, and beginning a family.

There are important differences, though, between Chomsky's and Harris's work in this area, as in others, because as Murray Eden notes, "a large portion of Harris's later work was to identify an overarching scientific procedure in an attempt to reduce discourse to some logical form." The idea that underwrote this approach, which will be discussed at length in Section II, was relatively straightforward, says Eden: "If you could take some piece of text or discourse which is intended to direct your thoughts in one way or another, then one should be able to be put into a logical form, and demonstrate connections or contradictions that are not obvious." Harris's last work, after retiring from Penn and working New York, exemplified a way of using this methodology to regularize chemistry texts. But long before then, in around 1949, Murray Eden had worked on a similar project, aiming to discover some standard logical form. For Eden, "Harris's work in this regard was much closer in its procedures and objectives to engineering than to the philosophical approach taken by Chomsky."

Chomsky-Harris

Noam Chomsky met Professor Zellig Harris, the Benjamin Franklin Professor of Linguistics, at the University of Pennsylvania, but he had known him through family connections since childhood. Shoshanna Harris recalled that William Chomsky, Noam's father, and Zellig Harris, "saw each other socially," and they published articles on Semitic language issues in some of the same journals. The Harris-Chomsky link expanded when Chomsky became a student and research assistant to this family friend: "The primary teacher of Noam was Zellig Harris," says Henry Hiz, emeritus professor of linguistics, who also taught Chomsky at Penn. "It's very difficult to describe the profound influence Harris had on him—and on me, too." "Zellig Harris was a primary influence on Noam, perhaps *the* primary influence back then," agreed Carol Chomsky (who went by Carol Schatz until she and Noam were married in 1949). "Noam admired him enormously, and I think it's fair to say that Zellig Harris was responsible, in so many different ways, for the direction that Noam's intellectual life took then and later."[20]

The linguistic text around which the early Chomsky-Harris dialog took place was initially *Methods in Structural Linguistics* (1951), an attempt to organize descriptive linguistics into a single body of theory and practice. On the back cover of the Midway Reprints edition (1986), Norman McQuown writes: "Harris's contribution [is] epoch-marking in a double sense: first in that it marks the culmination of a development of linguistic methodology *away* from a stage of intuitionism, frequently culture-bound; and second in that it marks the beginnings of a new period, in which the new methods will be applied ever more rigorously to ever widening areas in human culture." This book played a vital role in forging the Harris-Chomsky relationship, as Chomsky himself maintains in the introduction to his early work, *The Logical Structure of Linguistic Theory*:[21] "My formal introduction to the field of linguistics was in 1947, when Zellig Harris gave me the proofs of his *Methods in Structural Linguistics* to read. I found it very intriguing and, after some stimulating discussions with Harris, decided to major in linguistics as an undergraduate at the University of Pennsylvania. I had some informal acquaintance with historical linguistics and medieval Hebrew grammar, based on my father's work in these fields, and at the same time was studying Arabic with Giorgio Levi Della Vida" (25). But for Chomsky, the real interest was in Zellig Harris's approach to political and ideological issues, what Leigh Lisker described to me in correspondence as "Harris's interest in exploring alternative ways of describing the world which, despite Harris's tenacity and clearly-defined approach, was multifarious, suggesting that there was not ONE correct method or answer to the hardest questions." It is in this approach, said Lisker, that one found a link between Harris's linguistics and his politics, "even if he was friendliest with those students of his whose political attitudes were close to his" (something people often say as well of Noam Chomsky).

One of the clearest ways in which this link was manifested was in the work on discourse analysis, and another member in that period, Fred Lukoff, was involved through his master's thesis on the aforementioned discourse analysis project. Using some of Harris's linguistic techniques, he studied how certain very influential US magazines slanted discussions of the new Labor government in Great Britain. Lisker also described to me the ample time that he had spent trying to apply Harris's notions of discourse analysis, which he found to produce "revealing observations in the case of scientific and political texts, to some writings concerned with fine arts exhibitions," with what he described as "chaotic" results. Closer to his own interest was when he carried out, at Harris's request, a study to determine how accurately word and morpheme boundaries are reflected in the elementary statistics of phoneme distribution in Telugu, a Dravidian language of southeast India.[22] This work coincided with other studies and teaching related to several modern Indian languages.

Murray Eden's reflections concur with Lisker's on man of these matters. He had first met Harris when he was 18 years old, and although he had no formal training in structural linguistics, he undertook with Harris's encouragement a discourse analysis project. He attempted to rewrite English texts, originally from newspaper articles, into a standard form that was consistent with formal logic. Eden recalls that both Harris and Noam Chomsky, whom he himself had met through Zellig, "were championing quite different procedures, but were both were wedded to a formal approach." Eden's own taste was much more eclectic, an "engineering approach" that in his description "might fit some significant part of a text or utterance, but it failed to handle all the text." Later on, Eden, with Morris Halle, did develop a full formalism for cursive scripts that seems to work for any well-formed script, notably Cyrillic, Sanskrit, and Hebrew. He also used some of the ideas in the analysis of other symbol systems and even images of natural objects, and, with his students, he made trials to analyze degenerate (sloppy) handwriting. Eden's last work in linguistics, again inspired by Harris, was to return to the issue of discourse analysis, this time attempting to reduce papers in chemistry to logic governed statements. Harris's own last efforts, subsequent to his retirement from Penn, were at Columbia University, following his own formalist methods, but with essentially the same textual material.

On the more political side, Harris and his students applied descriptive methods to political and journalistic discourse, in part to bolster Harris's work on "attitudes" and how to modify them in the quest for the good society. Norman Epstein, a professor of engineering who had been a member of the McGill Avukah, recalled in a speech he gave in the Ridge Theater on March 5, 1996 (in the context of an introduction to Noam Chomsky, the invited lecturer) that Zellig Harris was a person of extraordinary brilliance and political understanding who "was interested in the media and popular culture representation of the dominant or mainstream ideology." From Epstein's perspective, "for Harris, the function of this ideology is to confuse and even deceive or fool people about the real state of affairs under which they live; and that one of the principal tasks of literate, articulate and educated radicals is to help reverse this process, i.e. to first of all unfool themselves, and then to contribute to unfooling others." The phrase that Harris used to describe this process was not "unfooling" but rather "defooling," so the proper job of a radical was to contribute to the defooling process, something that Harris worked on with his students as part of a project known as "frame of reference." This work, as we'll see in the next chapter (and again in section III), underwrote Harris's general approach to worker relations and the transformation of capitalist society throughout his life.

3 Frame of Reference

In spite of Zellig Harris's interest in the framework that underwrites people's approach to the world and his studies of political discourse, he had no overt interest in contemporary politics, such as elections or current events, because he considered them to be manifestations of deeper tendencies that could be studied more thoroughly in work on general attitudes. As such, the essence of his lifelong efforts, particularly in the work that he did under the auspices of what he called the Frame of Reference project,[1] FoR, to which I will return in detail in section III, was to understand and eventually motivate changes in underlying social attitudes. This work, partially represented in his posthumous book titled *The Transformation of Capitalist Society*,[2] allows us a glimpse into the relationship between his own work and the related studies of Noam Chomsky, Seymour Melman, and, from a very different perspective, Nathan Glazer.

The unwieldy set of notes and writings that constitute the current state of the FoR project was the result of it having been written by different people, who would contribute pieces on the basis of their respective expertise and interest. The text that remains, which takes the form of a 1,000 or so page diffuse collection of unsigned and largely unorganized observations, was mostly written by Harris and by people of the generation before Murray Eden and Seymour Melman. This group is described by Murray Eden as "the oldsters," a half dozen or so colleagues and friends who in some cases did not know one another. Fred Karush (who became a distinguished immunologist, eventually teaching microbiology at Penn) was an important member of this group and a key contributor to the text, including much that has been described to me as "unbelievably opaque." Another important contributor was Lawrence B. Cohen, who investigated decision making on production by industrial workers, an important antecedent to the work of both Zellig Harris and Seymour Melman. People involved in the project came to feel strong resentment toward Harris for withholding the work, and this led to a souring of relations among some of the key contributors, who consider to this day that Harris held the reigns of this small group too firmly in his own hands. From all indications, this sectlike character was typical of other small radical groups, and it produced remarkably close relations, including marriages (and divorces) within the group. It also of course produced dissension and diversity of opinion, about approach and even recollection of major events.

I had the opportunity to interview some of the members who contributed to the FoR project, including Murray Eden and Seymour Melman, and both of them described a process whereby a discussion relating to the project would be elaborated and developed by members of Harris's circle who, based on their respective perspectives and expertise, would then turn their findings over to Harris at their next meeting or send them to him through the mail. The process unfolded on the basis of an elaborate outline that provided a road map, so that each contributor would know where things were supposed to fit. But the project was never completed, and because each contribution was undated and unsigned, and clear sections were not set out in the text itself, it is very difficult, particularly in hindsight, to assess what issues are being addressed. Nevertheless, the sheer scope and volume of the existing manuscript reflects the grandiose ambitions that Harris had for the project, including his plan to follow up on the FoR with appropriate actions, to be undertaken on the basis of the analysis presented.

Regrettably, nobody ever got that far; the only publicly available product of this work was the book, *The Transformation of Capitalist Society,* which, as far as Eden recalls, was never circulated in manuscript form among those who had worked on the FoR project. Its existence only came to be known even to FoR collaborators after Harris's death, when Murray Eden, William Evans, and Seymour Melman prepared it for publication by Roman Littlefield (1997). And consistent with the idea that there were different and sometimes cordoned-off facets of Harris's life is the fact that many people who knew him very well knew nothing about the FoR project, including Meyer Rabban, Chava Rapkin, Irene Schumer, and William Schumer.

Many of the Avukah and FoR efforts described thus far relate to Harris's attempt to assess the general attitudes that prevail in a given society, and then to direct actions that would lead toward a "good society." To this end, Harris worked with friends and colleagues on approaches that he considered important to the task. As we have seen, such figures as Albert Einstein, Erich Fromm, Arthur Rosenberg, and a range of individuals in left-wing groups with which he had interactions, including those surrounding

Dwight McDonald, were deemed significant in this regard. Notable too, according to Seymour Melman, was "Harris's interest in the influential analyses of Ber Borochov, the Eastern European sociologist and political analyst who defined the occupational class analysis of Jewish societies in Eastern Europe and the 'necessity' for occupational productivization of Jews on a large scale, including co-ops, kibbutz, territorial concentration, and so forth."[3]

Harris also knew all the important Zionist figures, and he introduced many in the Avukah circle to major Zionist personalities, notably Louis D. Brandeis. Many of those I interviewed were deeply marked by their meeting with this great figure, a leading judge on the U.S Supreme court and an active "elder statesman" in the Zionist Organization of America. Harris fostered a yearly pilgrimage to Washington D.C., so that a chosen few would have the opportunity to meet with Brandeis in his home on Connecticut Avenue. Avukahites knew of these meetings, and those who participated in them, including Seymour Melman and Robert Wallerstein, described their meetings as an exceptional event in their lives. Harris had a lot to do with picking who would go to see Brandeis, and Wallerstein, for example, recalls that he was somewhat surprised by this honor, since he had little direct contact with Harris.

The Fall of Avukah

It is perhaps not surprising that the FoR project was kept under wraps, considering Harris's fear of discovery by the authorities of his more radical political and Zionist beliefs; but it is surprising that the little Zionist organization Avukah disappeared from the scene so quickly, particularly given Harris's investment in it. According to Glazer, there were among the directors of the New York office of Avukah "exaggerated expectations of the role of the vanguard," this inner educated circle that Harris created and sustained. In 1942, Harris was increasingly worried that so many of the leading members were donning uniforms and heading for Europe, and there was a growing sense among those charged with day-to-day activities that the objectives of the organization needed to be reoriented in the face of the unfolding annihilation of European Jews. It is incredible to consider, in light of the prevailing attitude many people hold about how ignorant the Allies were about the Final Solution, that in 1942 and 1943 groups of people, in institutions such as the Jewish Labor Organization (Bund), the BBC, the Vatican, the Red Cross, and organizations such as the State Department, and other officials from different levels of government in

Europe and the United States were being provided with descriptions of the death camps and the Nazi ambitions. People like the young Jews in Avukah were informed by different means about what was transpiring in the camps, notably through face-to-face meeting with Moshe Shertok (later Moshe Sharett, who became Prime Minister of Israel) who described narratives of two women who had escaped from Treblinka. Both Seymour Melman and Irene Schumer have described with profound chagrin this revelatory moment that would shake their respective faith in actions being taken by Avukah, and by the Allied forces.

The representatives from Avukah for the meeting with Shertok were Irene Schumer and Al Kahn; Melman, who was not present, learned about it from others shortly thereafter. Says Schumer, "when we heard Shertok tell us what these two women had said, we were stupefied. We were with a group of people from Jewish youth groups, and for us there, Al Kahn and myself, if we were going to do something for someone, it had to be for ourselves. That's what set us on our course." Melman recalled that subsequently, when word was spread, a huge group of Jews walked to a rally at Madison Square Garden in New York to discuss what could be done. At this point in my interview with him, conducted in his office at Columbia about two years before his death in the fall of 2004, he began sobbing. His voice shaky, he recounted that "no decisions were made at that meeting, but rather people gathered for what looked like a wake, replete with Jews wearing prayer shawls to remember the Jews who died, and, moreover, those were to die subsequently." Schumer recalls that this mass rally in Madison Square Garden was deemed necessary because "the official people [government officials, in particular] were not saying anything. They already knew these things, the leadership knew, it wasn't only women from Treblinka, but they knew. The Yishuv [the Jewish population in Palestine at that time] changed course, though, in the face of the news from Treblinka." For Schumer, this confirmation of what had long been suspected about Nazi intentions meant that the organization Avukah would have to reorient itself toward saving Jews, and this decision marked the beginning of the end of Avukah. "Zellig and the more radical elements didn't see the world in this way, and he didn't wish to become co-opted to the Allied cause, which would undermine the broader effort towards a radical overturning of society." He, like others in the inner circle, "thought that Avukah was a group of intelligent people, who shared the same world view as they did." And in this context—of the camps, the unfolding Holocaust, the destruction of Europe—"I didn't have a lot of sympathy for Milty [Milton Shapiro, a member of Avukah] starving himself, I didn't have a lot of sympathy for studying Swahili to avoid fighting. Not that I thought they should volunteer, particularly. But who is this? Whose fight is this? And there were other people who felt as I did."

Several Avukahites believe to this day that Harris and Melman decided in early 1943 to disband Avukah in the face of impending changes to its orientation toward saving Jews from annihilation rather than creating Jewish-Arab cooperation in a socialist Palestine.[4] But this decision reflected as well some of the prevailing attitudes that Harris and others held about Avukah being controlled by the women, who stayed behind in the United States while growing numbers of Avukah men were enlisted to fight in the war. From 1941 until early 1943 "things had been fine," recalls Schumer, but during this period the "boys" who had been running things were in heading off in ever larger numbers to fight in the war and "no matter how smart the girls were, and no matter how much control they were gaining in this period," they "deferred to the boys" for everything, and there was no thought that the girls could "do things themselves." The boys were "much more assertive, the traditional roles made us girls more retiring, and there were only certain areas where we were deemed to do well, like the housekeeping. But none of us would have ideological discussions, even though we all knew the program. And I think it was a wonderful program, I still do, it made a great contribution."

The dearth of "boys" in the leadership led to Avukah being increasingly directed by Schumer and Lillian Schoolman, and "we represented moderate voices" who challenged Harris's perspective, leading to the engineering of a "'blow-up' by Zellig and by Seymour Melman." Harris didn't want Avukah to change direction, in part because he favored small, easily controlled groups over more active ones that might make them targets of investigation (as happened, for example, during the Mitch Palmer episode in the 1920s[5]). The situation "became more critical as more Americans were sent overseas," and Harris and Melman presumably thought it better to dissolve Avukah than lose control of its leadership to a group of women who were considered, in addition to somehow incompetent, insufficiently radical. William Schumer, who worked with Seymour Melman at Columbia, claimed that "the girls would have done a better job than the boys, in particular the leadership of Avukah at this time." Be that as it may, the "boys" engineered what William Schumer called a "revolutionary coup" to dissolve Avukah.

A plan was devised in late 1942 to ensure control of Avukah by the inner circle, and on the basis of different conversations I had concerning the demise of Avukah, it was this idea that brought dissension, disarray, and eventually the end of the movement. Harold Orlans remembered that Seymour Melman came into the meeting wearing a khaki uniform (he was presumably on leave from military service), full of advice on how to keep the activities of the inner circle secret. Someone then came in and said that in the course of a meeting in Washington (of some unnamed group), Murray Wax had described Avukah's little inner circle in New York. This revelation created significant consternation and, with very little further discussion, the decision was taken to disband the group. This may have been a reflection of the fear that Harris had of being discovered in his radical activities, and the concern many members felt that they would risk the entire cause if they were investigated. Glazer recalls similar fears from Max Horkheimer, who "masked his allegiance to communism in dialectical materialism" and feared more direct engagement. "Horkheimer's carefulness and uncertainty reflected his position, and his fear of exposure as a Marxist. His work was all filled with negative dialectics and so forth, so his ideology was not so overt. In Harris too, you can find this whole notion that the political doctrines have to be concealed. It took his disciples to finally publish anything by Horkheimer on the politics," and the same applies to Harris's political work recorded in his book, *The Transformation of Capitalist Society.*

Whatever the motivation(s) that guided Harris and Melman, when members came from all over the United States to attend the annual national convention of Avukah in June, 1943, they were to be met with a proposal for dissolution. As Glazer recalls, by the time the summer convention convened, "Melman was already in the army, but he had been consulted on the plan to bring fundamental changes in how the Avukah would be run henceforth. Both Al Kahn and Meyer Rabban, the other two members of the trio that had been running the Avukah office in New York, were by then overseas. Glazer recruited Marty (Seymour Martin) Lipset to join the organization to strengthen the radical inner circle, and so he was brought in on what Glazer called the "plot."[6] "Harris was intent on preserving this elite. Where this idea came from? It could only have come from Melman. The plan was that they had to assure the offices of Avukah at the next Convention, which was in 1943. The notion was that they would have to control the elections. At that time, whether independently of this or just thinking it was a good idea I'm not sure, but I asked Marty Lipset to join Avukah, and he joined. . . . So it is true that we were a kind of Cabal in the group, and we had our candidates, and in retrospect you might say we represented a faction."

Zev Schumer's recollection was that

they wanted the New York elite, the intellectuals, to call all of the shots. Nathan Glazer was assigned to me, and I was the then president of the Michigan chapter of Avukah for the mid-winter conference of 1942. Nat and I went to lunch at the automat, where you put the coins in. He took me to lunch, and he was set on explaining to me why all the political power should be centered in New York. He said that they were brighter, they were at the center of things, and so forth. But we had the membership, and these central people in NY didn't have the membership, so they could be outvoted in plenary sessions. Of course I didn't fall for this crap. I was a Midwesterner. At Michigan we must have had a couple of hundred members, it was a strong chapter. So I had the votes. Then at one of the meetings, Irene was chairman, and she was very fair in conducting the meeting, she permitted everyone to talk, for which she got into trouble with her left-wing group. Afterwards they complained to her, "why did you let everyone talk?"

Irene Schumer recalled in response to her husband's recollection that "Bruria was beside herself, she was jumping up and down like a jumping jack!" As a result of that meeting, Zev described himself as "impressed with Irene, I had never met her before, and I asked her out to dinner, that was our first date."

The plan was hatched, therefore, to dissolve Avukah, since there seemed to be no way to ensure the continued control of the organization by the New York office. That summer, at the Avukah annual meeting of 1943, Lipset called everyone together to discuss a new plan that had been prepared by Harris in conjunction with the inner circle. Irene Schumer remembers having learned of the "cabal" in a meeting held on the Friday night before the election—in a cave near the location of the summer camp! "Present for the occasion were Tzvee, Margolit, Nat, Ruth, Shush, Lillian, Margolit, and Seymour 'the serpent', Marty Lipset." The view presented from Marty was in the form of a "confessional," as Irene Schumer recalls, that all of the "unreliable elements," the "counter-revolutionary elements," would be "eliminated from the leadership," and Avukah would continue with other people who were more "ideologically pure." In reflecting upon why Lipset decided to reveal the plan to some of the members, Glazer speculated: "At that time he was part of this offshoot of left socialism or Trotskyism, which took this whole notion of democracy very seriously. They were reading Gaetano Mosca, Wilfredo Pareto and Robert Michels, on why socialist parties turn into bureaucracies," something that presumably he tried to stop in the case of Avukah by revealing the plans of the leadership.

For Irene Schumer, this confession was "a shock, in particular because the Avukah members had all been very close, they enjoyed activities in NY together, they took care of each other" in part, in 1941 or 1942, because, as she told me in an interview,

We didn't know that we were going to win the war. In retrospect, we were able to do 50,000 planes, but who knew it? And then of course they started taking people into the army, so everyone began to disappear, and it was a hard thing to hold the organization together. We got $2,000 per year from the ZOA, one dollar per member. When Seymour and Al and Meyer left, Lillian became the Secretary General, and Margolit Shebulsky and I ran the office. And what were we to do? We were against the White Paper,[7] we wanted Jews to go to Palestine, this was the biggest thing, and we recognized what was going on in Europe, and this was overwhelming, what could compare to that?

Lillian and Irene Schumer had been brought into the Avukah establishment by Margolit, and they thought that some of the Avukah ideas were "out in left field. To not want to fight in the war? Now that to me was heinous," said Schumer. So when Seymour Lipset "exposed the plan for the putsch, the work of an inner circle that was trying to take over the organization," she describes having been "dumbfounded." She remembers that whole night as being "so awfully dark. It couldn't have been as dark as I remember. I said, 'what are you talking about? I cannot believe it!' We left that meeting, and we were wandering around at camp, and we had such wonderful times at camp, and here was this happening at camp, it was incredible."

Nathan Glazer recalls the same evening, saying that "Martin exposed us during the meeting as a secret group that was trying to control everything, and that he had known about it, and he had changed his mind. The whole thing broke up in total confusion, or a separation," but one "in which both sides ultimately forgave each other." Before the forgiveness, though, there was the devastation, in particular for Irene Schumer who thought that "no matter what divisions there were between the people in the New York office and the people out in the various chapters, the people in the chapters still had a point of view which was that we were all one group, and we had an attitude of tolerance. For instance, I felt that at that time Nat was so naïve about the world, but I loved him! The City College boys were very unfinished, they were crude, not crude sexually, indeed they were very puritanical in that regard, but a bit rough and brash." In any event, the night of the breakup, Irene Schumer called Al Kahn, the executive secretary at the time, to seek advice on the night after the meeting, but there was no turning back, so the group just fractured and dissolved.

The Legacy of Avukah

This was a breakup that a many Avukahites regretted long afterward, and for the most part, those with whom I have spoken blame Zellig Harris. It was, for Schumer, "the end of a kind of family—not for Bruria and Zellig," who she felt were more aloof, "but for others." Glazer suggested that "for Irene Schumer, who comes out of a more traditional Zionist household, and Lillian Schoolman (Kaplan) and others, how terrible this was, and they could attribute it all to Zellig or to Melman, but in fact there was always a willingness to go beyond it. Avukah overcame this split in terms of personal relations over the years after. These feelings of warmness of having been involved, . . . there was something incredibly intense and shaping, even though it was a short period. You can't make sense of it, you can't say why." Irene Schumer even recalls that when the story came out, Tzvee Harris was crying. "I couldn't believe it, Tzvee is crying! And we wandered around all night, and we didn't know what to do, I don't recall how we went home, but I remember that the organization moved to New England after that. It was so wrenching. It turned into an organization called the Intercollegiate Zionist Organization, which dissolved within the year."

When I first discussed this breakup of Avukah with Melman, he attributed it to pressure from the Zionist Organization of America on account of the "overly radical" nature of Avukah's positions. Chava Rapkin commented that Melman's position was too strong: "It disbanded because we each went our separate ways. We got married, and so forth, and we no longer gave support to up-and-coming young people. There were other issues that came up at that time, and some others took precedence. You have to be pretty committed to a thing like this, like Zionism. For one reason or another, because I was away from home, because I had just come from Palestine, Avukah was very important. But as time went on, even with the State of Israel, young people moved away. I cannot explain what happened. But it wasn't the pressure of the ZOA. I think that they lost membership, or interest." Even Irene Schumer agrees that "in and of itself it would have been difficult to maintain this organization, it was a real struggle. But why did they feel that they had to cut it off at that point? I understand that what the leadership wanted was small study groups, like cells, so that if the government came around you'd only know the people in your cell. I do think that this is what they wanted, because they had this notion that fascism was going to take over and people were going to be at risk for having these ideas."

This give-and-take in perspectives on the demise of Avukah–in which Melman described fears of being censored or investigated by the government or by the Zionist Organization of America, Irene Schumer recalls an ideological breakup, William Schumer calls it a "coup," and Chava Rapkin considers the inevitable development of a student organization–helps clarify a crucial point: these were monumental times, which required decisive and strong action, and Avukah, which had started more as a kind of social Jewish student organization, was thrust by the rise of fascism and the outbreak of the war into a different role. The different perspectives, which I am certainly not here to arbitrate, do demonstrate that Zellig Harris was a crucial lynchpin for many of the individuals and viewpoints discussed in this book; it is also clear from this discussion, though, that he was "a," but not "the" lynchpin, and there were very strong personalities and tremendous work undertaken by those with whom he worked, closely and at a distance, on very complex and controversial matters.

Members of Avukah had taken their program and their ideology very seriously, and many of them went on using some of the approaches that they had learned in Avukah, long after the demise of the organization. Everyone I have spoken to remained resolutely antifascist, and many adhered to the belief that fascism was a development of late capitalism, and as such was a threat to both the United States and Germany. This idea, which was certainly near and dear to people like Seymour Melman, was described by Glazer as an "error" that was typical of the left at the time. For him, "there was a sense that war would lead to the end of civil liberties in the US and possibly a fascism as terrible as that in Europe," a view that had been promoted by Harris. From this perspective, Harris concluded that the war was being fought by two imperialistic-capitalistic blocs, and as such there was little reason to choose between them. For Glazer, this was the import of a 1941 article in *Partisan Review* by Dwight MacDonald and Clement Greenberg titled "10 Propositions on the War."[8]

There is some background to this view of the Second World War, which comes from Robert Wallerstein. For him, many people in the New York Avukah group, in particular those who were attending City College in New York, fell into the intense politics of the period, as reflected in their specific milieu. Those politics were "very left wing" and "very factionalized, divided into Stalinist, Trotskyites, . . . and each faction would have lunch at its own table in the City College dining room," as was portrayed so clearly in the film "Arguing the World." Students would "talk politics, and derogate the other factions, at other tables, who they felt were off on the wrong track," and several important members of Avukah—Nathan Glazer,

Seymour Melman, and Al Kahn—were part of this. These people "absorbed that political climate and, like most youth in New York City at that time, children of immigrants, growing up in relative poverty, they were all imbued with left-wing politics." By way of example, Robert Wallerstein recalls that in his own high school, there had been a very active "Oxford Oath" group:

In the 1930s, people all over the country were taking an oath to never support a war again, the war to end all wars, WWI, had failed, and didn't bring about an enduring successful peace. Everyone was very disillusioned, across the country, but especially in New York. And then of course when World War II came, things were very different, and that got abandoned, that concept of being against all war, so instead we thought of the socialist revolution.

This sheds interesting light upon Harris's reluctance to join the war effort, and to direct his energies toward his own vision of radical politics. But at the heart of the Avukah ideology was, for Robert Wallerstein, "Zionism and socialism. There was going to be utopia in Israel, built around the Kibbutzim. It was going to be a bi-national state with the Arab and Jewish workers working together to overthrow the capitalists." There was as well a belief in the possibility of a greater degree of self-rule by groups of equals, and it is much more in this vein that Harris's student, Noam Chomsky, would follow later on (through the perspective of anarcho-syndicalism and anarchism). For Glazer, though, that "certain key members of Avukah put all imperialists and capitalists in the same boat, is deeply problematic," and he, like many members, changed his view after the war. He felt there was no specific moment that led to the evolution in his thinking but more of an unfolding of a new perspective over time: "That moment began to emerge at *Commentary*, under the influence of Irving Kristol more than anyone else. I also recall the influence of somebody named Martin Diamond, who wrote a thesis, which may have been a Master's, on why socialism is wrong." For Glazer much was tied to the whole question of America: "It's part of the appreciating of America, that we think better of it than you do, even if we are involved in Vietnam, even if we haven't solved the problem of African American-White relations, and so forth."

So for Glazer, reality modified the political vision whereas, according to Judith Wallerstein, the approach that Zellig Harris and also Seymour Melman took to society was

unmodified by reality. They had very little personal contact with other ideas, and they didn't try to. They were convinced, in the way that adolescents are convinced, that they knew the right way. I never thought of Zellig as a man with a broad education and I knew that Seymour didn't have one. The world of intellectual ideas was foreign to both of them, and any other world was foreign to them. I don't think that Seymour had a single friend that wasn't Jewish, and I don't think that Zellig had any friends. These people had an isolated social and intellectual life, and they talked to people who thought they were important. I loved Seymour, but I didn't even like Zellig, I thought he was a bore.

In his many writings about Pentagon capitalism and the military-industrial complex, Melman continually derided those aspects of the United States that were in his eyes imperialistic and, from an economic perspective, akin to Bolshevism. Various members of Avukah also held firm to Zionism, in varying forms, and this may help explain some of the approaches taken by members after Avukah's demise, according to Glazer: "How to tie up the overall ideology with Zionism is interesting, and it was done through theses, fashionable statements that we would publish in *Avukah Student Action* that maybe Zellig wrote with Seymour, but I'm not sure. These were odd positions, because Avukah's approach wasn't quite labor Zionism, it wasn't Hashomer Hatzair because we weren't idealistic, it was an oddity, and the only way to explain that oddity is through Harris himself." According to Robert Wallerstein, the oddity of Harris's approach was kept alive through Melman's work, long after most Avukahites had modified their positions. "Seymour, and Zellig as well, maintained their socialist utopian ideology to the end of their lives. Most of the others did not, they gradually shifted."

Action and Inaction

It is difficult to believe that figures as divergent as Murray Eden, Nathan Glazer, Al Kahn, Harold Katz, Bruria Kaufman, Millie Kravetz, Seymour Melman, Harold Orlans, Meyer Rabban, Chava and Chester Rapkin, Irene and Zev Schumer, and Judith and Robert Wallerstein could once have been part of the same organization, largely united in ideological approaches, or that the legacy of Zellig Harris would be invoked by people who have pursued such divergent paths. It is also astonishing to consider the stakes of what was being discussed, and the level of seriousness with which Harris and his counterparts worked, particularly when we recall that the key players in the inner circle were mostly in their teens, twenties, and thirties. These young people were struggling to understand movements that quite literally threatened the survival of entire nations, religious groups, and political approaches. And as Jews who saw themselves as part of an intellectual and cultural vanguard, they took it upon themselves to understand and to act in the face of the fall and rise of new regions and countries, of threats to the very existence of the Jewish peoples, of the destruction of entire political organizations and parties, and, by the time of Hiroshima and Nagasaki, of concrete threats to the future of the entire human race.

But where did this all come from? Why would Harris, who was so involved in antifascist activities through Avukah and his own political ideology, build up a vanguard that he hoped would direct the actions of others? And why would he in particular resist direct action in World War II, and then later on in civil rights, antiwar actions, and the New Left? And why was he so steadfastly secretive? We've looked into some of the motivations to this point, but Irene Schumer adds, crucially, that Harris feared that the United States was going to turn fascist, and much of his work was motivated to arrest that possibility. But in her opinion, his fears ran too deep. "Yes, we had trouble with Coughlinites [adherents to Father Charles Coughlin who publicly espoused an Americanized version of Fascism], and we had trouble with the people from Yorkville, and we had trouble with the German American Bund [an organization supported by Nazi Germany that promoted anti-Semitism and had a strong following among some of the population of, for example, Yorkville, in New York City], and there was always in our generation, anti-Semitism. But to hell with it! That's how we felt. I couldn't believe that people would cower, or be afraid of who they were." And finally, Schumer notes that Avukah members were active, they wrote about current events, they organized rallies and they lobbied, but Zellig Harris didn't engage in such efforts because he didn't consider such work "intellectual." "He thought it wasn't worth doing. But as naïve and as clumsy as we were in the things we were doing, we were still trying to do something. I'm sure that Harris considered that what we were doing was inconsequential."

Judith Wallerstein is even more blunt, describing Harris as disconnected from the concerns of people other than himself. This is in some way born out by Irene Schumer's reflection that he did not build the chapters, he did not hold the meetings, he did none of the day-to-day work that was done by Seymour Melman, Al Kahn, and Meyer Rabban. But it was not just a reluctance to engage in grunt work, in my opinion; the aforementioned documentary "Arguing the World" sets out a crucial distinction between what came to be an anti-Bolshevik but pro-American Old Left and a more activist New Left that was more committed to bringing the fight into the streets. For Harris there was also his lifelong commitment to science and rationality over activism, underwritten by the idea that people could be brought through rational inquiry to understand the logic of one position over another. Indeed, the fact that Jews like Harris found their strongest ties to science over religion may suggest why, when anti-Semitism threatened to annihilate the whole Jewish community, many Jews responded with incredulity and inaction, expecting that rationality had to prevail over madness and evil. Michael Stanislawski, in his book *Zionism and the fin de siècle: Cosmopolitanism and Nationalism from Nordeau to Jabotinski,*[9] traces some roots of this belief and the ways in which they influenced Zionist thinking: "Most western and central European Jews . . . [b]elieved that the anti-Semitism they were witnessing was not new, but merely a recurrence of traditional Jew-hatred in a new guise, a retrograde obscurantism deliberately cultivated by scurrilous politicians supported by the reactionary forces of society, particularly the Church. They thus committed themselves to re-emphasizing their fealty to the Enlightenment values of universal truth and the unstoppable march of progress; the good guys, they genuinely believed, would inevitably and eventually defeat the bad guys" (12). The strong reliance upon secular and Enlightenment values was reinforced in the New York Avukah approach by a version of Zionism that was distinct from Judaism, an approach bemoaned in a December 26, 2003, letter to Murray Eden from Al Kahn:

Avukah undoubtedly fortified my Zionist commitment, and it certainly gave me the comfort of group belonging. . . . I would, however, make one comment with the hindsight of my own experience since our college days. The vision of a labor Israel did not include the religious, the spiritual factor. Indeed the Jewish religion was seen at best as irrelevant and, more to the point, as something inimical to the development of a Jewish socialist state and to the "new" Jew. It was, ideologically, short sighted. . . . The lack of identification with our history and the absence of a sense of the sacred is a failure which has led to the "New Historians," to those who would easily give away our patrimony, and the "left" in Israel, now discredited, whose Zionism is attenuated to some clever concoctions on paper.

This is a fascinating point, nowhere present in Harris's writings, but also absent from the debates within the *Avukah Student News* and other organs of that organization. Judaism was about culture and about Zionism, and serious work was about science and rigorous, systematic study. To move into spirituality was to adopt an undue mystical irrationality, and to move into the streets would hardly advance the intellectual work that he thought was required to change America. This attitude may help explain why Zellig Harris's work against fascism didn't translate into an engagement alongside American troops in the Second World War, or even into active struggle on behalf of Jews under Nazism, and it may also help explain why Harris refused direct action against McCarthyism, the Korean and Vietnam Wars, the student movements, and so forth, favoring instead a reason-based radicalism that superseded the categories of race, nationality, or religion. History did not seem to support such a view, but there was always room for optimism, a tendency in some ways reinforced by appeal to universalistic ideals of science and justice. Stanislawski writes:

Contrary to Herzl's and Gomperz's conviction in the eternity and unstoppability of Jew-hatred, even in the homeland of Enlightenment and Emancipation, and thus their search for a radical solution to the *Judenfrage*, the most common reaction of central and western European Jews to the Dreyfus Affair was a belief that, in the end, French justice would triumph. After the Affair, they knew they had been right all along–the good guys did vanquish the bad guys; the true France of *égalité, fraternité* and *liberté* beat out the forces of reaction and hatred. This, most were convinced, was the verdict of History. (12)

Vichy and the Holocaust proved that progress in some domains does not imply social advancement, but there is a sense of optimism that runs through Harris's work, that despite the setbacks a "good society" could emerge from the rubble of destruction and disparity, just as a more valid theory of the social world could emerge from the inadequacies and failures of earlier models.

Science and Ideology

Harris was not the only person who had confidence in his and others' abilities to solve complex problems, including social problems, through science. His structural linguistics research received extensive funding by the U.S. government, and his results provoked significant interest from key people at a range of organizations, including IBM and Bell Laboratories, who thought that his approach might underwrite the coming revolution in communications technology. This optimism grows out of a broader faith in the sciences and in the potential for new technologies that many people shared. From this standpoint, research into behaviorism was not only a "new scientific approach to all human phenomena," it was an "ideology," which according to Seuren "fitted in with the brash belief, prevalent in the period between 1920 and 1960, that all social, political, economic and psychological problems would soon be overcome by the results, to be expected shortly, of science and technology."[10]

In 1945, Bell Laboratories openly declared that in the wake of both the challenges and avenues opened up by the war, they were actively seeking out work that could help them in their desire to develop new communications systems. "The pressure during World War II to develop rectifiers acting as crystal detectors for radar provided a strong impetus, as did an old hope of making amplifiers that avoid the power drain of vacuum tubes, and switching devices without the usual problems of corrosion and slow response. The work was 'problem focused'; it depended as much on the expectation of relatively short-term payoff as it did on the quantum physics of the 1920s and 1930s."[11] Zellig Harris's scientific linguistics provided the tools that would be required for the purposes of machine translation, decoding, content analysis, and so forth; and his political work, aimed at providing a more adequate description of capitalist society and a science-inspired method for its transformation, was similarly ambitious and all encompassing. Harris's efforts on both fronts led him to work in a kind of master-apprentice relationship that was aimed at fostering a vanguard of like-minded students and colleagues, an approach that is apparent even in his approach to teaching in the university.[12]

Zellig Harris as Teacher

In the opinion of many with whom I have spoken during the past fifteen years, Zellig Harris had the kind of personality that could help foster these interests and develop methods for understanding and analyzing them on both the linguistic and political fronts. Consistent with my conversations with a host of former students, Avukah members, and colleagues was Leigh Lisker's description of Harris as "approachable, intense and, moreover, inspiring, particularly of course for those in the inner circle. At a time when it was very rare, Harris was on a first-name basis with other students, and he frequently met with them in restaurants or at his home, for linguistic and political discussions." His approach to working with students was akin to the mentor-apprenticeship relation outside of the classroom. Konrad Koerner, in his aforementioned bibliography and homage notes that "as a teacher he was an unconventional man, dispensing with all classroom formalities such as course requirements, grading and exams, as several of his students reported in their tributes circulated shortly after his death on the Linguist electronic bulletin board" (509).[12] In terms of his style in the classroom, W. C. Watt beautifully captures many comments I have heard: Harris "taught many, myself included, to probe deep and to respect the data; he was a merry but exacting taskmaster; he was venerated by all who knew him, surely, and by many was held in warm affection. He was quick; he was wise; he held scholarship to be a calling worthy of one's best efforts and one . . . from which the personalities of its practitioners are best held apart. Oddly, perhaps, given his expressed wish to suppress personality in science, his own individual character was strongly expressed and strongly felt."[13]

Watt adds further color to the image of Harris as teacher, describing his unusual and legendary lecturing habits.

Some minutes before the time allotted to close a lecture he would sometimes pause, say "And that's all," and leave the room; and on occasion—still another legend—he would, on the first fall meeting of one of his courses, ask which of us were also registered for his other two and then, having discovered that we all were, announce that they would therefore be neatly combined into one. This was fine, since all of his courses, however titled, covered a vast domain. (In my Penn graduate catalog for 1967, the year he awarded me my degree, Harris is listed as being sworn to teach "Formal Linguistics" and "Mathematical Systems in Linguistic Structure" in the fall semester and "Seminar in Linguistic Transformations" in the spring. His courses tended to merge one into the other; and the first and third of those just listed are specified in the catalog as "may be repeated for credit." Which they were, and justly, since their contents overlapped and varied with Harris's latest advances).

Michael Kac, a contemporary of Watt, was a student of Harris's from 1965 to 1967 and described him as an "unconventional and in some ways troubling man" who was "at times frustrating to deal with," but "inspiring nonetheless." Kac recalls in Linguist List 3.453 (June 1992) a story that for him was emblematic of Harris.

In the summer of 1969 I decided, for a variety of reasons (some having nothing to do with anything academic), to leave the graduate program in linguistics at Penn and finish my Ph.D. elsewhere. I did regularly attend Harris's course that following fall, knowing that this would likely be my last chance to have any sort of personal contact with him. But I did not have a paper ready by the end of that semester and an outstanding item of business during the few months that intervened between my departure from Penn and my arrival at UCLA in March of 1970 was to produce one. This I did, and shortly after getting to Los Angeles, I finished it and sent it off. No more than a day or two later—soon enough so that it was clear that it had crossed my paper in the mail—I received my last transcript from Penn indicating that I had received an A for the course. It struck me as a very Harrisian thing to do and I would have a bad conscience about it but for one thing: I did write the paper!

With the passage of time, Harris became more distant from his students, and also from friends and colleagues, which suggests that to know him well meant knowing him in the early days. Even his more prominent students, such as Richard Kittredge, found access to Harris in those later years rather sparse.

I did my PhD work with Harris, and I had a couple of occasions after I went to Montreal (1969), especially in 1976 and 1981, to see him briefly on my visits to Philadelphia and New York. Zellig was quite stimulating as a teacher in both class-room and one-on-one sessions during my research. Nevertheless, he was seldom on campus, rarely gave any written comments on papers or thesis drafts, and did very little (by today's standards) to prepare his students for the give and take (including preparing stand-up talks or publications) of current academic life."

There remains, though, a strong legacy, for Kittredge and many others. "I still don't regret the time I spent with him since his ideas sent me in fruit-ful directions and have weathered well the test of time. He was always very friendly to me and interested in my Montreal work in machine translation (where we specialized in sublanguages) and sublanguage description."

Another related project with which Harris had ties was Naomi Sager's computational linguistics work, including major contributions to the NYU linguistic string project aimed at developing computer methods for struc-turing and accessing information in the scientific and technical literature. Her approach and methods are clearly related to Zellig Harris's approach, and in fact his relationship with Naomi Sager went beyond professional and entered the personal; but this was a relationship that, according to Ted Live, was kept quiet even within the Harris family. Although himself a family member, Live knew Harris as a teacher as well, and he offered in the course of an interview a rare look at Zellig's personality: "I took a seminar course in linguistics with him on discourse analysis, and my sense was that the whole class was well-run, he encouraged students to come up with ideas and examples to fill out the ideas he was talking about. It didn't seem to me particularly different from other classes I'd had. But after the course, he suggested that linguistics was not a field I should consider after graduate school, there wasn't a lot left to be done in it. Little did he know!" Live had been debating with himself; he liked linguistics, philosophy, and chemistry, and he thought that there was a lot more room in other sub-jects, since linguistics was pretty much laid out. "This was a generic strug-gle, that most of the work had been done, and there wasn't a lot left." On the political side, Live recalled, "I knew that Zellig was politically active more than other members of the family, since other members were more interested in domestic politics and traditional Zionism, while he seemed very devoted to the kind of life that existed on Kibbutzim as an example of how people could work together and exemplify the ideals that he upheld."

Other stories about Harris as a teacher and colleague were recorded just after his death in the Linguist List 3.462 (1992). In a section called "How did we become linguists?," Alice Freed recalled how she chose linguistics out of the catalog, eventually becoming one of only three undergraduate majors therein. In the course of her studies, she worked with Harris for two-and-a-half years and, she writes:

Despite his debated standing in our field today, he was an inspiration to me as a student. Whether or not he did us a disservice by his intellectual and professional isolationism, he talked to us about language in ways that were stimulating and exciting. He typically started his seminars, always held in his office, (which was always uncomfortably crowded), by asking if there were any questions. A single question would then become a two-hour lecture. His stream of consciousness lecturing style, which included a description of whatever piece of linguistic theory he was mulling over at the time, was more organized than many carefully prepared lectures I have heard. He covered the small blackboard in his office with his tiny handwriting and dispensed with all classroom formalities such as course requirements, grading and exams. He devoted his life to the study of language and assumed that his students were doing the same.

Later in his life Harris traveled regularly to Israel, so his classes were held much more sporadically, meeting several times weekly when he was in Philadelphia, suspended sometimes for months while he was, in Rabban's words, "driving a tractor or an ambulance in northern Israel." Even colleagues, like Leigh Lisker and Henry Hoenigswald, saw him less and less frequently. Lisker recalled that by the 1960s and '70s, "Harris's relations with the students enrolled in his classes became much more formal and distant than those he had maintained with the students of earlier generations" when, for example, he would have conversations with the likes of Chomsky, Lisker, Melman, and others at lunch hour, in Philly or New York. Lisker had regular meetings with Harris near Penn Station, because he was doing work at the Haskins Laboratories on East 43rd Street. These conversations were "intense but also congenial, since Harris had a ready laugh and was rarely 'in the dumps'; but he was also not given to idle chitchat, and conversation with him, whatever the subject, was always serious."

From Guru to Husband

Zellig Harris was instrumental in molding linguistics studies at Penn, but his work resonated in settings within the United States and beyond—particularly France. In an internal undated document describing "Linguistics at the University of Pennsylvania," Henry Hiz recalls that

it was literally the case that in the beginning years Harris *was* the department, and its formation involved no more than bringing together, as a program in 'linguistic analysis,' a number of courses that Harris had developed during the war years under the aegis of either the Anthropology or the Oriental Studies Departments of the University. In sum these courses were remarkably broad in content for a one-man department, ranging over linguistic field methodology and practice, the theory and practice of structural analytic description, the descriptive study of specific Semitic and West African languages, and what may be considered the precursor of the presently cultivated areas of ethno- and sociolinguistics, the 'language and culture' domain of interest.

What is clear here is that linguistics had, and maintained, important ties to anthropology and to Oriental studies. Harris himself "gave instruction in the grammars of Fanti, Swahili and Hausa for several years in the mid 1940s . . . as a program of African studies in the Oriental Studies Department rather than in Anthropology." So even if, as Hiz notes, the program in linguistics as an independent discipline at Pennsylvania "was essentially the achievement of one man," it had both antecedents and ties to other programs, and it grew and has flourished from those early days.

As we have seen, in later years Harris became much more reclusive and distant from the department and his students, and this may in part have been because of how he related to Bruria, his wife. Ted Live never noticed this, but there were certainly issues in the relationship that weren't visible to everyone in the family. Said Live, she "remained very devoted to Zellig," and never took her new husband's name after his death, but he, in particular, was very discrete about his emotions, even as regards his own wife. Harold Orlans commented about the surprise he felt when he learned about the marriage, because he had always found Harris "self-contained" and, in camps where pairing-off was common, he had no known girlfriend. "Bruria Kaufman attended at least one camp but I noted no hand-holding or other sign of affection," and when Orlans recalled that he'd later heard they had married, he was astounded and pleased at this "evidence of Zellig's humanity." Murray Eden didn't go this far in his description of Harris's discretion, but he did describe Harris as "very complicated, subtle, guarded,—and increasingly so with the passage of time."

Ted Live was not surprised at the distance or "coldness" that people observed between Bruria and Zellig because "nobody in my family held hands, as far as I know. I just saw them as a pair, like all of my aunts and uncles were pairs." For Live, all of the couples in his family were "well matched, and tolerant, and trusting of each other, sharing a lot of the same interests." And so, said Live, "Zellig was just another one of my relatives, and not particularly different from the others. Everyone went to Penn, everyone got a PhD, everyone went on to academia!" Live chatted about things with Harris, but he wasn't around all that often; he did spend a fair amount of time with Bruria, but only knew her as Harris's wife. One connection they had was through music, since Live played the flute and Bruria the piano. "I would go to the apartment on Walnut Street and play music with her," and she was very accomplished. "I would bring a Bach sonata with a complicated piano part, and I would arrive there having studied the flute part. She would just play the piano, without ever having seen the piece before. She was a good pianist, and she was an extremely good singer. Between that and the Kibbutz, I had a fair amount of contact with her. I always thought of her as fairly warm; she was certainly intolerant of fools, but she also had a fair amount of friendliness."

Eva Rapkin, who had many friends and relations in Avukah, described the couple, Zellig and Bruria, as "cold, without warmth"—but manifestly "brilliant." Nonetheless, she recounted one episode when Tzvee and Shoshanna had a baby. Zellig was once caught cooing over the baby, which was such unusual behavior for him that it became a joke among all of his friends. "Nobody had ever heard him cooing before!" Harris was, in her description, "very somber, a difficult person to be with," even for those people who actively sought him out for his brilliance and his leadership. Sometimes, this leadership quality could be oppressive to others around him, and he was more likely to direct the flow of communication. Rabban recalls, "We were visiting [Zellig's brother] Tzvee and [his wife] Shoshanna in Philadelphia and Shoshanna said to him: 'Zellig gave us this draft of a book he was writing, to edit, and it's unbelievable! I cannot comprehend a single sentence of what he is writing!' So I said, 'why are you doing this?' and Shoshanna replied, 'Because Zellig wants us to!'" Elana Rabban added that Shoshanna did everything for Zellig, anything that needed to be done. "'What can I do?' asked Shoshanna. 'He's bright, he's brilliant!'" Indeed, "the whole Harris family thought that he was a genius." But Rabban noted that "Shoshanna is herself a brilliant lady, and she herself could have managed a lot of things, but Zellig had to be the one who would tell everyone what had to be done." Meyer recalled visiting Tzvee, "who was a very different kind of guy, very warm and bright, but he too thought that his big brother was 'out of this world'." Ted Live added that he himself never knew how important Harris's work was, even if he knew that Enya, his mother, considered him "close to God," which Live discounted as being typical of family relations. In fact, said Live, "he took himself a lot less seriously than other people did." And while other people in the Harris family were bothered by Chomsky's having, from their perspective, "taken over some of Zellig's work," Zellig himself "paid no attention to that, he didn't care." For Live, those in the family who held Chomsky in a degree of contempt generally didn't know anything about the linguistics, so for them it was just a "family loyalty" issue.

Irene Schumer also found that when Zellig was around his wife Bruria, and even his friends, he was often "off-putting" and distant. "There was nothing forthcoming from him, on a human level. Everything was intellectual, in a way that was similar to his wife, Bruria." The net effect, as Lillian Kaplan suggested, was to make some people "very self-conscious, particularly in his and her presence." Judith Wallerstein described Bruria as a kind of shepherdess: "She wore the most amazing clothes, and she would sort of float around. I know that she was a physicist and mathematician, but she was sort of in the air. She, like Zellig, was not walking on the ground." For Schumer, this was especially true of Bruria, who would exhibit surprise when people who were not from more esoteric or cosmopolitan backgrounds (the "stratosphere"), were able to understand things. Kaufman was by Schumer's description "awkward, and had difficulty socially, she was very different from other women around her at this time." Schumer recalls a meeting of Avukah that she chaired, and, true to her democratic principles, she allowed the opinions of others present to be heard—"against the protestations of Bruria, who didn't feel it necessary to hear the others." It was on the basis of Irene Schumer's handling of that meeting that William (Zev) Schumer asked her out, the beginning of a relationship that continues to this day.

Meyer Rabban reinforces some of these sentiments on the basis of an anecdote: when he returned home after World War II, he went to Israel, and later pursued his PhD. In the course of his work, he had occasion to go to Princeton. Bruria and Zellig were there because "at that time Bruria was working as an assistant to Einstein, at the Institute for Advanced Studies, and, accidentally on the street, I met Murray Eden, who suggested that they go together and visit the Harrises." They went, uninvited. "Bruria, as always, was very pleasant," while Zellig "was very distant and very cold." "Perhaps," thought Rabban, "he was angry because I hadn't stayed in Israel, that I'd come back for an academic career." Rabban remembers thinking

To hell with this guy. He spouts off all of these ideas, and he sticks to his brilliant academic career, but all of us other guys also have good academic careers, and he puts us down if we don't stick to the program that he thinks other people ought to follow. I soured on his aloofness, on his preciousness, on his being above everyone else, his guru status, he was always in the right, and he knew what was best. His mental faculties were far beyond those of the common folk, this was true, but it led to the way that he interacted with other people, and I now look upon him with sour feelings. But I don't want to erase that initial impact of those years, 1935, 36, 37, 38.

Harris's own family felt this aloofness, and distances grew within the milieus. Ted Live recalls dinners on Friday night at the Harris household in Philadelphia, which were frequently held sans Zellig and Bruria. Shoshanna and Tzvee Harris recall a growing estrangement, as people in what was once this tight circle became involved in their own work, their own lives, at a distance from early ideals. Shoshanna said that "Zellig's mind went in many directions, he could do anything. But as time went by, people felt detached from what Zellig believed, and from the way he looked at things. He was a very different individual, very, very different. And it was very hard to match up to him, in any way. Eventually, people distanced themselves from him, they had to; they went on with their ordinary lives, and not this highfalutin existence." Once again there's this sense that Harris became increasingly aloof, even from friends and family, and as his isolation grew, so too did his distance from political action and, as we'll see in section II, from work in his own field of linguistics. As Judith Wallerstein noted, so many people in Avukah remained the closest of friends throughout their long lives, but "at no point was Zellig Harris part of our love or our friendship. He bored me, and he was divorced from reality." For her, this applied also to his professional work.

The closeness of the milieu has of course exacerbated or even exaggerated the importance of particular events; nevertheless, anecdotes are revealing in terms of what they suggest about the overall atmosphere of the time and of the intimacy of this group. For instance, Eva Rapkin, who had dated Murray Eden, recalled that her eventual husband, Chester Rapkin, had dated Bruria Kaufman before she married Zellig Harris. "She would come and visit Chester in the period in his life when he was living on a commune. When Chester was dating her, he scrounged up enough money to bring her to the Monte Carlo Ballet. Excited, and glowing with enthusiasm, he turned to her during the show and said, 'aren't they wonderful'? And she replied that they were, and that she'd known them all in Monte Carlo!" This was the first indication to Chester of the type of family from which she'd come, "but Bruria was more unassuming, and certainly more forthcoming than Zellig Harris." She considered that "for him, life was work, and he didn't relate well to people, perhaps on that account, whereas she was capable of deeper human emotions."

W. C. Watt adds to the picture of a reclusive genius amid a tightly knit group, suggesting with a retrospective and often philosophical air that around such a personality as Zellig Harris, legends inevitably abound. One of them, probably the most frequently noted, concerns his reclusiveness. "Few of his students had ready access to him, and I was once importuned by one of them, after he'd spent a full year at Penn, at least to point Harris out (I was able to direct his attention to the receding taillights of his aging gray Mercedes as it vanished up Walnut Street); and in my day (1959–1963) he had appointed the formidable Miss Sparagna to serve, outside his office, as a sort of Cerberus. This she did with great relish. In fact, as time went on her blinds were often drawn and the lights turned off, lending further weight, there in the gloaming, to Harris's inapproachability."[14] W. C. Watt's relation to Harris is interesting since he completed the PhD in 1967, one of the latter groups of students, a generation after the likes of Eden, Lisker, and Orlans. Watt recalls that

like all of my fellow students, I think, I revered Zellig Harris as mentor and as resident genius; like more than a few, I had a warm affection for him, in my own case as a sort of intellectual father. This affection was only increased by my personal interactions with him, not just in his office, once regularly admitted, but also, more casually, on the streets of Philadelphia. An accident of residence—his apartment and mine were only a block or so apart—led me often to find myself afoot behind him crossing the Walnut Street Viaduct to the Penn Campus, he not infrequently in his greenish outdoorsman's jacket, with wooden toggles in the stead of buttons and, armed against Philadelphia's blustery weather, a prominent hood. As he marched along across the Schuylkill [river] he would sometimes reach into the side pockets of this capacious garment and fish out various pieces of paper on which, presumably, he had written notes to himself on this or that linguistic point. He'd examine these without breaking pace and then, about half the time, toss them into the river. They fluttered down like the inscribed leaves that, in legend at least, some Chinese poets, uncaring of posterity, used to toss into the nearest creek. Sometimes I wondered how many potential dissertations, by us his epigones, floated down those then-noisome waters, to be swept eventually into the Delaware and then out to the Atlantic.

Watt completes this poetic description with an actual inventory of the notes he has saved, a cataloguing reminiscent of the kind of work that Harris might have done with a Native American language, for the Smithsonian, in the years that he worked with them (in ways reminiscent of Edward Sapir).

Some of these notes, though, have survived, for I still have a few in my possession, since he at one point delegated me to be his inquirer into the tangled web of English adverbs and so passed on to me his jottings there anent. They make interesting reading. First, they contain brilliant aperçus—if not yet analyses as such—and secondly they consist in large part of stray scraps of paper saved from the Schuylkill. They comprise as follows: (1) a note on formal University of Pennsylvania letterhead addressed to "Dear Watt"; (2) six notes on 8 1/2 × 11 brown-flecked blue-lined notepaper; (3) two notes on 5 1/2 × 7 notepaper; (4) one note on a different 5 × 8 notepaper; (5) twenty-nine notes on 3 × 5 sheets torn from some tablet; (6) twenty-three 4 × 6 sheets excised from some other tablet; and lastly (7) two notes on the reverse (flap side) of two University of Pennsylvania envelopes, one small and one letter-size. They constitute a set of casual records of a superbly talented linguist's cogitations on language—probably, given the ordinary evanescence of such things in the destructive course of time, among the best we'll ever have.

Bruce Nevin described what it was like to work with Zellig Harris in the later years in, for example, his "A Tribute to Harris,"[15] that is in accord with the impressions of many others during the period. He has also assembled a two-volume work,[16] well worth examining for readings from an international array of specialists on the importance of Harris's work in the philosophy of science and in theoretical linguistics, and on Harris's profound influence in formal systems and applied mathematics, in demonstrations of the computability of language, and in informatics.

Harris eventually worked on a range of fronts with his wife, Bruria, because she was interested in the sciences as well as Zionism and Palestine, and they even ended up collaborating on matters relating to language, particularly as he turned his attention more directly to uncovering a mathematical basis for communication. And yet despite how impressive and accomplished they were, individually and as a couple, and despite the number of times interviewees described to me how "powerful" a couple they were, there was also an oft-mentioned tension between them, apparently, because of Harris's belief in more open relationships. Nonetheless, Bruria's work with Zellig intensified in the later years of their marriage, particularly when she became a research associate at Penn for an NSF research project in mathematical linguistics, from 1957 to 1960, just prior to her leaving for Israel in 1960, where she became professor at the Weizmann Institute of Science in Rehovot (1960–1971) and then Haifa University (1972–1988).

From Penn to Mishmar Ha'Emek

Many interviewees, including Harris's own family members, had infrequent contact with him as years unfolded, and much less contact subsequent to Bruria's return to Israel. She became a member of an Israeli kibbutz, Mishmar Ha'Emek, the labor Zionist kibbutz, and from that point forward, Harris developed the habit of shuttling back and forth between Philadelphia and Israel three or four times a year. Ted Live, who visited for two summers, recalls Mishmar Ha'Emek,

one of the older, wealthier kibbutzim, a place that was really pretty. As far as I could tell, and I wasn't really that integrated into their social life, it seemed pretty egalitarian. Kids had their own dorm, and the school, where they spent most of the day, and they would hang out with their parents after 3 or 4PM. I actually thought that it was an ideal kind of civilization, it had a lot of advantages over standard American family practices. I like the fact for instance that I had professionals raise me, from day 1, instead of having parents who knew nothing about it. I also like the quality of time that parents had with their kids, because parents didn't have to be disciplinarians, so when they did have time for the kids they were pretty much 100% there for them. They weren't busy doing other things, and even TVs were pretty few and far between.

Live recalls visiting with Bruria; she was a kibbutz member, but he never was, so he would go and visit her. And he donated his salary, or some portion of it, to the kibbutz, and another portion went to a kibbutz-run teacher training school.

When Live went to live on the kibbutz for two summers, Zellig and Bruria were there on and off. One time when Live went to visit Bruria, their adopted daughter Tami Harris was there, after 4PM when the kids were back from school. "We were talking in English, which Tami knew, but she stopped us in our conversation and said 'Hey, this is the time when you are supposed to be with me, not with Ted!' And she was right, structurally that was the way it was supposed to be. And she knew it." At that time, Zellig spent roughly half the year there, and Live recalls him doing orchard work of some sort. "It wasn't specialized work, so I'm not sure what he was doing. A lot of the work was with orchard, and I don't remember him working with cattle, another big thing." Bruria, on the other hand, was working in the accounting office, "which I always thought to be ironic," while teaching computers in the kibbutz. "I remember her trying to convince me to learn programming, and I didn't have a computer at the time and I replied 'why should I learn programming? There are other people who are experts in it and I can just rely on their stuff'."

Zellig never taught on the kibbutz, in Live's view, because what he was doing was "not part of the curriculum. I don't think he would have objected at all to teaching, though, given his willingness to teach classes at Penn, I'm sure he would have been happy to teach there." His other great interest, Zionism, was not really a subject on the kibbutz, according to Live, because "you didn't need to talk about it, you were already there.

I remember people in Israel saying, 'I don't need to be a practicing Jew, I'm an Israeli citizen. People who were on Mishmar Ha'Emek didn't need to practice Zionism, Zionism was why they were there." At night people would be home, or they would go out and visit at the clubhouse where there was TV and games. Harris didn't work on linguistics there, as Live recalls, but he would often stay in and read, with Bruria and Tami. The kibbutz was a self-contained agricultural cooperative, but there were people who worked outside the community, and in fact there was one person who was a member of the Knesset and was never around. Live was housed in a cabin a few hundred yards from Harris's house and would see Harris every day when he was around. Live was not terribly close to Zellig, but he did not find him terribly aloof in that context. "I never had the sense that he was standoffish, or antagonistic to people who didn't agree with him. He always seemed to me quite even tempered, friendly but a little more formal than, say, Tzvee, who was always the jokester, much more outgoing. But he always seemed to me friendly, willing to talk, but very opinionated about political things. I thought that he would go overboard with his analysis of capitalist society. As an 18 or 20 year old, I thought that I saw things that he was missing." At one point, Live recalls Harris talking him out of going into linguistics, for reasons frequently mentioned by Chomsky. "Zellig told me that all the good work had been done already. This was in one brief conversation we had. He said that there wasn't much left to do. He must have told me this when I was in college, and uncertain as to whether I should go into psychology, or biochemistry, or linguistics, so this would have been around 1961 or 62."

W. C. Watt notes that "unlike Chomsky he [Harris] was no sailor, his physical activity being mostly confined to his working on a kibbutz in Israel during many summers, in which purviews he was apparently known simply as 'Carpenter Harris.' Prompting one to picture this great scholar, elegantly balding, slightly stooped and with thickish rimmed spectacles, astride a beam into which he was driving, with a framing hammer, a 10-penny nail." Tzvee and Shoshanna Harris remember Zellig's work on the kibbutz as multifarious; indeed, consistent with the ideal of communal living, he worked toward the greater good. "Whatever was needed on the kibbutz, he did. He didn't teach, he really just worked." Meyer Rabban commented on this engagement in kibbutzim: "With all the preaching of Aliyah [the immigration of Jews to Israel] and Hityashvut [agricultural settlement that is founded on collective, cooperative principles and based on self-labor] as the solution to the Jewish minority problem, no one made that a personal decision. I think I was the only one who joined Hashomer

Hatzair and was a member of a kibbutz. Zellig himself held on to his tenured academic position until retirement before he spent his time as a 'simple' carpenter in Mishmar Ha'Emek. We were all essentially careerists, even Seymour Melman, who held a life-long affection for Ein Hashafet [a kibbutz founded in 1937, named in honor of Louis D. Brandeis] as he held onto his job at Columbia."

Tami Harris, the adopted daughter of Bruria and Zellig, was "ambivalent" about contributing her perspective to this book because her parents were "inspiring in their humility," seeking neither fame nor fortune and shunning "public exposure." But, she said to me in discussions, "my father is long gone, and my mom died recently, less than a year ago. They are gone, but their spirit will always be part of me, and their spirit includes adherence to the truth. In confronting the trade-off between humility and truth, they chose humility. I see this book as my chance to tell the truth, while still respecting their privacy and other values and sensitivities." Tami's mother, Bruria Kaufman, was for several years affiliated with New York University and the University of Pennsylvania, but she returned to Israel, and during the period when she was a professor at the Weizmann Institute of Science in Rehovot (1960–1971) she and Zellig Harris adopted a three-year-old girl, Tamar (Tami), who was raised at the Mishmar Ha'emek kibbutz, in light of her parents' commitment to its socialist ideals. Zellig Harris had another child, with Naomi Sager, named Eva Harris, who is a faculty member at University of California Berkeley's School of Public Health. Zellig Harris became more receptive to the idea of having his own children later in life although, as Tami Harris notes, as a young man he was against having kids. "I understood from my mom that he found it selfish, bourgeois, and just another norm to doubt. In my twenties I told him that I think childbirth is part of the nature of women, unless they are deeply wounded by life. He was furious. He did adopt me though, and was a great father. Not without shortcomings, but loving, caring and finding ways to express his love despite being away—or with us but busy writing." His conscious and uncompromising effort to live by his ideology is a key characteristic of Zellig Harris, as Tami recalls:

My father was not easily defined. His thinking was original and independent. But he was definitely a socialist. I have heard cynical capitalists making fun of socialists like my father, claiming that Marx himself was wealthy. In my opinion, people who starve seldom have the luxury of coming up with revolutionary ideas. I think history tells us that civilizations flourishes in places where living was neither too difficult (where people didn't have to focus entirely upon survival) nor too easy (where people had no incentive to invent or develop). In the case of my father, he knew poverty. At the age of thirteen he was sent by his family in Philadelphia to live in Palestine. This was a rather peculiar way of expressing Zionism, but the times were different, and who am I to judge? He studied at the *herzeliya* gymnasium and worked to support himself. I think he lived in a youth hostel with some twenty kids in a room. At the age of seventeen, his aunt and uncle moved to Tel Aviv, and he finally had a home and the means to study more and work less. His uncle, Yehuda Kaufman Ibn-Shmuel, was a well-known writer and philosopher. His cousin, who was eight years old at the time, was Bruria Kaufman, who later became his wife, but in a way was always more of a loved family member and less of a wife or a woman to both of them.

Zellig Harris had little interest in wealth, and Tami Harris noted that "my father always gave every penny he made as a professor to the kibbutz. My parents gave the kibbutz their car, piano, and apartment. Even when he knew he was about to leave the kibbutz for good, he still gave his salary to it, right up to the end. My parents left the kibbutz in their old age with about $500 and borrowed money from my uncle to buy an apartment. There were times when my father had more money, but he still lived simply, never accumulating possessions or even thinking in terms of making money." While in Israel Zellig Harris's commitment to the kibbutz even superseded his professional work. Tami Harris recalls that "for years he was living in Israel as a kibbutz member. He worked just like everyone else, as a farmer, a driver or a factory worker. He never neglected his scientific work, but he did it only in his spare time. Never, never did he take one minute off his work on the kibbutz in order to do his scholastic work. He initiated, and then worked for many years to establish a kibbutz university. His objective was to combine his socialistic ideology with academia; but even that was only on his spare time."

That Zellig Harris placed his responsibility to the kibbutz collective above his scientific work was all the more remarkable in his case because, says Tami Harris:

My father was willing to pay a high personal price for his work—or science, for politics—which was aimed at making a difference in this world in the best way that he could. He was not important; humanity was important, and he kept working, he never stopped working. He used to go to his armchair saying, "Harris is writing books." Once in a while he would insert a word, like "Puyallup-Nisqually," which years later I discovered were the names of two Indian tribes in the Pacific Northwest. This was like a comic relief, a way of reminding himself, and us, that he took the work seriously, but not himself. That was so cute, childlike and human. So heartwarming. This was an aspect of his personality not many people knew about. We would be listening to Mozart Requiem and he would raise his head and say at just the right time "tuba mirum." Or else he would get up, prepare baked apples with cinnamon, and then forget all about them. Only when the fire alarm went off we were reminded that they were in the oven. He had the smallest handwriting. Sadly, I have many letters that I cannot possibly decipher. He would write until drifting off to sleep, and the line slanted down. He startled and kept on writing until it happened again. On the third time he would stop and go to sleep, not before.

This level of intense work defined Harris throughout his life, but as Tami Harris insisted, it was "the work itself that was important, humanity was important. But he, Zellig Harris, was not." In a moving and telling anecdote, she recalls:

His heart was weak at old age. He had a heart attack, and was about to have a triple bypass surgery. I was serving my mandatory army service in Israel and took a leave of absence to go with my mom to the States. On the way there, her feet got tangled in the taxi seat belt and she fractured her ankle in three places. We went straight from JFK Airport to the hospital, where my mom had to undergo surgery at the very same time as my father, but on another floor. My dad was always the oldest dad around, so from childhood I always feared his death when we separated. But this time it was real. The doctors were not sure he could make it. I told him that he had to make it, that I love him more than anything, and that I need him around. He replied—"Don't worry. I still have work to do." He made it, and lived eight more years. Maybe because the doctors were good, or because he was lucky. Maybe even because we loved him. But most likely, he made it because he had more work to do.

Tami Harris described her intense bond with her father, and also revealed aspects of his personality that he clearly guarded from others, including his sense of humor, and his sensitivity to art and culture. On the former, she recalled:

He had the greatest sense of humor, and hearing him laughing was one of my greatest joys. When I was a child, he read me a book by Dr. Seuss that had a seesaw with Mr. Brown on one side of it. The person on the other side hit the ground hard, sending Mr. Brown flying. The words were "Mr. Brown is out of town." My father couldn't get enough of that. Anything he found funny was funny to me as well. When I was in the army, he went with me and my friend roller skating. He was watching us, and my friend was so scared of falling backwards that she ended up falling forwards. He took us to the nearest hospital, as we were pretty certain her arm was broken. The hospital staff refused to help since, they said, "soldiers are not supposed to get treatment in civilian hospitals, unless it is a matter of life or death." My father replied, "It is. It is a matter of life . . ." On another occasion, a friend of mine was having dinner with us and refused to eat vegetables. In his broken English he explained that "it came from the child," meaning that he hated vegetables since childhood. We all burst out in laughter, but we never mentioned it again. Some twenty years later my dad was taking his daily walk around the block in Philadelphia and shared with us later that he was rather slow. "It came from the old man . . ." he said.

These moving passages suggest warmth and sensitivity that he kept back from most others, including his students. He also kept from view his strong interest in art, and in beauty, which play no role in his scientific or even political work. Tami Harris described another side to his personality when she recalled:

I always knew him as a rational person, angry about injustice but otherwise calm and never sentimental. He used to be too busy or preoccupied to appreciate beauty, but this changed when he grew older. He was once somewhere in the Alps and was touched by the scenery. Years later he told me the story and was choked by tears. Another time he was working and living in Oxford, and I was visiting. We were talking about art, specifically cubism and Braque, and he was describing his favorite painting, a grey beach and a small boat on shore. His eyes filled with tears again. In his last year we stood by a river in Philadelphia, watching the swimming ducks. At that time I was just about to begin my study for the PhD in clinical psychology, and I was dealing with some very painful personal stuff. I told him that we all have a void inside us, even people who have had a relatively good childhood. We try in different ways to fill it up—through work, sex. hobbies, family, drugs—but we are doomed to fail. Our only chance is to realize this, and accept the inevitable pain. He looked at me with tears in his eyes and said, "Those are the most intelligent words I have ever heard."

Of Festschrifts and Biographies

Many of those who contributed to Nevin and Johnson's *The Legacy of Zellig Harris* also wrote for a Festschrift, a story that W. C. Watt, the instigator of the effort, recounts as part of his revealing reminiscences about Harris that further demonstrate some of the characteristics we've seen described.

We come now to a still more revealing incident in Harris's life, and for that matter my own, that has not hitherto been disclosed to the public eye. In 1969, having become aware that on October 12 of that year (Julian calendar) Harris would celebrate his sixtieth birthday, I conceived the notion that the occasion mustn't pass unremarked, and gained the assurance of Mouton & Company, in the Netherlands, that that concern would publish a Festschrift should I be able to garner the requisite number and quality of participants. Accordingly, I wrote some of the prominent linguists of the day, therefore including a good few of Harris's onetime students, asking if they'd be interested in contributing. The response was overwhelming, and the Festschrift, to be entitled with maximum simplicity "To Honor Zellig Harris at 60," was thereby set in motion. The 31 who agreed to submit tributary articles ranged widely over the fields to which Harris had made major contributions, but they were naturally concentrated in linguistics and its computational applications.

As an indication of Zellig Harris's personality, and as a cautionary tale about writing biographies of such individuals as Harris or Noam Chomsky, for whom the work and the values are paramount, Watt continues: "Readers need not cudgel their wits for memory of this volume, for it never appeared. Harris aborted it. He learned of the planned Festschrift, just in advance of his returning to the States and there receiving my letter apprising him of it (these things are supposed to be a surprise, after all), while passing through the Netherlands offices of Mouton & Company. His refusal of the intended honor was at first acerbic. "Dear Watt," he wrote me on October 20, 1969, in his tiny longhand,"

I am sorry to intervene in your actions, but I am writing in a matter in which I have human rights. It has come to my attention that you and Mouton are planning a Festschrift for me. Such a publication would be a deep personal affront to me and to my sense of values. I have managed to live this long with the principle that scientists can be people who do the best work they can for the sake of knowledge and of its human value. Any special—and unavoidably invidious— recognition of their work, such as honors, prizes, and Festschriften, is abhorrent to me, and would violate what I feel is a human right and dignity. Therefore, I ask you to withdraw this activity. . . . Many years ago, during Bloomfield's lifetime, I had to get a similar project stopped for Bloomfield's sake, and I am sorry that now I have to do it for myself. I am sure, however, that you will understand me, and will respect my principles even if they may seem excessive. With best regards, Zellig Harris

P.S. I have just seen your letter [a greeting to him announcing the occasion], after writing the above. Thanks for writing me, & I will answer your letter tonight, although the above (for which I apologize again) will indicate how I feel in the matter. Yours, Z. S. H.

I had long heard of Harris's reclusiveness, discretion, and abhorrence of public honors, so the story is not surprising; and it was only after speaking with dozens of his friends and colleagues that I have pursued this project, in part because this book is not meant as an "honor" or even as a tribute specifically to Harris, but rather the marking of a long era to which Harris and many others contributed, from a range of perspectives. The Festschrift, now ostensibly present in the aforementioned Nevin and Johnson collection, is a welcome addition to a long but somewhat elusive career and a profuse but somewhat disparate array of contributions to a range of fields.

Watt's characteristically imagistic and exact prose helps us, as we learn of the follow-up to the story, to have a sense of how Harris understood his own work and his relation to the field(s) to which it contributed. Considering Harris's words, Watt writes

Here, beyond cavil, was a response to a prospective honor—and one granted to few—from an honorable man. Moreover, one couched in such a way as to cause me, the offender, the least pain, partly by basing his declining the proposed honor on his having scuttled a similar tribute to Leonard Bloomfield, one of the earlier gods of linguistics. My reaction, besides of course immediately resolving to cancel the projected Festschrift and to write its promised participants to that effect, was also to arrive at a new respect for the opinions that Harris had just evinced and to conclude that, in his sense, Festschriften are indeed an abomination of a sort. Having canceled the Festschrift, I so informed Harris. Before he could receive my notification of withdrawal he wrote me again, as promised, in a way still more indicative of what he held to be "human values" and also of his sensitivities to a very junior colleague (whom, after all, he might rightly have suspected of an activity not wholly divorced from self-aggrandizement).

Harris then wrote a second letter, on the same day, in light of having read the first, to which he responded as follows: "Thank you for your kind letter, and I would never have been able to write as I did yesterday had I seen [it] first—though it may be just as well for my earlier letter represents my feelings. . . . Small as the whole issue is, I think you too see that there are values involved. As for me, anything that I could have gotten from the Festschrift, I think I have gotten from the tone of your letter, for which I thank you." This is a crucial point, since the idea of the Festschrift is indeed to honor the man and his work, an action virtually committed by the very invitation initiated by Watt, and it draws an important distinction between the biography and the Festschrift, assigning different roles to each. In the end, with the official notice that "the abominable Festschrift had indeed been aborted," Watt received a third letter that concluded by saying "anyway, it is good sometimes to air one's feelings about the culture we live in (I don't mean only ours, or only now—the others are even worse)."

Zellig Harris's resistance to such honors as the Festschrift was, for Tami Harris, consistent with her perception of him as being a conduit for ideas rather than a subject in himself.

He, as a person, or an ego (spiritually speaking, not psychologically) was not there. He was like a hose. You turn the tap on, and water comes out the other end. The hose has no ego, the hose needs no recognition, the hose needs nothing, it's just a hose. The hose is a conduit through which knowledge, wisdom, talents, or human values can come to life. 'Shoot the messenger,' they say. My father was the messenger, totally indifferent to being shot. Actually, these metaphors are not precise either. A hose or a messenger would not avoid recognition or acknowledgement the way my father did. I guess metaphors convey ideas in a vivid fashion, but they cannot capture the totality of human complexity.

The Anxiety of Influence

The Festschrift, and the aforementioned relations between Noam Chomsky and Zellig Harris, are interesting examples of teacher-student or master-disciple relations, and the different approaches they employed toward advancing their work reveals different ideas about how intellectuals can work to effect change. The differences between their approaches have received special attention in linguistics, if only because so little has been revealed about Harris's political efforts. In the study of language, though, it is clear that the course of their projects, differently construed from the outset, became increasingly so in time. The linguist Richard Kittredge, who worked with Zellig Harris, gives us Harris's perspective, recalling in correspondence with me that

I remember asking Zellig, around 1967, what he thought of Noam's work in *Aspects* [Chomsky's 1965 MIT Press book called *Aspects of the Theory of Syntax*]. He clearly respected Noam immensely, but said he didn't really understand the model he [Noam] was developing. When pressed, he said something implying that he was troubled by the inaccessibility of Noam's theoretical constructs, not subject to verification, like the Whorfian hypothesis. (He might easily have said the same about the syntactic and semantic representations I later used in computational linguistics, although we were doing engineering, not science or philosophy!) At the same time, Zellig was aware of the importance of Noam's ideas in formal language theory and encouraged us to take Aravind Joshi's courses for a view of that work and its relation to linguistics.

Some of the details of this divergence are discussed in section II, while others, more technical, are beyond the scope of this book.

There are certainly many points of overlap between Harris and Chomsky, if only through their respective milieus. Even Chomsky's mode of speaking bore some resemblances to Harris's. Harris has been described to me as engaging, and serious, and predictably, there is even a linguistic description of how he sounded, again from W. C. Watt, whom he trained: "To my ear he had virtually no foreign accent, sounding just like any native Philadelphian (meaning that he spoke one of the half-dozen or so equally distinctive Philadelphia dialects), except that his 'filled pause,' as linguists term it, rather than the usual 'uh,' was something like 'eh' (linguistically, a simple long /ɛ:/ with a bit of nasalization and a hint of an 'h' at the end)." On a physical note, Eva Rapkin recalls Harris as being quite strapping, and she recalls that there had been a great snowstorm in New York City, and she'd gone down to the street to look at her car, wondering how she was going to extricate herself. She spotted a man with shovel, digging his car out, and she decided to ask if he'd loan her his shovel when he was finished. She went over to him, and, lo and behold, it was Zellig Harris! He looked at her and said "Chava [her Jewish name], isn't this a mess!" as though he hadn't seen her in two days; in fact, they had not seen one another in many years. Chomsky is similarly known for his robustness and determination, obvious in the remarkable dedication with which he pursues his lectures around the world right up to today and, of course, his memory is legendary.

Tami Harris also mentioned her father's relation to Noam Chomsky and, consistent with Ted Live's observation about the Harris family, she was very sensitive about the subject. She recalled that "Noam Chomsky was like a son to my parents, to Bruria and Zellig Harris. For years my father and he worked together scientifically and discussed politics. My father had a great influence on Chomsky's science and political- social thinking. At some point though, Chomsky turned against him, like Oedipus, and was publishing their joint research, without even mentioning my father's contribution. For around twenty years my father's career was seriously restricted by Chomsky, mostly in the U.S." This Freudian interpretation of the relationship is consistent with a certain line of thinking among family members, and in the second section I will revisit this issue as regards the linguistic work. For the moment, though, it is important to note Zellig Harris's own view on the matter, from Tami Harris's recollections: "I heard the whole story when I was fifteen years old. I asked my father why he didn't somehow correct it. He looked at me as though I were asking the dumbest question imaginable, and, very typical of his thinking, he replied "naah, I have work to do."

The Later Years

For all of the excitement and enthusiasm Zellig Harris generated around him, there was also a sense in most of those with whom I spoke that Harris could be a difficult person, for some of the reasons named,—his reclusiveness, his introverted character, his sometimes unmovable convictions, his playing favorites—and most interviewees suggested that these more abrasive characteristics grew more pronounced in later years. Richard Kittredge told me that "Zellig was definitely reserved (as I was, so I didn't draw him out) and not one to stray far from the topic during our classes or meetings." Harold Orlans went further, suggesting that "every person who knew Zellig Harris well harbored some sort of disagreement with him. We [those in his immediate circle of colleagues and students] hardly ever disagreed with him tête-à-tête because Harris talked so much better than we did, and could be more than just a little overpowering, and even Chomsky has expressed as much, although more about the linguistics than the politics." No matter where one stood with regard to Harris's views, however, everyone felt as though he was serious, and committed, sometimes to a fault. He was also stringent in his expectations about how one should engage the serious matters with which he and his group had truck, and he spent a lot of time thinking about how to do this. Murray Wax recalled that as Jewish radicals, he and his group needed to have a sense of their Jewish identity, rather than, to use Wax's own phrasing, "pretending to be cosmopolitan intellectuals"; as such—and this is clear from the political work in which Harris ended up becoming engaged—Zionism in one form or another was intrinsic to his own ideals and to his advocacy. On the complex issue of how Chomsky diverged from Harris, in politics and linguistics, we have here one key insight. For Chomsky, the work to be done is the reverse of an identification, leading him to be particularly aware of the crimes of his own state, and that of Israel which, particularly for the group in question, became such an important (if sometimes wayward) beacon of hope.

And yet despite Harris's convictions, Harold Orlans confirmed something that became clear in the plethora of interviews I undertook for this book: Harris was reluctant to be public about his politics, to the very end of his life. Orlans did not consider this to be linked to Harris's timidity, but rather to what so many remarked upon—his caution, his suspicion—which kept him from wanting to associate himself with any of the activities that he pressed others to undertake. Murray Eden suggests that the reason Harris never joined any specific political initiative, even those he advocated to his students, was because of his more basic interest in the attitude or the program of individuals in society. Harris was very careful to avoid saying anything in public that touched on what Chomsky would consider "real politics," and it is an important distinction between the two men. According to Eden, "when Harris talked to a congressman, or when he talked to Brandeis or to big wheels in the Zionist organization, he did so with a purpose, but he never tried to become a political animal, actively engaged against some government action or another." His approach was to establish a "frame of reference," first to establish the grounds within which to work, and second, to determine what the outcome would be. This reticence became a sore point among some of his colleagues, who called it a sort of paranoia about what the state would do to him if he were to get directly involved in resistance or commentary. He once remarked that "they" (the University of Pennsylvania "brass") felt he should engage in some outside activities, that he was excessively occupied with linguistics. He said this humorously, recalled Orlans, "in order to show how well he had concealed his other activities." I can vouch for this on the basis of the interviews I conducted with some of his former colleagues at Penn who quite literally could not speak at all to Harris's political convictions, or indeed to what it was that he did in the many months he spent every year in Israel. For Orlans, in contrast to Eden, it was as though Harris thought that "he and his compatriots were plotting a revolution, and had to keep it secret lest the FBI learn of their plans. When one of his initiatives, called "Social Analysis," produced its first and only publication, "The Harlem Riot," the group suddenly had a problem; where was it to be published? How and where could it be bought? They had no office or contact person. Finally they got a post office box, and so a note inside of the cover of their publication read "Communications should be addressed to Social Analysis, GPO Box 399, New York 1, NY." This level of fear, justified by the fact that government agencies were indeed paying close attention to the likes of Franz Boas and even Albert Einstein, as we will see later on, led in Orlans's view not only to the disbanding of Avukah, but to a whole series of abandoned or unfinished projects.

One of the struggles that these episodes underlines is between ideological and scientific work. What is clear, above all else, is that Harris was interested in science, and his legacy in linguistics remains tied to much of the scientific and mathematical work. As Richard Kittredge suggested to me, "the most important thing I took away from Zellig's discussions was a sensitivity to the full paraphrase system in English, and its use in discovering the compositional semantics of sentences. This served me well in machine translation, as did his work on transfer grammar." But for all of the different projects he directed, or to which he contributed, he was in search of verifiable results, and perhaps he never satisfied that requirement when it came to work on social issues. Orlans recalled that a great many social scientists, and even historians, and certainly scientists, believe that the scientific method or methods could and should be extended to the fields of society and even political and social action. This is evidenced in the one political book that was published, posthumously, based on Harris's writings, *The Transformation of Capitalist Society* (to which I will return at length in section III). This scientism lends an air of seriousness to everything that Harris published, such that it is difficult to imagine him in social interactions.

Interviewees confirm this, but with some notable exceptions. Orlans recalled that once he was witness to Harris showing some emotion. "I had just entered Harris's New York hotel room. Lying on his back, silently, Harris said that he had heard Sapir was dead." Sapir, Harris's mentor, had purportedly designated Harris his intellectual heir and successor as leader of American linguistics (although, according to Orlans, "Sapir was considered far more brilliant amongst many, including the group at Yale that had included Sapir and also Malinowski"). Said Orlans, Harris was in his own way "entirely friendly and kind," and "he didn't put on airs, he didn't have a sense of superiority, he was even tempered, even under provocation, and he was, in all things of interest to him, very informative." And yet, and this certainly remains in the memory of many, Harris was remarkably unemotional and, sometimes quietly, very critical. For Irene Schumer it was beyond that. In her words, he had "bloodless views" and was "without affect," even though "Zellig Harris couldn't possibly have garnered more respect," whatever one's political affiliations.

In all things, as Shoshanna Harris recalled, Zellig's efforts were "very intense," and she remembers him being preoccupied by Avukah, and with the whole idea of it as an organization. But even with its demise, so many former Avukahites spoke to me of its residual effects. As Shoshanna Harris said, "You couldn't get into Avukah without getting a lot out of it, a feeling, and an outlook." At a reunion of Avukah members in New York, in 2003, Irene Schumer recalls "conversing with Ruthy [Ruth Slotkin], who had great animosity toward Zellig Harris," whom she accused of using his position "to mesmerize, to unduly influence young people." For her, "this was a real character flaw." In my many conversations with Seymour Melman around that period, he didn't agree, and indeed he spoke to me with great fondness and real seriousness about Harris as a person, and the continued importance of his work. These disagreements went beyond ordinary relations between friends and colleagues; during this Avukah reunion, Ruth Slotkin and Seymour Melman had an argument about Harris's legacy that was so vehement that Avukah members (in their 80s, most of them) had to restrain them—more than fifty years after the fact!

Zellig Harris died in 1992, and Tami Harris offered recollections concerning his last days.

He lived a full life till his last day. He had some medical problems and was naturally deteriorating in some aspects, but he was still young in spirit and cognitively intact. He died in his sleep like a saint. I choose to believe he was simply tired of his full life and subconsciously feared deteriorating mentally or physically and becoming a burden on others. I choose to believe this because it eases my constant pain and longing. Not a day passes without my wish to still have him around so that I might hear his opinions on recent events, listen to him as a mature person, share with him the beauty of music, art, or nature. I know this is universal. My pain is universal, yet so private, so personal.

At a memorial service for Zellig Harris, held at the University of Pennsylvania, family members, former Avukah members, and colleagues came to speak on his behalf. Ted Live recalls that Chomsky was one of the speakers, but that other than a few words about his mentor at the beginning, he never really spoke about Zellig. This was of course a disappointment for the Harris family, but not atypical nor surprising, since Chomsky's nonlinguistic talks are motivated by the desire to change the status quo toward a fairer society. Live recalled that the reaction of various relatives ranged from "this cheats Zellig of his due," to "I never took this very seriously." Tami Harris's perspective on this event has shifted over time: "I came all the way from Israel to attend, and other family members and friends came from all over the world. Chomsky was the guest of honor. The whole place was full of people giving flyers and collecting money to help with the situation in East Timor. Chomsky went on stage and made a whole speech about East Timor without even mentioning my father once." A number of people, including some Harris family members, have expressed their frustration to me about this event, and Tami Harris recalls that "at the time we were furious. It was disrespectful, and even more so considering their common history and his betrayal. Today I see another side of it. Maybe in his own way Chomsky was following my father's wish to focus on humanity and not on Zellig Harris?" Then, in a moving note of reconciliation, Tami Harris told me the following:

I have an outstanding three-year-old daughter. I named her Noam. Noam in Hebrew means pleasantness. I chose the name for many reasons, but Chomsky was part of it. It symbolizes my wish that the future will heal past wounds and correct injustices. Actually, this is not a wish, it's a commitment toward myself and my daughter. My daughter and my father never met, and I regret this every time I see her, or think of him. But I do know what he would have said if he knew her. When something was good, he either said it was "not bad" or, when he was really enthusiastic, he would mumble "nhnhnana," meaning it is very successful. If Zellig Harris had had the privilege to know Noam Harris, he would have said "nhnhnhhna, it is very

II The Language Work

4 From Semitics to Structuralism

The purpose of this section is to briefly present the work that Zellig Harris contributed to the study of language with reference to his writings, supplemented by personal insights gleaned from letters, interviews, and other sources. I further complement this material with reviews of Harris's works from both the published records and from some reviewers who assessed his research projects for the National Science Foundation. Right or wrong about Harris's approach and legacy, some of these reviews or comments (from individuals such as Bernard Bloch, Franz Boas, Noam Chomsky, Morris Halle, Henry Hiz, Henry Hoenigswald, Fred Lukoff, Margaret Mead, Paul Postal, and Edward Sapir) are of interest because they offer a sense of how Harris's writings were considered by his own contemporaries. I present this particular set of language-related material to further illuminate Harris's (and others') attitudes toward what he was doing professionally, as it were, and to continue in the quest to understand the guiding principles according to which Harris worked.

There are many controversies stirred up in this material, even today, and different assessments of how to understand it all are addressed in the professional literature. In terms of his contribution to linguistics, *The Legacy of Zellig Harris*,[1] and also the video of a conference that was held by some of the contributors, by the same title[2], are of great value, particularly for specialists seeking specific details concerning the language work. I do not wish to overlap or recall these or other works available in the public domain, but instead I hope that, when considered alongside the first section on Harris's character and the third on his politics and ideology, this section will contribute to a sense of who Zellig Harris was, and why we might want to know more about him. Most of the technical discussion is rather opaque for nonspecialists, so I have tried to stick to more general overviews from the field and, following the idea that Harris's research built on insights gleaned along the way, I've organized the material in a roughly chronological fashion, with some digressions when, for example, later works help describe earlier efforts, or earlier work points to later insights.

Zellig Harris's published language studies began with his 1933 master's thesis on the origin of the alphabet, the core of which was published in the *Journal of the American Oriental Society*.[3] He contributed to the field of Semitics studies in a range of works,[4] beginning with his 1934 article "The Structure of Ras Shamra C" for the *Journal of the American Oriental Society*[5] and, in 1935, *The Ras Shamra Mythological Texts* (with James A. Montgomery), published by the American Oriental Society.[6] The latter was reviewed by Edward Sapir,[7] which is significant given his prominence in the field at this time and the close affinity that Harris felt to him as a person and a scholar: "The present work," writes Sapir, "contains, in addition to the first five mythological texts to appear, a valuable section on the location and discovery of the Ras Shamra tablets, preliminary contributions to the phonology and morphology of the Semitic dialect in which they are composed, material in the form and meaning of the texts as religious poems, a useful bibliography, and, most important of all, a glossary, with references to all the Ras Shamra texts then known to the writers" (326–327). According to Sapir, the advantage of Harris and Montgomery's approach was that "connected English translations have been wisely avoided, for the difficulties of interpretation are still numerous and there is great danger of a premature certainty induced by too great reliance on Hebrew parallels" (327). On the other hand, "the reviewer confesses to some dissatisfaction with the method [of transliterating into the Hebrew character], for he believes it is not as innocent as it seems to be. It unavoidably suggests phonetic identities or relationships which a closer study of the material may show to be illusory." Instead, says Sapir, "it is to be hoped that scholarly usage will eventually agree on an adequate transliteration into Latin characters, such as is used in Bauer's edition. There is no reason why Ugaritic (Ras Shamra) should come to us with a Hebrew mask. It should be presented, either with its own alphabet or in the type of transliterated form which the civilized world has agreed upon as conventionally acceptable" (327). In his obituary for Zellig Harris, Henry Hiz mentions this early text, suggesting that "already manifest in all these works is the peculiarly precise, yet flexible, scholarly style that was to remain his for the rest of his life."[8]

There are parallels here with some of the work that William Chomsky was doing during this period, and they demonstrate the strong alliances within the community of which Harris was part. A *Jewish Quarterly Review* article by Chomsky dated January 1935 titled "An Intermediate Hebrew

Grammar,"[9] discusses "the literature of scientific Hebrew grammar" and the "disregard" on the part of many Hebrew scholars "for some of the most fundamental principles of Hebrew grammar, with the result that some flagrant errors find their way into the language and become sanctioned by usage." The reasons for this are related to other strands of the Harris story, notably to "the zeal and eagerness with which Hebrew is popularized and secularized, rapidly becoming a living language in speech and in writing, under the influence of Zionism and modern Palestine," and "the lack of practical and simple, yet scientific, Hebrew grammars" (311). Through his work with Avukah, Harris himself was very much involved with Zionism and modern Palestine, although the language politics that were a part of these discussions do not figure in the work he was doing.

Zellig Harris's doctoral thesis, *A Grammar of the Phoenician Language*, was published by the American Oriental Society, Yale University, in 1936, and it too was reviewed by Edward Sapir,[10] Vojtěch Sanda,[11] Charles François Jean,[12] and Maria Höfner.[13] Sapir's 1939 comments are positive, suggesting that Harris has "used all the relevant literature on Phoenician" and has also "gone carefully through all the scattered sources. . . bringing his accurate knowledge of the Canaanite dialects and his superior linguistic competence to bear on the peculiarly refractory, fragmentary, essentially unsatisfactory materials which constitute our source for the phonology and morphology of Phoenician, one of the most important Semitic languages from the historical and cultural point of view" (61). The Harris text, says Sapir, offers a "clear sense of dialectology, both of time and place" (61), as well as an "excellent glossary, including proper nouns, which covers all the material in both native and foreign sources" (62). Sapir once again takes issue with the transliteration, which come out "far more crisply and interestingly if the Greek and Latin transliterations are completely utilized" (64), and with the problem of spirantization [turning into a fricative], the product of Harris's being "too hasty" and not taking "sufficient account of the transcriptional evidence" (65). In a December 10, 1937, letter to Sapir, Harris thanks Sapir and his wife for having him over to stay, and he also makes reference to the review: "I have just seen our review of our little Ras Shamra book; you have some very nice points in it. Götze just sent the JADS a beautiful long article on the RS tenses."

Harris actively contributed to anthropological studies of language from early on in his career, beginning with such published works as a 1934 review of Raymond Philip Dougherty's *The Sealand of Ancient Arabia* for the *Journal of the American Oriental Society*,[14] and a 1935 review of Edward Chiera's *Joint Expedition [of the American School of Oriental Research in Baghdad] with the*

Iraq Museum of Nuzi for *Language*.[15] The Chiera text contains copies of over two hundred tablets found through excavations at the site of ancient Nuzi, near modern Kirkuk in Iraq, archives of four generations of a prominent Nuzi family that, according to Harris, "constitute an excellent source for the study of social conditions in Nuzi at the middle of the second millennium B.C." These tablets were of special linguistic interest because although "written in Akkadian they are the work of a non-Semitic group,"—Hurrians. Therefore, "the Nuzi material thus becomes an important source for this Asianic language which was used over a wide area, occurring in records from Mitanni, Boghazköi, and Ras Shamra, in Syria." This material was of special interest to Harris, who in 1936 published an article titled "Back formation of 'itn' in Phoenician and Ras Shamra" for the *Journal of the American Oriental Society*.[16]

Anthropology and Politics

Harris had been lecturing as an instructor at University of Pennsylvania since 1931, and he was promoted in 1937 to the rank of assistant professor, largely on the basis of his contributions to Semitics (which he taught at Penn from 1931 to 1938). He also lectured at the Linguistics Institute of the University of Michigan, beginning in the summer of 1937 until 1939. Along with key figures such as Leonard Bloomfield, Franz Boas, and Edward Sapir, Harris was concerned with critical issues linked in various ways to the matter of anthropology as science. One of the interesting debates of this period can be found in a correspondence that Einstein had with Boas in 1935, concerning the case of one Dr. Zollschan who had requested considerable funds ($500) from Boas to travel to the United States to discuss the nature of Jews from a racial standpoint. In a letter dated October 31, 1935, Boas wrote that he felt Zollschan's work was in some ways objectionable because "his whole attitude has been to set up the Jews as a particularly gifted and excellent group as over against other groups," suggesting that they were being treated here as a potential vanguard. For Boas, "this is the one thing to be avoided," and instead he should make his assessments "on the basis of an objective investigation of different social and racial groups." In a November 3, 1935, reply, Einstein agreed that "an authoritative office should initiate a survey in scholarly institutions such that these say something about those points of the theory of race, which are currently misused demagogically by certain politicians." Nevertheless, says Einstein, "I believe that a sensible execution of this plan could only be advantageous," and "therefore I am not at all able to share your reservation that this concerns the attempt at a glorification of the Jews, which would certainly be disadvantageous from the political standpoint." For him, "the plan does not concern a glorification of a particular race, but rather the prevention of an objective certainly unjustified, overrating of the concept of a race in general." On November 6, 1935, Boas wrote back, saying that his "doubts" were about Zollschan's plan "to undertake scientific studies about racial peculiarities. . . . For months, I've already made efforts to obtain a very brief declaration from American anthropologists concerning what we know and what we do not know regarding races. . . . After many negative replies, which were given with the explanation that such a purely factual declaration would be inopportune, one of the Harvard anthropologists has drawn up a statement, and it remains to be seen how the people whose signatures we wish to have will react."[17]

Zollschan himself wrote a very interesting reply, given how anthropology was used by certain figures in Germany (and elsewhere) to bolster the idea that there exists a Master Race. He noted his disagreement with Boas, but then pointed out that he was not looking for unanimity from the American anthropological community on this issue; rather, "our task would . . . have to be to bring it about that the intellectual public *demands* from the scholars the statement of their opinion." For him, "our goal must be to find ways and means that such a public demand arises and that it is sufficiently vocal." The project would thus be multifaceted, such that "individual experts are to prepare the material, individual personalities and interested institutions are to provide the financial means, writers are to create the public opinion and political offices must work towards the actualization of the whole thing." As to the issue of whether Jews should be singled out for this effort, he notes that "it is not the place of Masaryk [the first president of Czechoslovakia] or of Pacelli [elected to become Pope Pius XII] or neither the place of the Anglican clergy to stand up for the interests of the Jews; we must count ourselves fortunate to have their valuable help. It must simply not be that, due to the indolence on the part of the Jews, even the most valuable help evaporates into thin air." The role of people like Einstein, Boas, or Harris in matters like this one is to lend their name to valuable efforts, contributing to the idea of intellectual responsibility beyond the ivory tower.

This debate had palpable implications given the social setting within which Zellig Harris, Franz Boas, and (eventually) Albert Einstein worked, as Jews in the American academy. The University of Pennsylvania, Harris's alma mater and workplace, was during this period quite conservative, in which little good could come of waving Semitic flags; the same was true of virtually all higher education institutions, including Franz Boas's own university, Columbia. Ernst Harms, the editor of the *Yearbook and Library for the Idealist Philosophy*, wrote to Boas on April 28, 1936, with a copy to the president of Columbia University, to describe the cold reception he had received from his colleagues when he came to do research there. Says Harms, they wished to "rid themselves as quickly as possible of every collegial relation to me." Harms suggests that Boas would probably wish to "communicate this 'being on the move' of American anti-Semitism to personalities who are interested in it." Incidents like this one help provide a backdrop to the environment within which these people were destined to work and the importance of the political and academic struggles they engaged, and it provides a basis upon which to consider Harris's activities within and beyond language studies.

New Linguistic Techniques

One way to avoid such ideological conflict implicit in the study of language and its relation to race or class or intelligence, as the formalists learned in Russia after the Revolution in 1917, was to work from an objective paradigm, such as the physical or natural sciences. Harris's work as a Semitist had been influenced by the new techniques in linguistic analysis, and it attracted the attention and personal interest of Edward Sapir and Leonard Bloomfield. Henry Hiz, in his aforementioned tribute to Harris, notes the common threads that link the three of them.

Both [Bloomfield and Sapir] strove to understand the phenomenon of meaning in language, just as Zellig Harris always did. However, they knew that at present there are no scientific ways to examine meaning in all of its social manifestations. But, as Harris repeated after Bloomfield, "it frequently happens that when we do not rest with the explanation that something is due to meaning, we discover that it has a formal regularity or 'explanation.' It may still be 'due to meaning' in one sense, but it accords with a distributional regularity.' For Bloomfield, Sapir, and Harris, the primary datum for the scientific study of language is the relative position of the segments of speech utterances. (519)

Harris's work thus follows in the tradition of both Bloomfield and Sapir, and came to be consistent with certain elements of formalist and structuralist approaches to language, which were premised on the idea that meaning and form (the distributional information about the discrete elements—phonemes, morphemes, words—that comprise sentences) are two sides of the same phenomenon. Harris would eventually review Sapir's writings, in the course of which he suggested such concordances with his own work. His system would also be influenced by mathematics, as we will see when we look to his 1947 work, published as *Structural Linguistics*,[18] and of course to his work on computability of language; but even at this time he ascribed to rigorous and scientific methods that are often referred to in the literature as "modern." We find as early as his 1936 review of Louis H. Gray's *Introduction to Semitic Comparative Linguistics* that "within the last few years Semitists have begun to analyze their data with the rigorous method of modern linguistics."[19] The nature of this method becomes clear later as he shifted his research emphasis toward the elaboration of a methodology of a science of language, on the basis of a theory of language that he describes in some of his writings.

In 1937, Harris was invited to lecture at the influential Linguistic Institute, held that year at the University of Michigan.[20] Edward Sapir came as the star speaker, which would have some unanticipated and far-reaching implications for the whole field of linguistics. In his obituary for Bernard Bloch, Martin Joos provides a sense of the occasion.

In the 1937 Linguistic Institute he [Bloch] was apparently influenced most strongly by the Sapir course in field methods and the other participants in it. The official attendance list is now irrecoverable, but it would not have named the non-credit participants anyhow; from the memories of three of the group, we have this partial list: Bernard Bloch, John B. Carroll, J. Milton Cowan, Zellig Harris, Fred W. Householder, Jr., Norman A. McQuown, and Kenneth L. Pike; Henry Lee Smith, Jr., was in the group at first, and at the end Morris Swadesh arrived and probably visited it. An editorial footnote of Bloch's, Lg. 42.90 [an article in the journal *Language*] (1966)—perhaps the last he ever wrote—testifies to some of the Sapir impact on him. The association with Harris for rather more than a decade after that is documented in the published papers of both.[21]

Harris's work during this period followed up on some of his graduate studies and included, in 1937, "Ras Shamra: Canaanite Civilization and Language" for the *Annual Report of the Smithsonian Institution,* "A Conditioned Sound Change in Ras Shamra," for the *Journal of the American Oriental Society*,[22] and "Expression of the Causative in Ugaritic" in the same journal the following year.[23] Henry Hiz recalls in his tribute to Zellig Harris[24] that Montgomery's influence led Harris to decipher and then read the Ugaritic texts that were coming to light at this time, and in the 1938–39 *Jewish Quarterly Review*, he reviewed two books under the title "The Ugaritic Texts of Daniel and KRT."[25] These are of great importance not only because they offer descriptions of two long newly discovered legends, but because both of them "exhibit linguistic forms which will help us to unravel the structure and history of the 'North-Canaanite' language of Ugarit" (191).

Although he disagrees with some of the interpretations, Harris finds this text to be of great importance because "the scholarly world depends for its knowledge of Ugaritic upon Virolleaud's reading of the alphabetic tablets," which are "exact" and "clear" (193).

On April 11, 1938, Zellig Harris wrote to Albrecht Goetze, who became an important interlocutor with Harris, for reasons that are described in the following letter:

> I want to tell you that I read the manuscript of your long article on the Ugaritic tense system, and think it is one of the finest pieces of linguistic analysis I have seen. I am still not completely sure of the present tense: you have built up an overwhelmingly probable case, but just for certainty's sake I see no form-group which may not perhaps be differently explained. In any case, the analysis and arrangement of evidence that you give is the only basis for methodological work. . . . I also saw your letter about honorary memberships in the Oriental Society, and wish to congratulate you on making the point about German nominations. It is unusual to hold such a position in the exaggerated impartiality of scientific bodies, but I think neither science nor social justice is promoted by hiding ourselves from the social implications of our "objective" actions.

This raises important points about the link between Harris's Zionism and other "implications" that grew from his analysis of society, because it is increasingly evident that Harris's language research had overlaps with some of the ideological interests he was pursuing at that time, through Avukah in particular, and with his work on Semitic languages, notably Hebrew. In a letter to Goetz dated January 26, 1939, Harris commented on a new paper on Hebrew accent and vocalism that he had received from Goetze. His critique was of Goetze's historical explanation, pointing out that "at the present moment I cannot see that either my statement or yours can be invalidated; I think both are possible, though I prefer mine." The argument is highly technical, summed up in the last paragraph with Harris's admission "that in all these things my explanation may not be the historically true one. In one point, however, I tend to strongly doubt your explanation—that is in your treatment of pre-stress long vowels. You say that they occur in those nouns which were originally stressed on the first syllable. To me it seems that they are very late, and have no connection with the original stress."

In 1939, Harris published *Development of the Canaanite Dialects: An Investigation in Linguistic History*, once again for the American Oriental Series. It was reviewed widely, by William Foxwell Albright,[26] Max M. Bravmann,[27] Marcel Cohen,[28] René Dussaud,[29] Harold Louis Ginsberg,[30] Albrecht Goetze,[31] Alexander Mackie Honeyman,[32] Franz Rosenthal,[33] Gonzague Ryckmans,[34]

Raphaël Savignac,[35] Bernard Baron Carra de Vaux,[36] and Ronald James Williams.[37] Rosenthal calls Harris's methods of dialectology "sober" but admirable in their historical approach. Further, "every attempt to synchronize the study of Semitic languages with current progress in linguistic research is in itself highly commendable," and when, "with a side glance at the historical and economic problems of the area are covered, this attempt aims at clarifying the linguistic situation in a very controversial, and yet inadequately treated field . . . it is all the more welcome" (179). Williams further notes that the "new era" in linguistics research was ushered in by Sapir's *Language: An Introduction to the Study of Speech* and by Bloomfield's *Language*, and in recent years Semitic studies has been able to "share in this advance." Williams specifically calls Harris's work scientific but points to areas of possible dissension between Harris and scholars in the same field; nevertheless, he says admiringly, "this in no way detracts from the value of [Harris's] investigation."

Honeyman finds this text important because "in research into Canaanite philology, to which the discovery of the Ras Shamra tablets has given a fresh impetus in the last decade, America leads the world, and in a group which includes the names of Albright, Ginsberg, Goetze, Gordon and Montgomery, Dr. Harris holds a high place" (263). Despite the "newness" of this approach, Honeyman nevertheless calls the book's methods "strictly philological," inspired entirely "by his master," Edward Sapir. "His purpose is to mark the phonemic, phonetic, morphological, syntactical, and lexical changes characteristic of groups within the Canaanite family, to date and localize them, and thence to elucidate the processes by which the several dialects evolved." Harris's contributions are described as "twofold": first the methodology is valuable for students of language, and second, the work contributes to Semitic studies because one of the chapters "offers as complete a list as the nature of the evidence permits of some sixty-four linguistic changes occurring in the Canaanite group." Nevertheless, the "paucity" of the material is such that Harris makes statements that can have "a specious precision and simplicity." De Vaux's review is positive, although he does suggest that the text may be "un peu prematuré," (329) on account of the limited knowledge of those texts at the time and the lack of other texts from that same period. Ginsberg agrees on this point in his review, suggesting that the book is "almost entirely" a work of interpretation; indeed, "the author has had to reconstruct as much as possible of the history of the changes that took place in the Canaanite languages, individually and collectively, in the course of their existence" (346). Nevertheless, he finds Harris to be gifted with "wonted industry," which allowed him to produce a "valuable work," even if he disagrees on a number of points relating to Ugaritic grammar, the Tiberian vowel system, and other details.

Goetze's review begins with a statement that is echoed in most assessments, that "Harris's statements are always based on a complete survey and a well-considered appraisal of the facts; moreover, they are invariably presented in an extremely attractive way" (168). Nevertheless, he expresses qualms about Harris's belief "in the Canaanite character of Ugaritic" (168). Harris had seen the review before it appeared because Goetze had sent him a copy, and he commented on it in a letter dated December 27, 1940: "Thanks for your paper and review. I have just read them hastily, and will soon go over it point by point. Let me assure you that not only do I not consider it "unpleasant" but am glad of the controversy. No person, certainly not I, can be sure of his judgments as "always right"; the best way to get closer to the 'truth"—after I have figured out whatever I could— is to get the divergent opinions which arise from a different scientific analysis. The only fun in science is finding out what was actually there." This statement is a strong articulation of Harris's approach to the field, and to scientific inquiry more generally, and it is in evidence in his language research and, as we will see in section III, in the political work as well.

Albright's review was published after (and in light of) Ginsberg's and Goetze's criticisms, but emphasizes instead that Harris's methods are "thoroughly up to date," and that his book is marked by "the influence of the late Edward Sapir on nearly every page." Further, although "a resolute exponent of the diffusion school of linguistics," he "does not carry its principles to absurd lengths, as has been done by certain members of the Meillet school."[38] Indeed, Harris is "intimately versed in the individual dialects, from Biblical Hebrew through Phoenician to Ugaritic" and he shows "exceptionally good judgment" in his datings of inscriptions." But the study itself is in Albright's view "premature" because "a judicious analysis of the data will help us solve the problems which they present" (414). Harris's work was also reviewed in France and published in the *Bulletin de la Société Linguistique de Paris*,[39] the beginning of what would turn out to be a strong interest on the part of the French, still today, in Harris's work. Marcel Cohen, the reviewer, suggests that "tous les sémitistes devront tenir compte de cet ouvrage" [all Semiticists should take this work into account] because of the detail it provides, and the clear grasp that Harris thereby exhibits of pertinent issues. Raphaël Savignac, also reviewing in French, describes Zellig Harris's "minutieux et ardu" [careful and arduous] work, noting the general lack of information available about this important area.

In 1939 Harris published "Development of the West Semitic Aspect System,"[40] which he described in the following passage:

The late Proto-Semitic system of objective aspects of the verb changed, in the course of West Semitic history, into a pattern of subjective aspects. Within Proto-West Semitic there first developed a) two modes (out of the imperative: jussive, subjunctive); b) the internal passive form; and c) the perfective use of the nominal. Later, this was elaborated in the separated West Semitic languages into a consistent morphologic pattern: d) development of the active perfect; e) disuse of the preterite; f) development of the indicative imperfect; g) disuse of the present. Possible date and causes of each development were given in this paper. (409–410)[41]

He also made a contribution to the Linguistic Society at Baltimore's "Near East Group Meeting: Linguistic, Epigraphic, and Historical," and in that same year completed, with Charles F. Voegelin, *Hidatsa Texts Collected by Robert H. Lowie*, with grammatical notes and phonograph transcriptions by Z. S. Harris and C. F. Voegelin, an important contribution to the document-ing analysis of native American languages in the United States.[42]

Language Studies at the Brink of War

As war broke out in Europe, some of the implications of the work that was being done by anthropologists and linguists took on a different meaning, since there was so much tied up with questions of superiority of race, coding and decoding, and the transmission and analysis of useful informa-tion (in a multiplicity of languages). Harris was working on a number of projects at that time that would bear fruit in the coming years, notably studies of a whole range of Semitic, native Indian, and African languages. Further, he was involved with a project on Hebrew grammar, described by Alfred J. Kahn (the executive secretary of Avukah) in a December 6, 1939, letter to Solomon Goldman[43] (a director of the Jewish Theological Semi-nary of America) for which he requested $750 to help bring it to press. The text was funded by the Zionist Organization of America (ZOA) and was announced in the *Avukah Student Action* of February 16, 1940. This same issue includes an article by Bruria Kaufman, who eventually became Zellig Harris's wife. Her ties with Avukah came early, with the previously cited letter on the Avukah Plan and this article entitled "How to Write a Hebrew Grammar; Co-Author Tells Secrets of Trade," which recalls that "every language has a set of sounds (consonants and vowels) peculiar to it," and that "certain combinations of these sounds are recognized within the language as words." The grammarian is, according to Kaufman, "in the position of the hearer," with regard to the sounds that make up a sentence, so "a segment of the series between two consecutive pauses may be analyzed and found to contain independent units, i.e. units which can occur in various combinations with other units" making up words. Among these words, the grammarian "finds families related in form and meaning," with the common element being the "root." Clarifying the role of phonology, she recalls that "the section of grammar dealing with sounds synthesizes the rules for changes in sounds due to their positional relations to other sounds." Of further interest is the ordering of these sounds, these words, to make up the grammar of the sentences, or syntax. "Any scientific description of a language should contain the rules governing the changes in these three elements: sound, words, and sentences" (3). It is interesting to consider the rigor of Bruria Kaufman's approach to language in light of what we know about the clarity of her work in physics and mathematics, for which she was much admired by Albert Einstein, in evidence in this anecdote from a biography of Einstein:

Once he [Einstein] greeted a new and awestricken assistant, Bruria Kaufman, with some equations which had been tormenting him for two or three weeks. Within a half-day she discovered that a factor of 2 was missing and, in disbelief, went to one of his former assistants to see if it was possible for the great man to have made such a mistake. She learned it was. "So I got used to the fact that I could correct him." Another time she quoted some known theorems to him which struck him as very beautiful, and which, he was convinced, she had invented.[44]

These comments suggest intersections between Harris's and Kaufman's work, and given his early interest in physics and his eventual work in mathematics, there are some interesting areas of overlap in their respective realms.

The Underlying Structures of Human Language

On January 20, 1940, Harris wrote a letter[45] describing a week he spent with a frequent collaborator of his, the anthropologist and linguist Charles Frederick Voegelin, during which time he gave a couple of lectures on linguistic structure: "While looking over our forthcoming Hidatsa grammar, we took time out to plan an American Indian linguistics course. It is so planned as to constitute incidentally a general introduction to linguistic science, but its central subject matter is the structure of various American Indian languages and the methods of field work." Harris and Voegelin delivered the course together at Penn, expecting the students to work out, "in laboratory style, typical structures out of linguistic material that we'll arrange for it, etc." At that time Harris also completed an important review of Louis Herbert Gray's *Foundations of Language*,[46] and then commented on the book in personal correspondence with the linguist Bernard Bloch, a frequent correspondent and friend to Harris for many years. In a January 30, 1940, letter, Harris confessed that he had been hesitant to review Gray's book because "some two years ago I wrote a very negative review of Gray's *Comparative Semitic*. He was pained by it, and we had a long (friendly) correspondence thereafter. As a result, I simply couldn't write a harsh review now. On the other hand, I have this in favor of writing a review: that it is an opportunity to argue that all linguists should know what language structure is, which Gray doesn't seem to." The review itself provides a sense of Harris's thinking on crucial issues, notably, "the nature of language, . . . phonetics, morphology, and etymology, and . . . the classification of languages" (216). He takes issue with an array of Gray's presuppositions, notably that the linguist's sources must be written texts, rather than conversations. For him, spoken utterances are "not only more direct, numerous, and normal, but also have greater laboratory value, since in speech we have opportunities for controlled observation, and even for experimental conditions" (216). More important, according to Harris, Gray neglects "the structural method," which "cuts the linguist off from the organization of all non-historical facts. By constantly deferring to historical texts, says Harris, Gray must always make appeals to history, "which are beside the point, since the meaning of forms and of their arrangements is necessarily given by a complete description of how they are used, i.e. of what they mean to the people who use them" (217). This is an interesting take on structural linguistics because it challenges the assertion that structuralism is (necessarily) ahistorical; if the description of the structure is taken to correspond to a particular moment in time, and if individuals employ or study it with an awareness thereof, then it is tied to a historical moment. In the Boas files (held by the American Philosophical Society), Harris refers to oral conversations of native Americans, captured in some instances on phonographic recordings, and similarly notes that "failure to organize data by their place in the structure often leads to unsatisfactory classifications," a point that he would eventually drive home with his meticulous classifications in *Structural Linguistics*. Gray neglects the structural method, says Harris, in statements such as: "Some scientific terms [are] 'linguistically correct, both elements being drawn from the same language,' while others are 'linguistically unjustifiable, whose components are taken from different languages'" (218). Says Harris, "one need hardly point out that for the speaker it makes no difference if the elements come from one language or two, but only if the phonological and morphological structure of the form is the same as that of other words in his language" (218).

Harris's method revolves around phonemic analysis, which is "necessary in any discussion of linguistic regularity" (219). A study of this regularity is essential to structural analysis because when such classification is made of phonemes, "we can briefly identify the sounds of any utterance in that language" (219), which is the very basis for Harris's structural method.

The structural method is basically the placing together of any formal features of a language which in respect to any criterion are similar. Sounds in each language may be grouped according to certain phonetic features and certain complementary distributions in respect to the other sounds in the flow of speech; we find this classification into phonemes particularly convenient because in terms of it we can briefly identify the sounds of any utterance in that language. The phoneme may be grouped according to the positions they can occupy in respect to other phonemes, and insofar as this yields distinct classes, such as consonants and vowels, we may describe in terms of them the shapes of linguistic forms in that language, and the relations between certain partially similar forms." (221–222)

This is where we find the quest to uncover underlying components in human language, an ambition which is in some ways interesting to consider alongside the Einsteinian quest to uncover relations between, for example, subatomic particles. This is not to say that Harris's linguistics were inspired by Einstein—it would perhaps be more appropriate to consider constructivism and intuitionism in mathematics and some of the work by Gödel—but Einstein's ideas were certainly in the air at that time, and there was for many people an allure in the idea of finding the workings of complex phenomena in the actions of unseen structures or particles. With this in mind, it is interesting to read such statements as: "We call this 'structure,' because all these statements and classifications for any given language can be organized in terms of particular units (phonemes, morphemes, etc.) and relations existing among them. We call it 'pattern' because many of the relations crisscross each other, often in parallel lines. Some linguistic facts will escape the investigator who does not try to arrange the initial classifications into possible networks, who does not look for relations between the relations" (222). Structural linguistics, which Harris himself defines in "The Background of Transformational and Metalanguage Analysis"[47] as an effort aimed at "formulating this hierarchy of distributional classifications," is a project that "made it necessary to establish procedures for determining the primitive elements at the bottom of the hierarchy, for their simplicity and objective characterizability is as important to the system as are the classifications and sequences that state the departures from randomness of the entities at each level" (2). In the review of Gray's work, Harris goes beyond the rationalization or ordering of related elements and into the much more complex issue of what defines a language.

It is important to recognize that language is a system of units and their relations, because that often serves as our criterion of what material is language and what is not. Only on this basis do we exclude at present the vast and as yet unorganized fields of expressive modifications (e.g. anger-modulations, intonations of sarcasm, etc.), and of the linguistic differentiae used by particular sections of the community (e.g. characteristic intonations of girls, etc.). All these have conventional phonetic forms and meanings, no less than language proper, and are marked off from language only because we cannot analyze them structurally in the same way. (223)

Harris assesses Gray's approach by emphasizing his own sense that "the structure of language can be described only in terms of the formal, not the semantic, differences of units and their relations" (223). This helps explain Harris's idea that linguistics cannot be the study of meaning through, for example, semantic classification. And studies of linguistic details also undermine the psychological approach, sometimes present in Gray's text, because it "adds nothing" and "is often circular" (225), just as the "mentalistic approach" is of no value because we know very little about "mental processes" (226). Harris's negative review seems to have been strongly felt, because the editors of the journal made the very unusual move of adding a second, more positive review after his "as a valuable supplement."

Harris's status in the field was firmly established during this time, leading to some significant invitations; on February 26, 1940, for example, he wrote to W. Edgerton, H. L. Ginsberg, A. Goetze, A. Jeffery, and E. A. Speiser, saying that "Professor Ginsberg had suggested that I take the secretaryship of the Steering committee [of the Group for Hamitic and Semitic Linguistics]. I have waited some time to see if this would be possible, but know now that I will not be able to do it." The motive for his refusal is not given, however it may be on account of his increasing work in native American languages, with which he clearly had some involvement already. On April 10, 1941, Harris received a letter from J. Alden Mason asking if he had a student with some "spare time" who might assist him in the writing of the section on native languages for a proposed book called *Handbook of South American Indians*. The problem for Mason was that "as I promised Kroeber to finish a grammar of Papago before I did anything else I haven't begun on it yet, and *tempus fugit*. The Chairman writes me from Washington that there are some small funds available for help in this work and wants to know if I can use some before the fiscal year ends and all is allocated. A student might do some of the background work for me."

The study of native American languages in America dated back to the last quarter of the eighteenth century, and "had been fired by a number of prominent citizens of the newly founded United States of America who stayed in Paris for long visits, imbibing the ideas of the Encyclopedists and the Enlightenment that were popular there. These they took with them when they returned (together with a great many books) inspiring others who had not been so fortunate as to have visited Paris." As we will see, Harris in this sense worked in a way that was consistent with a tradition that saw "many philosophers and amateur historians and antiquarians . . . collect[ing] data, especially word lists, from languages spoken by far away nations and tribes, including the aboriginal peoples of North America."[48] The American Philosophical Society, a source for many archival documents cited in this book, was also an impetus; founded in 1769, it was a rallying point for linguistic activity in America and it focused upon native languages in the United States.

The other major development in this wartime period was the U.S. government's intensified interest, for strategic reasons, in linguistics research, including a program to encourage the study of foreign languages.

In 1941 the American Council of Learned Societies (ACLS) sought contact with the LSA to set up an Intensive Language program (ILP). When the US did step into the war, in December 1941, the ILP was greatly intensified and soon merged with the Army Specialized Training Program (ASTP), which commissioned the writing of materials and crash courses in a number of languages that were considered strategically important, notably Russian, German, Dutch, Spanish, Italian, Japanese, Chinese, Thai, Burmese (this was the beginning of a period of collaboration between the American armed forces and the linguistic world, which would last for over twenty years, the former playing Dutch uncle to the latter). (Seuren 194)

This was significant both for what it produced and what it suggested about wartime (WWII and the Cold War that followed) funding; no matter what the eventual importance of the work done during this period is, there is a social history to be written about Cold War linguistics, which would reveal much about what the military thought it could achieve through research. Elements of this will be discussed in the pages that follow, but without full access to government archives, the full story will remain untold.

Regularity, Basic Units, and the Common Language of Science

During this period Harris was named editor of the *Journal of the American Oriental Society*, a position he would hold from 1941 to 1947. Although still involved with Semitic studies and native languages, according to Peter

Matthews's obituary that divides Harris's life and work into "phases," he was entering his first phase of work, the central aim of which was to "establish the basic units of a language on the evidence of distributional patterns." In this project, "phonemes are identified to account for regularities over sounds that can be distinguished in speech; morphemes to account for patterning over longer stretches; syntactic units to account for patterns over morphemes." In 1941, the year in which William Chomsky published "The History of our Vowel-System in Hebrew" for the *Jewish Quarterly Review*,[49] Harris published the "Linguistic Structure of Hebrew," for the *Journal of the American Oriental Society*,[50] a review of Nikolaj Sergeevic Trubetzkoy's *Grundzüge der Phonologie*[51] in *Language*,[52] and, from 1941 to 1946, "Cherokee Materials."[53] In 1942, his work included "Morpheme Alternants in Linguistic Analysis," published in *Language*,[54] "Phonologies of African Languages: The Phonemes of Moroccan Arabic," read at the Centennial Meeting of the American Oriental Society and published in the *Journal of the American Oriental Society* (JOAS).[55] Two publications from that period, on "The Linguistic Structure of Hebrew (1941)[56] and "Phonologies of African Languages: Phonemes of Moroccan Arabic (1942)[57] are cited in his aforementioned article, "The Background of Transformational and Metalanguage Analysis" (hereafter "Background") as "intellectual background" for the general methodological program that aimed to find "the maximum regularity in the occurrence of parts of utterances in respect to other parts" ("Background" 2). He also worked during this period with William E. Welmers on "The Phonemes of Fanti,"[58] a highly technical phonemic analysis of a language native to the southern part of the Gold Coast, in British West Africa. In the same issue of *JOAS*, he coauthored, this time with Fred Lukoff, a much shorter text on "The Phonemes of Kingwa Swahili," as well as "the Phonemes of Moroccan Arabic,[59] which he read at the Centennial Meeting of the Oriental Society in Boston, in 1942. These technical texts are examples of the type of work he undertook with students who would have extremely important impacts upon intellectual life in the United States. Lukoff, for example, began the work on Swahili with Harris, and he was later replaced by a key figure in the Avukah movement: Nathan Glazer.

It is striking in reviewing the work from this period that Harris moves from European to Semitic to American languages, and indeed he continued to do so through much of his career, in part to discover interconnections between languages not typically studied together. The importance of this effort to his overall methodological ambitions is driven home in a February 3, 1942, letter to Robert Lowie. Writing as the editor of the *Journal of the*

American Oriental Society, Harris notes that "several persons have suggested that scientific groups dealing with Old World cultures should have some understanding of the historical interconnections and methodological similarities between Old World and New World areas. In some cases this would help break down artificial boundaries, in others it would broaden the understanding of scientific workers. . . . And I wonder if you could give us an article on Circumpolar problems,[60] or on some other matter of this character." Lowie, like Harris, studied both Native American groups and European cultures, and this during a period when, as John Goldsmith notes

linguistics was split between the traditional, Europe-facing historical linguists who studied Indo-European and couldn't imagine working on languages without a long written tradition, and the anthropologically oriented linguists who were most interested in learning about indigenous cultures without a written history. It was Sapir and Bloomfield who, though trained in the first tradition, were the heroes of the second, and proved that the two traditions could be merged. Harris, too, followed a similar trajectory, though he wasn't all that much of a field worker.[61]

Other traditions of study were also being considered in juxtaposition at this time, particularly as Harris pursued his work on different fronts. The Jewish student organization Avukah crisscrosses this narrative, for example, as figures from the realm of Socialist Zionism undertake work that can be linked into Harris's approach to the study of language. In addition to the aforementioned work of Murray Eden, Nathan Glazer, and Bruria Kaufman, some further overlaps between Harris's and Einstein's approaches are suggested by a talk that Einstein gave on the relationship between words and thoughts, recorded for the Science Conference, London, September 28, 1941 (and then published in *Advancement of Science*[62] shortly thereafter). Einstein's talk began with the foundation of language, the first step for which is "to link acoustically or otherwise commutable signs to sense-impressions," a process which most "sociable animals" undergo. The higher level occurs "when further signs are introduced and understood which establish relations between those other signs designating sense-impression. At this stage it is already possible to report somewhat complex series of impressions; we can say that language has come to existence." The next issue concerns the analysis of linguistic mechanisms, for which Einstein's sense is that "if language is to lead at all to understanding, there must be rules concerning the relations between the signs on the one hand, and on the other hand there must be a stable correspondence between signs and impressions." Children grasp these rules and relations by "intuition," but "when man becomes conscious of the rules concerning the relations between signs, the so-called grammar of language is established."

The next issue is how this language relates to perceptions and ideas, such that language can become an "instrument of reason in the true sense of the word" (335). In Einstein's view, "the mental development of the individual and his way of forming concepts depend to a high degree upon language. This makes us realize to what extent the same language means the same mentality. In this sense thinking and language are linked together."

In scientific discourse, Einstein finds a strong link between statements and sensory data and suggests that science is "supernational" because scientific language and concepts "have been set up by the best brains of all countries and all times." But their work is not purely empirical or quantifiable, rather "in solitude, and yet in cooperative effort as regards the final effect, they [the scientists] created the spiritual tools of the technical revolutions which have transformed the life of mankind in the last centuries. Their system of concepts has served as a guide in the bewildering chaos of perceptions so that we learned to grasp general truths from particular observations" (337). The issue for Harris would be to establish a methodology to study scientific discourse with his linguistic tools, whereas Einstein completes his observations with the optimistic sense that the scientific method yields great fruit, but the goals of science ought to be carefully considered to ensure "the safety, the welfare, and the free development of the talents of all men" (337).[63] So despite their many differences, it is interesting to recall some of the overlapping concerns between Einstein's and Harris's work, especially given their connections through Zionism, Avukah, and Bruria Kaufman.

Harris corresponded during this period with the archaeological anthropologist and linguist J. Alden Mason, who was working on a section about native languages for the proposed *Handbook on South American Indians* (letter to Harris dated April 1941) and a linguistics project for the Smithsonian (letter to Harris dated June 1942), and was soliciting Mason's assistance in finding help for both. He was also in contact with Franz Boas, a towering figure who had supervised Sapir early on, and who undertook considerable work on native Indian languages, making it a respectable effort in a period dominated by the renowned linguist, philologist, and lexicographer William Dwight Whitney, who was arguably somewhat less interested in such endeavors than Sapir or Boas.[64] Boas was working by that time to political ends as well on, for example, a center to reunite scientists who, on account of their descent or political convictions, were being expelled from central and Southern Europe. In a letter to the historian Salo Baron dated December 29, 1939, Boas notes that a large number of these scientists had been forced to settle in foreign countries, leaving them "isolated and unable to make known the results of their researches," the reason for his wishing "to establish a center which can give them help and new inspiration."

These considerations have led a number of scientists in Palestine to consider the establishment of [a] society of sciences, without any desire to make this a specifically Jewish enterprise. It seems appropriate to take action in Palestine because Jewish scientists form, without doubt, the majority of the victims of persecution. On December 16, 1938, the scholars of Palestine met in Tel Aviv and decided to work for the creation of such an institution. The president of the curatorium of the Hebrew University (Professor Ch. Weizmann) is lending his moral support to this plan. It is conceived as an academy of sciences with its seat in Jerusalem and membership throughout the world, without regard to race. Its purpose will be to contribute to the enrichment of human culture and also provide for the cause of better international understanding.

The concrete results of this effort included the *Scripta Universitatis atque Bibliothecae Hierosolymitanarum* and the new series, Scripta Academica Hierosolymitana (in English). From Baron, Boas sought "moral support" and consent to be among the committee for the establishment of an international academy of sciences in Jerusalem. Many of those asked to join in this capacity are by now familiar to us through Zellig Harris's story, including Cyrus Adler, Max Ascoll, Albert Einstein, Louis Finkelstein, Felix Frankfurter, Louis Ginzberg, Walter Landauer, Phoebus A. Levene, Emanuel Libman, Immanuel Velikovsky, Max Werthelmer, and Harry A. Wolfson. On January 12, 1940, a number of these persons (and others) attended a meeting to discuss the plan; an agreement was reached to work in the direction outlined by Boas, and twenty-five professors agreed to work as members of the Committee for the Academy.

Zellig Harris, Roman Jakobson, Franz Boas, and Threats to American Security

Zellig Harris's correspondence also documents his efforts aimed at finding a job for Roman Jakobson, whom he had previously assisted by helping him be admitted into the United States (from Sweden, in 1941). The August 2, 1942, letter Harris wrote to Boas is worth citing at length.

I have for some time been trying to get Dr. Roman Jakobson appointed at the University of Pennsylvania for Russian. We finally got a very strong statement from Graves that if any university asked for intensive Russian courses under Jakobson, the ACLS would almost certainly supply the necessary money in the form of scholarships whose income would become Jakobson's salary. I think we can finally count on the ACLS for this. Here we had gotten all departments concerned to ask enthusiastically for Jakobson, with the approval of the graduate Dean. Yesterday, however, I learned that the administration refused the project, claiming administrative reasons.

While we shall try to appeal, it may be assumed that the brutality of American universities, and the indifference of most of them to scientific work, cannot be overcome.

The question is whether another university may be found which would request the ACLS for intensive courses with Jakobson. Might I impose upon you to ask if there is anything you could do in this regard? You might be able, more than any one else, to get faculty members in other universities working on the case.

Regrettably, the archives of Boas material do not contain Boas's response, although it is interesting to note that Jakobson did get a permanent position in 1946, but at Columbia, not Penn, before moving to Boston. But there is another Boas connection that bears consideration in a study of Harris, notably the United States government's interest in his work. If there are FBI files for Harris, they have not been declassified, but based on what is found in other files from this period, Harris would have been a likely target for investigation. I have obtained through the Freedom of Information Act parts of the Boas FBI file,[65] and a brief inspection and discussion of its contents provides some sense of why the FBI would be interested in anthropologists or linguists of this period.

Susan Krook, an anthropologist who has used the Freedom of Information Act to study FBI work, informs us in an unpublished document that is in the Boas file that, not surprisingly, the FBI's Boas file "is just one of a number of dossiers kept on the activities of anthropologists." The domain of anthropology was not clearly delineated, and Boas, like Sapir, Harris, Bloch and many others, undertook a range of work that could fall under several different departments, including anthropology, ethnic studies, history, native studies, linguistics, or sociology. This is of more than passing interest in terms of what it says about the "interdisciplinarity" of the period, and about the range of work that was employed in certain circles to attack fascism. For instance, a January 16, 1939, *Avukah Student Action* article included a discussion of Boas's work that demonstrates, as the page 2 headline blares, the "theory of Nazis on 'Aryanism' is false."

Deploring what it termed the conscription and distortion of anthropology "in many countries" to "serve the cause of an unscientific racialism" the American Anthropological Association formally attacked the Aryan theories of racialism declaring that the terms Aryan and Semitic have "no racial significance whatsoever," but "simply denote linguistic families." Though the anthropologists did not single out Germany, Italy or any other countries, Professor Franz Boas of Columbia University, dean of American anthropologists, who moved adoption of the resolution, declared in a statement made after the meeting that Germany was the most "crude" offender and that American scientists must strive to preserve Academic and intellectual freedom in the United States.

The resolution was backed by three factual assertions: first, "Race involves the inheritance of similar physical variations by large groups of mankind, but its psychological and cultural connotations, if they exist, have not been ascertained by science"; second, "the terms Aryan and Semitic have no racial significance whatsoever"; and third, "anthropology provides no scientific basis for discrimination against any people on the ground of racial inferiority, religious affiliation or linguistic heritage." The opposite views were propagated, of course, even by allies; an article in the January 10, 1940, *Avukah Student Action* (3) notes that "anthropologists have become disconcerted lately, through reading of recent dispatches from the democracies. All their fire had been vented at the fascist abuse of the concept of 'race,' but it appears that the same concept now prevails in England and France." In the type of investigative journalism style that sometimes marked this paper, writers for *Avukah Student Action* found that "the influential *London Times*, organ of the Conservative Party, has this to say on the scuttling of the Graf Spee: 'The Germans were a brave race and this would not have happened in the old German Navy. The episode showed that the behavior of the British ships was admirable and it revealed to the world the vitality of the race.'" As for the French, the article notes that Premier Daladier "expressed a similar viewpoint on the race question, when, in his Christmas Eve broadcast to the nation, he spoke of the 'Asiatic barbarity' of the Russians."

The FBI's specific interest in anthropology seems to reflect the sense that anthropologists might through their work uncover useful information concerning the workings of human language or perhaps the behaviors of certain groups. In Boas's case (and it applies to Harris as well), the added interest was in Communist or anti–status quo activities, of great concern to the FBI under J. Edgar Hoover, who directed the agency from 1924 until his death in 1972. Krook notes that "the Bureau's interest in Boas began in 1920, in the aftermath of his criticism of 'scientists as spies' and his censure by the American Anthropological Association—and was apparently precipitated by his chief antagonist in that episode, as part of a general campaign against him." According to this file, it would appear that the FBI's active interest in Boas's activities was initiated following a January 20, 1920, letter from Charles D. Walcott, the Secretary of the Smithsonian Institution, who complained about a December 20, 1919, article in *The Nation*, that was signed by Boas. A. Mitchell Palmer, the U.S. Attorney General, responded to Dr. Walcott's letter with the following assurance: "I desire to express to you my appreciation of your courtesy in calling this matter to the attention of the President and I have the Honor to advise you that the Bureau of Investigation of the Department of Justice has been instructed to make a thorough inquiry into the past and present activities of Franz Boas, in order to ascertain whether or not he has been identified with any of the pernicious radical activities in this country." It is unclear exactly how this follow-up occurred, however, since Krook has found that the official initiation date of file number 100–15338 on Boas's activities was in fact July 24, 1936, that it had data placed in it until December 1942, and was officially closed on July 4, 1942 (a federal holiday!), and then was declassified, in part, in 1983.

As much as one-half of the forty-nine pages that make up this file have been blacked out pursuant to Title 5 of the United States Code, Section 552, which says that "Information which is currently and properly classi-fied pursuant to Executive Order 12356 in the interest of the national defense or foreign policy, for example, information involving intelligence sources or methods."[66] In what remains, we discover that "Franz Boas had agreed to operate 'under Communist discipline' but this was largely due to the influence of [BLACKED OUT], he asked me to tell you that Boas, who is connected with Columbia University in New York City, is one of the leading 'stooges' for Communistic groups in the United States. He is eighty-odd years of age and is used by these Communistic groups to put over propaganda for them." One FBI agent reported that "Professor Franz Boaz, also known as Professor Franz Boas, is considered to be one of the 400 people, most of them prominent, who were classified as concealed Communists and were thus sectioned to Internal Security with FBI inves-tigative categorization." The criteria for being classified Communist, cited from an office memorandum dated July 14, 1950, from SAC [the Special Agent in Charge] to Hoover, would certainly have made Zellig Harris suspect (as he himself feared), especially given some of the links made by Avukah members and also its detractors between Avukah-style Zionism and left-wing politics. For instance: "Did individual ever write anything that could be considered Communist literature for *The Daily Worker*, *New Masses*, or *Political Affairs* and any front publications or other publications." "Was individual active in front organizations. Which organizations? How active was the individual?" "Was individual ever involved in secret work. What work; who knew it; did individual ever do any special work for party?" "Is individual still active or sympathetic to Party?" "Is the subject working for the U.S. government or is he affiliated in any way in Confidential [sic] Government work at this time?" "Was this individual employed in vital industry?" "Do you know other members of his family who are Communists?" "Do you know of any other activity on the part of the individual which would indicate that the individual is a concealed Communist?"

The answers came in a letter from J. Edgar Hoover to Brigadier General Edwin M. Watson on April 13, 1940, accusing him of being involved in a whole range of "dubious" organizations, including the New School for Social Research, the New World Resettlement Fund for Spanish Refugees, Spanish Intellectual Aid, the American League to Abolish Capitol Punishment, the National Committee for the Defense of Political Prisoners, the World Congress Against War, the American Committee for the Struggle Against War, the National Committee for the League Against Fascism, the Committee for Victims of German Fascism, World Peaceways, the American Committee for Democracy and Intellectual Freedom, the American Committee for the Protection of Foreign Born, the American Committee to Save Refugees, the National Emergency Conference to Save Spanish Refugees, and so forth. That this list would be different from one that could be compiled for Harris seems certain, but it seems clear that Harris had some involvement through his work in the kinds of "radical organizations" that raised the suspicion of FBI agents in the Boas case.

Dr. Boas had served on various committees of a radical nature for several years, being at one time active in the American League for Peace and Democracy, Eastchester County and Riverside Branch. The source reported that Dr. Boas is alleged to have spoken on many occasions for radical organizations and reportedly helped considerably in the Spanish Loyalist cause. The informant indicated that Dr. Boas felt the Dies Committee was dangerous to American institutions, and that the attacks of the Committee on trade unions, together with the alleged practice of rating organizations, should be stopped at least in another period of war hysteria. (3)[67]

Boas (like Harris) was aware of the FBI's interest in people like him, as is evident from a letter in the FBI file which he wrote to friends and colleagues in 1939.

You are undoubtedly aware of the apprehension with which intelligent people throughout the country have realized the dangerous nature and scope of the FBI's activities as recently exposed by Senator Harris and the Senate Interstate Commerce Commission. We have learned that the FBI's uncouth and violent raids in Detroit are apparently only one phase of the undemocratic procedure of the tapping of wires, spying on labor committees and establishing for the future a nation-wide index file of progressive individuals who have never been either convicted or accused of a crime. It would appear that nothing less than a thorough investigation of these ominous activities of the FBI can prevent a repetition in 1940 or 1941 of the organized national witch hunt that horrified the country in 1919 and 1920. Prominent Americans from various parts of the country, some of whom will represent organizations, are therefore planning to meet in Washington on Sunday, April 14th, to plan an appropriate appeal to the administration. It is proposed to seek interviews on Monday, the 15th, with President Roosevelt, Attorney General Jackson, Senators Wheeler and Norris and other Senators and Representatives to request a thorough official investigation of the FBI.

The list of people to whom this letter was sent is not in the file, but the FBI was concerned about it, and in an April 4, 1940, memorandum it was noted that it was sent to "quite a number of individuals."

Questions are raised in the file about Boas's age and involvement in Communist activities; for instance, in an April 13, 1940, letter from Hoover to Brigadier General Edwin W. Watson, Secretary to the President, Hoover writes: "Professor Boas is not a member of the Communist Party, according to reports which I have received. He is over eighty years of age and is said to be paralyzed and seldom comes to his office." Despite his age, and his being considered a pawn in a larger game, it is clear that Boas carried out an extensive correspondence of over 1,500 letters from 1940 to 1942 alone, including some to Albert Einstein (Boas's books were some of the first to have been burned by the Nazis, but the honor was bestowed as well upon Einstein, Freud, and Helen Keller). The brunt of the letters from this period were political, some touting pro-Communist Party views, but others that were more innocuous, such as one to the Union Theological Seminary President Henry Coffin, in which he wrote that "the only thing in which I am interested is complete intellectual freedom, and I am trying to defend the rights to a free expression of opinion" (March 31, 1941). He was right to be concerned, of course since, in a confidential letter to the director (undated) that is part of the file, we learn that "since the individual such as the subject of this case [Boas] are [BLACKED OUT] concealed Communists and since they are, in most instances, persons of some prominence, it is suggested that if the information appearing in the attached blind memo is reported, then Mr. [BLACKED OUT] should be given a temporary confidential informant symbol." Further, "for the information of the Bureau the subject [Boas] is one of the 400 concealed Communists whom [BLACKED OUT] stated he knew. The names of these concealed Communists were sent to the Bureau in the case captioned "Communist Party, USA, Internal Security—C [Communist]."

An April 15, 1940, letter from [BLACKED OUT] notes that Boas, who belongs to "extreme left-wing organizations" and engages in "subversive" work, had as well some hand in the effort by the National Emergency Conference for Democratic Rights to challenge FBI powers. In the document called "The People of the U.S. vs. the FBI," included in the file, we find complaints including the facts that "Wm. J. Burns, who along with Hoover heads the FBI, is a 'notorious labor spy';" "the General Intelligence Division compiles elaborate index of 450,000 liberals and radicals;" that "the Sacco and Vanzetti 'legal murder' was part of a collusive effort between the District Attorney and agents of the Department of Justice"; that Hoover "invites banks, corporations, railroads and individuals to 'cooperate' in 'intelligence work';" that "430 "plants" receive FBI protection and benefits"; and that "these activities are illegal according to the rules of the U.S. Congress and according to a number of U.S. Codes."

A number of points regarding Boas bear mention here as well, since they help shed light upon the nature of his work, and upon the areas that were of special concern to the U.S. government. First, in an editorial from the Kansas City *Plaindealer*, dated August 1, 1941, (and clipped for the FBI file), Boas is said to have written in the journal *New Masses*[68] that racism is founded upon obvious scientific untruths: "Racial prejudice is as rampant as ever. No matter how clearly it may be proved that mental character is not determined by racial descent and shared by every member of the race, or how definitely it may be shown that the low estimation of the ability of certain races is due to ignorance of their achievements, the prejudice remains and has to be fought over and over again." His conclusion is that "we must demand equality, not equality on paper, but equal rights in life, equal opportunities, and a breakdown of the social barriers that oppress even those who in character and achievement are often infinitely superior to those who will not acknowledge for them the claim that is so often heralded as the basis of ours society, the claim that all men are born with equal rights." This application of scientific ideas toward the liberation of oppressed people helped Boas cross interdisciplinary lines, the importance of which is driven home in an article from the *New York Times* (December 23, 1942), again clipped for the FBI file, which mourns Boas's passing.

With the passing of Dr. Franz Boas, anthropology loses its most distinguished interpreter. He was a measurer of skulls and bones, who proved that the human race is very unstable and that since the first settlers came to this country the American physical type has changed; yet he declined to reduce his subject to mere physical measurements. He was a linguist; yet he realized the limitations of language in tracing cultural origins. He saw the immense value of psychology, yet he rejected the application of European modes of thought in explaining the reasoning of savages. He was a geographer before he became an anthropologist; yet he refused to consider environment as the one determining factor in the shaping of cultures. He was a geneticist; yet he made much of the importance of nutritional and environmental influences in accounting for 'racial' differences. He was a statistician; yet he warned his colleagues against the alluring pitfalls of the statistical approach. In a word, he was a universalist, a scholar of immense learning who insisted that man and his culture demand a study which embraces every phase of life, even animal life, if we are ever to make anthropology a discipline that can be of practical importance in shaping human social destiny.

Many of these comments reflect back onto the memory of Zellig Harris, and although a much more private figure, we can adduce that Harris's legacy is similarly that of a universalist scholar with broad ambitions based upon radical questioning of prevailing norms.

In a letter to the University of California (Berkeley) anthropologist Alfred. L. Kroeber, dated October 15, 1945, Harris responded to many questions concerning the plight of Boas's research and writings in ways that point to his own interests.

I should very much like to discuss these things in some greater detail with you. That could occur in connection with the meeting on American Indian linguistics. . . . I have suggested to the American Philosophical Society that I make this trip the opportunity for detailed discussion with you on the future of the Boas collection and of the Philosophical Society's interest in American Indian linguistics. If it would not be an imposition on you I should like to bring some of the manuscripts to show you, so that you would be able to give me some specific suggestions as to what can be done with them.

The materials to which Zellig Harris referred here had been collected by the Committee on Native Languages, formed in 1927, of which Boas was chairman.[69] Harris and his anthropologist-linguist friend C. F. Voegelin eventually arranged the materials by language, but they also listed much miscellaneous nonlinguistic material, such as data on folklore and mythology, and general ethnology; their index was published in 1945.[70]

As editor of the *Journal of the American Oriental Society*, Harris was also considering publishing Leo Oppenheimer's "Catalogue of the Cuneiform Tablets of the Eames Babylonian Collection—Tablets of the Time of the 3rd Dynasty of Ur," about which he asked the advice of Goetze in a letter dated January 1945. Papers in the Yale University archives include a number of letters by Harris written in the latter stages of World War II, with intricate comments on issues of this nature, including decisions of whether to publish papers such as one "South American Indian Languages" by J. A. Mason (February 12, 1945). The archives also contain a longer correspondence with William M. Austin, beginning on March 19, 1945, which includes passages that illuminate Harris's approach to the field of anthropology at that time and to his views of the scientific method.

I feel that I owe you and Sturtevant and the others some explanation on the Bonfante-Gelb article. You know that a rather dangerous situation is developing within linguistics and careful handling is required, if the rift is not to harm the standing of linguistics. In particular I feel rather strongly that the old division of opinion must be placed on the merits of the case, I deem it as a question of scientific method . . . rather than as a question of personality or of an in-group or an out-group (the out-group referring to persons who are not American or do not follow a particular school of thought). I need hardly tell you where my scientific sympathies lie, I think it would defeat our purpose if we used editorial instead of scientific debate to determine what is linguistics, the best thing that can happen is for each side to be given real freedom of explanation, at least for a time, until its validity or lack of validity has been made a matter of explicit public record.

On March 22, 1945, the matter continued with Harris's letter to Goetze, in which he reiterates that he deplores "the introduction of personalities on either side," and his view that "both Bonfante and Gelb, as well as any other serious research worker, has a right to be heard." And in a telling remark, adds that "I not only want to protect Sturtevant from unjust criticism, but also want the scientific truth (in so far as there is such) to come out as a result of this."

Harris's anthropological work continued in this period with, for example, his training of students such as Diana Luz Pessoa, who was studying Indian languages, and on behalf of whom Harris wrote to John Alden Mason on November 15, 1945, of the University Museum, to solicit suggestions for an American Indian with whom she could work. Mason replied on November 28 that he was "not personally familiar with any Indians resident in Philadelphia," although "there is a little organization in Philadelphia known as the neighborhood Indians in Philadelphia who are, I believe, affiliated with the International Institute at 845 N. 15th Street." Harris was also vetting Mason's paper on Papago grammar, on behalf of the Publication Committee of the American Philosophical Society. He had a burgeoning interest in Central and South American languages, and wrote in July 1945 to J. Alden Mason asking for suggestions on how to increase the society's holdings in this area. Mason promised to look into it, but wrote again a year later, on June 6, 1946, to express with dismay that they had not been able to devote sufficient resources to that goal.

Thomas A. Sebeok mentions in the 1948 issue of the *International Journal of American Linguistics*[71] the publication of Harris's "Developments in American Indian Linguistics"[72] which begins with Harris's description of the irregular course of American Indian linguistics and then offers the promise that considerable advances will be made as a result of new linguistic techniques. Harris was also continuing work in the Boas Collection, evidenced by the notes about Seneca linguistics that have been preserved, including grammatical word lists and utterances, skeletal grammars, verb suffix notes, phonological materials, morphological notes, transcribed texts, ethnographical texts, autobiographical texts, utterances, and miscellaneous materials (including some rather humorous doodles). There are as well some conclusions relating to how texts can be analyzed, based upon studies of phonemes of North Carolina Cherokee or Seneca utterances, some by his coworkers, Ernest Bender and John Witthoft, or his informants, Will French and Molly Sequoia. For instance, in an October 5, 1946, letter to Carl Voegelin about North Carolina Cherokee, Ernest Bender wrote that "according to the material we [he and Harris] have collected up till now I would say: There are morphemes, indicating person, which can be analyzed as specifying inclusion or exclusion of certain persons." He gives a series of examples, such as "o (exclusion of second person (you))," "ad (two persons + 'he'. Both can be subject or object)," and so forth, with the conclusion that "the material isn't sufficient enough to allow me a more definite statement. The pronoun markers occur, for the most part, in this order: subject, object, pluralizer (-ni-). Utterances such as 'I kill you' and 'you kill me,' which have the same form in Cherokee (and are relatively few), leave us uncertain." The paper that follows the analyses also notes that the work "is based on material collected several years ago by Professor Zellig Harris," and in the footnotes Bender provides a sense of Harris's supervision when he explains that

my work on North Carolina Cherokee was begun in 1944 under a fellowship granted by the American Council of Learned Societies for the study of the techniques of linguistic analysis under the guidance and supervision of Professor Zellig S. Harris. The gathering and analyzing of material obtained from Mrs. Sequoia was made possible by a grant from the American Philosophical Society. I take the opportunity here to express my gratitude to the American Council of Learned Societies and to the American Philosophical Society, and to Professor Harris for his help and encouragement.

That year, Harris was traveling, for his work and research, to the Linguistics Institute of the University of Michigan. He was also working as a research associate with the American Philosophical Society, a position he held from 1944 to 1947. Other people in ever-widening Harris circles were engaged in overlapping projects, and some familiar faces are recalled through common projects and related insights. William Chomsky published during this period a history of the study of Hebrew grammar with a conclusion that recalls statements we have seen elsewhere concerning the science of language: "The use of Hebrew in traditional houses of Study and Prayer has never been interrupted. Linguistic study cannot, therefore, be scientific unless cognizance is taken of actual usage in all the successive stages in the process of the development of the particular language question." For this reason, "to base the study of a language and its grammar exclusively on classical models handed down from antiquity is to violate a most fundamental tenet in modern linguistics" (301).[73] Chomsky was also writing on "Some Irregular Formations in Hebrew"[74] with discussions on "grammar, as the science of language" (409).

Along the way, Harris followed through on his efforts to publish Franz Boas's "Kwakiutl Grammar with a Glossary of the Suffixes," edited by Helene Boas Yampolsky.[75] In his review of this text,[76] C. F. Voegelin announced that "phonemics has won the day, and Boas' objections to phonemics (or rather to complete phonemicization of an entire language) is now a matter of historical interest, rather than contemporary discussion" (415). In Morris Swadesh's more extensive review,[77] ample praise is heaped upon Boas's method and this text that stands "as a further monument to a great pioneer and leader in scientific thought" (63).[78] This link between the science of language studies and anthropology is recalled as well in Harris and Voegelin's article "The Scope of Linguistics,"[79] which aims to assess "the place of linguistics in cultural anthropology" and "trends in linguistics" (588). They begin with the statement that "the data of linguistics and of cultural anthropology are largely the same" because "human behavior, as well as (or rather, which includes) behavior between humans, is never purely verbal; nor, in the general case, is it non-verbal." In terms of approach, "cultural anthropologists often segregate the non-verbal from the verbal, relegating the latter to special chapters or volumes (such as folklore), as contrasted with chapters devoted to various aspects of material culture, such as house types; one might infer from some ethnographies that houses are built in sullen silence" (588). Exceptions to this are the ethno-linguists, who attempt "to integrate the verbal and non-verbal aspects of behavior," although they admit to being more indebted to the ethnographic side than the linguistics one for this combination. This will to interdisciplinarity is reinforced in this article with reference to Sapir, who shows interrelations between languages, cultures, and populations, and who thought of linguistics as second only to archeology in its importance for the study of relative chronology. But linguistic work requires "great exactness," and enables "a worker to state the parts of the whole (for any one language) and to give the distribution of the parts within the whole," to provide a "criteria of relevance" (590). Further, linguistic analysis "provides an exhaustive list of its elements" and then explains them, that is, "makes statements about sets of phonemes and sets of morphemes . . . by giving their distribution relative to each other within the utterances of a single language" (593). All of this can happen in ethnology, but not necessarily, and the range of ways that a cultural anthropologist can decipher texts is even more vast, thus making the choice of primary data much more difficult to narrow down. "Throughout the formulation of linguistic structure there are problems of a mathematical or logical nature; in determining the physical bases of phonemes and the manner in which phonemes are produced by speakers, linguists turn to physics and physiology. Problems of the type here mentioned do not occur in cultural anthropology which has, however, other points of contact with those fields, as in the study of diet (physiology)" (594).

The critical question for our purposes is what Harris (and Voegelin) considered to be current trends in linguistics in 1940, since these will offer a way of reading *Methods*. We have seen Harris's assessment of Gray's work, in which he suggested that linguistics should be descriptive, as opposed to Gray's prescriptive account, with an emphasis upon phonemics. In "The Scope of Linguistics," he and Voegelin describe the need for rich diachronic analysis because "increased experience with linguistic structure, which characterizes twentieth century linguistics, has led investigators in both Europe and America to think about the use of the comparative method and historical analysis on whole genetically related language structures rather than merely on groups of cognate words." This is particularly important for languages and cultures about which we know too little, such as those of native Americans. "For American Indian languages, where historical research has been meager though successful, the controlled reconstruction of both groups of words and language structure will no doubt yield much information" (598), notably descriptions of whole language structures that are sufficiently commensurate with one another to support comparative reconstruction of their ancestor structure, which also points to the need for study of different languages as a means to help the researcher understand language more generally.[80]

One way to deepen our understanding of Harris's interest in these anthropological and comparative linguistic projects is to refer back to his long review in *Language* of *Edward Sapir: Selected Writings in Language, Culture and Personality: Essays in Memory of Edward Sapir*,[81] which was, in the words of his March 21, 1951, letter to Bloch, "as hard a job as any I have ever undertaken." This volume was supposed to have been a collection of studies in honor of Sapir, begun in 1938, but when Sapir died in February 1939, it became his memorial. Contributors to it were Harris's contemporaries and in some cases his friends, including Murray B. Emeneau, Mary Haas, George Herzog, Harry Hoijer, Morris Swadesh, George L. Trager, C. F. Voegelin, and Benjamin Whorf. For Harris, "this volume is far from representing a continuation of his work," which is not a "stricture upon the editors or the authors" because "such spade work has to be done along the many lines suggested by Sapir before the fruitful results which he foresaw can be explicitly and exactly formulated. And the deep influence which he had, as person and as scientist, upon his students and friends cannot readily be made to appear between the covers of a book. Rich as this book is in scientific work and in individual influences from Sapir, it is strongly to be hoped that its success will make possible the publication of the omnibus volume of American Indian grammatical sketches which he began to edit and which is now in Swadesh's hands, and of Sapir's own remaining manuscripts" (245).

Harris's method for his contribution, consistent with what he was working on at the time, was to view Sapir's work from a linguistic point of view and to "try to trace how his methods in culture and in personality were related to his linguistics." Harris spent "a lot of time on it for 9 months," producing 23,500 words, which he considered to be "probably the only complete job that will be done on Sapir" and could even merit a separate monograph. Bloch took it without cutting it, since in his opinion forty pages of *Language* devoted to the subject was "by no means an excessive length for the sort of article that I know this must be" (March 22, 1951). Harris wanted the review be available to people in other fields, which Bloch assured with his promise of 100 offprints and with the conclusion that "monograph publication would be a mistake . . . for this type of job: It belongs in a journal—specifically, in LANGUAGE. Let's say no more about it." Interestingly enough, a Linguist List 3.457 posting from Anna Morpurgo Davies makes the following comments about this article, in 1992:

After Ellen Prince's announcement no one has written anything about Zellig Harris's death. Probably few people knew him. It is natural to say that with him ends an era. But he was also a man of astonishing intellectual power (that he kept to the end), of very wide and deep culture and of total devotion to his subject. In a period when departments of linguistics may be proposed for closure at a moment's notice, we ought to remember that he founded the first department of linguistics in the United States. Those who (wrongly) see Harris as a man only concerned with narrow formalisms may try to read his 45-page long review of Sapir's *Selected Writings* (*Language* 1951) and see how natural it is to apply to him what he said of Sapir: "So refreshing is his freshness and criticalness, that we are brought to a sharp realization of how such writing has disappeared from the scene."

A brief survey of this work is instructive, and Peter Swiggers offers an excellent assessment (from which I've extracted a numbered list) of what Harris highlights in the preface to *The Collected Works of Edward Sapir*[82]

(1) Sapir's overarching interest was in discovering the *structure* of language;
(2) Structure in language is, from the viewpoint of language itself, the result of processes (in fact, linguistic entities are the result of processes of change); this explains the 'process-like' nature of Sapir's statements;
(3) The structure of (a) language is, from the viewpoint of the linguist, the result of the structuring of structure in language' by the linguist, who characterizes relationships between elements and processes in specific ways;
(4) Apart from being characterized by a process oriented approach, Sapir's work is characterized by the recognition of *patterning* in language; the greatness of Sapir's work lies in the establishing of 'total' patterns, and in showing the interplay between organized structures at various language levels;
(5) The combination of *process* and *pattern* allowed Sapir to move constantly from form to function, and from structure to history: much of his work is both syn- and diachronic, and his linguistic analysis is never confined to pure forms, but always starts out from forms and their use(s). (24)

Citing Harris, we see the move from Sapir's 'functional' conception of form, that in Swiggers's view "followed from his approach to language as a form of behaviour, defined by its use as a symbolic system of reference. This system of reference is constituted by content-units and by form-units, as well as by syntactic relationships and contextual insertion" (24). This structuring of language, and structuring in language are, according to Harris, complementary, pointing from the more anthropological in Sapir (behavior, symbolic system) to logic and mathematics. Harris writes in his review that "the formal analysis of language is an empirical discovery of the same kinds of relations and combinations which are devised in logic and mathematics; and their empirical discovery in language is of value because languages contain (or suggest) more complicated types of combination than people have invented for logic" (301). This is a very helpful overview of Harris's approach to language as regards categories of relations and combinations, and as a statement concerning the formal study of language it is of particular interest as we turn to a key moment in Harris's life and work, around the period when Noam Chomsky enters the scene.

5 Structural Linguistics

Harris's efforts at this time culminated with the publication in 1951 of *Methods in Structural Linguistics* (hereafter *Methods*), a landmark in the field that attempted to describe languages consistently and without presuppositions, and a key text in the development of discourse analysis, studies of information representation, mathematics-inspired theories of language, the attempt to derive formulas of science information from science reports, and the attempt at discovering the linear distributional relations of phonemes and morphemes. In the retrospective article ("Background," 2002), he distinguishes between "generating (or deriving, synthesizing, predicting) as against analyzing (or describing, recognizing the structure of a sentence), which issue is commonly associated with transformations" (6). He then suggests that: "the difference between the analysis of a sentence and its generation is not substantive for the theory except in a limited but important sense . . . but rather is a matter of presentation. The analyzing of a sentence in structural linguistics allows both for a description which directly recognizes the structure, and alternatively for a grammar as a deductive system that synthesizes (generates) sentences . . . or for generating it as noted in the Co-occurrence and Transformation" paper. . . . In the later case, the analytic statements of successively entering components of a sentence, or its decomposition, can be used almost directly to generate or predict sentences of that structure. In any case, analysis of the language precedes synthesis" (6–7). The work set out here is, by this description alone, hugely ambitious. There was a considerable lag between the writing of this book (completed January 1947, the year Harris was promoted to full professor) and its publication in 1951, but it was long awaited in the field, and for some it represented a true landmark. I should add that it is widely agreed that the importance of Zellig Harris's work grew as he focused upon a more general approach to language, and in the view of Nathan Glazer, attention to the earlier work may give the impression that

Harris was a more important figure than he was in this earlier period. But it is the case that some of the work mentioned to date related directly to *Methods,* and some of this research began very early in his career.

Because the work on *Methods* coincides with the most significant encounter in contemporary linguistic history, I also describe the impact that Harris would have upon a certain Noam Chomsky, at that time a nineteen-year-old student at Penn. Although nineteen years younger than Harris, Chomsky was nevertheless known to the whole Harris family and, because Noam's parents William and Elsie Chomsky were friendly with the Harrises, Noam himself had visited the Harris family home as a child. Now, years later, Noam Chomsky was commuting to Penn from his parents' house in the East Oak Lane section of Philadelphia, teaching Hebrew School on the side, and during that period he met Zellig Harris in the university setting. Noam was poised to become not only Harris's most famous student but ultimately, according to some versions of the (many) stories, a challenger or even a usurper to his dominant status. From the beginning, this was no ordinary teacher-student relationship: "The primary teacher of Noam was Zellig Harris," says Dr. Henry Hiz, emeritus professor of linguistics, who also taught Chomsky at Penn. Carol Chomsky, who went by Carol Schatz until she and Noam were married in 1949, agrees: "Noam admired him enormously, and I think it's fair to say that Zellig Harris was responsible, in so many different ways, for the direction that Noam's intellectual life took then and later."[1]

Harris himself was no ordinary teacher, as we have seen, and Chomsky, no ordinary student. He was one of that small number of students described in chapter 1 who entered Harris's world through the very intense and personal courses Harris gave, in what would today seem like an unusual and remarkably uninstitutional fashion. The unfolding of the eventual Harris-Chomsky relationship is of considerable interest for the development of both of these thinkers, but because of the eventual importance of both linguistics frameworks, and because of a well-publicized "rift" between the two of them, there are a number of camps that exist to describe, criticize, attack, challenge, or belittle one side or the other. I avoid comment on this tendency (a cursory look at reviews offers sufficient examples for those who are curious), and I will steer clear of rendering judgments of this sort. I will, however, begin by suggesting that from my perspective the claim made by some people (particularly in the realm of linguistics) that Chomsky may have popularized some of Harris's ideas and dressed them up for a larger public consumption seems to me to be inaccurate at its very base, and even a cursory comparison of their output (linguistic and political), combined with some of the information presented thus far, makes this case. It is true that some of the questions they ask, about underlying structures, the possibility of addressing certain questions, and the ways in which language is generated, are at times similar. And the considerable overlap between respective milieus means that there is bound to be a series of shared assumptions about what constitutes, say, linguistic methods and scientific research. Furthermore, there are crucial overlaps in the ways that these two radical Jewish linguists from Philadelphia think about political issues, and there are very important links between the fundamental value systems that guide their respective approaches to society. The differences are significant; but there are varying views in the field about how substantial they really are. The University of Chicago linguist John Goldsmith provides insight with reference to other noted influences on Chomsky when he suggests that "certainly the differences are substantial, but for all the reasons you pointed out, here and elsewhere, Noam was Harris's student, and he learned much of his linguistics from Harris. That he went forward and in his own direction is a given, it is a certainty. What is equally certain is that Chomsky's linguistics is far more influenced by Harris than it is by Descartes, Humboldt, or Sapir, by orders of magnitude." I put more weight on the overall objectives of the respective enterprises and the attitudes they reflect, which for me brings Chomsky closer to Humboldt, but in terms of the technical details of the linguistics work, Goldsmith makes a powerful point.

Despite his original plans to drop out of college to work on one of the Kibbutz Artzis (a federation of kibbutzim associated with the socialist Zionist organization Hashomer Hatzair), Chomsky eventually decided to prolong his studies at Penn, largely on account of his having met Harris, stating "[his] was a very powerful personality, and he was very interested in encouraging young people to do things." Along with teaching him a "tremendous amount" about political matters, Chomsky recalls, Harris "just kind of suggested that I might want to sit in on some of his courses. I did, and I got excited about that." So much for dropping out. "In retrospect, I'm pretty sure he was trying to encourage me to get back in," says Chomsky,[2] and one of the ways this occurred was through the work Harris was doing in connection to his book, *Methods in Structural Linguistics*.

The range of people involved in working through the implications of this methodology was wide, and in Harris's circle includes Murray Eden, who was associated with work on discourse analysis for ten years. Eden employed his competence in chemistry and his intuition of meanings in the English language to parse chemical sentences and represent them in a form reminiscent of logical statements. "Nothing much came of it," he recalls, although he was working on other projects concurrently, which may have impeded his progress.

The approach that Harris takes in the *Methods* book flowed in part from a general enthusiasm about using mathematical formulations for basic processes, about which Chomsky comments in *Language and Mind.*

For those who sought a more mathematical formulation for the basic processes, there was the newly developed mathematical theory of communication, which, it was widely believed in the early 1950s, had provided a fundamental concept—the concept of "information"—that would unify the social and behavioral sciences and permit the development of a solid and satisfactory mathematical theory of human behavior on a probabilistic base. About the same time, the theory of automata developed as an independent study, making use of closely related mathematical notions. And it was linked at once, and quite properly, to earlier explorations of the theory of neural nets. There were those—John von Neumann, for example—who felt that the entire development was dubious and shaky at best, and probably quite misconceived, but such qualms did not go far to dispel the feeling that mathematics, technology and behavioristic linguistics and psychology were converging on a point of view that was very simple, very clear, and fully adequate to provide a basic understanding of what tradition had left shrouded in mystery.[3]

Harris considered that even with his own advances in the field, much remained to be done in order to complete the task that he set for himself, in this book and elsewhere; in "The Background of Transformational and Metalanguage Analysis," (2002) we read Harris's notes that "although decades of work were needed for applying the methods, and for further directions that grew out of the book, it is indicative of the intellectual background cited above that the general program could be stated from the beginning, e.g. in a paper in the *Journal of the American Oriental Society* 61 (1941) pp. 143, 166; also in 'The Phonemes of Moroccan Arabic,' ibid 62 (1942) sec. 4; (*Methods in Structural Linguistics* p. 364) (the latter was completed and circulated in 1946, though it appeared only in 1951)" (2). This personal assessment emphasizes a continuum in Harris's work, which challenges some of those who have remarked upon the "phases" of Harris's career and output. To read Harris's descriptions of his own work is to have the sense that he would undertake analyses that in some cases lasted many years, and would publish them when he felt they were ready.

Despite the importance of the project Harris had set up for himself, and the wide array of people who awaited its appearance, it nevertheless took a long time to find a publisher, and he was still looking for suggestions as to an appropriate outlet in the late 1940s. In an undated letter[4] to Bernard

Bloch, which turns out to be the most playful and creative letter in any archive I saw, he writes:

dear

sir

bernard

your article III will begin at t

o

p

of

p

a

g

e

this g—d——d (for the hyphens, substitute od, and amne) methods in descriptive linguistics book was revised by me for the (n+1)th time last spring. several people who saw it said i ought to try a couple of commercial publishers before sending it to you (even though, as I explained to them, i had an informal understanding about it with you), in order to see if a wider audience (of non-linguists) could be reached, and in order to become a filthy plutocrat via royalties. i didn't know whether i should follow their advice, but after thinking it over (and figuring that perhaps you wouldn't mind being spared an editing job), i decided to give the commercials a fling. in particular, one of the people who saw it, prof of formal art at Columbia and friend of george herzog's, who has been much interested in modern linguistic methods as possibly suggestive for his own field, knows the oxford u press editor and wanted me to show it to same, which i am therefore doing.

so if i get a bite i will discuss matters with you. if i dont i will send ms to you with my (or its) tail between my (or its) legs. i assume all this is ok by you, or i wouldnt have done it....

cheerio and all

that sort of rot

The hope that there would be commercial interest, or at least interdisciplinary interest, was founded upon the idea that this methodology could be applied to a range of fields; indeed, structuralist (and formalist) approaches were viewed as universally applicable, since they described underlying structure and form of complex systems such as language or, in the literary realm, narratives (especially poetry). Bloch suggested that Harris try Ronald Press. In a December 19, 1950, letter to Charles Hockett of Cornell, Harris mentioned his (at that time still-unpublished) manuscript, and also referred to the student [Chomsky] who had read it in manuscript form, before revealing that he had at last settled on a publisher: "As you may know the University of Chicago Press is printing my 'Methods' manuscript. They took it exactly as is and refuse to send it back to me for any additions so that I have not even been able to bring the bibliography up to date. However, I am glad to be rid of the thing."

From the Psychoanalytic Approach to the Anxiety of Influence

Methods serves as an important link to the Harris-Chomsky relationship, as Chomsky himself recalls in the introduction to his own important early work, *The Logical Structure of Linguistic Theory* (hereafter LSLT):[5] "My formal introduction to the field of linguistics was in 1947, when Harris gave me the proofs[6] of his *Methods in Structural Linguistics* to read. I found it very intriguing, and, after some stimulating discussions with Harris, decided to major in linguistics as an undergraduate at the University of Pennsylvania. I had some informal acquaintance with historical linguistics and medieval Hebrew grammar, based on my father's work in these fields, and at the same time was studying Arabic with Giorgio Levi Della Vida" (LSLT 25). So there is an interesting student-teacher relationship here that has some elements of a filial tie, through the relation between Harris's and William Chomsky's work. It bears mention in this regard that in addition to his politics and his linguistics, Harris had also developed a burgeoning interest in psychoanalysis, including the work of Erich Fromm, who, Harris hoped, would help address the very complex issue of workers' attitudes. But it was to Freud's writings that Harris directed most of his attention, a point that was made by a number of interviewees and in some of his correspondence, particularly with Bloch. In the August 20, 1949, letter acknowledging Bloch's idea of sending the *Methods* book to Ronald Press, Harris picks up on what seems to have been a long-standing discussion of Freud's works and offers a rare glimpse into his own perceptions of himself and his work. He begins by acknowledging Bloch's suggestion and then picks up on Bloch's inquiry about the length of time that had passed since Harris had finished his book.

Point is I am neither patient nor nursing a violent grudge; I am merely oral-receptive. This last is only partly a joke. Though I don't [illegible; support?] the data on which the Freudian typology is based (oral-sadistic, oral-receptive, anal, and so on, you know), some of the typology descriptions fit various people I know, including myself, fairly well. I get my main interest or pleasure out of consuming—in my case it's specialized not into food but into subject-matter and information. It is quite important for me to find out what gives—whether with linguistics, or with human language, or with politics, or with physics. But I don't have much interest in producing whatever results I get. It's a chore which I go through only because it is the way of the world. Hence I simply lost interest in my Methods ms after writing it. There are other things bothering my little head, and I practically never remember the existence of the ms. Of course, such books are items of status; but I have such a deep disrespect for the status structure of our society (or of any other) that I just don't react. I'd much rather live and find things out. So the delay in the appearance of the book has no personal meaning to me.

This quality of resisting formal honors or even the recognition that a published book provides, in favor of this quest for knowledge, is present in a host of ways in Harris's work. He did not leave behind much in the way of personal correspondence, and a good deal of his political work was not signed. He enjoyed discussion (in his very intense courses, and with a small number of close relations from the different realms to which he contributed), but described the writing process in rather arduous terms: "My not writing chatty letters is partly related. I like to talk, exploratorily (that is what Carl also does, hence our talking with each other). Writing is just too slow and inhibited, hence somehow I don't get around to doing it."

Harris's next letter to Bloch, dated November 3, 1949, begins with apologies about his inability to keep up with his own desires to maintain a constant communication with his friend. He also makes a few crucial points, in relation to recent discussions Bloch had been having at that time with the linguist Leigh Lisker, Harris's colleague at Penn. "First, the real difficulty in making technical matters like mathematical logic or acoustics clear to the linguist who doesn't deal with them (you must have met it in your excellent Postulates which I enjoyed but which many people passed up); second, the psychological interpretation—I don't think I feel any snobbishness and certainly not Lisker who is quite shy and plain-feeling—it's primarily a tendency to shortcut the hard work of explaining something beyond the point required by the nearest technical group (I can usually explain linguistics to logicians in a half hour, and linguistic acoustics to physicists in much less).

A November 11, 1949, letter from Bloch picks up on these missives, stating that since "you [Zellig Harris] are by nature oral-receptive, I hesitate to ask you to do a chore for LANGUAGE that might be more attractive to an oral-sadistic; but, on the other hand, having had fairly good luck with my requests to you in the past, I ask it anyway. As you doubtless know, Zipf[7] has published a fat book called HUMAN BEHAVIOR AND THE PRINCPLE OF LEAST EFFORT—the culmination, he says in his preface of 25 years of work." Carl Voegelin had already turned down Bloch's offer to review it, with a note recommending that *Language* not review it, both on account of its statistical approach and, moreover, because the "rest of the book is silly." Bloch seemed disappointed, suggesting to Harris that Zipf's statistical methods should be "evaluated," and, as he says, "if Zipf's other remarks on language are silly, it is probably necessary, in the interests of all sorts of things that most of us cherish, to say so and show how and why." In short, "though you claim to be no altruist, you are surely no curmudgeon[8] either; so please, if you possibly can do it, do it. Let me know, may I send you the book?" In a rather playful manner, Harris replied on November 25, 1949, that "since we are talking Freud, the Zipf job needs not an oral-sadistic but an anal-sadistic review. Too far from my line. I looked through the book a half year ago and got the impression that he demonstrated that a number of things could be graphed on a straight line. Period. The book is a natural for Joos to review." In the same letter, Harris goes on to describe his own work, stating that "I don't go in much for statistics (my line is combinatorial things like algebra and group theory). And I am so involved in the extended discourse stuff that I couldn't wallow through Zipf. Incidentally, I am trying to pull both cultural and mathematical logic sometimes out of the extended discourse work, and will soon have something to submit." And so Harris refused Bloch's offer, saying that such a review would be "a destructive and critical job which probably ought to be done but for which I don't have the heart. I do, however, think linguists ought to try to explain and present linguistics—but in their own terms rather than by criticizing others."

The Ronald Press saga was not over yet, and months later, on March 15, 1950, Harris wrote to Bloch in despair.

Point is that inquiries, jokes and even pressure about my Methods book have become embarrassingly (or happily) large: a couple of mathematicians (at Indiana and at Penn) a couple of psychologists (at Swarthmore and at Harvard), several logicians, and many students. I'd like very much to get the damn thing out. If it can't be done at the present moment by LSA (I presume Ronald Press—if this was their name—didn't take it), do you think I could try various commercial presses? Any idea which might be interested? Random House? Harcourt Brace? Incidentally, although I couldn't go back and review the book, there are some improvements I want to put in as a part of my work during the last few years. If you have any idea what can be done—by you or by me—to get the book out in 1950, I'll be all ears.

Besides some of the psychoanalytic references, direct and indirect, evident in this correspondence, the link between psychoanalysis and linguistics was explored in a host of ways during this period, relating to behaviorism, authority, attitudes, the source of human language, and through the works of people like Fromm, Jakobson, Rapaport, Sapir,[9] and Sullivan. It has been claimed by some of my interviewees, in discussions about Chomsky and Harris, that the psychoanalytic influence in Harris's work could also be considered when thinking about his relation to Chomsky, and vice versa. This is not an avenue that I will follow, but there are lots of ways to talk about the influence that Harris had on his young student, through his support and his ideas. Chomsky's BA honor's thesis, which set the stage for some of his later work and which is taken to be the first example of modern generative grammar, was completed in 1949 when he was twenty years old. Harris himself, then chair of the department, wrote a note on June 3, 1949, to the dean, indicating, that "Mr. Noam Chomsky has successfully fulfilled all the requirements for an honors major in the Linguistics Department." He sent a second memo to the dean on March 14, 1950, indicating that "in giving you the departmental report on the application for scholarships in Linguistics I neglected to add that the department recommended Mr. Chomsky very strongly and considers that he is exceptionally deserving of a scholarship." On December 18 of that same year, Harris signed a memo admitting Mr. A[vram] N[oam] Chomsky to candidacy for the degree of master of arts, the only MA (or PhD) degree offered that semester in linguistics. This degree was actually delayed, at Chomsky's request. Chomsky recalls, "I was 1-A. . . . I was going to be drafted right away. I figured I'd try to get myself a six-week deferment until the middle of June, so I applied for a Ph.D. I asked Harris and Goodman, who were still at Penn, if they would mind if I re-registered—I hadn't been registered at Penn in four years. I just handed in a chapter of what I was working on for a thesis, and they sent me some questions via mail, which I wrote inadequate answers to—that was my exams. I got a six-week deferment, and I got my Ph.D."[10]

Inspired by Harris, and increasingly engaged intellectually by the kind of work he had undertaken for the BA thesis, Chomsky decided to extend his studies into graduate school, once again at the University of Pennsylvania. He began in the fall semester of 1949, and within a short period of time wrote a master's thesis (degree granted in 1951), which was a 1951 revision of the BA thesis, and which was edited further in 1951 and then published in 1979 as *Morphophonemics of Modern Hebrew*.[11] Harris was clearly impressed since he wrote to Bernard Bloch on December 19, 1950, with the following question:

A student of mine, A. N. Chomsky has been doing a great deal of work in formulation of linguistic procedures and has also done considerable work with Goodman
and Martin. Last year I [sent] him the morphological and morphophonemic material
which I had here. He added to it a great deal by means of informant work and
turned out a rigorous detailed morphophonemic [analysis] which I am sending you
under separate cover. I thought you would be interested in it for its own sake. In
addition I wonder whether you think there would be any point in publishing it and
if so, in what form.

On the same day, Harris wrote to Dr. Charles Hockett of Cornell, using
exactly the same first paragraph, and then adding: "In addition, I remember that you once asked me about doing a general analysis of Hebrew for
a volume on European languages. Is that volume still being considered? If
we do any work that would include Chomsky's morphophonemics, that
would be included in such a volume." Furthermore, Harris wrote to the
Graduate School Dean to solicit further support for his promising young
student on February 28, 1951.

I wish to write in support of Mr. A. N. Chomsky's application for a University
Scholarship in Linguistics. Mr. Chomsky has just received his M.A. in this department and is continuing his work toward the Ph.D. He is one of the best students
we have ever had and is highly regarded by men in various departments with whom
he has worked, in particular, by Professors Goodman and Martin of the Philosophy
Department. He has taken a considerable amount of work in logic and mathematics
and has come to the attention of the Rockefeller Foundation as a possible key man
in interdisciplinary research between linguistics and mathematical logic.

Chomsky has always reported that Harris manifested little awareness of his
work, but it is clear from these memos at least that Harris did respect him
and was working on his behalf in the background. Further support for
Harris's request was found in the person of Henry Hoenigswald, who considered that "in spite of his youth it has already become clear that he
[Chomsky] will develop into an original worker in our field" (March 9,
1951).

During this period Chomsky's work with Harris developed, taking on
mythical proportions, at least in the context of linguistics studies. Chomsky
might have been expected to follow up on and expand the work of his
teacher, and Harris represented both a kind of role-model and, perhaps,
someone against whom Chomsky could measure his own achievement.
Chomsky's early work in linguistics was in the Harris framework, the early
fruit of which was his first published article in *The Journal of Symbolic
Logic*.[12] Chomsky described these efforts to the French linguist Mitsou
Ronat:[13]

For a long time I thought that the discovery procedures appearing in the literature were correct in the essentials, that is, that the methods employed by structural linguists like Zellig Harris . . . were in principle correct, and that only some refinements were necessary to make them work. I spent quite a lot of time and energy, for about five or six years, I guess, trying to overcome some obvious defects of these procedures so that they would be able to produce a correct grammar with infinite descriptive scope from a finite corpus of the language; that, evidently, is the proper formulation of the task, if we think of these procedures as in effect a 'learning theory' for human language. (115)

Chomsky's undergraduate thesis also applied some of Harris's ideas, but he had by then abandoned Harris's methods, adopting instead what he described to me as a "completely non-procedural, holistic (in that the evaluation measure proposed was a measure applied to the whole system), and realist' approach" (March 31, 1995).

Phrase structure rules can generate representations of syntactic structure quite successfully . . . for quite a range of expressions, and were introduced for this purpose in the earliest work on generative grammar. It was at once apparent, however, that phrase structure rules . . . are insufficient in themselves to account properly for the variety of sentence structures. The earliest approach to this problem, which has a number of subsequent and current variants, was to enrich the system of rules by introducing complex categories with features that can "percolate down" to the categories contained within them, expressing global dependencies not captured in a simple system of phrase structure rules. . . . I adopted this approach in an undergraduate thesis of 1949, modifying ideas of Zellig Harris from a somewhat different framework.[14]

And so even if Harris's letters to Bloch and Hockett suggest that Harris recognized the importance of Chomsky's work, it remained, in Chomsky's words, "radically at odds with everything in structural linguistics, to my knowledge, which is why [it, and LSLT] were published only 30 years later." Nonetheless, a number of texts discuss the proximity of Chomsky's linguistic theories to those of Harris, including "The Fall and Rise of Empiricism," published in *An Integrated Theory of Linguistic Ability* (1976), in which Jerrold J. Katz, D. Terence Langendoen, and Thomas G. Bever write. "[C]ontrary to popular belief, transformations come into modern linguistics, not with Chomsky, but with Zellig Harris's rules relating sentence forms. These are genuine transformations, since they are structure-dependent mappings of phrase markers onto phrase markers. That this is so can be seen from the examples of transformations Zellig Harris gives."[15] Even the *New Encyclopedia Britannica*[16] has something to say about this relationship: "Since Harris was Noam Chomsky's teacher, some linguists have questioned whether Chomsky's transformational grammar is as revolutionary as it has been taken to be, but the two scholars developed their ideas of transformation in different contexts and for different purposes. For Harris, a transformation relates surface structure sentence forms and is not a device to transform a deep structure into a surface structure, as it is in transformational grammar." Chomsky assesses his own relation to this work in *Language and Responsibility*.

That grammar [in his *Morphophonemics of Modern Hebrew*] did . . . contain a rudimentary generative syntax. The grammar associated phonetic representation with what we would now call "base-generated" syntactic structure. Parenthetically, this was a pre-transformational grammar. Harris's early work on transformations was then under way and as a student of his I was familiar with it, but I did not see then how this work could be recast within the framework of generative grammar that I was trying to work out. In place of transformations, the grammar had a complex system of indices assigned to syntactic categories, which indicated syntactic relations inexpressible within the framework of segmentation and classification that was later constructed, in somewhat different terms, as the theory of phrase structure grammar. (112)

Harris's colleagues considered that the work on transformations was very important, and a number of them made connections to some of the work that Chomsky was doing as a student in their department. Henry Hoenigswald, for example, suggested to me that Harris's "linguistic achievement has no equal. The discovery of syntactic 'transformations' by him and then by his pupil Noam Chomsky in the '50s of the century was profound in a way for which there are few parallels in any discipline. Transformations—the basis of generative grammar—were new concepts in the sense in which the great discoveries in the history of science were 'new.' They made things that had been known after a fashion, as well as things that had hardly been known at all, fall into place in dazzling fashion. To be sure, he disdained to talk descriptively *about* them, leaving it to those who would study his work to develop it or attack it as they saw fit. In that he wasn't always lucky, but such was his temperament." In an unpublished internal document for the University of Pennsylvania, "Linguistics at the University of Pennsylvania," Henry Hiz makes a clear distinction between distributional description and transformational theory, such that "the first characterizes each linguistic entity as a class of some lower-level entities, whereas the latter derives a sentence from another sentence or sentences, thereby deriving a sentence from entities of the same level." Pursuing his history of the Penn department (and the field), Hiz noted that "in 1952 Harris introduced procedures of sentence transformation into discourse analysis, as a method of regularizing a text and of finding equivalences between its segments." Soon afterward, recalled Hiz, "transformational theory was divorced from discourse analysis and became an autonomous part of linguistics." For him, "Noam Chomsky's dissertation connected to many things. Sentences are related and their relations are to be studied by a grammar. It may be done without much semantics when transformations are only sentence-preserving." The other interesting connection to Chomsky in this realm is the discourse analysis work that he had been doing with Harris in the late 1940s, about which Chomsky said:

If you look at his discourse analysis papers that were published in the early 1950s, they're all about chemical abstracting, but that's not what we had been doing. What we were doing was political analyses. I remember a project that I was assigned to and worked on, which was to take Sydney Hook's writings during the transition period, from the time when he was a communist to the time when he was anti-communist, and to do discourse analysis of them, to see if you could tease out the changes that were going on through the kind of linguistic-style analysis that Harris was working on. That was most of the work, not the scientific stuff that got into print. As you know, Harris was very cautious about making his political positions known. It was particularly striking during the 60s when things were heating up, and all of that group just pulled out. For example, Bruria and I used to be very close friends, but we couldn't talk to each other by the mid-60s. She had been a committed anarchist, but by the mid-60s it all changed.

The interview with Chomsky that appears in the appendix reiterates this point with further evidence and examples.

When finally published in 1951, Zellig Harris's *Methods* book became a landmark and, as Hiz points out in his obituary for Harris, it was

a book that made him famous, often for the wrong reasons. It was considered a unified and systematic presentation of the achievements of the Bloomfieldian school to which Harris himself had contributed several papers. The book establishes both a new standard of rigorousness for structural linguistics and a very broad scope for linguistic study. The linguist's job is to study the entire structure of a language as a system. But the results of Harris's book are contrary to some tenets of many followers of Bloomfield. Formal procedures to establish phonemes or morphemes do not lead to a unique result. There may be several ways to assign phonemes to a language, depending for instance on whether we want to minimize their number or minimize their distributional anomalies. The twentieth-century physicists introduced operational definitions that led to the splitting of traditional concepts according to the method of measurement. Furthermore, Harris argued that the rigidity of linguistic levels, phonology first, then morphology, then syntax, is not defensible; instead of composing morphemes from phonemes one can begin with morphology and then decompose morphemes into sequences of phonemes.

On the back cover of the Midway Reprints edition (1986), the anthropological linguist Norman A. McQuown asserts that "Harris's contribution [is] epoch-marking in a double sense: first in that it marks the culmination of a development of linguistic methodology *away* from a stage of intuitionism, frequently culture-bound; and second in that it marks the beginnings of a new period, in which the new methods will be applied ever more rigorously to ever widening areas in human culture." Henry Hiz recalled in the aforementioned University of Pennsylvania document that Zellig Harris's Bloomfieldian-inspired *Methods in Structural Linguistics* "establishes both a new standard of rigorousness for structural linguistics and a very broad scope for linguistic study" (519).

For Hiz, this approach was original in many ways, running at times "contrary to some tenets of many followers of Bloomfield" (520) for a range of reasons, often revolving around the issue of meaning. In a January 19, 1945, letter to Kenneth L. Pike, Leonard Bloomfield complains that "it has become painfully common to say that I, or rather a whole group of language students of whom I am one, pay no attention to meaning or neglect it, or even that we undertake to study language without meaning, simply as meaningless sounds. . . . It is not just a personal affair in the statements to which I have referred, but something which, if allowed to develop, will injure the progress of our science by setting up a fictitious contrast between students who consider meaning and students who neglect it. The latter class, so far as I know, does not exist." This charge—that those linguists who work in the Bloomfield paradigm pay no attention to meaning—is a frequent refrain from people like Robert A. Hall Jr., who suggests that Harris's work contains the "thoroughly mistaken" idea, shared by American linguists Bernard Bloch and George L. Trager, that "descriptive linguistics was in theory (but only in theory) limited to the enumeration of patterns of distribution of phonemes and sequences of phonemes, with meaning taken into consideration only as a factor serving to differentiate between sequences" (48).[17] Other assessments from the aforementioned *The Legacy of Zellig Harris*[18] offer more nuanced considerations of how Harris can account for meaning and, more broadly, for the value of the approach. In "Method and Theory in Harris's Grammar of Information," for example, T. A. Ryckman writes that

Harris's hypothesis is that additional structures of language emerge as further conventionalizations of usage from this original, and primitive, referential function, producing constraints that only indirectly, or distantly, or not at all carry referential meaning. Within the additional latitudes of expression provided by new syntactical constructions are opened up new possibilities for purely symbolic or abstract vocabulary. Not incidentally, these further structures provide as well the wherewithal both for the development of abstract thinking, and for the formation of 'nonsense' (as opposed to ungrammatical) sentences. This is a highly plausible accounting of language as a self-organizing system developing in tandem with the complexity of thought.[19] (34)

Paul Mattick Jr., in "Some Implications of Zellig Harris's Work for the Philosophy of Science,"[20] discusses the issue of "meaning" as regards Harris's attempts at formulating an abstract system. Says Mattick, "while this abstract system is in the first place formulated in purely combinatorial terms, its elements in their relations can be seen to have clear semantic properties. In particular, all occurrences of natural language can be described as word-sequences satisfying certain combinatory constraints, and these constraints can be given an informational interpretation." (44). And in the same volume, Richard Smaby, in "A Distributional Semantics Applied to Computer User Interfaces" discusses "meaning features" at length, describing different aspects of meaning described by Harris" (274 ff.). Harris himself adds what Robert E. Longacre calls in his contribution titled "Some Implications of Zellig Harris's Discourse Analysis" a "very quotable" point on semantics: "for each word, what the learner or analyzer does is not think deeply about what the word 'really means' but to see how it [is] used, keeping in mind the fact that various life-situations in which it is used are largely reflected in the various word combinations in which it occurs" (118).

These texts offer crucial complements to Harris's work in part because it is so difficult to read so much of Harris's own words; indeed, Pieter Seuren begins his assessment of *Methods in Structural Linguistics* with the observation that although "remarkable," it is "among the dullest [books] ever published" (213).[21] Especially compared to the wonderful array of recent works that have popularized interest in the relationship between language and the mind, or even the aforementioned descriptions of Harris's work by John Goldsmith or Paul Mattick Jr., much of the Harris corpus is dry and painful to peruse. A review by Knud Togeby[17] also notes that the reader of Harris's work is constantly interrupted by the need to consult notes and appendices throughout the text: "Without any evidence of necessity, it has been composed in such a way as constantly to trip the reader up. It is a sort of house with three floors, and one has the tiresome task of running up and down the stairs all the time: from the text itself to the notes (which often fill half a page), from the notes to the text, from the text to the appendices, which must always be sought far away from the chapters they belong to, back to the text, and so on" (190–191).

Nevertheless, as Seuren points out, Harris is driven by the "consistent and inspiring" idea that "it should be possible, in principle, to record a large corpus of actual utterances and then, by careful comparison, set up a tentative inventory of minimal recurrent sound units later to be grouped together as phonemes on the basis of their complementary distribution." (213–214). In terms of the style he uses for this effort, Jane Robinson has suggested, "If I have an idea what he's talking about, I can understand him. As someone said of Quine, once you've understood what he means, you realize he couldn't have said it any other way. Harris is that way for me. It's just that what he's trying to say is difficult."[22] Goldsmith agrees; in personal correspondence (2010) he adds that this same comment has been made of Chomsky's linguistics too, and that "linguists who don't have a background of reading mathematics don't have much experience in reading really hard technical material, I suppose."

An example of Harris's writing tendencies can be found in the following passage from *Structural Linguistics* when he elaborates on the study of minimal recurrent sound units. "As the first step towards obtaining phonemes, this procedure represents the continuous flow of a unique occurrence of speech as a succession of segmental elements, each representing some feature of a unique speech sound. The points of division of these segments are arbitrary here, since we have as yet no way of enabling the analyst to make the cuts at precisely those points in the flow of speech which will later be represented by inter-phonemic divisions. Later procedures will change these segmentations until their boundaries coincide with those of the eventual phonemes." (25). Reading such descriptions carefully makes one realize that the apparent opaqueness is in fact a very economical and terse form of writing, and intense focus on what Harris says reveals a real clarity and logic. Seuren follows up on this passage by noting that subsequently, "recurrent phoneme combinations will be recognized as morphs, whose distribution will make it possible to set up an inventory of morphemes. . . . Until all combinations (constructions) have been exhausted" (214). Harris's work provides a whole series of these operations, with examples from different languages, making it "one massive discovery procedure for a maximally compact, i.e. simple, statement of all possible constructions of the corpus at the various different levels of phonemes, morphemes, words, phrases, and, finally, the sentence" (214). This work was an application of mathematics to the study of linguistics, "an idealized procedure that should be applied in an ideal world of science" (214). In a 1951 review of *Methods*,[23] Stanley Newman suggested the Harris method can be described as a two-step procedure, "identifying the phonological and morphological elements, and describing the distribution of these elements relative to each other," tasks that would proceed as follows:

The first procedure . . . takes up the method of dividing utterances into arbitrarily segmented elements of sound; the second describes the techniques for determining whether or not a segment is equivalent to (i.e. can be substituted for) another segment; and the remaining phonological procedures present methods of analysis leading to a description of the total phonological structure of a language. There is a smoother transition from phonology to morphology in Harris' approach than in the more traditional treatment: he identifies the morpheme, not as a unit of form that carries meaning, but as a restricted sequence of phonemes showing the distributional character of a unit in being replaceable, within utterances, by other phoneme sequences. The morphological procedure themselves deal with the methods of describing morphemic segments, morpheme alternants, morphophonemes, morpheme classes and sequences, morphemic long components, constructions, and, finally, the total morphological structure. (404)

One indication of the paradigm within which Harris's work was received came in another review, this one by Charles F. Hockett that assesses the nature of scientific inquiry.[24] As regards the science of language, he suggests that "in the nineteenth century our predecessors managed to clear away most traditional misunderstanding about the relation of language to writing, and to excise the latter as not properly a part of our subject matter." The hero of this story is Leonard Bloomfield, whose "system recognized two initial criteria for the analysis of a language: sameness or difference as to *sound*, and sameness or difference as to *meaning*, of utterances and parts of utterances" (117). For Hockett, Harris's book is important because therein he "takes two steps beyond Bloomfield's system." The first of these is that "we are quite explicitly told how to determine sameness or difference in sound ["whether or not they sound the same to a native speaker"]; the second is that Bloomfield's other fundamental element—meaning—is eliminated entirely." Thus "Harris both narrows and more sharply defines our starting point; also, of course, he describes and illustrates in considerable detail the operations which can be undertaken, one after another, after this start, in order to reach a description of a language" (118). Hockett then makes clear why Harris's system seemed to offer so much to those interested in machine analyses, while also explaining why more sophisticated computing machines would be valuable to the approach Harris described.[25]

Once we have discovered all the elements of sound which are capable of making utterances sound different from each other to the native speaker, have devised symbols to represent these elements, and have collected a sufficiently large sample of speech transcribed in these symbols, we need no further help from the informant. Indeed, all the further operations which Harris describes could be performed just as well, if not even better, by a battery of computing machines rather than by a live analyst and his card files; what further use is in practice made of the informant (save for enlarging one's sample) is by way of short cuts to compensate for the slow speed at which a human being can perform the operations of distributional analysis as compared to computing machines. (119)

This is part of a general optimism about the perspectives for machine analysis, which is regularly recalled in Noam Chomsky's assessment of that period. For instance, in *Language and Mind*[26] Chomsky speaks of a kind of general euphoria about the possibilities that machines could offer those interested in machine analysis of human language, particularly in places like Cambridge, Massachusetts.

The technological advances of the 1940s simply reinforced the general euphoria. Computers were on the horizon, and their imminent availability reinforced the belief that it would suffice to gain a theoretical understanding of only the simplest and most superficially obvious of phenomena—everything else would merely prove to be "more of the same," and apparent complexity that would be disentangled by the electronic marvels. The sound spectrograph, developed during the war, offered similar promise for the physical analysis of speech sounds. The interdisciplinary conferences on speech analysis of the early 1950s make interesting reading today. There were few so benighted as to question the possibility, in fact the immediacy, of a final solution to the problem of converting speech into writing by available engineering technique[s]. And just a few years later, it was jubilantly discovered that machine translation and automatic abstracting were just around the corner. (3)

As he describes it, Chomsky was cynical about such work, which led him in directions that were different from those of his teacher, and it is certainly the case that they did not remain interlocutors in any sustained way once Chomsky's career took off; nevertheless, they did maintain contact as Chomsky completed the requirements for his degree, including passing examinations in French (September 29, 1950), German (September 30, 1950) and his preliminary exams (December 14, 1953). Harris remained supportive of Chomsky during this period, as is evident from memos he wrote during that period describing his progress, and Harris also hired Chomsky's girlfriend (and later wife, Carol Schatz) for research. An April 29, 1952 memo to the Director of Personnel at Penn authorized a payment of $200 from one of Harris's research grants for her research in Boston "which will aid in completing my project." One of the last formal points of contact between Harris and Chomsky is documented in a June 8, 1955, memo from Harris that states that "Mr. Chomsky was examined in problems of structural linguistics and in the use of mathematical logic and abstract algebras for a formalization of linguistics. He passed the examination with a high order of excellence." There is also mention of his having been examined by Professor Goodman in epistemology and logic, via four two-hour questions. From the mid-1950s, Chomsky had little contact with Harris, and from the mid-1960s Chomsky recalls none at all, but an interesting anecdote that suggests a kind of passing of the torch from teacher to student: in 1962, Zellig Harris stood aside as the keynote speaker at the International Congress of Linguists and nominated Chomsky in his stead. Chomsky downplays Harris's eventual influence upon his work but has nevertheless always described Harris to me as an extraordinary person who inspired his thinking about a whole range of issues.

The Reception of *Methods*

The work that had brought Chomsky and Harris together on the linguistic front was of course *Methods*, and the range of reviews of that book provide a sense of how it was understood at that time. Whatever the individual reviewer's opinion of the overall project, there was a unanimous sense that the publication of *Methods* represented some kind of landmark in linguistics. Stanley Newman set the tone in his aforementioned 1954 *American Anthropologist* review, in which he stated that "there will be little disagreement among linguists that this book is the most important contribution to descriptive linguistics since the publication of Bloomfield's *Language* in 1933."[27] Its significance was that "it makes explicit the direction in which linguistics has been moving," employing Harris's characteristic "bold" and "original" mathematical approach to linguistic analysis, and "its coherently reasoned and clearly formulated sequence of operational procedures for analyzing linguistic data" (404). Of particular import for nonlinguists, according to Newman, is that Harris's method eliminates meaning as a criterion of linguistic analysis, a point raised by most reviews but more clearly stated in this text than elsewhere.

C. F. Voegelin suggested in his 1952 *American Oriental Society* review that with this book, Harris "becomes the spokesman for the "new linguistics," which may be said to have had its opening on the American stage in 1933 (with the publication of Bloomfield's *Language*).[28] Fernand Mossé found the "scientific" method overly obtuse in terminology and inordinately dependent upon logic and mathematics; nevertheless, it could be useful if it could be shown to be applicable to the "grandes langues bien connues," notably French, German, and Spanish.[29] A review by Fred Householder in the *International Journal of American Linguistics*, reiterated that whatever one might think of the book, *Methods* "will remain an indispensable part of every linguist's library for many years to come," partly because it mentions virtually every method of descriptive linguistics previously attempted."[30] The review is not altogether favorable at the outcome, however, finding numerous inconsistencies, which he ascribes to the number of years devoted to writing the text. Further, although most of the book is an attempt to describe a structure of human language (which he describes as "God's truth" approach), it sometimes falls into the realm of "hocus-pocus," which involves the imposition of a structure upon a human language that he describes as simply a hodge-podge of incoherent, formless data. Nevertheless, in an important passage Householder does credit Harris with understanding "the pretense which we make," in presenting linguistic descriptions,

that they have been arrived at by performing a series of humanly impossible operations (impossible even with the aid of any electronic computing machines now in existence and financial support far beyond our most enthusiastic dreams). The rigor of linguistics is strictly fake rigor in many instances. And a failure to recognize this fakeness can have (for our poor students) some unfortunate results. We demonstrate that it is possible to determine the phonemes and morphemes of a language entirely without reference to meaning (*if* we had an infinite corpus and a second-order infinite amount of time and money), but in practice we all use meaning and no one makes any efforts to refine our techniques of using it to avoid error, because of the theoretical possibility of doing without it. (261)

Thus, he considers that linguistics is an art, not a science, so "the best linguist is the man with the best hunches, the most natural talent for the job, and the best unreasoned and inexplicable feel for the language."

Margaret Mead, famous for *Coming of Age in Samoa* (based on field work she did on the suggestion of Franz Boas), reviewed this text, also in the *International Journal of American Linguistics*.[31] Her assessment was done in the name of cultural anthropology, as a scholar "who has used the analysis of language only as a research tool on other aspects of culture." Harris focused on language, but as we have seen, there were important overlaps with contemporary anthropological work by the likes of Boas and Sapir. And J. Alden Mason, according to a March 4, 1949, letter to Zellig Harris, even called upon Harris's anthropological expertise to assist him in the preparation of his course on museum technique and research at Penn. Furthermore, Harris's assistant was busy with copies of Mason's Tepehuan wire records (of songs) according to a September 20, 1949, letter from him. But it is Mead's review that is compelling in regard to the anthropological aspect of Harris because it is both far reaching in its analysis and conclusions and, moreover, remarkably contemporary in tone and emphasis.

The student of culture cannot be called "lay" in respect to the study of linguistics, except with regard to those refinements of method which are also peculiar to any other specialization within the broad field of culture, whether it be the arrangement of potsherds into types, the analysis of the zonal-modal sequences of expressive play in young children, or the special determinations necessary for comparative musicology. Yet, with the sort of fatality with which students of culture become captives of the very categories through which they have sought to escape culture-bound provincialism, there seems to have been an increasing tendency within the broad field of cultural anthropology to perpetuate and accentuate the division between a category called "language" and a category called "culture." Such a tendency may be assigned historically to the very old human recognition that a language (in contradistinction to the rest of culture) has such systematic qualities that it can be "learned" by the immigrant and the bilingual specialist who retain the food habits and even the postural systems of their own cultures. This recognition, which is found all over the world and at all levels of cultural complexity, has now assumed a quasi-scientific form in which the "science of linguistics" is regarded (especially by non-linguists, but lamentably by linguists themselves sometimes) as separate from the study of the rest of culture. This is not the case with Dr. Harris' book, where the "rest of culture" is systematically included in a most thoroughgoing, although often condensed, fashion." (257)

For Mead, it seems more profitable to consider that linguistics provides "a model for other divisions of the science of culture," so Harris's work "could be used to specify the possibilities of attaining a like precision and rigor in the study of other aspects of culture, especially of the other sensory modalities, considering the degree of systematization that is imposed on them through the circumstances of learning and the demands of communication" (257). She adds to previous descriptions by pointing out that the essence of his method "consists in combining the 'objectivity' of machine recording (which stands in back of the linguist's pencil as a kind of validating mechanism to ensure another linguist's 'hearing' the same sounds at a different time and place) with precise body-based descriptions, and with objective determination of the subjective experience of discrimination, in order that the linguistic informants may be subject to a series of 'experiments' or repetitive, controlled situations by which this discrimination may be codified" (258).

Mead has real problems with Harris's approach for cultural analysis, since "the same cultural materials can be analyzed with different sets of categories"; furthermore, Harris's method is built upon the assumption that "the analyst of language is dealing with a body of material within which there is a structure, a structure so complexly built that it may be revealed by a series of comparably rigorous operations which are not necessarily identical" (258). The problem for Mead is that this quality of language may be due to "the circumstance that a language's quality of being systematic may be related to a wide range of different human capacities for systemization." So what appears through analysis of phonemic, morphemic, and grammatical analysis to be a "kind of redundancy of precautionary discriminability may actually be capable of being related to the requirement that a human natural language must be learnable and usable by human beings with varying and different types of discriminatory capacity, of which only the human ability to systematize and generalize may be held entirely in common" (258). Nevertheless, the method has much to offer, because "by taking the methods of structural linguistics as a model, and asking of any cultural study, what is the corpus? How many of the units can be distinguished? What are the morphological equivalents of utterance and environment and analysis of different levels such as phonemic and morphemic levels? How may the corpus be recorded for independent analysis, and in what way is it to be related to systematic properties of human beings?—any cultural analysis can be checked for possibilities of precision and rigor" (260).

Norman A. McQuown undertook a major review of *Methods* in *Language*,[32] noting that this project, familiar to most people in the field before the book was released (because the manuscript had been in circulation in mimeographed form prior to publication, and a number of articles published in *Language* in the 1940s became parts of *Methods*), employs the principle of relative distribution and the method of controlled substitution to undertake the most ambitious project since Leonard Bloomfield's. Harris's work is based upon the hypothesis that the logic of distributional relations constitutes the basic method of structural linguistics, a logic that is based on two previously described suppositions, "that the investigator is able to perform an initial segmentation of the speech continuum (on any one of a number of levels), and that he is able, by substituting his initial segments one for another and by observing a native speaker's reaction, to judge which segments are equivalent for that speaker and which are not" (495). This work expands our intuitive grasp of similar ideas by allowing results to be "subject to multipersonal check." McQuown admired the effort, and looked forward "to the day when similar descriptive systems will be applicable with equal rigor to all aspects of human behavior."

Nevertheless, he found Harris's attitude objectionable because it turns structural analysis into a "game;" for Harris, elements are reduced to

"logical symbols" that can then be subjected to "operations of mathematical logic," which falls into what McQuown refers to as the "culture-of-the-
informant-be-damned-approach" (496). He questioned as well Harris's
limitation of which linguistic material should be admitted into the analysis, the further restrictions imposed on certain criteria and techniques of
analysis, the fact that there is "little specification of procedure for shorten-
ing the process of distribution hunting" and "little comment on interpret-
ing the informant's reaction," and, finally, that there is little discussion of
the "psychological reality of linguistic patterns" (503). McQuown does
suggest that Harris is aware of some shortfalls in the approach, which he
believes could be addressed by complementary work that would focus
upon "the analysis of other elements of culture reflected in the medium
of language" and by bringing to bear "extralinguistic cultural systems and
all the correlations we can perceive between such systems and the system
of language" (504). In the end, though, Harris has "provided us with the
tool" for extending linguistic methodology, and it remains for the practitioner "to use it" (504).

In the same issue of *Language*, the linguist Murray Fowler complements
McQuown's anthropological critique by focusing upon the problems that
arise when an object within a distributional study is isolated from its environment. After a careful review of the approach, Fowler sums up his review
by stating that

the conclusion that must be given here is that, as stated, Harris's procedure cannot
be used to isolate a single morpheme. The proposal is to make morphemic distinctions on a phonological level by the use of statistical—i.e. distributional—criteria
alone. That is impossible. A group of phonemes in a phonemic environment can
be called a morpheme in a morphemic environment only by the addition of function or of meaning. That addition is concomitant with the privileges of occurrence
of the phoneme sequence: it is that addition which makes the morpheme. It is this
additional element which the trained linguist and the naïve informant alike use as
the prime criterion in isolating morphemes. It is this prime criterion—the additional
element of function or of meaning—which Harris would put aside in favor of 'distributional investigations'. Until it is brought back and placed in first position, the
job simply cannot be done. (509)[33]

The question of the feasibility, and indeed the value, of Harris's method
came to occupy a central position in this narrative, in part on account of
the emergence and spread of Chomsky's paradigm; other discussions, concerned with the relationship between Harris's approach and other (European) methods, further emphasize the differences between Harris and
Chomsky. Knud Togeby's review, for example, suggested that one advantage

of Harris's methods over European ones is his complete rejection of the "mentalism" with which Europeans "are so deeply affected." Nevertheless, Togeby, like other European reviewers, found consistencies between Harris's approach and the one developed by Jakobson. R.-L. Wagner followed the European ties to Harris, suggesting from the outset that "Il ne faut pas perdre de vue que la Linguistique est né en Europe et qu'elle s'est développé à partir d'une comparaison historique des langues classiques anciennes et des langues romaines" (637).[34] Goldsmith asserted that this point is important if we wish to understand the previously-mentioned relationship between the European-based philology–classical language approach and the anthropological linguistics approach, which eventually merged in the United States. Furthermore, and consistent with the French view (even today, in certain milieus), Wagner emphasizes Harris's links to Saussure, suggesting that the whole approach proceeds directly from the arbitrary nature of signs and the idea of differential oppositions. Indeed, Eugene Dorfman recalls Harris's own acknowledged debts not only to American structuralists but also to Saussure (and Trubetzkoy).

I have noted ways in which Harris's later work emerged from the earliest writings, but P. H. Matthews draws a clearer distinction between phases of Harris's work, and in the obituary for Harris suggests that this period's work was not consistent with the first phase.

A second phase begins in the early 1950s, with the analysis of "equivalences" in distribution within texts. For example, the sequences *there is often snow* and *it is very cold* would have equivalent distributions in a text in which both precede *in January.* But analyses of individual texts will often reach an impasse. In one, we might have the sequence *the weather is cold at the beginning of the year.* Then in the same text, we might have a further sequence *the cold weather after Christmas.* On that evidence alone, no further progress can be made. But we can establish more generally that, in the language as a whole, any sequence of the form *the weather is cold* (schematically, *the N is A)* is related, by what Harris called, for the first time, a TRANSFORMATION, to a sequence *the A N.* Given that, we can then speak of a distributional equivalence, within the text itself, between *at the beginning of the year,* which follows the sequence *the weather is cold,* and *after Christmas,* which follows a "transform" of it.

Some of these observations refer to notions that occur in earlier writings, but it is the case that *Methods* formally sets out this methodology in a rigorous and sustained fashion. But there is evidence in the correspondence and the writings that Harris believed that significant work remained to be done, and that there were considerable grounds for criticism. Throughout this period, Bernard Bloch remained a constant correspondent and a conscientious editor. In a letter dated February 15, 1951, we find

Harris replying to one of Bloch's long commentaries on a recent piece, which in Bloch's opinion needed some refinement. Harris replied: "Thanx for your letter, and please don't think that I assume that anything I write ought to go in as is, or even ought to go in at all. I am seriously interested in any criticism you have (and why should I not be) and particularly in improving its status as communication." He then offered a series of corrections, based on Bloch's ideas, which satisfied Bloch, according to a February 19, 1951, reply: "In revising, don't spare the horses: please make all changes, both of style and of organization, that seem to you called for in view of my carpings; this is the kind of thing, in view of the novelty of the project, that only you can do at this stage." Bloch also pointed to a growing problem relating to the distance between Harris's work in the fields of logic and mathematics, and the kinds of knowledge taken for granted in the field of linguistics. "In particular, please expand your proofs even to the point of laboriousness: remember that you have to satisfy not only the demands of logic but the quite different demands of linguists untrained in logical forms. (As a hobby I read, in a desultory way, whatever I find I can understand of mathematics and logic; but unhappily I have to stay always pretty near the surface—e.g., just at present, Tarski's *Einführung in die mathematische Logik*; and of course even my dabbling is a good bit more than most linguists do in these fields)." Harris's work may be difficult for most people to understand, but from this perspective it would require further elaboration, even on its own terms, to meet the requirements of what Harris is trying to describe and accomplish.

During this period, Harris set forth the transformational system at the Linguistic Institute at Indiana University, 1951–1952. This work brought him into conversations with a range of individuals including the psychologist David Rapaport, whose work had been of interest to him for his understanding of attitudes, as well as with the Swiss developmental psychologist Jean Piaget, the philosopher Rudolph Carnap, the philosopher, mathematician, and linguist Yehoshua Bar-Hillel (who met Harris in Israel), the mathematician Max Zorn (who attended linguistics talks at Indiana), the University of Pennsylvania linguist Henry Hoenigswald, the French mathematician Marcel-Paul Schutzenberger, the linguist Maurice Gross (who did his PhD at Penn under the supervision of Harris), the mathematician and linguist André Lentin, and, most closely, with the aforementioned Henry Hiz, who worked in the *Methods* framework in close association with Harris.

There are indications as well of Harris's orientation toward and approach that emphasized procedures and instructions, in evidence in, for example, in a letter he wrote on October 27, 1954 to Dr. Warren Weaver of the Rockefeller Foundation.

Some years ago you sent me your memorandum on translation. At the time I was working on a method for reducing translation to a fixed procedure, which might ultimately be put in the form of instructions for a computer. A preliminary report on this work has just been published, and I am sending it to you for your possible interest. I think that any practicable method of mechanical translation will require a considerable amount of linguistic structure to be built into the programming. Work has to be done to find ways of putting language structure into the machine program. I am interested in setting up a research project for this purpose, and would be glad to discuss it with you if you are interested.

This is an interesting passage in terms of Harris's interests and objectives and also in terms of what the computer and communications industries thought possible as regards the linguistics–mechanical language field overlap. It is also notable that attempts to follow this program have yielded comparisons between the grammars of two languages. One such effort is described in "Some Results on Transfer Grammar," by Morris Salkoff, in which he notes that

I have completed a detailed comparative French-English grammar (Salkoff 1999) as a necessary preliminary step for a program of French-English machine translation (MT). In this grammar, French syntactic structures are translated into their English equivalents. This procedure extends Harris's proposal for defining transfer relations between two languages by providing a wide coverage of French syntax. This work was carried out independently of the results of Harris's paper, which I had read many years before. It was only after the comparative grammar had been completed and published that I re-read his paper and realized that I had fleshed out his proposal for the pair French-English.[35]

This is an early indication of how Harris's "legacy" would play out in future work on language and communication studies, using insights developed early on in his work.

On a Whole Other Plane

The complex circle of relations between Harris and his different counterparts continued to develop through the 1950s, and the constant reappearance of familiar critical figures from the Jewish intellectual realm speaks to the world that surrounded Harris throughout his life. There was, on the one hand, a series of milieus brought together by such organizations as Avukah, or in vibrant intellectual institutions of the time, like the University of Chicago, Columbia, CUNY, University of Michigan, Penn, Harvard, and Yale, but on the other hand there remained a quest for other "homes" for Jewish intellectual work. One example is the Hebrew University of Jerusalem, which was in 1954 still "in exile," and later was to unite key intellectual figures, as Avukah had once done. Albert Einstein encouraged this effort by writing to Salo Baron on August 10, 1954, in support of Hebrew University. Einstein noted in his letter that Hebrew University "had been close to my heart for many years" and "it occupies a position of great responsibility for future generations"; indeed, "when Israel becomes a fully independent state one day—independent economically as well as in the political sense—it will be the scientists and scholars of the University, in very large measure, who will have made it possible." For them, notably the scientists who had done such "outstanding work" despite the terrible conditions, the university was in dire need of new laboratories and classrooms.

At this time, Noam Chomsky was in his early but nevertheless enormously productive years, while his father, William Chomsky, was commenting upon newly released scientific approaches to language,[36] and Noam Chomsky's institutional father, Harris, was keeping him on track, to ensure he would finish his thesis. In a February 17, 1955, letter to the Local Board 146 in Philadelphia, he wrote:

We understand that Mr. Avram Noam Chomsky, a graduate student in this Department, while a member of the Society of Fellows, is subject to induction to the armed services. Mr. Chomsky has completed his class work and is now completing his dissertation. He is to graduate in June of this year. He would not be able to graduate unless he completes his dissertation, and his dissertation is of such a technical nature that it would be impossible to hold it over until he returned from the services. We, therefore, hope that this call will come only after his graduation. I might mention for your information that Mr. Chomsky's dissertation, the product of several years of hard work, is a major bridge between two sciences. Mr. Chomsky happens to be a man of exceptional academic abilities, who is obviously destined to make unusual contributions to knowledge.

Chomsky prefaced his dissertation in linguistics, titled "Transformational Analysis," submitted in 1955 (and signed by Zellig S. Harris both as Supervisor and Chairman of Group Committee), with the following:

This study had its origin in certain problems that arose in attempting to extend linguistic techniques to the analysis of discourse. This extension naturally presupposed standard linguistic analysis, but in the attempt to develop effective techniques of discourse analysis it was found necessary to assume certain knowledge about linguistic structure which was not in fact provided by existing methods, though it seemed within the range of distributional study. In particular, these methods failed

to account for such obvious relations between sentences as the active-passive relations. Systematic investigation of this problem exposed other gaps in syntactic
theory, and led finally to this attempt to construct a higher level of transformational
analysis. This is basically a study of the arrangement of words and morphemes in
sentences, hence a study of linguistic form. Thus it is a syntactic study in both the
narrow sense (as opposed to phonology) and in the broader sense (as opposed to
semantics). (ii)

He then noted that "this study was carried out in close collaboration with
Zellig Harris, to whom I am indebted for many of the fundamental underlying ideas. I have also received suggestions and criticism from Morris
Halle" (iii). So during this period, which corresponded to his departure
from Penn, Chomsky was setting out his differences with the framework
in which Harris worked, differences that became increasingly pronounced
over time. His last contacts with Harris were for a couple of days in 1964
in Israel, followed by a frequently mentioned silence between them. This
"schism" has become the stuff of much discussion and, on a lighter note,
some academic fantasies, generally not worth reading, but there are some
humorous texts that can be examined in this realm.[37]

"Linguistic Transformations" and "Information Retrieval" for the National Science Foundation (NSF). At the same time, there were residues of the anthropological work he had done; in 1957, for example, came a review of a 1956 book, by Dorothea F. Bleek and edited by Harris, titled *A Bushman Dictionary*.[3] This rather remarkable text contains 15,000 Bushman-English entries and, as we learn from E. Westphal's 1957 review in volume 27 of the journal *Africa*, Harris's specific role is not mentioned "but we may be sure that he has made no small contribution," and that "those who admire the work of Miss Bleek will feel grateful to him for enabling this book to stand as a memorial to her" (204).

Work done during this period was deeply affected by what had been learned in the course of the Second World War, and what was expected from the emerging technological revolutions in communication, computing, and mechanical discourse analysis and translation. "In the beginning of the 50s Harris was a professor of linguistics at the University of Pennsylvania. . . . Around this time there was increasing interest in mechanical information processing and machine translation along with the development in cybernetic communication theory, automata theory and related areas. The Cold War between America and Russia took place also on the scientific level. Computer sciences, logic and formal languages gained special interest in this connection" (Plötz 11).[4] The implications of this newfound interest in and, moreover, excitement about, mechanical and machine work has been discussed by Stephen O. Murray,[5] Senta Plötz, in her 1972 preface to *Transformational Analysis*,[6] and by Konrad Koerner.[7] Murray Eden's approach to the machine translation work helps explain how there might be such divergent approaches to judging its potential value among people in the field. Chomsky, as we have seen, was very skeptical about the value of machine translation and deemed Eden's own efforts to parse chemical sentences and represent them in a form reminiscent of logical statements as "fruitless," a consequence, in Eden's view, of the fact that Chomsky's main intention is "philosophical rather than linguistic." Accordingly, Eden told me, Chomsky "holds to a perfectionist view of inquiry. I have spent most of my professional life as an engineer. Engineers, as you probably know, rarely worry about perfection. If some procedure or theory or device works most of the time, that's good enough. Future adjustments will probably lead to improvement. Again, as you undoubtedly know, machine translation will never be perfect, but there are companies making significant money by doing a job good enough for human readers to correct or at least identify mistakes." This sheds considerable light upon a particular oft-cited quote from Chomsky about this work:

"It may have [had] some utility; it could be on the par with building a bigger bulldozer, which is a useful thing. It's nice to have big bulldozers if you have to dig holes."[8] From the perspective of Eden's statement, this is a very important observation since it calls our attention to the overall task at hand and the appropriate tools for undertaking it. "Digging holes" is in this sense akin to a menial and mechanical project, far less lofty than uncovering the universal grammar and the creative uses of language that would largely resist this kind of excavation.

A perspective more sympathetic to Harris's structuralist or computational linguistic projects comes from Stephen B. Johnson's "The Computability of Operator Grammar," in which Johnson points to the value but also the challenges of working in Harris's paradigm.[9]

The most radical departure of Operator Grammar from other linguistic theories is the representation of meaning in a statistical model rather than through interpretation in a logical model: the information carried by a sentence is given by the probability distributions of arguments under their operators. Integration of this perspective with conventional symbolic representations of grammar is a daunting task. In particular, it suggests that any serious investigation into the computational aspects of the theory would require access to a large body of linguistic data in order to understand the actual distributions of operators and their arguments. Corpora with formats sufficient for this kind of analysis have only become available very recently, and appropriate tools are still lacking. (144)

This notion of developing these "tools" is what Eden refers to as the engineering task that stands before us, on the one hand, and the value of new technologies to make manifest Harris's ambitions, on the other.

Another effort in this direction relates to work on transformations, and there was much excitement about this approach from on the start, including discussions of the relationship between Zellig Harris's and Noam Chomsky's versions thereof. Bloch wrote in a letter to Robert Lees, dated July 31, 1959, that "I am an admirer of Chomsky's from way back and an admirer of Harris's of even longer standing; and I'm convinced that transformation theory (or whatever you want to call it) is a tremendously important advance in grammatical thinking. Though I don't know the ins and outs of it well enough to use it myself, or even to lecture on it, I expect great things of it."[10] Bloch also wrote to William Locke, in a letter dated October 26, 1960, that "Chomsky has not only contributed to the literature of structural linguistics, he has fired the imagination of dozens of scholars throughout the country. It is interesting to note that young workers in the field, especially the most brilliant among them, are particularly susceptible to his spell. One of the liveliest and most promising developments in grammatical theory in recent years is transformational grammar. I call it Chomsky's even though Zellig Harris was perhaps the original proponent. It is above all Chomsky who had developed the theory and had given it its current vogue."[11]

This emerging linguistic paradigm was—and still is—the subject of some debate, as Murray points out in a passage of his work that recalls earlier mention of Einstein's influence upon scientific research.

The emergence of a transformational-generative "paradigm" in linguistics has been heralded by some Americans as a "scientific revolution" in the Kuhnian sense, with Noam Chomsky as the "Einstein of linguistics." One founder of this perspective told me, "our little Kuhnian revolution was in some ways actually more typical than his physics case." Other linguists, however, have objected to such claims by detailing continuities in assumptions and concepts between the *ancien régime* and the self-styled revolutionaries. Dell Hymes has even suggested that transformational grammarians attempted to act out Kuhn's scenario of a scientific revolution, distorting their historical accounts to conform to the model.

Whatever the intentions of those who pioneered this work, the point here is that "the expectation was that it could be developed into a powerful instrument in language analysis which would eventually make mechanical information analysis and translation possible. The results in mathematical logic additionally increased the hope that natural languages were also accessible to a precise and explicit description with the same standard as found in the grammars of formal languages" (Plötz 11). This emergence of the field in directions linked to Harris's approach, and to Chomsky-inspired Transformational Generative Grammar (TGG) during the late 1950s and into the 1960s was a consequence, according to Koerner, of the funding of university programs during that period, facilitated in part by the passage of the National Defense Education Act in 1958 (Mildenberger 1962; Newmeyer and Edmonds 1971). Cold War institutions invested heavily in linguistics research because many people believed that it could yield important results.

I maintain that government subsidization of research and education, regardless of how benevolently and fairly it is administered, increases the likelihood of scientific revolutions for the worse, since it makes it possible for a subcommunity to increase its membership drastically without demonstrating that its intellectual credit so warrants. The kind of development that I have in mind is illustrated by the rapid growth of American universities during the late 1950s and 1960s, stimulated by massive spending by the federal government. This spending made it possible for many universities to start linguistics programs that otherwise would not have been started or would not have been started so early, or to expand existing programs much further than they would otherwise have been expanded. Given the situation of the early 1960s, it was inevitable that a large proportion of the new teaching jobs in linguistics would go to transformational grammarians. In the case of new programs, since at that time transformational grammar was the kind of linguistics in which it was most obvious that new and interesting things were going on, many administrators would prefer to get a transformational grammarian to organize the new program; in the case of expansion of existing programs, even when those who had charge of the new funds would not speculate their personal intellectual capital on the new theory, it was to their advantage to speculate their newfound monetary capital on it, since if the new theory was going to become influential, a department would have to offer instruction in it if the department was to attract students in numbers that were in keeping with its newfound riches. And with the first couple of bunches of students turned out by the holders of these new jobs, the membership of the transformational subcommunity swelled greatly. (McCawley 1976b, 25)

To help understand such developments it is interesting to consider how Chomsky replied when asked by the linguist Konrad Koerner about linguistics funding and the relationship between the U.S. military complex and linguistics research. "Ever since the Second World War, the Defense Department has been the main channel for the support of the universities, because Congress and society as a whole have been unwilling to provide adequate public funds [...]. Luckily, Congress doesn't look too closely at the Defense Department budget, and the Defense Department, which is a vast and complex organization, doesn't look closely at the projects it supports—its right hand doesn't know what its left hand is doing."[12] The effect of this funding, particularly from the military side, was to bolster language studies throughout the US, with a strong measure directed toward the type of work that Harris was doing.

In 1956, Harris began a pilot study, financed by the National Science Foundation, to develop the possibility of developing transformations, and in 1957 he received funding to establish the Transformations and Discourse Analysis Project as well as a further $20,000 from the Air Force Psychological Research Division to add to a project that was already underway. This latter project gained some importance as Harris tried to examine the structure of discourse by using features of linguistic analysis for discourse analysis. This funding was the inception of the federally funded Transformations and Discourse Analysis Project, which he developed in tandem with ongoing applications of linguistic work, such as machine translation and automated information retrieval. Discourse analysis is a cross-disciplinary field of research that, like conventional philology or rhetoric, establishes discourse as a specific body of knowledge. Unlike traditional studies of discourse, however, discourse analysis does not favor studies in literature, philosophy or history (the traditional "high-culture" disciplines), but rather it employs methods developed in areas such as content analysis, English and American discourse analysis, French *analyse du discours,* narratology, textual semiotics, *Ideologiekritik,* and social discourse to permit (if not favor) studies of all manifestations of discourse in everyday life.

The earliest work in discourse analysis can be traced back to Harris, in 1939, and the first published work appeared in the beginning of the 1950s, including Harris and Voegelin's work on the Hidatsa material. In his pioneering study *Discourse Analysis Reprints,*[13] Harris described "a method of seeking in any connected discrete linear material, whether language or language-like, which contains more than one elementary sentence, some global structure characterizing the whole discourse (the linear material), or large sections of it" (7). Irene Markaryk summarized the project in an encyclopedia that surveys a host of approaches to language theory: "Harris was interested in the ways in which *segments of discourse* (utterances, sentences, parts of sentences, words, parts of words) recur within a whole constituent or a sequence of constituents, and as such he concentrated upon the structure in discourse which can be studied without reference to other information, such as the pattern or relations of meanings in the discourse."[14] Thus, according to Harris, "discourse analysis finds the recurrence relative to each other of classes of morpheme sequences, given a segmentation into morpheme sequences by a suitable grammar, and having the intention that the classes set up are such that their regularity of occurrence will correspond to some relevant semantic interpretation for the discourse" (*Discourse Analysis Reprints* 7).

An earlier paper called "Discourse Analysis," published in *Language*[15] provides Harris's overview of the method, notably the fact that it deals with two types of related problems. "The first is the problem of continuing descriptive linguistics beyond the limits of a single sentence at a time" and the second is "the problem of correlating 'culture' and language (i.e. nonlinguistic and linguistic behavior)" (1). Both of these concerns persist in discourse analysis work, and there is much confusion among students in trying to work out the relations among these different discourse analysis projects from one discipline to another, for good reason. As Henry Hoenigswald pointed out to me, there are significant differences between literary structuralism or literary discourse analysis and that which was promoted by Harris. Says Hoenigswald, "the late Jakobson, on the other hand, would fall for every mistaken analogy. Individuals working in a mathematics-oriented intellectual world [i.e., Zellig Harris's linguistics] don't have this particular problem (though they do have other problems)" (personal correspondence, November 10, 1997).

Some of the Discourse Analysis Project's findings were published by Penn in the Transformation and Discourse Analysis Papers series, and the overall project, to which a range of researchers contributed, is described by Plötz as having an organization akin to the organization of society which Harris would come to advocate in his book, *Transformation of Capitalist Society*. "In order to avoid the impression of a strictly organized research organization, it should be mentioned that a number of researchers from various universities and countries worked on this project at various times (among them Irena Bellert, Maurice Gross, Jerold Katz, Zeno Vendler) and that their participation amounted to a loose association rather than a strict membership, characterized by the possibility to become acquainted with the linguistic work at the University of Pennsylvania and to follow, within this frame or deviating from it, one's individual interests and questions" (11). This "loose association" permitted, according to Plötz, a certain range of perspectives and approaches, appropriate to the many complex issues in question. Consistent with his views of society, and in line with the kind of organization we saw in Avukah, Harris oversaw but did not dictate modalities of research.

Harris did not create a school or admit disciples; instead he was tolerant toward work done outside his framework. This fact is directly mirrored in the linguistic work that came out of the University of Pennsylvania: it is not reducible to, and determined by, a single position; there are always deviances and divergences from the particular stand of Harris (e.g. the development of the decomposition procedure by Aravind K. Joshi and Danuta Hiz), there are directions becoming independent (e.g. the string project headed by Naomi Sager), and there are loose associations (e.g. the periphrastic analysis of Henry Hiz or the philosophically oriented investigations by Beverly Robbins and Zeno Vendler).[16]

The first number in the TDAP series was a reprint of the 1957 "Co-occurrence and Transformation" paper in *Language*. What followed included a 1959 paper on investigations of machine analysis of language ("Computable Syntactic Analysis"), and the development of a program for the grammatical analysis of sentences, which, according to Plötz, successfully analyzed a newspaper article on Univac I, also in 1959, making it "the first functioning computer program for language analysis" (13).[17] Work into the 1960s was directed toward trying to analyze more complex sentences, to work out parts of the English grammar, and to describe transformations that led to a more and more mathematical characterization of language among this group. Of fundamental importance here, according to Plötz, "was the concept of elementary transformation and an investigation of other languages with respect to their elementary transformations was started." The various subdivisions of Harris's project pursued different but related work: Henry Hiz investigated problems like paraphrase, disambiguation, and reference, James Munz studied chemical notations with linguistic analysis, and Naomi Sager worked on mechanical string analysis.

During this period we see as well precursors to Harris's interest in rendering systematic scientific knowledge by looking for methods of comparing and compiling scientific data from reports. In a letter dated December 14, 1960, to Dr. Arnold B. Grobman, the director of the American Institute of Biological Sciences, Harris explained his interest in Grobman's Curriculum Study research: "In the analyses of scientific writing [for the NSF], we are interested in working with the courses and materials prepared by the BSCS [Biological Sciences Curriculum Study]. We wish to use this in order to compare the structure of writing in such presentations with the structure of scientific reports." For his interest in relating linguistics to medicine, we also find him following work on discourse analysis of mental illness, sponsored by the U.S. military. In a September 29, 1961, letter to Dr. Agnes M. Niyekawa, he mentions Dr. Herbert Rubinstein's work on discourse analysis of the discourse of schizoid patients for the Operations Applications Laboratory, Air Force Cambridge Research Center, Air Research and Development Command. This development in Harris's work can be traced through the 1960s, as we can see from his faculty activities reports that note that in 1961 he supervised Anatol W. Holt's thesis "Methods of Language Computation," pursued research into mathematical operations in linguistics, lectured at the Courant Institute of Mathematical Sciences (NYU), and corresponded with the Minnesota School of Mathematics Center to pursue new work in mathematics teaching. In 1962, he supervised A. W. Holt's doctoral thesis on linguistic programming and researched linguistic transformations for the NSF. In 1963, he researched Transformations, Discourse Analysis and Chemical Notations for the NSF. The legacy of this work, described and recorded by (among others) Bruce Nevin, can be seen still today with insights from Harris applied to computerized management and presentation of information in scientific reports, interest in automated abstracting and in information retrieval, and in applications of information formatting and automatic text generation derived from Harris.

On February 13, 1962, John W. Tukey, the Associate Executive Director, Research, for the Communications Principles Division of Bell Telephone Laboratories, sent a most interesting letter to Harris, which I'll cite in full.

As I told you briefly on the telephone some time ago, we now have someone, namely Dr. Manacher, working full time in the area that might *broadly* be described [as] structural linguistics. Together with Jon Pierce, who is Executive Director, Research–Communications Principles, and one or two other interested people, Manacher has visited both Oettinger's group at Harvard and Yngve's group at MIT. I write to inquire whether there is any chance of our visiting your group at sometime when this would not be too much inconvenience to you. I would hope that if this were arranged, it could be done on a day when I could come also. Please do not hesitate to be frank about the difficulties of a visit from your point of view. We understand the need for getting on with the work and look forward to trying to be of help to you if we can when we come.

Harris replied three days later, with another key indication of the way that he saw his work and its overall relation to the ambitions of the field at that time.

I must confess that in general we avoid individual discussion with research groups, because we receive more requests of this kind than we can possibly handle. However, I would not want to refuse a request from you. In addition it is possible that some form of cooperation might be some day possible and desirable between your group and our Department or some of our graduates. I would therefore suggest that some day be chosen in late March or in April when you could speak with the people who are working here. The people most relevant to you are those who are currently making a computer program for transformational analysis of English sentences: Aravind Joshi, Naomi Sager and Anatol W. Holt. I suggest that in fixing the date that you write to one of them, perhaps to Dr. Joshi at the Linguistics Department.

Bell Telephone had been part of the linguistics program at Penn since 1948 when Leigh Lisker wrote a dissertation involving the use of the then revolutionary new instrument developed at the Bell Telephone Laboratories, the "sound spectrograph." In Henry Hiz's "Linguistics at the University of Pennsylvania" document, we learn that "the Department at Pennsylvania was among the first to acquire such an instrument once it became commercially available, and with its acquisition, instruction in the area of acoustic phonetics became a regular part of the linguistics curriculum." A broad-ranging assessment of these developments is offered by Chomsky in his 1968 book *Language and Mind*,[18] an overview from his perspective of where the field was going at that time.

In the United States at least, there is little trace today of the illusions of the early postwar years. If we consider the current status of structural linguistic methodology, stimulus-response psycholinguistics (whether or not extended to "mediation theory"), or probabilistic or automata-theoretic models for language use, we find that in each case a parallel development has taken place: A careful analysis has shown that insofar as the system of concepts and principles that was advanced can be made precise, it can be demonstrated to be inadequate in a fundamental way. The kinds of structures that are realizable in terms of these theories are simply not those that must be postulated to underlie the use of language, if empirical conditions of adequacy are to be satisfied. What is more, the character of the failure and inadequacy is such as to give little reason to believe that these approaches are on the right track. That is, in each case it has been argued—quite persuasively in my opinion—that the approach is not only inadequate but misguided in basic and important ways. It has, I believe, become quite clear that if we are ever to understand how language is used or acquired, then we must abstract for separate and independent study a cognitive system, a system of knowledge and belief, that develops in early childhood and that interacts with many other factors to determine the kinds of behavior that we observe; to introduce a technical term, we must isolate and study the system of *linguistic competence* that underlies behavior but that is not realized in any direct or simple way in behavior. And this system of linguistic competence is qualitatively different from anything that can be described in terms of the taxonomic methods of structural linguistics, the concepts of S-R psychology, or the notions developed within the mathematical theory of communication or the theory of simple automata. The theories and models that were developed to describe simple and immediately given phenomena cannot incorporate the real system of linguistic competence; "extrapolation" for simple descriptions cannot approach the reality of linguistic competence; mental structures are not simply "more of the same" but are qualitatively different from the complex networks and structures that can be developed by elaboration of the concepts that seemed so promising to many scientists just a few years ago. What is involved is not a matter of degree of complexity but rather a quality of complexity. Correspondingly, there is no reason to expect that the available technology can provide significant insight or understanding or useful achievements; it has noticeably failed to do so, and, in fact, an appreciable investment of time, energy, and money in the use of computers for linguistic research— appreciable by the standards of a small field like linguistics—has not provided any significant advance in our understanding of the use or nature of language. These judgments are harsh, but I think they are defensible. They are, furthermore, hardly debated by active linguistic or psycholinguistic researchers. (4–5)

The distinctions between Harris's ambitions and Chomsky's approach are herein made explicit, particularly in this focus upon "competence" as the task deserving of attention. This work on the system of knowledge and belief, referred to variously as a mentalist approach, is in sharp contrast to the study of output, upon which in Chomsky's view so much of Harris's work focuses.[19] Whatever concordances do exist between Harris's early work and Chomsky's projects, a number of assessments do dispute Chomsky's harsh characterization of Harris's approach. Harris was arguably the foremost structural linguist of his generation because, as N. R. Cattell wrote in his otherwise rather critical 1962 review, "The Syntactic Procedures of Zellig Harris," "No one else has provided such a complete and unified methodology, and few have analytic ability to match his."[20] And László Antal, in his 1963 review of *String Analysis of Sentence Structure*,[21] goes so far as to suggest that his *Methods* is "a kind of Bible on the whole subject" (97), and that "Harris can be compared to a chemist who discovered in nature an element, the existence of which was already long suspected" (104).

Murray Fowler, in his review of Zellig Harris's *String Analysis of Sentence Structure*,[22] points to the problem that took on growing importance as linguists considered the relationship between natural and artificial languages: "Most important of all for the task of transfer is the contrast between the closed and open systems of artificial and natural languages: by design, a language prepared for use by a computer is in a finite state or in a succession of finite states; all natural languages are open-ended and infinitely expandable in other than a linear dimension by self-contained, self-perpetuating devices, such as methods and rules for derivation and for compounding" (245). Harris has various notes in his texts during this period and elsewhere concerning the fact that a finite state recognizer will necessarily make mistakes or leave certain types of items unrecognized;[23] nevertheless, says Fowler, string analysis is "almost infinitely more rigorous and more objective" than transformational analysis, whatever its "insoluble" problems.

Robert B. Lees notes in his own review of the string analysis text that this work is "a detailed description of the research and results of the NSF project which Harris has conducted for several years now to develop an automatic English-sentence-analyzing program for a general-purpose digital computer."[24] However, even "if he and his colleagues do succeed in showing that for a certain computer application string-analysis excels, it will still not follow, despite an eager desire in some quarters for it to be the case, that either an IC-analysis or a string-analysis of sentences will meet widely accepted standards of adequacy for grammatical description" (415); for this reason, "string analysis is not a feasible alternative to the most sophisticated kind of syntactic description now available to our field of study."[25] In his introduction to the second volume of *The Legacy of Zellig Harris*, Stephen Johnson offers a more positive assessment of "the impact of Zellig Harris on the study of language pertaining to formal systems, computability, and computer applications," beginning with string theory: "The effect of Harris's work in these fields stretches back almost 45 years, to 1957, when the first computer program to perform syntactic analysis of

English sentences was developed on a UNIVAC computer" (ix). A description of string grammars, and their continued value, appears in Sager and Nhàn[26] and, moreover, in Joshi.[27] beginning with the description, elaborated with examples, that "a string grammar is a grammatical formalization of the grammar implicit in Uniparse. A string grammar consists of a finite set of elementary strings of terminal symbols and possibly the nonterminal S. A subset of these elementary strings is called center strings" (129). There is an important relationship between string grammar and transformations, such that a transformational grammar can be developed from a string grammar by refining its subclasses, as Sager and her colleagues suggest. Joshi describes how much hierarchy is needed for grammatical description, which helps explain the importance of Harris's insight.

There is an advance in generality as one proceeds through the successive stages of analysis. This does not mean increasingly abstract constructs; generality is not the same thing as abstraction. Rather, it means that the relation of a sentence to its parts is stated, for all sentences, in terms of fewer classes of parts and necessarily at the same time fewer ways ("rules") of combining the parts, i.e. fewer constraints on free combinability (roughly, on randomness). But at all stages the analysis of a sentence is in terms of its relation to its parts—words and word sequences—without intervening constructs.[28]

Harris's book *Discourse Analysis Reprint* received substantial attention, and it has influenced the more sociological or literary theory–inspired analyses of, say Edmond Cros or Teun Van Dijk. It was based upon four papers, reissued from the *Transformation and Discourse Analysis Papers*, mimeographed at the Linguistics Department of Penn and dating back to 1957. An early review of the book was published in *Lingua* by Fred C. C. Peng who worked at the Bunker-Ramo Corporation of Canoga Park, California, a computer company with a history of work on electronics research.[29] The link between linguistics concerns and the military industrial complex demonstrates, once again, the optimism placed in Harris's research in this field. The review begins with the interesting remark that "the use of transformations in Harris' sense differs significantly from that in Chomsky's sense" in, for example, the fact that "while Harris allows for reversible transformations there is no reversible transformation in Chomsky's sense" (326). Peng's tone is quite negative, and he finds "numerous errors" in Harris's work, but this is deemed less consequential because the papers "no longer represent the current state of work in discourse analysis" (4). His less than glowing conclusion is that he "has not enjoyed the book" on account of the many errors, but that it is, nevertheless, "not without value" (330). Regrettably, Peng's specific interest in the work, and its relation to whatever it was he was doing at Bunker-Ramo, is not described in this review.

G. Hell, in *Acta Linguistica,* insists upon the nature of the Harris project, that is, to discover "whether a discourse has a structure or not," and does end with some discussion of the implications of this work for computer applications.[30] From Hell's perspective, to discover if a language structure could be uncovered, and to find ways of applying its implications, Harris builds a system "on the recurring characteristics [morpheme relations] of certain segments and ignores the intrinsic relation asserted in the entire discourse" (233). In an overview of the technique, Hell writes: "These discourse segments must be related to the grammatical analysis of the sentences for they are either identical with one of the grammatical constituents of the sentence or with a series of constituents. Naturally these segments do not recur in a discourse so frequently as to provide a characteristic structure, therefore we form such classes of them whose regular recurrence results in a clear structure. The main goal of discourse analysis is precisely to formulate these characteristic classes or to find a universally valid process for this" (233–234). Hell concludes that the structures Harris uncovers are often of a logical rather than grammatical nature, which is notable because it means that the relations are not formal and, therefore, "are impossible to use in computers." Nevertheless, "discourse analysis deserves to be taken note of in this field of research more seriously as it has been until now" (235).

A similar point is made by Tae-Yong Pak in his in-depth 1970 review in which he complains that Harris's "stringent method, using nothing but distributional data, turns out unusable upon closer examination" because "there is no mechanical procedure for obtaining an optimal transformation without an indiscriminate dismemberment of the text."[31] Indeed, "no explicit criterion is suggested for the procedure of selection," so "one can conclude that there is none other than semantic intuition arising from the reader's understanding of the text," and it's "a specious quantification of an essentially intuitive, 'qualitative procedure'" (759). These critiques have been made not only in linguistics but also in literary theory, where structuralist theorists such as Algirdas Julien Greimas, Julia Kristeva, and Tzvetan Todorov had hoped to systematize their reading of literature. One of the salient overlaps here noted by Jonathan Culler who, in his seminal analysis of structuralism,[32] assesses a range of structuralist projects including the work of Greimas. Culler carefully works through the selection procedure of the smallest meaning-bearing units in a literary text, called sèmes, and then talks about how they are organized into lexemes (words), which can then be classified into classèmes on the basis of shared sèmes. This rigorous process ultimately leads the reader to a series of isotopies (themes) which group together the units, from the smallest to the largest, and indicate the broad meanings present in the text. Culler points out in ways similar to Pak that at the end of the day, readers' intuitions and subjective judgments are critical to the analysis, pointing, here again, to the role of what Pak has called the "intuitive, 'qualitative procedure'." There are of course crucial differences between Greimas's and Harris's respective approaches, but some of the observations and critiques of structuralism do apply across disciplines.

In 1965, Harris published his second paper on transformations, which in the linguist Peter Matthews' view, marked an important turning point, "The paper in 1965 was also, sadly, his last contribution to *Language*. I have not thought it my business to inquire into the circumstances; but from then on, for whatever reason, a journal for which he had written so much for a quarter of a century, and so much of such influence and importance, published him no more."[33] This is a point of interest upon which a number of informants speculated in discussions with me; Richard Kittredge notes, for example, that

I'm unaware if Zellig submitted any ms to *Language* after 1964, which is the year I came to Penn for grad study. I used to run the mimeograph machine for a couple of years, for TDAP papers, so I did have some opportunity to hear about potential material during 1964–66. Mostly I remember that a number of MIT-aware visitors who gave talks during 64–66 and 67–69 (I was abroad on a Fulbright in 66–67) were puzzled by what they had heard of Zellig's work, and he was rarely at talks to engage the visitors. That may have been different for the longer-term important visitors like Zeno Vendler, who must have had ample opportunity to interact with him—the students certainly absorbed Vendler's work. We grad students were a bit uneasy about the lack of engagement in theoretical debates, although Henry Hiz did encourage us to read Chomsky through 1965, and had some comments of his own. Still, when I went to U Chicago for a job interview in spring 1969, I was very poorly prepared to discuss my work and Zellig's in terms and frame of reference that were attractive to the audience, which included Jim McCawley.

However insular his work was in an American context, it is remarkable how many of Harris's later writings were to appear in Europe, with the Éditions du Seuil, in the *Journal of Linguistics*, or with the Clarendon Press, and not, as hitherto almost exclusively, in America. I can speculate here that it was on the basis of European interest in structuralism and more formal approaches to language studies that this shift occurred. Researchers working in Harris's paradigm, and many who weren't but who wanted the kind of credibility offered by science, would find in his work a sophistication, rigor, and also an antidote to elitism and authority that was, particularly in places like France, de rigueur in the 60s and 70s.

Harris's contributions to the field continued with his development of Operator Grammar, a comprehensive theory of language and information, and he worked on a detailed analysis of the sublanguage of immunology, including its vocabulary and grammar of information structures, and he even lectured at the International Congress of Mathematicians in Moscow in 1966. In 1966, Harris was working on *Linguistic Transformations and Chemical Notations* while supervising Carlota S. Smith's "Mutually Exclusive Transformations." And in 1967, he pursued his "Transformations and Discourse Analysis Project" for the NSF and, "in recognition of the distinguished contributions that [he] made in linguistics and in the training of graduate students in this area," the Provost of Penn accorded to him the position of University Professor of Linguistics. For Hoenigswald, the directions that Harris's work were taking remained exciting, and indeed, he told me in personal correspondence (August 7, 1997), that "in his later production he once again surprised everybody by turning in a completely unexplored theoretical direction, leaving a good many others behind, open-mouthed. What he never abandoned, though, was a severely formal approach—mathematicizing, but never exhausting itself in the 'application' of any particular ready-made mathematics."

Harris also developed "Objective and Subjective Components of Grammar" for a grant application (for the National Institute of Health, not funded). The first major product of this prolonged reflection was *Mathematical Structure of Language*, a "landmark in the field of formalized linguistics" and a work "which appears in a context of discoveries that have entirely transformed linguistics in the past fifteen years" (380),[34] including, for example, Chomsky's approach, which Maurice Gross mentions.

Chomsky's approach focuses on certain essential features of language; some of these features have been studied from an abstract point of view, and they lead to structures that have deep mathematical and linguistic significance. The theoretical views that Harris develops in his book, although based on the same empirical material, are completely new, and the relationship with what is called mathematical structure in Chomsky's framework is quite indirect. In fact, Harris's approach has many facets. While Chomsky made one main hypothesis about language structure, namely, that it is describable by means of certain types of formal systems (in the sense of mathematical logic), Harris looks at various phenomena as being of distinct natures; as such, they require distinct treatments. Thus, for Harris, linguistic theory does not have to be unified for the time being" (381).

The implications of this for a mathematical approach to language are numerous, and it's interesting in light of this brief overview of Harris's work to consider this idea that different linguistic phenomena require distinct approaches. On the one hand, mathematicians "will not find axiomatized theories with proved theorems, or even precise definitions that promise immediate new results;" nevertheless, "they will be given a general framework for mathematical studies that have linguistic significance."[35] So, in accordance with what many commentators were saying at this time, there is a mitigated success in that program in terms of rendering the scientific study of language. Indeed, Gross's view was that this book "is a sign that linguistics has become an autonomous scientific domain, with its own methods, where formal features have been extracted that already indicate many important directions of investigations, both empirical and theoretical" (389).

As we have seen, there was growing interest in Harris's work in France and other European countries during this period. Richard Kittredge noted in discussions with me that "it was clear that Maurice Gross had considerable prestige and influence through his lab and students describing French verbs (cf. *Méthodes en syntaxe*) and adjectives at Paris VII. Probably also, the initial generative grammar models fit the reality of French syntax less well than they did English (old problem of freer word order, clitics, etc.)." Harris's work was often mentioned by eminent French figures outside of linguistics as well, such as Roland Barthes, Gerard Genette, Algirdas Greimas, Julia Kristeva, and Tzvetan Todorov, who used his work as a starting point for their efforts to establish some kind of empirically valid approach to language research for the purpose, primarily, of literary analysis. The literary theorists were certainly aware of, and perhaps contributors to, the fact that Harris's work was reviewed systematically and generally warmly in France. Furthermore, in addition to his frequent travels to Israel, Harris was a lecturer as well at the Université de Paris VII and VIII from 1963 to 1966. Jean-Claude Chevalier, author of the hugely successful grammar book for French students *Grammaire Larousse du Français contemporain,* was inspired by Harris's *Methods* and attended Harris's Paris VII lectures, remembering his "great kindness" as well as the great clarity and simplicity of his talks. Yves Gentilhomme,[36] who clearly fell under Harris's linguistic spell finds, in his review of the French translation *Structures mathématiques du langage,*[37] that Harris's work is original for a range of reasons:

1. the desire to render each operation "calculable" and to not be satisfied by a simple objective description of language actions or of a conciliatory explanation.

2. the importance of the mass of facts relevant for the theory.

3. the account of the degree of acceptability of utterances, susceptible to continuous variations (and not just *all or nothing*, grammatical or a-grammatical).

4. the treatment of the metalanguage as an essential part which integrates the language.

5. and, moreover, the systematic utilization of transformations related to sentences and which end up as phrases (this last view sometimes eclipses the many other important contributions by this author).[38]

In short, Gentilhomme considers that this is a vastly important book, which has the "great merit of opening up new perspectives on properly linguistic work by inserting it into a solid theoretical grid" (53, my translation). Harris expanded his ties to France when, in 1974–1975, he taught a course at the Linguistics Department of the Université de Paris VIII Vincennes, the notes for which became the basis for *Notes du cours de syntaxe*[39] in which Harris offers a series of formal analyses based upon mathematics, the logic of distributional relations, the logic of set theory, and a systematic methodology. This, like previous texts from this period, attracted significant interest in France, where Jean-Pierre Descels,[40] Danielle Leeman,[41] and others explained and elaborated upon Harris's work for a French audience. French interest in Harris's work would culminate in September 1990 with the publication in the journal *Langages*, an issue on "Les grammaires de Harris et leurs questions," by Anne Daladier, Maurice Gross, André Lentin, and Thomas Ryckman.[42]

In 1992, the year of Harris's death, Catherine Fuchs and Pierre LeGoff published "Du Distributionnalisme au transformationnalisme: Harris et Gross."[43] This text is of special interest because Harris's aforementioned survey of his own oeuvre appears within it through a discussion of "The Background of Transformational and Metalanguage Analysis." Among many interesting passages, he notes that "the work began as an attempt to organize the analyses made in descriptive linguistics, and to specify and formulate its methods." The "background" for this work came, as we have seen, "from the foundations of mathematics and logic, and the analysis of formalisms," which "was relevant to language because in all of these systems there were sentences (propositions, formulas) with partially similar structure (syntax)." In the realm of linguistics, Harris situates his work with regards Saussure's phonemic analysis and the "'distributional' method" that "was followed by Franz Boas, and more explicitly by Edward Sapir and Leonard Bloomfield, analyzed likewise the occurrence and combination of grammatical elements in the particular environments of other elements"

(1). Tellingly in light of previous discussions, he then notes that "I think, and I am glad to think that the intellectual and personal influence of Sapir and of Bloomfield colors the whole of the work that is surveyed below. It seemed natural to formulate all the methods above in the spirit of the syntax of mathematics and logic noted here" (1–2). As for the objectives themselves, Harris notes, quite simply, that "this methodological program involved finding the maximum regularity in the occurrence of parts of utterances in respect to other parts. In its most general form it required the description of the departures from randomness in the combinations of elements, i.e. the constraints on freedom of occurrence of elements in respect to each other" (2), which as we saw earlier was already present in his own work in 1941. The rest of this article sets forth in quite accessible ways the projects Harris followed in his linguistic study, and it bears careful consideration for those with a special interest in understanding how Harris perceived his lifelong corpus (and for this reason I have made mention of it in several sections of this chapter).

In 1970 Harris published a volume of papers, written from 1940 onward, titled *Papers in Structural and Transformational* Linguistics. Although most of these papers had been published elsewhere over the years, there are some notable texts, including a paper on report and paraphrase and, moreover, "a Cycling Cancellation-Automation for Sentence Well-Formedness," which addresses Harris's efforts to use string analysis as a tool for computation work in linguistics. Ferenc Kiefer noted in his *Linguistics* review of the book[44] that Harris's work "has received wide acceptance among mathematical linguists, especially in Eastern Europe," where in fact the whole idea of structuralism came to be closely associated with him. David Cohen's (French) review[45] also spoke to the vast importance of Harris's work for the field, in America and in Europe, where its impact "cannot be overstated" (507). Harris's work is of seminal importance in part because many works in computational linguistics "are based on the principles set forth in Harris's work." Indeed, "immediate constituent analysis, once a common practice in American linguistics, has received a more precise and rigorous formulation in Harris's work. Quite a few concepts widely used in computational linguistics are also due to Harris (classification of morpheme inventory, syntactic categories, sentence types, etc.)" (61). Michael B. Kac's in-depth review of the same book[46] added further discussion of the importance of Harris's work on string analysis for machine computation, especially his work on "A Cycling-Cancellation Automaton for Sentence Well-Formedness" in which, according to Kac, "it uses an extension of string analysis to implement a procedure for computing the well-formedness of sentences on the basis of comparison only of pairs of adjacent—thus requiring a device with an immediate memory only one symbol long" (468).

Continuing his work in Europe, Harris lectured at Oxford University in 1977, the year he began inquiries about a new research project on the theory of information. On June 5, 1977, he wrote to Edward C. Weiss, Program Director for the Information Science Program of the National Science Foundation, to propose his new project on the relationship between syntax and meaning. "Recently, I completed a theory of syntax in which it is seen that when the syntax of a sentence is analyzed in a particular way, the meaning of a sentence is obtained directly from its syntax." This correlation, in Harris's view, "has had important computer applications in the works of some of my former students especially in the science-information works of [blacked-out, but probably N. Sager] at NYU; also in the computer translation work of [blacked-out, but probably Richard Kittredge] at Montreal. It also underlies the medical-report computer program of [blacked-out, but possibly Irwin D. J. Bross] at Roswell Park, Buffalo" (these names may have been blacked out for reasons related to the adjudication process for an eventual grant). For Harris, the "theoretical work on syntax" was now complete, and it was now time to "explore its inherent application to an analysis of information." He proposed to do this by investigating "the nature of the syntax-semantics correlation," and then "to evaluate the semantics that this brings out" to determine: "How we can formally (syntactically) distinguish objective information from subjective attitude to the information; what are the distinctions or boundaries between whole-language meanings and subject-matter (sublanguage) information; etc." And finally, Harris proposed "to relate language-borne information to the meanings carried by other vehicles (mathematics, illustrations, gestures, etc.), and so to prepare ground for a general view of information, especially in science." The assumption he worked under for this project is that "just as previous theoretical work in syntax has paved the way for practical possibilities in computer processing of information and language, so the theoretical connections of syntax and information can lead to useful techniques." Edward Weiss replied with great enthusiasm on July 12, 1977, because he had "heard of" Harris's work and since the NSF was at that time "pursuing a line of research aimed at 'knowledge' or 'fact' delivery systems," and thus "the three stages" suggested in Zellig Harris's letter "seem appropriate to this line of research."

Shortly thereafter Harris sent in an abstract of "The Correlation of Language Structure with Information," which set out the parameters of the work he was pursuing at that time.

This project seeks to establish a computable structure for factual information, based on recent studies showing the structure of language to be essentially an informational structure. The intent is to establish classes of words having special informational character, and combinations of these which constitute assertions. The crucial point is that all definitions are to be precise and combinatorial, so that human judgment is not needed in the individual case, and so that a computer program could operate and even extend the system. The main methods required for such an investigation are known, and involve combinatorial analyses within the language-structure categories. The development of a systematization of factual information on the basis of a computable formulation of language structure should be of major service toward computer processing of the actual information contained in factual, and especially in scientific, material.

The research plan Harris proposed involved, first, "checking the informational character of a large body of members of every operator class . . . to see if a common informational property can be stated for the words in each class"; second, "investigating the informational properties of the words in the domain of each reduction"; and third, "search for special syntactic-semantic relations among the words of a domain." Time permitting, Harris also proposes a "large additional task" of finding the "contextual constraints on the reference of words," that is, discovering "what previous word is being referred to" in a text. The research proposal was sent to six reviewers, of whom three rated the project "excellent," two "very good," and one did not reply. Although there were some questions raised, concerning methodology and the availability of personnel for the tasks, the NSF looked favorably upon the proposal, and Weiss himself commented:

I agree with the reviewers that the research is timely and meritorious. The Principal Investigator is uniquely qualified to carry it out. The budget is modest in terms of the tasks to be performed. The research is of the most basic nature in information science but at the same time it has the potential for broad applications. Thus, it will contribute to the foundations of information science and its application to information systems can be of immediate value. The fact that this is the first venture by one of the most outstanding linguists of our time into the field of information science is in itself a recognition of the maturation of this emerging discipline. This is a most important and significant proposal which fully merits support.

The project was funded, with $18,540 requested for Harris, $92,933.28 for other personnel, $2,100 for computer services, and $56,727 for indirect costs; the final award was for $164,000 payable over two years, from 1978–1980, the exact amount that Harris requested.

In 1980, Zellig Harris retired from his long career at Penn, and was named Professor Emeritus as well as Senior Research Scientist at the Center for Social Sciences, Columbia University. This was a period of intense research activity, and in 1980 alone he applied to the National Science Foundation for two grants, for $74,989 and $115,471 (on "Information Correlates of Basic Language Structures"). Three years later he applied for another $197,269 ("Conjunction-Hierarchies in the Structure of Arguments"), in 1984 another $141,998 (to continue the 1983 project) and then, in 1985, $469,781 for a pilot study on "Informational Representation in Survey Structures." These later projects provide a sense of Zellig Harris's linguistic work from the perspective of what he thought to be useful and possible during this period, and the reviews thereof, both published and not, provide an (often contrasting) sense of what people in the field thought of his approach and his methods.

In his obituary for Harris, Matthews suggests that his 1981 collection marked Zellig Harris's "last phase":

The basic ideas of Harris's last phase became clear in the 1970s, in papers in English (1976a, 1978) and more fully in translation into French (1976b). In the collection published at the beginning of the next decade (1981), papers from our earlier periods are grouped in sections headed 'structural analysis' and 'transformational analysis'; those of this period under 'operator grammar'. But we are concerned in reality with two complementary insights. The first is that of the progressive simplification, or reduction, of sentence structures. Thus, to take an example whose point it is sadly easy to misunderstand, *The paper was written by Mary* stands in a crucial relation not to the former kernel structure *Mary wrote the paper*, but to an unreduced *The paper was in the state of the writing of the paper by Mary*. The second idea is indeed that, in the description of unreduced forms, a straightforward operator-argument structure will suffice.

In 1982, a book was published that Hiz referred to in his obituary of Harris as his capolavoro: *A Grammar of English on Mathematical Principles*. Says Hiz, "this comprehensive and subtle study of the syntax and weak semantics of English uses the report-paraphrase and operator-argument approach. At the same time it is the most detailed presentation of this theory. As always, Harris tries to write a grammar of the entire language, not of an aspect or fragment of it. Does he succeed? Of course, not quite. He was aware that the book fails to take into account that the indicators form what are called "paradigms"; also, that it does not sufficiently deal with intonation." Eric S. Wheeler (an employee at IBM Canada) described this work as "a novel version of (transformational) generative grammar" applied to English sentence structure.[47] Bruce Nevin disagrees, suggesting that: "Altogether, we have here an impressive analysis of the grammar of English as a whole, embodying a model of language and a paradigm for linguistics that is clear, explicit, and verifiable. Linguists of all persuasions would do well to study it carefully and on its own terms."[48]

Zellig Harris himself wrote that "the essential feature of the method of analysis presented" in this book "is that words and sentences can be characterized by a syntactically defined operator-argument relation, with different likelihoods for particular words as operators on particular arguments and with reductions in shape (in some cases to zero) for words that have high likelihood with respect to their operator or argument in a given sentence" (88). The approach is of little interest to Wheeler, however, who finds that it does not help with semantics issues, it cannot be considered mathematics, and "it comes late to the problem of syntax" (90–91). It is interesting to read this perspective on Harris's work because it is set up in contrast to that of his most famous student, Noam Chomsky:

As a vehicle for research into the structure of English (or language in general), I doubt it will ever supplant the Chomskyan paradigm. First, it covers largely the same ground—the generation of sentences; it does not talk about phonological patterns or the place of Japanese in the Ural-Altaic family or how to parse text. The large investment that scholars have made in researching sentence syntax in Chomsky's framework ensures that a replacement theory (as opposed to a supplementary one) will not be adopted unless there is a strong argument for it. There are no such arguments here. Harris does not compare his theory to those of others, makes no evaluation of its relative worth, and provides no motivation for preferring his theory at all. Were it the first generative syntax theory, these omissions would be understandable, but in the 1980s, they can only serve to isolate Harris's ideas more than their novelty does. (89)

This review is not peculiar in its views of Harris's work at this time; indeed, most commentators concentrate upon the degree to which this text recalls, rather than elaborates, upon theories from an earlier era. Frank Heny[49] finds that the book took him back "almost fifteen years," and "how far mainstream linguistic theory has come since then is made abundantly obvious by this book":

For Harris is still working in 1968. Not that he hasn't changed his theory. Like so many of us who were then operating with transformations in a different framework, he has virtually abandoned such rules. Only one remains—paradoxically, the rule of deletion, with some special cases like pronominalization (actually, this is a slight exaggeration, since he still allows a few marginal cases of permutation). Like many another grammarian today, too, he is explicitly working with an enriched categorical grammar. What dates this book is not the general framework Harris assumes but what he does with it (or doesn't): the analyses he proposes, the lack of systematic argumentation, the vagueness—but above all the goals he sets himself. (181)

After technical discussions of the failings of this work, Heny concludes on a rather mournful tone that this is an "extreme example" of how pontifical Harris's work is,

(and at the same time of how far he dissociates himself from all that is going on in linguistics today—which heaven knows he was largely responsible for) is the way in which despite the analyses cited throughout this review (and there are hundreds more) repeating or echoing analyses from the '60s, there is not one single reference to work done by anyone outside a tiny circle of his friends: Hiz, Hoenigswald, and less than half a dozen more. Pullum (1983) has recently drawn attention to the need for linguists, like all scientists, to keep in tune with the current scene. This book is a terrible warning of the dangers of not doing so. Whether Harris has read the literature he failed to cite is irrelevant. The point is, he hasn't learned from what came after him and the result, I fear, is years of virtually wasted effort and an unusable product at the end of it.

Reviews were not unanimously negative,[50] and, according to Bruce Nevin, this book would be of particular value "for those interested in the scientific study of language, and in particular by anyone working with computers to analyze or use natural language." The intrinsic interest Harris holds for computational linguistics stems chiefly from:

The simplicity and elegance of the mathematical model he proposes for language. Particularly attractive is its freedom from highly abstract hierarchies of grammatical objects and operations subject to change in the next gust of theoretical fashion.

The comprehensiveness of his grammar with respect to the semantic, syntactic, and morphological detail of natural language, as exemplified by English.

The use he makes of the observation that the metalanguage (the language in which the grammar is stated) must of necessity be contained in the object language being described. This is a principle reason his approach avoids building the hierarchies of grammatical and semantic mechanisms—and computational representations for them!—that many investigators have come to accept as necessary and even desirable. Of particular interest is his use of language itself to account for the indeterminately numerous and interminably complex issues of the context and use of language (pragmatics and all that).

His partitioning of semantics into "objective information" versus communicative and expressive nuance, relying only on formal linguistic criteria.

His notion of sublanguage; in particular, the sublanguage generated by his base, which is free of paraphrase yet informationally complete (albeit at the cost of being for most utterances "unspeakably" cumbersome in style).

His linking of "reductions" (approximately, transformations) to points of informational redundancy in discourse.

His identification of affixes and most prepositions as "argument indicators" and "operator indicators", and his exploitation of them as providing traces of derivation.

"Together, writes Nevin, "these characteristics suggest an approach to computational parsing and synthesis that could be both highly efficient and semantically sensitive. Beyond that, they indicate avenues for design of artificial languages and language-like systems that have yet to be tried."[51]

In spite of Nevin's positive review, however, there is recurring mention of the idea, in both the linguistic and the political arenas, that Zellig Harris was living in a previous moment in time. This trend continued, as did the negative perception thereof, with the publication of *A Theory of Language and Information*, in 1991, reviewed by Terence Langendoen in *Language*:[52]

Zellig Harris' linguistic career spanned seven decades, from the 1930s to the present one. For the last four however, he worked in virtual isolation, interacting almost exclusively with a few of his colleagues and former students at the University of Pennsylvania. In this, as in his other writings of this period, he cites only his own and their work, and that of a few eminent mathematicians and philosophers. On the whole, the favor has been returned. There are almost no citations of H's work in the mainstream linguistics literature, apart from references to his contributions to the founding of generative grammar. (585)

As becomes typical of reviews of Harris's work in this period, there are statements such as "H's reductions, and the sources on which they operate, will strike most contemporary practitioners of generative grammar as unprincipled and ad hoc," or "the concluding paragraph of section 10. . . . says something so outrageous that I am compelled to quote it in its entirety." He then quotes Harris: "Finally, it seems that the sign language of the deaf does not have an explicit operator-argument partial ordering, nor an internal metalanguage, but rests upon a direct juxtaposition of the relevant referents. This applies to autonomous sign languages, developed by the deaf without instruction from people who know spoken language." It would be valuable to discuss how Harris's work may be misrepresented here, particularly in light of Harris's statement that areas of investigation that remain to be undertaken should include "How does the operator-argument structure compare with the old deaf sign-language, which was not based on knowledge of spoken language?"[53] It is not my objective to adjudicate in these technical matters, however, so I leave it to those in the field, but a sense of what is being written in the professional journals, in particular the highly respected journal of the Linguistic Society of America, gives a sense of how Harris's work was portrayed and received.

At the end of it all, though, Langendoen does conclude with the statement that "there is much of interest in this book in addition to the development of a particular theory of linguistic form, including the analysis of sublanguages and the relation of natural language to mathematics and to music" (588). Despite these strong words, there was still significant interest in Zellig Harris's paradigm, and subsequent to his departure from Penn, Zellig Harris continued his research, but now with Columbia University. On April 12, 1983, he received $197,269 to support a two- year research project (with projected further funding of $141,998), to be undertaken at the Center for the Social Sciences and titled "Conjunction-Hierarchies in the Structure of Arguments (Information Science)." New York was another milieu, however, and although he certainly kept in contact with his long-time colleagues at Penn, there are a few people upon whom the limelight now falls more brightly.

Paul Mattick Jr. and Columbia University

Paul Mattick Jr., through his father and through his own work, serves as an interesting connection to various strands of Zellig Harris's world, in terms of political, linguistic, and personal interests. He was also a link between Zellig Harris and other figures who came to play crucial roles in Harris's work, including Naomi Sager, of NYU, with whom Harris had close working ties since 1948 and personal ties previously. In a June 12, 1985, letter to Dr. Murray Aborn, of the NSF, Sager notes that she had been in touch with Mattick regarding "a subcontract to the Linguistic String Project group of the Courant Institute for computer work on a Columbia University research project, 'Informational Structure of Survey Questionnaires,'" which was prepared by Zellig Harris, at that time a Special Research Scholar at the Center for the Social Sciences. This proposal was submitted by the Columbia University Projects Officer to the NSF on July 24, 1985, with the hope of securing $469,781 for twelve months. A review of the application, and of the assessments thereof, provide a view of Zellig Harris's late linguistic work and the reception of his ideas by individuals working in a whole range of related fields. Paul Mattick Jr., whose father had been a friend of Harris and who had been very engaged in thinking about the transformation of capitalist society (in favor of an anti-Bolshevik Marxist approach), also has knowledge of social movements. He has been a professor of philosophy at Bennington College, a Fellow of the Institute for the Humanities at New York University, and, more recently, a Professor of Philosophy at Adelphi University in New York. He had been a research

assistant for the Transformations and Discourse Analysis Project at Penn
from 1961 to 1967, had worked as a tutor at Harvard (1966–1968), an
instructor at the New England Conservatory of Music (1969–1972), project
faculty at the Goddard-Cambridge Graduate School (1972–1973), Instructor at Suffolk University and the University of Massachusetts (1979–1981),
and he worked in 1984–1985 on the "Fact Formulas and Discussion Structures in Related Subsciences" at Columbia. This research[54] provided a
foundation for his 1989 work on the structure of information in science,
and is described in the NSF awards as follows:

The purpose of this research is to develop a method for reducing the information
contained in a scientific article including data presentations, discussions, and conclusions to a system of formulas adequate to describe the information for any given
subscience. This system of formulas can be regarded as a "grammar" or informational structure of a subscience. This work is possible because methods now exist
for studying the word-combinations in scientific writing, which carry almost all the
information in science. This permits the discovery of fact-structures, argument
structures, and the relation of facts to arguments and the like. These methods are
not semantic. Because they are based on observed word-combinations they are
objective, testable by others, applicable in the real world, and eventually amenable
to computer processing. The reduction of the information to formulas has many
advantages for computerized information storage, manipulation, and retrieval
besides the obvious one of reduced storage space. It will permit the manipulation
of the information in order to retrieve facts, inferences, and hypotheses not previously possible. The significance of this work lies in its ability to provide a basis for
the computer processing of the specific information in scientific reports. The
research team including Zellig Harris have made numerous and important contributions to the field and the environment at Columbia provides a supportive setting
for such research.

Harris was also on Naomi Sager's "Linguistic String Project" at NYU in
1985, which was funded (in the name of Zellig Harris and Paul Mattick Jr.)
by the NSF for the period 1983–1986 in the amount of $557,504. Naomi
Sager's participation in Zellig Harris's new project is very important in
terms of eventual computer applications since she had worked on a range
of computer and mathematics-related projects at the Sloan-Kettering Institute for Cancer Research, the Computer Center at Penn, and the Courant
Institute of Mathematical Sciences (NYU). Arnold Simmel, a consultant at
the Office of Educational Assessment of the New York City Board of Education was also a member of the team, as was Tzvi Harris, Zellig's brother.

According to the technical abstract, the "first objective of this research
is an identification of the informational elements of which social science
survey instruments—to begin with, surveys dealing with income and

economic well being—are constructed." Harris suggests that his methods "which make possible the condensation of survey items into an informational schema, will allow us to address such issues as the description of the information requested or carried by particular instruments, the utility of particular survey material for secondary analysis, and how the collection and manipulation of survey data can be improved and made more efficient." This was based upon Harris's whole research approach, thus extending his efforts to study "the patterns of word-combination in scientific writing," under the assumption that they "carry the information of those fields." In the end, "this research should establish ways for controlling what information surveys are trying to collect." In addition, "the information structure analyzed by it can function as a database structure suitable for the construction of a computerized social-science survey database" which "should be of interest not only to social scientists but to database designers and information scientists generally." Through this work, Harris was combining his life-long interests in science and language with an objective on the part of the Social Science Center and the NSF's public objective of designing measurement methods and data improvement. It also responds to contemporary needs, and emerging technological tools, to bring about "a clearer understanding of the fundamental nature of the immense masses of social data which, as society moves deeper into the 'Information Age,' are destined to be increasingly used for both scientific and nonscientific purposes, and whose usage, owing to advancing technology, is apt to become increasingly remote from both generating sources and the intentions, designs, and techniques of the generators." There is a link in this effort to other initiatives of that period, including an NRC Committee on National Statistics report illustrating "how recent advances in cognitive psychology can contribute importantly to a major objective of the initiative, namely the survey-taking process, and which urges the start of a program of collaborative research involving cognitive psychologists, survey researchers, and other investigators associated with the field of cognitive science." The link to Harris's own institution existed as well through efforts over the previous years "in using certain formal methods to extract, codify, and organize the information in scientific articles, within a single field." Harris's hope was that his group "could address the issues raised by the memorandum on the basis of the methods that we have developed and used in other scientific subfields, and that in the process we would test and extend our methods as well as bring precise methods to the service of judging survey information." The question of the relationship between the research objectives and the budget were of considerable concern to the committee, and one is led to wonder how the research team proposed to spend almost half a million dollars in twelve months doing linguistics research, a question answered through a quick glance at the budget, which requested $70,833 for Harris's salary, as well as unstated amounts for researchers, for a total of $192,312; there was also $10,000 for travel to Ann Arbor, $105,000 in other direct costs, and $89,700 for subcontracts with the Courant Institute, which was to provide computer processing of questions in the survey questionnaires and the processing of the material.

The assessment of the project is extremely interesting in terms of the direction that linguistics has taken since Harris began working on the scientific structuralist linguistic approach in the 1940s. An NSF document suggests, under the rubric "weaknesses," that reviewers can find "no hard evidence or critical independent appraisal of success in the text of the proposal," and no "real discussion of standards for judgment of success." Further, "the cost is way out of line for a NSF pilot study," "the proposal is not well written," "no one in the proposed research team appears to have any substantial experience with surveys," "there is no familiarity with relevant procedures of survey researchers," "there is no relevant treatment of empirical research on relations among related items," and, finally, the problem that "a machine can identify information content of questions," but "how will the work produce improvements in 'data collection and manipulation'?" Among the twenty-nine "proposal evaluations forms," there were many other criticisms, including "the funding is quite extreme," there is no way to consider the relationship between questions and answers, the method cannot distinguish between different ways of saying the same thing, it is not clear what the study could produce in the way of valuable insights, and it is not clear what "the effects of the previously presented medical literature informational structure analysis on either the medical literature researcher and or the professional," it is not clear why focus is upon questions rather than responses, and relevant literature has not been considered. In the second evaluation, the reviewer adds that "it seems doubtful that even given the successful application of the method to the field of income and economic well-being survey questions that it would affect practice in the field or interface with the theoretical questions being asked in the traditional research," and, interestingly, "ideas about automated content analysis and machine aided language analysis have been around a long time and consumed a great number of research dollars," and even if this proposal is better than most, it "does not seem to warrant the enormous investment proposed." Another appraisal finds that the "informational structures" approach is "untried" and is not clearly computational, that the proposal shows "neglect of the literature concerning the design of survey questions" as well as that relating to "organizing survey question data," and that the cost of the proposal is "prohibitive." The next review finds that Zellig Harris's work has, of late, fallen outside of refereed journals and the field as a whole, suggesting that he no longer has "normal reaction" to the field. Further, the rest of the team has no publications in "relevant areas," and "Harris's proposed research is isolated, totally unrelated to other work."

Among those who were more favorable to the project (rating it "very good"), there was nonetheless the sentiment that "even if the project seems weak," the quality of the researchers "is strong enough to justify funding," but at a considerably lower level. There is hope among this group of reviewers that the work could indeed be applied beyond the literature to be studied in this project, and could serve as an example of what could be considered "basic research" in this field. Finally, among the four reviewers who rated it "excellent," there was one reviewer who noted that this "bold attempt to examine and categorize the information elements of which surveys are constructed . . . will affect the ways survey instruments are drawn up and analyzed," and "it will make possible to set up computerized databases of social science survey instruments." Another reviewer notes that "the development and use of computers as well as new applications in computer science depend essentially on the success of formal linguistic analysis." The third finds that this formidable group of researchers "hold out the promise of a solution to the problem of determining what might be called the informational primitives of social science survey instruments." And, finally, the proposed research will "extend some existing methods of extracting information in scientific reports to represent the information in survey questions" which "are based on the theories of language structure that have been developed by Professor Harris over a long period of time," which assures a high level of success. So in the end, of the twenty-nine reviewers, from psychology, sociology, linguistics, economics, mathematics, engineering, life sciences, social sciences, and computer sciences, there were thirteen replies ranging from excellent to fair, with considerable reticence about the proposed project. In the "review analysis," reservations were tabulated and found to center on the fact that "textual data employed in social science research . . . are not analogous to the narrow subspecialty of immunology, wherein the proposed methodology was perfected." For this reason, "a basic assumption of the proposal, namely, that classificatory schemes which are combinatorial rather than semantic in character can be importantly employed in uncovering the informational structures in survey questionnaires, must remain in doubt seated relations between singular elements (linguistic and beyond). That same year Zellig Harris also published a small book and, in 1991, an extensive one, which are in Hiz's words from his obituary,[56] "reflections on the variety of approaches he had been taking toward language."

These books are written in a clear, simple manner, almost without formulas. They must be read with the previous writings in hand, and our understanding of the previous writings should be enriched by these two books. Here the problem of meaning looms large. On the one hand Bloomfieldian social meaning is intuitively known to everybody. On the other hand, the meaning of a word is defined by Harris as its redundancy on redundancy in the information theoretical sense. By this Harris means the limitations of the class of admissible sequences of the word's arguments and further the limitations of the operators that take this word as their argument in turn. These two books also contain Harris's views on the development of language. Some are speculations, while others are sharp observations like "discreteness and repeatability of the elements (which reduces error compounding in transmission), and the lack of grammatical devices for direct expression of feeling, suggests that language developed primarily in the transmission of information within a public, rather than for personal or interpersonal use."

The disparity between the reports of several reviewers and commentators is reasonably representative of the range of views regarding such work and, for Zellig Harris, the place they ascribed for him in the contemporary field of linguistics.

To conclude this section on the language work, I will return to Harris's own sense of this legacy, as described in the aforementioned article, "The Background of Transformational and Metalanguage Analysis," which describes "a record of the background and the steps of analysis that led to grammatical transformations and to the recognition of the metalanguage as being a part of natural language, with the ensuing development to an operator-argument theory of language" (1). This work "began as an attempt to organize the analyses made in descriptive linguistics, and to specify and formulate its method." The background, as we have seen, "came largely from the foundations of mathematics and logic, and the analysis of formalisms," with the key references being Brower, Russell, Post, Goodman, Godel, Tarsky, Lukasiewicz, Lesniewski and Quine. In linguistics, again consistent with what we have seen, Harris mentions Saussure, Boas, Sapir, and Bloomfield and, as he says, "I am glad to think . . . that the intellectual and personal influence of Sapir and Bloomfield colors the whole of the work that is surveyed below" (1).

This article is especially interesting as we reflect back upon Harris's accomplishment in language studies, because therein he sets out the successes and objectives of this work, moving through *Structural Linguistics*, and then on from morphology to syntax, and toward discourse analysis and his *Mathematical Structures of Language* (1968).

While the machinery for transformations was provided by the "Morpheme to Utterance" equivalences, the motivation for developing transformations as a separate grammatical system was furthered by the periphrastic variation in sentences that was found in discourses. In 1946, with the completion of *Methods in Structural Linguistics*, the structure of a sentence as restrictions on the combination of its component parts seemed to have gone as far as it could, with the sentence boundaries within an utterance being the bounds of almost all restrictions on word combination. I then tried to see if one could find restrictions of some different kind which would operate between the sentences of an utterance, constraining something in one sentence on the basis of something in another. It was found that while the grammatical structure of any one sentence in discourse was in general independent of its neighbors, the word choices were not. (2)

Harris then traces the evolution of this work, with regard to the Skolem normal form in logic, for instance, "which made me think of the possibility of a canonical form for sets of periphrastic sentences," and through the differences in approach between work on the analysis of sentences and their generation. From there he moves on to his motivation in studying the metalanguage of natural language, drawing attention to "its different status from that of the metalanguage of mathematics," and then develops the ways in which linguistics is different from other sciences, notably in that "it admits an alternative to theory: an orderly catalog of the relevant data, sufficient to do most of the work that a theory is supposed to do" (5). This subject is of great interest, and leads him to discuss the "unique status of language as a system," which includes the fact that any description of a language must occur within language itself. For this reason, "we cannot describe a language without knowing how our description can in turn be described," which suggests that we must find a "self-organizing description" to avoid "infinite regress" (10).

This work produced "a system of predicates (operators) first on primitive arguments and then recursively on predicates, with reduction of words which had high likelihood in the given operator-argument relation," which "created a partial order of words in each sentence, and in the language as a whole. It was constructive, not only in the partial order of entry of words into a sentence, but also in that the reductions took place in a word upon its entry, so that each sentence could be defined as a particular kind of semi-lattice of work-occurrences and reductions. All further events in forming a sentence are defined on resultants of the partial order construction" (12). This method allowed Harris to go "beyond transforma-tions" in two ways, by using "likelihood information about word-choice both in the first-level operators that create the elementary sentences and in the similarly working second-level operators that create from them the enlarged sentences" and, secondly, "the operator grammar gives a single system of word partial order for forming both elementary sentences and other sentences . . . with reduction in shape to form the remaining sen-tences" (7).

On the overall contribution Harris made to linguistics, and to the success of this later work, the verdict is certainly still out, as we have seen; but there remained the political arena in which Zellig Harris had been working, more or less hidden from public view, for all these years, and which demands examination in light of his last work. To this work we shall now turn.

III   The Politics

7   From Avukah to Zionism

Zellig Harris's involvement in politics began when he joined a small American student organization called Avukah, which had a defining impact upon his and many others' social, political, and Zionist work. His family was involved in Jewish cultural affairs, and, he emerged from an active and engaged social setting. For Harris's own politics, however, I will focus on Avukah, the organization within which he expressed and developed a political approach that remained with him, in an evolving form, throughout his life. I will also emphasize Avukah because it has been virtually forgotten from history, even the Zionist history for which it was so important. To help remedy this collective historical amnesia, I will cite from the many publications it produced, paying particular attention to the work that Harris undertook in association with Avukah and many of its members. I will complement these written sources with the insights from the many interviews I have conducted with old friends and associates of Harris in order to offer the reader a privileged look into his overall approach to the world, which resonated long after the demise of Avukah in 1943.[1]

Assessing the work of Avukah brings us to four major political issues that would dominate Harris's political work: Arab-Jewish relations, the kibbutz movement in Palestine, Jewish immigration (to Palestine and the United States), and the problems of American Jewry. To understand the approach Harris took to each, it is important to recall some of the salient facts about Avukah itself.

Lighting Avukah's Torch

The story of Avukah began inauspiciously in 1925 at Harvard University, where a couple of students decided that a new Jewish student organization was needed on campus to address some crucial concerns. In the *Avukah Annual 1925–1930*, Joseph S. Shubow describes the moment when he and

Max Rhoade "lighted the torch" of Avukah. Shubow was a student at Harvard, concerned by "social smugness and complacency, the cowardly Jewish self-effacement and assimilatory tendencies on the part of so many of our fellow students" (37). To help initiate change, he and others involved in the Harvard Zionist Society invited speakers to Zionist meetings, even drawing an editorial in the venerable *Harvard Crimson*, the college daily, which helped stimulate interest and even made attending Zionist meetings on campus "fashionable." As a development, a number of students engaged in serious scholarly study of the Hebrew language, Jewish history, and Zionist affairs, to the point where their "entire college life was illumined by these thoughts and activities" (38).

Inspired by a visit to the campus by Max Rhoade,[2] Shubow began to think of a "sound, powerful student Zionist organization" to revive the nearly defunct Intercollegiate Zionist Organization. To begin, he sent out invitations "to students among the more active Jewish college groups to attend a national conference at Washington on June 27, 1925, immediately preceding the National Zionist Convention" (39). The call was answered, and "sixty or more students and graduates from about twenty-two universities attended our gathering at the Mayflower Hotel, and there we exchanged our views and experiences; and, guided and inspired by our guests from Palestine, we founded our present organization." With the idea came the need for a name, when Max Rhoade, present in the founding meeting, shouted out "Say Joe, what's the Hebrew word for torch?" and he and I thundered 'Avukah' almost simultaneously," a scene that evokes the creation of more than just a movement. Shubow describes how he and others were "warmed by the very word," how they felt they "had conjured forth a name that was to fire the imagination of the Jewish students of America."

We felt like alchemists, who after considerable mystical rather than scientific experimentation had discovered the magic flame that would transmute the spiritual apathy and indifference of American Jewish college youth. We were no doubt too optimistic but as we look back, though we are far from satisfied, even the most critical must admit that we kindled a spark which may yet flare into that luminous torch we originally saw in a vision. (39)

Avukah's "flame," this attempt at (re)kindling magic through Zionism, spread quickly through Harvard, and then through universities in New York, Baltimore, Philadelphia, Chicago, Pittsburgh, Buffalo, and Wisconsin. Says Shubow:

We founded the American Student Zionist Federation because we believed it was the sacred duty of the youth as well as of the elders to participate in the glorious privilege of the national redemption of our people. We also sensed that our elders were getting older and growing fatigued in the laborious task of national liberation and we desired to help train the younger generation to be prepared to carry on the work. We wanted to discipline ourselves, to charge into the breach and maintain the good fight. We did not care to wait until we were drafted, dragged or pressed into service. We were ready to volunteer. And we stood eager, like prancing vigorous young steeds, prepared to perform any kind of duty from the most menial to the most dangerous. (40)

During its early years, Avukah was a loose federation of Zionist clubs, each having "its own special program without any particular cooperation."[3] When in 1928 a new regime took hold, headed by James Watermann Wise, the organization was centralized and expanded, and it was at this moment that Harris joined.

Harris's involvement with the organization began in his early days as a student at the University of Pennsylvania. On March 29th, 1928, a little journal called *Rostrum* published its first issue, under the auspices of the University of Pennsylvania chapter of Avukah. On page 2, signed by an undergraduate student with the initials Z.S.H. [Zellig S. Harris], appears an article titled "The Torch Unlit," describing from another perspective this same foundational moment.

On a certain inauspicious afternoon in May 1925 two men were sitting in the offices of the Kerem Kayemeth at New York. It was after office hours, these two having remained to discuss their major task. Both were members of the "Palestine Youth Commission," sent to America to deal with the problem of Jewish youth here. Both being teachers, and closely in touch with Zionist youth in Palestine and Europe, they were thought the most fitting for the mission. Despite all the warnings they had received they expected to find here a youth more or less similar to that which they knew. Without entering into a tirade against the younger generation, it must be admitted that the human material with which they had to deal was not the best. They had not come with any clear-cut plan of what they were doing to do. Their mission was to influence organized and unorganized Jewish youth in the direction of Zionism. Here the problem of extracting Zionism from an unnationalistic youth resembled the ancient problem squeezing water from a rock.

This discussion led to the conferences and meetings that brought together heads of organizations, culminating in the 28th Zionist Convention in Washington, D.C., when Avukah was formally founded on the basis of the program already in existence in the Palestine Youth Commission. Harris writes: "Like most similar organizations, it had a two-fold purpose: to widen the ranks of the Zionists among the students, and at the same time to foster a deeper understanding of the movement among those who had already accepted the principle. From its ranks the future leaders should evolve—men with practical experience and close to the Zionist ideal. It would be comprehensively Jewish—thus filling a certain need in every national Jewish student; and above all it would be fair and open-eyed, nationalistic without chauvinism."

The reality was different because, according to Harris,

there can be but two types of Zionists. There is the Zionist by emotion, in whom nationalism is inculcated from childhood, and who, no matter how many reasons he may offer for the ideal is not a Zionist by virtue of them. And there is the Zionist by logic—the one who knows well the Jewish situation and who, from a purely rationalistic point of view, decides that the centering of a nucleus of Jews in a Jewish Homeland is absolutely necessary to the future well-being of the nation.

Harris would sympathize with the latter approach, but at this early point "too few had the training requisite for one of the first type, and too few had the knowledge and cold rationality requisite for one of the second." This is an interesting statement in terms of Harris's own propensities toward rationality and scientificity, and, in terms of his training, which had been rigorous and intense. But it is interesting politically as well, since he proposes by this description that there should be some kind of ideal "Zionist conception," which was to be in accord with the ideals of the founders, who presupposed "a wholehearted acceptance of Zionism," a "decidedly desirable" motivation. What was lacking in terms of the original organization, therefore, were the goals that had been set forth early on, and so it could be said three years after the founding of Avukah that, in Harris's words, "the torch—the real torch—is really unlit as yet. It is our task then to light it so that it may shine in the way it was first meant to shine."

This kind of quest for a Zionist vanguard is present throughout Harris's (and others') Avukah writings, and it ties Harris's approach to someone to whom Avukahites looked for inspiration: Louis Brandeis. On this issue, Brandeis, who wrote that "our main task must be to make fine men and women in Palestine, and it will be desirable to correct there, so far as possible, those distortions of character and mind which too much commercialism enforced by separation from the land many centuries, has entailed."[4]

In this same 1928 issue, there is discussion about how "some of the leading minds of Avukah" should go beyond the "cultural phases of Zionism" to focus on "the practical side [of] some appropriate and worthy Palestine project," like fundraising for the library at the Hebrew University of Jerusalem. This type of endeavor became important for Avukah, along with publishing (newsletters, newspapers, books), staging social events, and setting up forums to discuss Jewish or Zionist issues. For example, Harris spoke about Zionism at one such forum at his parents' home on November 6, 1927; Shoshanna Harris spoke on "Territorialism and the Return to Palestine Movement" on February 26, 1928; Zellig Harris spoke on "Ahad Ha'am and cultural Zionism" at the home of Rabbi and Mrs. S. Greenberg on March 25, 1928; Anna Harris spoke on "Social Zionism" on April 15, 1928; and Zellig Harris spoke on "Palestinianism," once again at his parents' home, on May 13, 1928.

In the second issue of *Avukah Rostrum*, dated June 25, 1928, the Palestine Project was described to representatives from the Chicago Avukah, as was the idea for "a colony of secondary-school graduates who wish to return to the soil." These types of projects were central to the overall Avukah mission: "As Lilion Blum's famous saying goes, 'the liberation of the spirit comes before liberation of the mind.' Avukah's work is educational. All its energies, and, if necessary, all its funds, are to be used toward its main end, the spreading of Jewish culture and nationalism in the universities and the creation of what is hardly possible here: a nationalist youth movement."[5] In another article titled "Third Party Zionism," Harris bemoaned the state of Zionism, conveying a sense that "American Zionism is bankrupt," partly because of the politics of competing Zionist parties.

When two parties exist, both of them powerful, and neither fit to rule, the time has come for a "third party." So it is in America and much to our sorrow it is so in American Zionism. The opposition [to the Lipsky administration] was wrong in the first case in creating a "second party"; that system is out of place in the Z.O.A. But now let a third party come—one with no politics, no tactics, no thought but Zionism alone. Let it be not a party but the Zionist movement itself. It is time. (3)

This rejection of the Party, but support for the movement, is the type of distinction that regularly appears in the writing of Avukah.

Politics does not properly come within the scope of Avukah. We cannot but evince interest, however, in a state of affairs so deplorable that it jeopardizes the spiritual legacy which the major organization will presumably leave Avukah. But destructive criticism alone is not sufficient. Avukah owes it to itself to know what is essentially wrong with the present situation, what factor is responsible for this unfortunate lack of anything spiritual in American Zionism.

The problem, according to Harris, is that when Zionism came to America, "too much of its old European idealism was lost," which led him to call for the types of changes he eventually instituted when he became an officer, and then president, of the organization. His early writings provide a sense of the direction toward which he thought the movement should be headed: "American Zionism has fallen into a rut of its own creation from which it must be extracted by a revival of spirit. And the reviver does not come. No one emerges from this humiliating affray to lead the organization—or rather to create anew a Zionist movement in America." What Harris wanted was a "straightforward Zionist" who "cares for Palestine and his nation and for that alone," whose "mundane honors are gotten in other fields and whose Zionism is purely objective, purely a matter of idealism." This discussion anticipates those that took place at the Third Annual Avukah Convention in Pittsburgh, immediately before the Zionist Convention of June 28–30, 1928.

There are some other interesting articles in this same *Rostrum* issue, including Anna Harris's "Religious Skepticism in the University," which suggests that religion cannot be dogma, "handed out as pills, to be swallowed at rising, before meals, and bedtime and on holidays, and its rules obeyed because of a vague fear of consequences" because according to this conception, God is relegated to the role of a "bookkeeper," and "the facts on which that religion is constructed are shown one by one to be doubtful or impossible, and the whole structure crumbles" (5). Instead, she suggests that "the only religion that can survive the buffets of impracticality of logic and science, is that religion which is emotional poetry: as impractical, as illogical, as unscientific as is lyrical poetry, but as relieving from the everyday, as uplifting and as emotionally beautiful." This science-spirituality distinction is present in Harris's description of "cultural Zionism" and its relation to Nahman Krochmal's Hegelian idea of the "national atheist," whereby a nation is "defined by its spirit," and has its own personality, individuality, and identity.

On the basis of this theory, cultural Zionism (Ahad-Ha'amism) teaches that Jewish Renaissance means a revivification and rejuvenation of the Jewish "Geist"—call it "Culture" or "Spirit." And learning from bitter experience that this can be effected in Palestine only. A thousand and more factors combine to make Palestine the sole possibility; tradition, natural beauty and variety, the feeling of "home" and much more. In Palestine alone can the Jewish spirit again develop Jewish culture in a way that is all its own. There only can the Jew attain his pure individuality in his way of looking at life, in his national geist. Palestinianism is a mode of life, the Jewish mode, and we believe it should be given a chance to develop as much as other earthly cultures. (7)

The February 1929 issue of the *Rostrum* has no articles by Harris, but it does contain a significant anonymous editorial about what role the United States should play for the Jewish community overseas, which bears his imprint.

After the fight for cultural liberation had been won the Russian center reached its height in the Hoskalah which corresponds to the Jewish science movement of Germany, and as the movement ripened it took an increasingly rationalistic trend and expressed itself in Chovevei Zionism desire to return to Palestine, a movement brought on by the Pogroms. The cultural creators of the Hoskalah movement were Smolevskin, the poets Bialik, Tschernichovsky, Shneik, and the great thinker Ahad Ha'am. When the pogroms of 1905 and subsequent outrages made life in Russia intolerable for Jews, a large part of its Jewish population left. Now Russia of all places can no longer be the Jewish Center.

Ideally, Palestine would be the new center, but "even with its aggregation of great Jewish minds (Binlik, Ahad Ha'am, and many others), a truly active, cultural center, one that would be a constant vital influence to the entire Diaspora, it cannot yet be." Hence, "history seems to have singled out a predecessor for it—a place where the Jewish population is large, where economic conditions are good, where the status of Jews is not bad but with enough anti-Semitism to be stimulating. That place is, of course, America. Fitted and necessary as America is, to be a great transitory Center filling in the gap between the Russian one of the past and the Palestinian one of the future, does America take advantage of its position?" The answer provided, with a few exceptions, is "no," because it is "hindered by competition from the rising Palestinian center."

In the September 1929 issue of *Rostrum*, there is once again much hand-wringing about Avukah, which is described as suffering from "bare hand to mouth existence, a plodding along, each season for itself, with no vision or plan of later work—that will not even suffice to keep the organization alive" (1). To remedy this situation, the issue contains a long list of proposed cultural activities for 1929–1930, including reading groups, historical work, publications, meetings, seminars, and work relating to practical Zionism. The reading group in history, for instance, includes Bernard August, Mary Brenner, Harold Ehrenskranz, Leonard Finkelstein, Joseph Goldenberg, Ruth Schimmel, Robert Siegel, as well as Shoshanna Harris, Anna Harris, Tzvee Harris, and Zellig Harris. Dr. and Mrs. Harris also hosted, in March 1929, a forum on "The Exiles," and in the same month an informal gathering of active members of Avukah to meet James Waterman Wise, the Avukah National Executive Secretary. In April, the Harrises hosted the first meeting of the Reading Group in Hebrew, led by Shoshanna Harris, on "Abad Ha'am—"the Sacred and Secular," as well as a talk by Leo Schwarz on "The Seventh Dominion." This issue features discussions as well on forums aimed "to give the foundations of Judaism as a national character, the starting point from which it had to work and the original basic elements which have always colored it."

This nationalistic program was supported by a talk by Zellig Harris on "The Ancient Hebrews," in which he describes the Hebrews as "kindred Semitic Bedouin tribes" who stayed in Egypt and Canaan, and then later "combined into a nation." Palestine was thus inhabited since the days of the "Earthdwellers" and the "Cave-dwellers," and was settled by Semitic Canaanitish agricultural and merchant tribes, having previously been long ruled by the Amurru (Amorite) nation from the North. Furthermore, "Babylonia had long had a great influence upon Palestine: Cuneiform in the Amarna tablets, Babylonia records of intercourse with pre-Israelite Palestine, Joshua 7:21. Egypt had great influence: Bedouins in the Sinai Mines, Bedouin trade, the Hyksos, Thutmose I, II, III conquer Palestine, Sinuhe, the Amarna Tablets, Ramases' wars, the Mohar; remains in Beisan, Geezer, Meggide, etc." As for the Hebrews, who lived as a patriarchal group, they were present as well, leading "an orderly nomad life, traveling to and from new land, much as an Englishman today goes to Colonies" (5).

In this issue Harris also described "The Messianic Idea" of a bodily resurrection of the dead (Jews), and their return to Palestine, and another "more natural" version featuring "the appearance of a Messiah who may be merely an inspired mortal and who would bring all the Jews (living) back to the Holy Land." Interestingly, wrote Harris, "as the years passed and the lot of the Jews became worse, and a revival of the ancient Jewish Kingdom became more and more impossible, the belief in the Messiah became more powerful, and thus we find still stronger evidence of this in the various Apocryphal writings." Harris also returned to the subject of cultural Zionism, in which he sets up an initial dichotomy between Zionists who are "born," that is, who are "inevitable Zionists who have no real reason for their belief" except upbringing and emotion, and those who are "made" by force of intellect, "who, knowing and understanding Judaism, accept Zionism because they find it worth the accepting." The latter group "prove the vitality and truth of Zionism" and "seek a justification of this idea" in terms of world application "that lies in the idea of national existence." This leads to a broader discussion about the relationship between human nature and the role of the State: "Man, being a gregarious animal, enters into gregarious groups, societies, which grow and change until his gregarious instinct has found satisfaction, i.e., until he has achieved that type and size of society which he desires." The question of how large the grouping should be is important, since "Krochmal, the Hegelian philosopher of Jewish history, stops at the national stage in organization of individuals, or nations. He saw the cultural interests of individualities integrated into a harmony. No single individual can be as rich as many sided as an organization of such" (10). In this regard, the nation is "a harmonious coordinating of peculiar abilities and tendencies, of reactions and orientation of life, of an attitude to the past and the future, of all the mores and morals of a group," and it is "the bearer of its culture, bounded by it, and like it, to be taken in reference to the whole world."

The originality of Harris's vision is in the idea that "a nation exists to teach, to teach its own peculiar contributions to world culture to its neighbors, whence it passes on." By the same token, the nation can lose its individuality by conveying its vision, and thus "no longer exist" as a "separate cultural group." Zionist Jews must therefore concentrate upon teaching, because "the Jewish principles of World-Unity (as in Monotheism) and Justice have not yet penetrated to the world (as the principles of Greece and Rome have)." This makes "the continued existence of the Jews as a cultural unit "desirable," but "the Jews should, by massing their forces and by centralization, make their culture more essentially a culture, and more essentially individual. For various reasons Palestine is the only place—and a perfect place—for that." Palestine is a "playground, a laboratory of ideas," in which all work to one end, "a newer, vital, individual Jewish culture, which, as a distinct unit of a perfect world whole, will give its new and vital and individual contributions to humanity" (10). This vision of the incomplete transference of Jewish ideas and the need for a space to cultivate them is at the basis of Harris's conception of Zionism during his undergraduate years and beyond.

Expanding Avukah

In May 1929, Avukah opened an office at 170 Fifth Avenue in New York, from which it published the first issue of the *Avukah Bulletin*. President Max Rhoade described it as "a modest leaflet, little different from many similar publications"; but behind it lay some lofty ambitions, notably to "remind us of our hopes of some day publishing a worthy Avukah journal of creative literary expression." In the meantime, its goal was to "flash a constant interchange of thought and action through the membership of our Chapters from New England to California, and mark the end of a period of communication restricted to mental telepathy, irregular items in a few friendly news columns, and laborious transmission of ideas through the post-box." As such, "the Bulletin is a new instrument in the high task we have set for ourselves of making the renascence of our people a vital force in the lives of the student youth." This publication printed news from the various chapters of Avukah, including announcements for Harris's March 3, 1929, forum on "The Exile Factor in Jewish History," and the April 14 history group talk on "Cultural Zionism," which was complemented by Anna Harris's "The Development of the Idea of Zionism." This issue advertised a forthcoming 1929 *Annual*, which would be dedicated to Albert Einstein on the occasion of his fiftieth birthday. It also contained some important discussions of Avukah's educational role, including Dr. Chaim Arlosoroff's suggestion that "Avukah is the reserve officers' training camp of the American Zionist movement," so it "must never seek to become a mass movement or organization" (3).

The members of Avukah included "newcomers," "citizen members," and "graduate members," those who had graduated from university but actively pursued an interest in Avukah through "knowledge, attendance and service." Remarkably enough, this article also proposed that "under the heading of knowledge a definite course of prescribed study is to be included, to be followed by all members of grade 'A'. At the end of these courses there are to be examinations and possibly the requirement of a thesis to be submitted by the individual applying for admittance to grade 'B'. For the 'B' and 'C' grade requirements of knowledge are to be fulfilled in discussion circles, particularly on current Jewish and Zionist events and study of Zionist problems and ideology." This illustrates the degree to which Avukah was designed as a vanguard movement that aimed to attract and train the very best Jewish students, and to submit them to rigorous training, as we have seen with Harris's identification of particular students for Avukah work. This marks a significant development since, as Michael Berkowitz notes in his very interesting discussion of early Avukah, intellectualism had been considered quite low among members this organization by people such as Maurice Samuels, Chava Rapkin's father.[6]

In 1930 Harris completed his B.A. at the University of Pennsylvania and enrolled in graduate studies. At the same time, he pursued his interests in Avukah, which was playing an increasingly important role on American campuses, and was encouraging the teaching of Hebrew in American high schools and in Palestine. Further, it was announced in that year that a new summer school camp would be launched, for which he would eventually be named faculty advisor. The first camp was held at Camp Scopus, on Lake George, New York, from June 26 to July 6, 1930, featuring informal roundtable discussions "led by men whose scholarship and experience in the various fields of Zionist thought and activity are outstanding."[7] In the March 1930 issue of *The Avukah Bulletin* we learn that Edward Sapir, who would play such an important role for Harris in his linguistic work, gave (with James Waterson Wise) a public forum under the auspices of Avukah and titled "The Jewish Ego," with proceeds of the talk designated for the Chizik Memorial Project.[8] Sapir's participation raises the point, which will become increasingly clear as the Avukah story unfolds, that so many of the Jewish intellectuals involved in language studies and radical Zionist work during this period had some contact with Avukah and, directly or indirectly, with Harris himself.

The October 1930 issue of the *Avukah Bulletin* announced that the Avukah Summer School was "a successful experiment in Jewish adult education," in which 65 registered students participated in songs, a "playlet" by Leah Kaplan, and lectures by Jacob De Haas, Arthur James Balfour, Dr. Mitchell S. Fisher, Dr. Shalom Spiegel, Simon Halkin, James W. Wise, Rabbi Samuel M. Blumenfield, Rebecca Imber, and Rabbi I. B. Hoffman. This issue announced as well the nomination of Harris to the position of secretary for the University of Pennsylvania's Avukah,[9] and he was also named to the cultural committee of the national office.

Albert Einstein, American Scientist and Zionist

In the next chapter of what is to become a remarkable story of friendships, colleagues, and intellectual links, we find Harris acting as a catalyst and a go-between in Albert Einstein's eventual decision to move to the United States. This would have considerable consequence and it was motivated as much by politics and Zionism as it was by science.

Einstein's personal world met Harris's on account of the former's eventual move to the United States, which was in some degree inspired by Zionism. Fritz Stern cites a 1914 letter from Einstein who was already refusing an invitation from the Imperial Academy of Sciences in St. Petersburg on grounds unrelated to his work in physics: "I find it repugnant to travel without necessity to a country in which my tribesmen are so brutally persecuted."[10] And in 1919 he wrote to a colleague that "the Zionist cause is very close to my heart. . . . I am very confident of the happy development of the Jewish colony and am glad that there should be a tiny speck on this earth in which the members of our tribe should not be aliens. . . . One can be internationally minded, without renouncing interest in one's tribal comrades."[11] In 1921 Einstein fulfilled his promise to his "tribe" by traveling to New York with Professor Chaim Weizmann, who later became the first president of the State of Israel, to raise funds for the Jewish National Fund and for the Hebrew University in Jerusalem. In a chapter of

Einstein's German World devoted to the relations between Einstein and the chemist Fritz Haber,[12] Stern writes that in 1921, "Haber pleaded with Einstein not to go to the United States just then, not to sail on an Allied ship or to associate himself with former enemies." Haber's words did not sway Einstein, even when he suggested that Einstein's actions had the significance of "the acts of princes" in earlier times, making his departure "treasonous." Stern cites a letter from Haber, recalling that

So many Jews went into the war [WWI], perished, became impoverished, without complaining, because they thought it their duty. Their lives and deaths have not eliminated anti-Semitism from the world but, in the eyes of those who make up the dignity and greatness of our country, have demeaned it to something odious and undignified. Do you want by virtue of your conduct to wipe out all that we have gained from so much blood and suffering? . . . You sacrifice definitely the narrow ground on which the existence of academic teachers and students of Jewish faith in our institutions of higher education rest.[13]

Ever consistent and persistent, Einstein reiterated his intention to travel to the United States, especially in light of the "countless examples how perfidiously and unlovingly one treats superb young Jews here [in Germany] and seeks to cut off their chances for education." On April 7 of the same year, Franz Boas wrote to Einstein to recruit his support for the Emergency Society for German and Austrian Science and Art on similar grounds.

You are familiar with the work that is being carried on by the Emergency Society in Aid of German and Austrian Science and Art. We want to be sure that the funds that we provide are used in such a manner that they will help in the best way possible, not only to prevent the threatened breakdown of intellectual work but that they will also help toward a reconciliation of the scientists who are still torn by political and racial antagonism. As you are aware, the funds which we provide are utilized for the maintenance of journals the existence of which is in danger, for the support of research that cannot be carried on for lack of funds and for the support of young scientists, who without such help may have to give up their scientific career.[14]

Boas considered that there was "urgent" need for "help" in this matter, and Einstein responded enthusiastically, on April 11, 1921.

It is with great pleasure for me to express to you my deep appreciation of the work of Relief to which you and your Society devote so much time and effort. This work I consider to be of the greatest importance in the struggle for the existence of the scientific research of the scientists themselves. In this time of acute crisis the relief that you can provide is most urgently needed if the advancement of science is to be maintained; also in these amongst the highly civilized countries which are now poverty stricken as a result of the war.

Einstein lent his name to many such causes, often in defiance of the patriotic chauvinism of the time: "I did this by the way not out of attachment to Germany but to my dear German friends, of whom you are one of the most outstanding and most benevolent. . . . Dear Haber, an acquaintance has recently called me a 'wild animal'. The wild animal likes you and will visit you before his departure."[15] This "wildness" seemed foolhardy given the political landscape, but it served to inspire many persons around him.

Neither Haber nor any of his other friends could restrain Einstein from his new political involvements. He took his fame as a warrant to make public utterances on a number of subjects; he had come to realize during the war as well as in his scientific work that the outsider, the *Einspanner*, may intuit truths that are at odds with conventional wisdom. Among academics, he had been almost alone in his absolute if quiet opposition to the war—and he had been right. After the war, and in a sense justified by its end, he espoused pacifism, internationalism, Zionism, and a mild brand of socialism. These were causes that his scorn for German imperialism had taught him: they were the reverse of chauvinism and German nationalism. Postwar progressives in many countries held similar views (with the exception of Zionism), and they were anathema to most German academics.[16]

Just prior to his departure in 1921 for the United States, Einstein wrote a prophetic letter, dated March 8, to Maurice Solovine: "I am not at all eager to go to America but am doing it only in the interest of Zionists, who must beg for dollars to build educational institutions in Jerusalem and for whom I act as high priest and decoy. . . . But I do what I can to help those in my tribe who are treated so badly everywhere."[17] His trip was very successful, and he was courted for positions in different universities, including an "extravagantly generous" offer from Columbia University. He was still committed to Europe, however, but upon his return to Berlin, he gave a talk, published along with four others given between 1921 and 1933 as *Mein Weltbild*,[18] which already set out a major theme of an approach to Jews and to Zionism which would place his ability to stay in Germany in question. In a prescient statement, Einstein warned:

We need to pay great attention to our relations with the Arabs. By cultivating these carefully we shall be able in future to prevent things from becoming so dangerously strained that people can take advantage of them to provoke acts of hostility. This goal is perfectly within our reach, because our work of construction has been, and must continue to be, carried out in such a manner as to serve the real interests of the Arab population also. In this way we shall be able to avoid getting ourselves quite so often into the position, disagreeable for Jews and Arabs alike, of having to call in the mandatory power as arbitrator. We shall thereby be following not merely the dictates of Providence but also our traditions, which alone give the Jewish community meaning and stability. For our community is not, and must never become, a political one; this is the only permanent source whence it can draw new strength and the only ground on which its existence can be justified.[19]

As the occupation and the current tensions claim their victims in Israel and Palestine, these words resonate with the weight of unheeded warnings and unfulfilled promises.

Einstein's Avukah

In 1929, Einstein decided to return to the United States, and in the December 1930 issue of Avukah's newspaper, we learn that en route he agreed to make an address from his ship, the *S. S. Belgenland*, as it approached the American shore. What is remarkable is that this speech, scheduled for 9:30 A.M., December 11, 1929, would be given to Avukah, "the only organization under whose auspices he would make a public pronouncement upon his arrival in the United States." In the address that preceded Einstein's talk, Avukah's Executive Secretary George M. Hyman recalled that "in the library of the Hebrew University in Jerusalem is deposited the original manuscript of Professor Einstein's 'Theory of Relativity.' This monumental document has revealed to the world a new truth, and it may well be that from Zion shall go forth to all humanity new values resulting from the development of the Jewish homeland in Palestine." Einstein then issued a general greeting from the ship, and upon his arrival he was given a reception arranged by the Zionist Organization of America, where he was presented with *The Golden Book of the Jewish National Fund*, the *Avukah Annual*, and other Zionist literary texts.

Two days later, Einstein gave another talk on the subject of Palestine from the National Broadcasting Company's studios over radio relays from coast to coast in the United States, as well as to England and Germany, this time preceded by an introduction from Dr. Mitchell Salem Fisher, chairman of the Administrative Committee of Avukah.[20] In his introduction, Fisher noted that Einstein has "rejoiced in his people" and sympathized with its difficulties, "has labored earnestly time and again on its behalf," and he has "gloried in its heritage and has shown special interest in those idealistically motivated minded men and women who have pilgrimed their way to Palestine and have lived in the historic land of their fathers, building a new Jewish commonwealth which will yet mean much to the peace and well-being of the world." Fisher also recalled that Einstein had for many years been interested in Palestine and the Zionist movement, and that Avukah has been "attempting to bring to the youth of the United States and Canada, both that romantic appreciation of the Zionist movement and the persuasive, compelling understanding that the Jews must have and be given an opportunity to recreate their national life in order that the Jewish people as a people may contribute to the culture of man" (2).

Einstein's speech, another in what came to be a long line of oracular statements, is worth citing in its entirety.

My dear friends:

I am very happy to have the opportunity to speak a few words directly to the youth of this land which has remained true to Jewish ideals.

Do not, I ask of you, allow yourselves to be discouraged by the difficulties which seem to face us at present in Palestine. Such experiences are the tests of the Jewish people's will to live.

Undoubtedly certain statements and measures, taken and pronounced by British officials have been just subject for criticism. We can not, however, be satisfied with this, but we must learn the lesson of what has recently happened.

In the first place, we must pay great attention to our relations with the Arab people. By cultivating these relations we shall be able to avoid a development in the future of those dangerous tensions, which can be exploited for the purpose of provoking hostile action against us. We can very well attain this end, because our upbuilding of Palestine has been so conducted and must be so conducted that it also serves the real interests of the Arab population.

And in the second place in doing this we will be able to avoid the unfortunate necessity—unfortunate for Arabs and Jews alike—of being obliged to call in the Mandatory Power to act as judge and umpire between us.

In this way we are not merely following the bidding of wisdom but we also remain faithful to our traditions which above all else give substance and meaning to the unity of Israel. For indeed this unity of Jews the world over is no wise a political unity, and should never become such. It rests exclusively on a moral tradition. Out of this alone can the Jewish people maintain its creative powers, and on this alone claim its basis for existence." (2)

These words are crucial for movements such as Avukah and the League for Jewish-Arab Rapprochement, the two key Zionist organizations to which Harris contributed his time and efforts. And unlike many individuals of the period, Einstein remained committed to his ideals, even when the views he put forth were unpopular. In 1929, the same year as his visit to the United States, he once again warned Weizmann:

If we do not find the path to honest cooperation and honest negotiations with the Arabs, then we have learned nothing from our 2000 years of suffering, and we deserve the fate that will befall us. Above all, we should be careful not to rely to heavily on the English. For if we don't get to a real cooperation with the leading

Arabs, then the English will drop us, if not officially, then *de facto*. And they will lament our debacle with traditional, pious glances toward heaven with assurances of their innocence, and without lifting a finger for us.[21]

In "Our Debt to Zionism," a speech he gave before the National Labor Committee for Palestine on April 17, 1938,[22] Einstein reiterated that: "I should much rather see reasonable agreement with the Arabs on the basis of living together in peace than the creation of a Jewish state." Einstein was certainly not the first to point out the dangers of imposing a Jewish state in the region, and indeed some even suggested that Jews ought to look elsewhere for sanctuary. Zachary Lockman recalls that in 1899, one year after Herzl's first visit to Palestine, France's chief rabbi gave Herzl a letter he had received from Yusuf al-Khalidi, former mayor of Jerusalem and member of the Ottoman parliament of 1876–1878, who warned that "large-scale Jewish settlement in, and ultimately Jewish sovereignty over, Palestine could only be achieved by force and violence, in the face of strong resistance by the local population, and he implored the Zionists to find some other territory in which to settle Jews and seek a Jewish state" (33). Of the major Zionist thinkers, Ahad Ha'am was among the first to raise the question of Arab-Jewish relations in the region, offering warnings decades before Einstein's that the existing Arab population must be carefully considered by the Zionists. Einstein's statement is significant, however, because of his extraordinary status, particularly among members of Avukah. The whole question of the relationship between those Zionists who wished to cooperate with Arabs in Palestine and those who insisted upon the need for a specifically Jewish homeland was of considerable importance to Harris, and it will be raised repeatedly in this narrative.[23]

Einstein's book on these matters, *About Zionism*, was published in 1931,[24] although much of its content would already have been known to people like Harris earlier on because it was composed of extracts from speeches and letters dated from 1920 to 1930. A review, published in the October 1931 *Avukah Bulletin*, recalls Einstein's devotion to the cause with which Harris felt such a strong affinity: "I am a national Jew in the sense that I demand the preservation of the Jewish nationality as of every other. I look upon Jewish nationality as a fact, and I think that every Jew ought to come to definite conclusions on Jewish questions on the basis of this fact. I regard the growth of Jewish self-assertion as being in the interests of non-Jews as well as of Jews. That was the main motive of my joining the Zionist movement" (5). According to Einstein, Zionism had three functions: "To Jews who despair in the Ukrainian hell or in Poland it opens out hopes of a more human existence. Through the return of Jews to Palestine, and so to a normal and healthy economic life, Zionism involves a creative function, which should enrich mankind at large. But the main point is that Zionism must tend to enhance the dignity and self-respect of the Jews in the Diaspora." This was to be done, as was clear from his Palestine speech, by living "as friends of the kindred Arab nation." As such, Great Britain's role should be to "promote the growth of friendly relations between Jews and Arabs, that it shall not tolerate poisonous propaganda, and that it shall create such organs of security in the country as will afford adequate protection to life and peaceful labor." Finally, from the "scientific" standpoint for which he is most famous, Einstein rejects assimilationist Jews because "nationalities" are a "law of nature." But the horrors witnessed by the Jewish population in Europe and Russia were only just beginning, and Palestine offered grounds for both concern and optimism, tending toward the former in the decade leading up to the Second World War.

Frame of Reference

This was an important period for Harris as he started working with a range of people on long-term projects, including the aforementioned "Frame of Reference" (FoR) work, which outlined a theory of society and its transformation. This is a monumental study, which spanned several decades but only produced one major publication, the (posthumous) book titled *The Transformation of Capitalist Society*. A number of friends and colleagues collaborated on the project and it is surprising, given the huge mass of material assessed and produced for this work, that so little came of it. This was a source of dissension among the various collaborators, including Murray Wax and Murray Eden, who grew frustrated in their attempts to convince Harris to promote and circulate the product of all this labor.[25] Murray Eden described the Frame of Reference (or "framework") project as an attempt at a grand synthesis of social planning for a democratic, egalitarian, noncapitalist structure for living. Harris led the effort, but a number of others participated, although most were eventually disturbed by the overly pedantic style.

As Harris pursued his goal of earning a position on the faculty of the University of Pennsylvania, the Avukah organization, to which he still contributed, continued to gain prominence. Indeed, Avukah members held their most ambitious convention ever in December 1930, in Boston, and the Avukah headquarters was moved to a larger space at 1133 Broadway, in New York. In the March 1931 *Avukah Bulletin*, the continuance of the

Avukah summer school was confirmed as well, with goals of "training Zionist leaders on the campus," and "the crystallization of the concepts underlying the Zionist movement and a deepening of the understanding of the values inherent in Zionist Ideology with special reference to Jewish life in America." The list of its Avukah faculty, according to the article, would "read like a roster of Who's Who in American Jewish Creative Thought," including Rabbi Samuel M. Blumenfield, Jacob de Haas, Mr. Simon Halkin, Professor Mordecai Kaplan, and Mr. James Waterman Wise. To that pantheon was eventually added another group of contributors, including Dr. Mitchell Salem Fisher, Dr. Nisson Touroff, Mr. Meyer Levin, Mr. Joseph S. Shubow, Mr. Moshe Burnstein, Dr. Otto Wolfgang, Mr. Elias Newman, Mr. Beryl Levy, and Dr. Horace M. Kallen.

The editorial describing the objectives of the summer school is revealing in terms of what it says about Avukah's orientation during this period.

The Avukah Summer School is a unique institution because its aim and its accomplishment include not only the acquisition of information but the development of personality. There are few schools at which the student lives according to the ideology which he studies—fewer in which the faculty teaches not by lectures alone but by personal inspiring contact. The Avukah Summer School of 1930 was characterized by these qualities, and the coming session promises an integrated, inspiring program of Zionist study and Zionist living. (2)

This approach apparently bore fruit, but may very well have been inspired by the amazing commitment of Jews in Palestine. A section of the February 1932 *Avukah Bulletin* included the type of column regularly written by Harris, in which we find mention of the fact that even though there were but 175,000 Jews in Palestine at this time, they published more than fifty Hebrew dailies, weeklies, monthlies, and quarterlies. One suggestion that appeared in the pages of Avukah's publication during this period was that the Jews would not necessarily be safe in most countries of Europe, so Palestine may be a better choice. In Poland, for example, Krakow University was closed in November 1931 on account of anti-Semitic clashes, which eventually spread to Warsaw and other university towns in Poland, and later on in the month in Vilna. By November 21, Jews were warned not to appear in the streets of Warsaw, and, for the first time in history, synagogues in that city were closed. Disaster, as we now know, was looming in the not-so-distant future, and signs abounded. On December 21, in Breslau, a court halted publication of inciting pictures of Nazi anti-Semites, and on January 5, 1932, it is reported in the *Avukah Bulletin* (of February) that German Jewish families had begun an exodus to France to escape Hitler's menace. Response was, of course, rapid, with the

French Report[26] calling for further reduction of immigration and legal measures against Jewish land purchases. Warnings were sounded to the Avukah community about impending disaster; in Volume 2.2 of the *Avukah Torch Bearer*, for example, we find mention of Dr. Nahum Goldman of Berlin, who gave a "short analysis of Zionism at the present time and approached the subject with an examination of the European situation today as it affects Jews and non-Jews, proving that Jewish difficulties and assimilation are growing, and that even America will inevitably develop along the same lines." The only solution, according to an article describing Goldman's views, would be the creation of a new center of Jewish population. "He stressed the tremendous possibilities for accomplishment in Palestine, and that the crisis of fulfillment is now. Our generation has a duty and responsibility to help solve the Jewish destiny, or our indifference will commit us of the great crime of bringing about a catastrophic situation more tragic than ever before in the annals of the Jews" (1).

This article raises a hugely important point in light of contemporary assessments of how America, and particularly Jews in America, responded to the rise of fascism and Nazism in Europe. First, this particular call came in 1932, one year before Hitler's party even assumed power, which challenges the idea that he was of little concern until 1933, and that his ascent to power was precipitated by an unexpected and anomalous confluence of events. Second, it was in no way taken to be a controversial statement by readers of *Avukah*, who were accustomed to thinking about the problem of how to save European Jews from the type of disaster unfolding at that time in Poland and Ukraine. Third, it points to an important effort made by a range of Avukah commentators, including Harris, that although America was a relatively safe place, it nevertheless had all the ingredients for rising fascism that could eventually endanger American Jews. In *The Holocaust in American Life*,[27] Peter Novick makes some very interesting points about how mainstream American institutions treated emerging anti-Jewish sentiments in Europe and beyond. But the fact that Avukah is left out of his discussion, as it is left out of virtually all discussions in histories of this period, makes us grateful that he qualifies some of his sweeping statements and calls attention to our need for continued prudence. For example, it is not true from the perspective of Avukah that "from early 1933 to late 1942—more than three quarters of the twelve years of Hitler's thousand Year Reich—Jews were, quite reasonably, seen as among but by no means singled-out victims of American gentiles." On the contrary, Avukah's leaders most certainly considered that Jews were, to recall Goldman's words, in for a truly "catastrophic" situation in the near future.

Novick's next sentence, that "this was the all-but-universal perception of American gentiles; it was the perception of many American Jews as well," (21) is therefore far more accurate. Reading Novick's book alongside Avukah materials leads one to focus upon the adjectives such as "many," and also leads us to reflect upon the relative importance of Avukah members as emerging Jewish intellectuals and eventual mouthpieces for views about Jews and Zionism in the United States.

In the meantime, the situation in Germany worsened, culminating with the naming of Adolf Hitler to Chancellor in 1933. To meet the crisis Avukah members, concerned for the survival of European and Russian Jews, heightened its efforts to bring Jews to Palestine. The intensity and urgency of this effort challenges Peter Novick's sense, that "before 1941, and surely before the outbreak of the European war in September 1939, it appeared to be a matter of Jews escaping from likely persecution, not certain death" (50). The challenge for Avukah was the difficulty of purchasing the land through the Jewish National Fund, and, critically, of working on the Arab-Jewish question, considered essential for the success of Avukah's plans. Harris was on the forefront of Avukah activities, as he assumed the role of Chairman of the Praesidium for the national movement (with other members named, including Rose L. Rosenberg, Sylvia Binder, Herman Charney, and Abraham H. Cohen). With his arrival came important changes, including a reorganization of the national office, and new efforts to create Avukah groups on the campuses of America through the elaboration of a new national program that, as described in the October 1934 *Avukah Bulletin*, required new training programs with rigorous study. The new administration also worked to establish Avukah libraries, local Hebrew work, a speakers' bureau, and new efforts to celebrate Avukah's tenth anniversary, in 1935. A series of letters from this period find Harris actively encouraging new efforts and modifying ongoing projects, including publication. In a letter to the October 1934 issue of *The Torch*, an Avukah publication, he wrote:

There is a basic shortcoming among publications dealing with Zionism. They show a natural tendency to superficiality and to a discussion of movements rather than social forces. No real work can be accomplished without facing actualities. *The Torch* should give you an opportunity to discuss clearly just what you see in Zionism and just what type of Palestine you want. You must decide what there is in Zionism that holds the interest of American Jewry. We are an independent group. *The Torch* is free to analyze every aspect of our movement and its social problems. I trust that you will invite a free discussion of fundamentals. I am sure that Chicago Avukah will do a good piece of work and I look forward to *The Torch* with great expectations. (4)

Harris also aimed to fulfill one Avukah's prime objectives, described in the November 1934 *Avukah Bulletin*, to encourage students to become "halutzim" (Jewish pioneers) in Palestine: "Such groups of halutzim have been leaving this country for Palestine for a number of years. The first organized group left from Detroit in 1931 and the flow has been steady ever since. Upon arriving in Palestine, these young people are sent to certain Kvutzot, communal farm-settlements, where previous groups have already been assimilated. Prepared as they are for kvutza life they fit in quite well and soon become an integral part of that movement which has been the backbone for Jewish Palestine" (1). According to this commentary, the advantages of this program include assurance of employment and the promise that the student will not succumb to "social uselessness." In short, "as a halutz in Palestine not only is his personal economic problem solved, but he also finds himself again in terms of the group. He becomes a productive and integral part of society, in a movement which has more or less definite ideas and aims." To the idea of social vanguard, therefore, comes promises of utility and the ability to earn in a society that does not suffer from the limitations and obstacles of contemporary (capitalist) America. This is an interesting point at which the social and the Zionist ideals meet, as will become evident further on when we find Harris living on a kibbutz, but it would became an urgent issue when World War II broke out. Again, however, this article recalls that Jews were fleeing places like Poland, but not necessarily to Palestine; in March 1934, 2,397 Jews did emigrate to Palestine, but 419 went to Argentina, 328 to France, 160 to the United States and, amazingly enough, 1 went to Germany. "Although not personally acquainted with him," writes the commentator, "we have been losing sleep and wondering and worrying about that solitary 'one.'" Einstein wrote to Franz Boas on February 4, 1934, to commit $50 he had raised at a charity concert to "be used to liberate valuable people from the German hell."

Overall, Harris expressed satisfaction with the work being done by Avukah during this period, particularly in the realm of publications, as he noted in this same March 1934 issue. The first work of the organization was the *Avukah Bulletin*, which he considered an "important medium for communication and expression for the whole membership." The second was the *Avukah Program*, which would appear in several editions through the years (the 1938 version is discussed further on). It was "intended to sum up the situation of the Jews today and, on the basis of the historical work of this term, to analyze the chief problems: antisemitism, assimilation, etc. In the treatment of this there is much room for suggestions both as to arrangement and as to subject matter; these should reach us while yet the essay is in the making." And finally, there was a series of Avukah leaflets, "to marshal all the important information on any one subject." On the other hand, says Harris, "we recognize, of course, that this purely intellectual work makes up neither the whole of life nor the whole of Zionism. There are a number of plans for activities which would involve the work of Avukah members and also bring them in closer contact with Palestine and modern Jewish life." Sending students to Palestine was one such project, as was raising money to buy land in Palestine (via the Jewish National Fund[28]), but there were cultural ones as well, including the idea that "Avukah may have records of Palestine songs made, and an exhibit of Palestine painting is being planned, to tour the chapters if possible."

He picks up on the theme of publication in the December 1934 issue, driving home the point that outlets like *The Avukah Bulletin*, published each month, was of value because "nothing reaches the truth so forcefully as honest and objective argument" (1). Plans were also afoot to make concrete the idea of making a leaflet series, which was to include titles such as "The Inner-Arab Parties," "the Situation of the Arabs," "The Interests of England in Palestine," "The Economic and Social Influence of Jewish Immigration," "The Stand of the Jewish Parties," "The History of the Conflict," and "Communist Activity Among the Arabs." The secondary goal of this series was to train people in gathering and preparing these materials, since "members of the staffs will be getting excellent training both in the Jewish field and in research methods and writing." There was also the idea of mentors, which would be important in the group: "The staffs should arrange occasional meetings with professors of history and sociology in their universities and with persons who can help them understand the problems upon which they are working." Finally, Harris was also involved during this period in rebuilding the links between the national organization and the individual chapters which had suffered from "laxity" and "sadly inadequate communications," something which had to be rectified because, in his words, "Avukah is in a position now to produce much valuable material, but it must have an organized body to use and to gain by it, and ultimately to help in creating it."

The national organization was also interested in finding appropriate individuals to travel to Palestine in order to become intimately acquainted with life there. In an article in this same 1934 issue of *The Avukah Bulletin* (p. 2), comes an unsigned editorial (probably Harris's) praising two new sources of Zionist news, both of which are found to contribute to help "form the vanguard in the development of intelligent Zionist opinion in America." The former project was announced beginning the following month and some interesting figures for our story, including Harris's close friend Seymour Melman, came to participate in this effort later on.

Einstein's Rejoinder

The year 1935 was an auspicious one for Harris, in terms of his Zionist efforts and his language studies. Following the annual Avukah conference, held in December 1934 in Cleveland, Ohio, he worked on a new plan to link individual chapters with the national organization. This effort, which led to chapters being grouped together by regions headed by a regional director, and the forming of a national organization director to coordinate the activities of the various regions, is interesting in terms of his eventual concern with the (re)-organization of workers groups under the auspices of his interest in self-governed production. The decision-making process would be based upon discussion meetings and executive sessions of all the national executive committee members from all regions, ensuring that each chapter would thereby have a voice in the decisions of Avukah, a model of cooperative organization among units that could find corollaries in other political or workplace realms.

That year Harris was also reelected as president of national Avukah, and, in that capacity, he communicated with Albert Einstein. The first letter known to exist between them came from Harris on February 5, 1935, and was addressed to Einstein's office in Princeton.

Dear Professor Einstein:

Avukah, the Student Zionist Federation, has just established a Palestine fellowship. By the terms of this award two students will be sent to Palestine annually, to study there and to work in a Kvutzah. The holders of the fellowship will spend some nine months in a Kvutzah, and upon their return will present an analytic essay on some of the cultural, social or economic problems of Palestine life.

You would honor us greatly and help us in our work if you would lend your name as member of the professorial Advisory Committee for these fellowships. Membership in this Committee would not make demand upon your time, and I sincerely hope you will find it possible to accept.

The first awards are to be made this Spring. May I hear from you therefore in the near future?

Very sincerely yours,

(signed) Zellig S. Harris, President

Harris asked that the reply be sent to the Office of the President, his residence at 5601 West Diamond Street, in Philadelphia. The response was rapid.[29]

Dear Sir!

I was very happy to receive your communication and shall be glad to become a member of the Advisory Committee of the Fellowships. I cannot let this opportunity pass without warning against the Sirens of Revisionism, who [sic] are as much a danger to our youth as Hitlerism is to German youth. This is a case of Jewish aping of this disgraceful movement which threatens our best moral traditions.

Very sincerely yours,

(signed) A. Einstein.

Again, very quickly, Harris responded and asked for permission to reprint the letter by Einstein in the *Avukah Bulletin*, in which it appeared the following month (March 1935).

February 13, 1935

Professor Albert Einstein

Princeton, N.J.

Dear Professor Einstein:

I wish to express to you my very deepest gratitude for your acceptance of participation in our work. I shall be happy to send you full information concerning these fellowships, and copies of our publications.

Your letter was one of the finest and strongest statements on Revisionism that could be made today. I am extremely anxious to fight this fascism to the end. You would be helping this work very much if you permitted us to publish your letter in our Bulletin. We are holding up the coming issue until I hear from you in this matter.

May I therefore have the permission to publish your letter?

Sincerely yours,

(signed) Zellig S. Harris.

The *Avukah Bulletin* reported, in its March 1935 issue, that Einstein "readily permitted the publication of his letter," writing "Hoffentlich hilft es!" And so came a new link between Einstein and linguistics, this time through the members of the advisory committee, formed by Harris, which had among its ranks Edward Sapir (Yale), as well as Professors Felix Frankfurter (Harvard), Isaak Husik (U Penn), Kurt Lewin (Cornell), Selig Perlman (Wisconsin), H. A. Wolfson (Harvard), W. H. Worrel (Michigan) and also Avukah's own James Waterman Wise, then editor of *Opinion*. The links between this complex world were growing, and Harris was about to enter the most fruitful period of his career, even as Spain was about to erupt in a precursor to a decisive war of horror and destruction that would lead to the undermining of so many social and political projects he held dear. As always, he would turn increasingly to reason and science in the hope of discerning some patterns of sanity in a world of war.

From Avukah to Mishmar Ha'Emek

Avukah in this period was working to expand Jewish immigration to Palestine, and increase emigration thereto from America and, moreover, from Ukraine, Poland, and Germany. The territory grew when a mosquito-infested Hulah swamp was transferred to the Jewish National Fund, which meant that drainage had to be undertaken so that cultivation and, eventually, Halutzim settlements could be established. The March 1935 *Avukah Bulletin* reported that "that which in Russia has so caught the fancy of people may also be seen in the Palestine of the national funds. It is the spectacle of planned construction, of a country building itself up, consciously and with a definite design" (unsigned editorial, p. 1). Unlike other booms, however, this one stood outside of the normal rules of land development and profit since

the Kvutzot and Moshavim, the collectives and co-operatives, are unassailable fortresses of sound economy and sensible life. They are built on unsalable National Fund land; they have set rules which preclude any false expansion. The fictitious values of prosperity cannot arise in them, nor will post-boom crises deeply injure them. It is this joint work of the national funds and organized labor that is holding Palestine down to realities in the wave of laissez-faire, and it is this joint work of the two that must be supported and furthered, at all costs, as the constructive basis of Zionism.

This link between Zionism and a kind of cooperative socialism is extremely important in terms of Harris's politics, as they would come to be articulated in his informal discussions and in his book on *The Transformation of Capitalist Society*.

The summer of 1935 was for Harris another occasion to participate in the Avukah Summer School, at Camp Cejwin in New York, where he presided with twenty-six representatives from Harvard, Radcliffe, City College of New York, Hunter College, University of Pennsylvania, University of Chicago, Wayne State University, University of Wisconsin, and University of Rochester. Following discussions, a statement was issued in the October 1935 *Avukah Bulletin* indicating the goals of Avukah, which included the following reiteration of principles we have seen emerging in the Avukah literature:

Avukah seeks to give its members a sound understanding of Zionism and of movements and conditions in which it is involved. Avukah sees in the collective and cooperative movement the most valid and most significant development in Zionism and works of the creation in Palestine of a collective society. Avukah reaffirms the resolution for the World Zionist Congress calling for the development of Arab-Jewish friendship and supports all the efforts of the Jews in Palestine for cooperation with the Arabs. (1)

This was the distinctive Avukah approach: a vision of a collective cooperative coupled with Arab-Jewish Cooperation.

Harris announced in a November 1935 *Avukah Bulletin* editorial that the December Avukah annual conference was to be "given over to a few basic discussions and technical conferences" relating to the goals of Avukah, the role of those who do not go to Palestine, extra-Zionist activities, the approach of students, program arrangements, Jewish National Fund work, and contacts with other groups. This sense that Avukah was in constant evolution is confirmed by a steady stream of discussions about its long-term objectives, evolving plans, and new programs aimed at fulfilling the obligations and desires of each chapter.

This whole effort fit into the Avukah general plan to make Jews in America as aware as possible of what was going on "on the ground" in Palestine, both through direct experience and through the communication of this experience by emissaries (for example, fellowship recipients). This was crucial, both for what Jews would learn about Jewish settlements, and for their learning about the Arab population, which was the vast majority of settlers in Palestine at this time. The ways in which these spokespeople experienced Palestine were communicated back to the Avukah group, and contributed to Zachary Lockman's idea that "the Zionist movement and the Jewish society it helped create in Palestine were shaped in crucial ways by their interactions with the Arab society they encountered 'on the ground' in Palestine itself" (2). These fellowships were expanded in 1938 from four to six, the increase being due to the naming of one fellow in a New England college, and one for a young man or woman in Canada. A range of sponsors helped with this endeavor, including Salo Baron who, in a February 7, 1938, letter from Adrian Schwartz (the fellowship chairman), was asked to reaffirm his sponsorship, which he did, in a letter dated February 14.

One of the crucial Jewish settlements that appears in discussions among Avukah members was the Kibbutz Artzi called Mishmar Ha'Emek. It is clear that by its link to such places as Kibbutz Artzis, and more specifically the Kibbutz ha-Shomer ha-Za'ir, which was founded on a belief in the kibbutz as an instrument for fulfilling the Zionist ideal, furthering the class struggle, and building a socialist society. As regards Harris's politics, we find in the idea of the kibbutz some basis of the type of society that he and others hoped to foster. This is made clearer in an article published in the March 27, 1939, edition of *Avukah Student Action*, which also describes kibbutz life from the perspective and experience in Hashomer Hatzair, recorded by Avraham Ben-Shalom in his book *Deep Furrows*. Titled "Toward a New Society," this article suggests links between the new economic structure of the kibbutz and the new social forms and relationships being set up as a consequence, issues which come to be of great concern to Harris. "The kibbutz aims to have that kind of community whose harmonious, integrated and balanced social relationships will permit the fullest possible development of human possibilities. It is an attempt towards rational planning, organization, and control of the community in order to set up the most adequate framework for the individual's growth and well being." Harris eventually spent considerable time on Mishmar Ha'Emek, and Jerry Cantor, a member of this kibbutz for many years, shared his recollections with me in an August 4, 1997, letter.

Zellig Harris was a member of Kibbutz Mishmar Ha'Emek for a number of years. He lived here with his wife Bruria Kaufman and their daughter. During this time I and a number of members came to know them well. Suffice to say that Zellig Harris was very much liked here. His very gentle and helping personality was always much appreciated by people here. To a certain extent it was a pleasant surprise to people here since he was known to be a world famous intellectual. His modesty was legendary. . . . I think his stay at Mishmar Ha'Emek was somehow related to the unusual productivity in his later years which is only now beginning to be appreciated. Perhaps this gave him a chance to mull over his ideas away from the necessities of teaching and supervising work for higher degrees.

Harris and his wife, Bruria, eventually spent considerably more time on the Kibbutz Hazorea, located in the Jezreal Valley midway between Haifa and Afula, which was founded by members of a youth group called Werkleute, originally a non-Zionist movement that changed with the rise of Nazism. This kibbutz is of special interest in terms of Harris's later concern for Employee Stock Ownership Plan (ESOPs, described at length in chapter 7), since its main economic activities centered around a factory for the production of plastic sheeting and bags, and a furniture factory (recently closed).

The May 1935 issue of the *Avukah Bulletin* contained news that the publication was to be retired and replaced by a new magazine and a newly inaugurated *Avukah News*, which would be published by the New England Council and headed by Leo Orris of Harvard. It also announced that Avukah had received funding to create a permanent site for its summer school on the Hashomer Hatzair Training farm in Liberty, New York.[1] On the political front, the *Avukah Bulletin* contained an article by Harris, addressing the question of Avukah's political orientation through a description of the growing urgency both among members and "outsiders" as regards its pro-Labor policy, summed up by the question, "Has Avukah become a political organization?" Harris's somewhat contradictory answer was that Avukah remained a "nonpartisan," pro-Labor group aiming to "bring a large number of Jews into Palestine," notably farmers and factory workers, for the simple reason that "if employers were Jews and the workers, Arabs, then for every Jewish factory-owner there would be a large number of Arab workers, and Jews would permanently be a small minority" (*Avukah Bulletin* 1). Furthermore, in Palestine a large population of Arabs was already living as serfs, working for a few cents per day with subsistence homesteads, so "between an Arab and a Jew (the latter's wages usually many times what the Arab asks), [an employer] will inevitably take the Arab." As such, "Zionism must, therefore, inevitably support a great trade-union movement among the Jewish workers in Palestine, an organization which will force wages to stay at the Jewish level and make it possible for Jews to come to Palestine, reasonably assured of finding work there." This, of course, is a gesture "toward a new society" in which the vanguard Jews work to promote the interests of all workers in the region.

All this is actually realized, if only semi-consciously, by the Zionists of the world. It is for this reason that the votes of Palestine for the Zionist congress go 70% to labor; that the last World Zionist Congress passed a number of Pro-Labor resolutions and recognized the Histadrut (Jewish Federation of Labor) as the only labor union in Palestine. It is for this reason, too, that the most anti-Histadrut group in Palestine, the plantation-owners group (which uses Arab labor), is actually outside the World Zionist Organization; that the Revisionist party, when it began to fight the Histadrut, was forced to leave the Zionist organization.

As such, says Harris, "every Zionist must be in favor of a strong labor-union in Palestine," which means that Avukah is simply consistent, rather than "partisan." Nevertheless, "there is no intention here to disparage political work," which he deems "necessary," and, further, "it is erroneous to confuse pro-Labor Zionism with Socialist views in America. A Zionist must support Labor Palestine because of specific conditions in Palestine; such support need not derive from his personal views on society" (2). But in the end, "the accent on the personal and social bearing of Zionism is, and will continue to be, the characteristic of the new movement" (2). All of this expresses the Avukah side, as though it had to be the Jews who would call all the shots; the Middle Eastern Studies scholar Zachary Lockman insists that this is overly partial, and finds that, in fact, "the complex relationship between Arab workers and labor Zionism must be seen as interactive and mutually formative, though perhaps not always in ways which are immediately obvious" (3).

Less than one year later, Avukah published an important letter from Palestine written by Mordecai Bentov, a prominent member of Mishmar Ha'Emek, providing clarification on the issue of Jewish-Arab relations from the standpoint of how the "left" envisions the Jewish homeland. The substance of this letter would have been in accord with Harris's own views, as will become clearer further on, and would perhaps inform his own interest in the reorganization of society beyond Zionism, described in *The Transformation of Capitalist Society*.[2] The letter came in reply to a piece by Fenner Brockway, former editor of *Labour Leader,* in which he attacked Zionism, and is taken by the editors of the *Avukah Bulletin* to be "an example of the some of the advanced thought on the relation of Arabs to Jews." It began with a statement that resonates even today: "I should like to state authoritatively that the left wing of the Jewish labor movement, though it is all for a maximal Jewish immigration, sees that Palestine will ultimately become an integral part of some kind of a Federation of the Near-Eastern countries. It is just possible that it may ultimately include also Turkey, Persia, and other countries" (2). The *Avukah Bulletin* article goes on to clarify its left stance, noting that for the imagined Federation, "one thing is clear: a socialist federation is one thing; a reactionary or fascist federation is another," so "the problem of including Palestine in such a federation must be solved not on the racial but on the socialist grounds of whether it would be helpful or detrimental to the advancement of socialism."

Bentov emphasizes that whatever side one takes in an Arab-Jewish conflict, "a socialist must always bear in mind that every state is an instrument of oppression, whether class or national, and consequently his goal is the socialist society in which the comparative numerical strength of any group would make no difference at all in its position." Even though he and others in Avukah supported emigration to Israel, it did not mean that he supported the domination of one group over another (at the time when this article was written, there was an estimated 800,000 Arabs and 375,000 Jews in Palestine). "If we are for Jewish mass immigration it is not because we want to dominate anybody, but because we want to save as many Jewish refugees as might be necessary under the circumstances. The Jewish worker will never understand a socialist's objections to his immigration into Palestine which while solving his problem as at the same time greatly benefiting the Arab toiling masses and socialists as well" (Bentov in *Avukah Bulletin*, p. 2).

This is extremely powerful, and is indeed consistent with some of the actions taken by Jews in Palestine during conflicts with Arabs. In the same issue of the *Bulletin*, an unsigned article (again, probably by Harris, in conjunction with others) describes the terrorist actions during recent Arab strikes, including random attacks against Jewish settlers and their property. Most attacks were against the trees that had been planted in an effort to take back a country that, on account of "Arab occupation," had become "almost a desert." The article made reference to the Jewish tactic of *havlaga*, nonretaliation against Arabs for terrorist acts, despite the apparent ability and will of the settlers. The reason for the restraint speaks once again to the idea of Arab-Jewish cooperation, because "the only answer would be to kill other Arabs, haphazardly to retaliate by similar acts of terrorism," something that "many Jews would not do as a matter of principle." Even more important, "the Jews refused to answer with terrorism because they did not see this as war between Jews and Arabs as such. Each Arab was not necessarily an enemy. The enemies were the instigators and leaders, the social economic interests, and the terrorist bands which were their tools. With the Arab people as such, the Jews still hoped to make peace, to reach an understanding" (Harris in *Avukah Bulletin*, p. 1). Once again we find this idea that the common Arabs had similar objectives to the common Jews, and that they must cooperate toward similar ends, instead of creating a climate of hatred. Havlaga, according to the report, left the Jews "in a far better position to talk to the Arab people with some home of understanding." This was not an uncommon position at this time, and it is surprising the degree to which it is left out in today's discussions of Zionism and of actions by the state of Israel, which so clearly defy such an approach. In 1936, the World Zionist Congress, the Histadrut, General Federation of Jewish Labor in Palestine, Hashomer Hatzair, and Avukah all held to the view that there must exist Arab-Jewish relations, generally on socialist principles. Even the *Manchester Guardian Weekly* suggested that "their [the Arabs'] leaders do not seem to consider the advisability—which may nevertheless appeal more to the rank and file—of 'living with' the Jews and awaiting the emergence of those economic and other lines of division which will in time cut across present national differences."[3]

In 1936 the Avukah summer school took place in its newly-inaugurated camp, and it featured long discussions about Arab-Jewish issues, alongside of habitual questions of organization, propaganda, and publications, and Adrian Schwartz (Chairman of the Program Committee for Avukah) reiterated many by now familiar points in a talk called "Arab-Jewish Relations in Palestine." Reporting on the event, David Furman wrote, in the first issue of the newly published *New England Council Avukah*, that Schwartz had advocated cooperation between Jews and England "until they have gained Arab friends. It is hoped that when the Arab youth movement matures, it will cease rendering aid to its own enemies, the feudal landlords, and join up with the Jewish workers for a cooperative Palestine," an idea that picks up for the first time the question of Arab youth movements.

Justice Louis D. Brandeis

The November 1936 issue of the *Avukah Bulletin* brought the news that Bernard Kligfeld would spend a year working and studying in Palestine as an Avukah Palestine Fellow. It also brought to the fore Justice Louis D. Brandeis, who celebrated his 80th birthday on November 13, 1936. To honor the occasion, the editorial on the front page, probably written by Harris, speaks of Brandeis as "one of the most thoroughly American persons in public life," who works from the "historical and accepted American ideal of democracy and equality of individuals, products of a time when the idea of laissez-faire was a socially progressive norm." He is also described as "one of the most ardent and active of Zionists," who had become a Zionist by studying the movement and, in the end, made "the same analysis of the Jewish situation that Zionism does. He recognized the meaninglessness of assimilation—not its impossibility in his case, but its lack of justification for the group. And granted the existence of the Jewish group, he correctly analyzed its problem—namely, that the Jews are everywhere a minority," and hence Zionism, "the forming of a Jewish center in Palestine." On page 2 we learn that Justice Brandeis has for a long time been actively interested in Avukah, and that for him, "the earnestness and sincerity with which Avukah approaches Zionism has more appeal than some blatant and better subsidized organizations. We don't have to look at Brandeis as a symbol because we know him as a friend. He would be happiest if we go to our work as Jews with much energy. Let the friendship continue on this basis."

As further testament to the link between Brandeis and Avukah, Avukah published the *Brandeis Avukah Volume of 1936, celebrating the Justice's 80th birthday: A collection of essays on contemporary Zionist thought dedicated to Justice Louis D. Brandeis*, edited by Joseph Shalom Shubow, associate editors Rabbi Michael Alper and James Waterman Wise.[4] Brandeis was a kind of spiritual leader, a shining light for the Avukah movement, and he served as a focal point for a number of interactions which, once again, linked people to Avukah, if only tendentiously. For example, on June 11, 1940, Alfred Kahn was trying to solicit comments about the Avukah take on the future of Zionism and Palestine from Salo Baron, who met with Albert Einstein on various occasions (including in March 1941), and Louis Brandeis (in April 1941). Further, in a letter to Baron from Alfred Kahn, dated May 6, 1941, we learn that Avukah had actively solicited Baron to act as a faculty member for the Avukah summer school, to discuss Jews in Europe "and what may be expected of the European Jewish descendants after the war." Baron refused on account of a heavy workload, and he made it clear that his refusal was "by no means a reflection on the value of [Avukah's] work," which he "highly esteemed."

In 1936 Harris was still president of the national Avukah organization, but in the December 1936 *Avukah Bulletin*, signals of change were announced in the leading article: "Zellig Harris, [who] has long expressed an urge to retire to his Philadelphia hermitage. We can expect," says the editor Jesse Orlansky, that he will emerge "in a few months with several of the Phoenician grammars in which he takes an ungodly interest" (!). Sylvia Binder, Harry Norbitz, and George Poster also voiced their intention of leaving their positions as of the next convention. The article finished with an uncharacteristically informal tone: "As Zellig Harris said, in what must have been an unguarded moment: 'this is a movement, and individuals don't count. No, sir.'"

The new Avukah Fellow for that year, who went by the name Sachkie, also had a letter (addressed to Harris) in this issue, which once again contained dire predictions about where things were headed for the Jews in Europe. He began by saying that he was "afraid" to write from Poland, where he had been before coming to Palestine. "I wanted to tell you how poor the country is, how despotic the government. I wanted to write about the concentration camps where political prisoners are tortured and where they are cut off from the world. I wanted to tell you how my cousin had to flee Poland because he had communist sympathies. Perhaps if I had written, nothing would have happened to me, but I might have caused trouble for my informers." By contrast, Palestine seemed a veritable oasis, leading Sachkie to suggest that persons hesitant to go to Palestine should visit Poland first!

Avukah itself would have difficulties on this very subject with the onset of the war; indeed, publications from the organization show that it was becoming increasingly politically engaged, which would in 1939 lead to a crisis provoked by an attack by the Young Poale-Zion Alliance on the basis that Avukah itself was becoming "Marxist." Peter Novick points out in his book *The Holocaust in American Life*[5] that the Jewish-Communist link had old roots, with popular associations of Jews with Communists dating back to the Bolshevik Revolution of 1917, and that "in the interwar years the Communist Jew was a staple of anti-Semitic propaganda in both the United States and Europe" (92). According to Novick, "Jewish organizations worked frantically to combat the Jew-Communist equation," even though "a great many—perhaps most—American Communists in these years were Jews" (93). Avukah's leadership acted similarly when, depicted as having manifest sympathies for Communism in 1939, they denied the charges. This seems odd now, because Avukah's sympathies for Marxist analysis frequently surface, and its overall leftist stance is in abundance in most issues. In the May 1937 *Avukah Bulletin,* the editor lashes out on a range of fronts and speaks out in favor of those fighting fascism in Spain, those standing up for Jewish rights, and, in an unfortunately neglected overlap, for those demanding equality for Blacks in the South. An example of the latter is an editorial describing the case of William B. Redmond, a "27-year-old Negro from Tennessee," who appeared before Chancery Court in Memphis with allegations of "colorline discrimination" in education. "He protests that since the State School of Pharmacy rejected his application for admission, the authorities ought either to reconsider his case or provide special instructions for him. Happily he does not go so far as ask to sit at the same benches with lighter skinned students—a statutory misdemeanor in his state." Carrying on in a tone of ironic outrage, the editorialist writes: "But his brash enough insistence on elementary rights guaranteed by the Fourteenth Amendment to the United States Constitution naturally outrages all sense of decency and reason in the chivalrous South."[6] This report, along with other discussions of oppression that goes on outside of the Jewish communities, is a trend that develops in Avukah publications with the passage of time, with the positive effect of creating links between Jews and other groups suffering under the weight of oppression. This article continues, noting that "the State defense takes its Bible oath that 'legislation is powerless to eradicate racial instincts or to abolish racial distinction.' It is indeed reassuring to learn that laws cannot cripple economic prejudice because they can change neither the shade of dark skins, nor, perish the thought! the contours of Jewish noses. Thus the world remains safe for the white men of Tennessee."

The hardening of Avukah's political stance grew out of overt signs that things were getting much worse in Europe, particularly for the Jews. For instance, against the oft-stated view that Mussolini's alignment with Nazi Germany was limited to particular spheres, we recall the news, recorded in *Avukah Student Action* on September 23, 1938, that Mussolini declared before a gathering of 200,000 people that "the world of Hebraism has been the enemy of fascism for the past 16 years." On the same day, it was recorded that Jewish stores were plundered and Jews were attacked in Sudetenland, leading 72,000 of them to move to larger Czech cities, part of their reaction to a growing anti-Jewish sentiment in the country which "dates back to 1931," two years before the election of Hitler. "Suddenly," we read in a November 28 editorial in *Avukah Student Action*, "the 'democracies' have awakened to the modern Jewish tragedy. Though this belated sympathy is welcome, it means virtually nothing in terms of Jewish improvement." Avukah's answer, yet again, was to lift immigration restrictions to Palestine. The official reasons for the British refusing this solution—the Arab Jewish conflict and the size of the country—are not legitimate because "the conflict is England's doing," and "Palestine has territory enough to absorb all of Europe's Jewish refugees" and is "ready for mass immigration" (2). To suggest today that the United States, Britain, and Canada were simply unaware of the German threat or the stakes of letting Hitler continue his tirade are not sustainable, and this is just one piece of evidence from one newspaper issue published by Avukah.

Avukah was not clearly associated with some identifiable left-wing stance, either in deed or in declaration, but it was nevertheless consistently anti-fascist. In a February 1, 1939, letter to Salo Baron, Lawrence B. Cohen, the executive secretary of Avukah, described an updated plan to arrange "a Roll-Call of American Jewish students, in support of (1) immigration of Jewish refugees into Palestine, (2) American preparation against fascism." The justification for the first plan was:

Because the position of the Jewish minority under fascist governments is such that migration is unavoidable; because plans of mass migration to undeveloped areas are largely schemes doomed to be unrealized and designed only to remove from the British and other governments the onus of meeting the situation; because in any case such migration would only continue that same minority status of Jews which makes them defenseless in a contracting capitalism and in the face of nationalist propaganda; because Palestine can absorb 100,000 refugees immediately, and many more later; because such migration will not harm the Arab population but will advance that very modernization and class-consciousness of Arab peasants the fear of which has led to the current anti-Zionism of the Arab ruling class; because American public and governmental opinion may be effective in opening Palestine immigration.

On Avukah's anti-fascism, the support provided was justified as follows:

Because fascism means persecution of the Jews and their elimination from the society in which they live, as is seen in the situation treated above; because fascism means the death of human freedom and democratic civilization; because fascism may develop in the United States out of attempts to hold back the existing economic system from change; because fascism here can be prevented only if Americans prepare and organize in advance against its local origins and manifestations.

The form that this newly articulated program was to take was through meetings on campuses, social pamphlets, a card-signing drive, and fund raising through a form of voluntary taxation in which donors indicate their support through a "roll call." The purpose of the effort was to reach otherwise politically unorganized students, to form a pressure group of Jewish students, to amass a tax to be used for political work in support of refugee immigration. The roll-call itself would be "an important factor in developing students' sympathy for fascist victims into fruitful political channels"; for this reason, Baron and others were contacted by Cohen on behalf of Avukah: "We are now asking a number of professors, without regard of whether they are Jewish or not, to indicate their approval of this roll-call; for this work, which will serve as an introduction to political activity for thousands of students, could not succeed, or would not have the desired character, without such sponsorship. We are very anxious to have your acceptance, and to hear your opinion and suggestions. If you would like to have further information about Avukah, we would gladly send it to you." Salo Baron answered on February 3 in a very telling letter in which he revealed that he had "been acquainted with the work of Avukah for many years" and "shall be glad to appear among the sponsors of your undertaking as outlined in your letter of February 1st." Nevertheless, "I have some misgivings with regard to the coupling of the two projects." Furthermore, wrote Baron,

If I may venture another suggestion, I should like to amend the passage on p. 2 referring to the use to be made of the tax "for political work in support of refugee immigration to Palestine." It would seem to me that the Avukah would do much better, if the money thus raised could be made use of for the purposes of establishing definite scholarships for Jewish students at the Hebrew University and other Jewish educational institutions in Palestine, rather than for political work which is, after all, primarily in the province of the Jewish Agency and the World Zionist Organization. However, if your plans are too far advanced for changes, you may list me as a sponsor of the project, even as it is in its present form.

So, once again, Avukah is asked to calm its political ambitions and, in a letter from Cohen dated February 14, 1939, the suggestion is adopted such that moneys raised would go "to one of the recognized agencies" Baron mentioned.

Democracy and Intellectual Freedom

Another effort undertaken at this time by those around Harris was Boas's work on behalf of "Lincoln Birthday Committee for Democracy and Intellectual Freedom," a copy of which was sent to Albert Einstein on January 20, 1939. The idea was to solicit answers to important questions from forty "outstanding leaders" in the fields of government, science, education, and religion, which were to be used in a publicity campaign. Einstein replied in January 1939 at some length, a text worth citing for its value as a treatise by a "public intellectual." The questions were: "First, how can the scientist insure freedom of research and socially useful application of the fruits of his research? Second, How can scientists and educators help to combat racial, religious, and other forms of discrimination which violate the letter or spirit of the Declaration and the Bill of Rights? Third, How can the schools best meet the obligations which rest upon them as fortresses of democracy? And finally, How can the government most effectively assist the expansion of science and culture?" Einstein responded as follows:

1. The freedom of research and the securing of the application of its results depend on political factors. Researchers have an influence on this development, not as researchers, but only as citizens. From this it follows that the researcher has the duty to be active in the political questions in the sense of the above-mentioned goals.

On political and economic issues, he must even as teacher and author have the courage clearly to defend his convictions established through studies. He should protect himself and the general public as much as possible against a deformation of the freedom of teaching and publication through joining together with others and through collective action and should always keep a watchful eye for a threat in this area.

2. & 3. Freedom of teaching and protection of the ethnic and religious minorities are the cornerstones of a free state. This truth as well as generally to keep alive the consciousness of the meaning of the inviolability of the rights of the individual in the consciousness of the people is one of the most important tasks of the school. An important opportunity for effective action has been placed into the hands of the teacher and a great responsibility rests on him. There is no special method guaranteeing success in this important matter; the spiritual [intellectual] atmosphere and example are more effective in this regard than knowledge and understanding.

4. Public authority can and should protect the teachers at all levels against influence on the basis of economic pressure, promote the publication of cheap enlightening books, generally promote popular education. It [public authority] should make possible the intellectual and professional development of gifted individuals without means. The administration of the school system should also without standardizing centralization be constructed in such a way that it is as little dependent on private capital as possible.[7]

Yet again, so much of what Einstein suggested, decades ago, seems applicable not only to the challenges faced then but also, regrettably, today.

As Avukah gained strength and membership, increasing effort was made to establish its links to kindred Arab, socialist, and Zionist groups. It also formalized a number of its proceedings, producing a "Diagram of Zionism" pamphlet that was to be read by all those planning to attend the 1937 summer school. The organization published key texts describing the aims and objectives of Avukah, including the March 1938 "Introductory Program." Both the "Diagram" and the "Program" offer overviews of Avukah's program, with some by now familiar theses, including the importance of finding a way to make a "territorial concentration" of Jews in Palestine. Critiques of the approach suggested in this document are offered in appended letters by Adrian Schwartz, Sylvia Binder, Larry Cohen, and several others.

Program for American Jews

The crucial document of this period, which sets forth in the clearest of terms the objectives and some of the accomplishments of Avukah, was the

Program for American Jews. This pamphlet, largely written by Harris, was published in 1938 and addressed to Jewish American students concerning the question of whether there were facts or problems that specifically apply to Jews, but "it does not assume that the Jewish group is a question apart." Its goals included "discussing the relation of the Program to these interests and attitudes, and seeking to indicate to what extent it coincides or differs with them." It speaks of the Jewish group and of Jewish interests and problems only to the extent that these are shown to exist, only to the extent that they *must* be dealt with. The premises of the group were multifold: that there existed at that time four million Jews in the United States who "constitute a group with special needs and special problems" (6), that Jews are curtailed in particular activities or, in the case of Nazi Germany, that Jews are thrown "out of their jobs and into concentration camps" (7), that there is latent and blatant anti-Semitism in American society, and that "*the whole Jewish environment,* the society which young American Jews find around them, is not suited to their needs" (8). Avukah also clarified its aims for those who might stand outside of its realm, suggesting engagement on three fronts: first, the "eventual liberation from the difficulties arising out of their minority position"; second, the creation of "a new type of organization"; and third, the provision of "such aid as they can to Jews in countries where anti-Semitism is strong" and, "far more important than such palliatives . . . the definitive construction of the new Jewish settlement in Palestine." According to Avukah, certain British, Arab feudal, and Italian interests were trying to use the situation in Palestine for their own ends.

The Palestine issue was leading to significant conflict between the Arabs and the Jews, which would ultimately work at cross-purposes to left-Zionists. For example, the *Program for American Jews* notes that "these interests have obstructed the Arab masses from the liberation which Jewish immigration can bring them, but they have not been able to stop the immigration of Jews." Accordingly, the Palestinian situation had to be "faced by the Jews and straightened out on the only possible basis of social equality. For the fundamental interests of Jewish and Arab people are the same." The pamphlet suggests that "the Jews who come do not displace the Arabs. On the contrary, they are necessarily leading the Arab peasants out of the feudal system which holds them as serfs. Such a change can not come without fighting, without the attempt of reactionary forces to thwart the liberation of peasants and to set them against the Jews. But the fall of feudalism in Palestine is unavoidable, and with it will come the basis for cooperation of the masses of Arabs and Jews" (16). In short, Avukah's program at this time was to "fight anti-Semitism," defend civil liberties, participate in "anti-fascist action," "liberalize and modernize the Jewish environment," and "organize for maximum assistance in the migration of Jews to Palestine." A second edition of the program was produced in March 1938, advocating a three-pronged approach—working for democracy, changing the Jewish environment, and promoting unrestricted immigration to Palestine—efforts described briefly by Nathan Glazer in "From Socialism to Sociology":[8]

> The three points of our program were to build a non-minority Jewish center in Palestine, to fight fascism, and to foster a democratic American Jewish community. This program represented a somewhat off-center Zionism. The term non-minority was meant to leave room to for a binational state of Jews and Arabs. In those days we believed it possible for the two nations to share power, with neither being in the minority in a political or cultural sense. Our notion was that if both nations were guaranteed equal political rights, the Arab majority of Palestine would allow unrestricted Jewish immigration. At a time when Jews were being hunted down by the Nazis, when the doors of the United States and other Western countries were closed to Jewish refugees, and when Palestine itself had been closed to Jewish immigration by the British, unrestricted immigration was the minimal demand of every Zionist group, even one as eccentric as ours. In retrospect, our views were naive. (195)

An in-depth critique of Avukah's objectives appeared as an unpublished paper called "Memorandum on Avukah," which was circulated in Zionist circles in December 1938 and which mobilized significant forces to defuse its numerous charges. A careful look at this document is in order since it called into question the evolution of Avukah under Harris's leadership and because it elicited a large-scale reply to which Harris contributed.

The Young Poale Zion Alliance (YPZA) was a youth labor Zionist organization, comprised of students attending American universities and colleges who were closest to the Lipsky or Weizman-style (which ostensibly implies politically liberal, nonradical Zionists). For them, Avukah represented a bunch of radicals, and the tone they adopted was far more conservative. Unlike Avukah, the YPZA never undertook to establish branches on campus because it believed that "the problem on the American college campus is to bring Zionism in its *totality* to the attention of the student, in such a way as to give him as full a knowledge and as warm an attachment to Zionism as possible. Once he has become acquainted with the character of Zionism, the student is expected to find his position within the movement in line with his special interests and social outlook." The version of Zionism promoted by the YPZA was not exactly mainstream, since it was specifically socialist, although campus Zionism was certainly more left-wing during this period than it is today, with much attention devoted to defending actions undertaken by the Israeli military. The reason for the YPZA's "memorandum" was that in their opinion (the authors of the report are not cited, which is not atypical for the period for organizations of this nature) is that "Avukah is no longer faithful to the role which by general consent in the Zionist movement was assigned to it, and since we are convinced that the situation is an unhealthy one and needs correction" ("Memorandum on Avukah," 1).

The problem according to this "Memorandum" was that over the last few years Avukah, under Harris's leadership, began to represent particular aspects of Zionism instead of speaking for the general characteristics of the movement. This is made clear in the contrast between YPZA's socialism and Avukah's Marxism: "Within the past few years, the program material issued by Avukah for use at chapter meetings has had a limited partisan orientation and has been not only entirely Marxist in its assumptions (thus tending to exclude many Zionists, even Socialist Zionists who are not Marxists) but has been based on a particular brand of Marxism, closely related to the Trotskyist point of view." As such, the Jewish "problem" is treated by Avukah "largely as a function of the Capitalist system." While the YPZA was in agreement that students of Zionism "should be acquainted with this view," they did "not think it permissible to use such a program as the staple education material, representative of Zionist thinking" because acceptance of it by the student would make him or her "antibourgeois" and "a partisan." (2). The basis of the affiliation to Marxism was likewise through Avukah's ties to organizations frequently mentioned in the Avukah literature, notably Hashomer Hatzair and Mishmar Ha'Emek. "It is a matter of common knowledge among informed Zionists that Avukah's ideological partisanship in Zionism has been a result of the identification of certain of its leading members with the Hashomer Hatzair organization, although we doubt whether the Hashomer Hatzair would be prepared to accept all the implications of Avukah's present point of view." The YPZA document also calls attention to descriptions of Avukah Fellows sent to Palestine where they spend most of their time on Mishmar Ha'Emek "and other Kibbutzim of the Kibbutz Artzi" because "when Avukah attempted to organize a Kibbutz Aliya for those members who were thinking in terms of Aliya, it was expressly organized in affiliation with the American Hashomer Hatzair (without the individual members being enrolled as members of Hashomer Hatzair here)." The YPZA doesn't come out against Hashomer Hatzair specifically here, but it does suggest that "such a direct tie with such a partisan point of view in Zionism tends to limit the possible effectiveness of Avukah" (3). This idea of there being a "direct tie" is a good example of the YPZA right-wing propaganda from this period.

The "three front program" was at the heart of the YPZA critique, since in their opinion it is "entirely irrelevant to the aims of Avukah as an all-embracing Zionist student [organization]." Further problems are found in other Avukah publications, including the new newspaper called *Student Action*, which will be described further on, and the previously-mentioned *Program for American Jews*. In the first issue of *Student Action*, for instance, the YPZA finds contradictions between the view that Avukah doesn't begin by presupposing the "thesis of preserving Jewish culture" or with preordained "Jewish problems," even as it speaks of the fact that "American Jews . . . are clearly a social unit with needs and problems"; for the YPZA, this "entire confused attempt to do away with the positive factors within Jewish life and the verifiable facts about the make-up and interests of American Jews is a reflection of the immaturity and irresponsibility of the authors" (4). Point two of Avukah's program attacks "the American Jewish Community by stating that "the only available Jewish education in the Jewish community is 'the religious and semi-religious schools which teach rote reading of Hebrew prayers, the importance of wearing a skull-cap and a smattering of Jewish history.'" This, according to the YPZA, is "insult added to gross ignorance," "libel upon the many community-wide systems of Jewish education" and "the large number of progressive congregational schools," and, moreover, "it overlooks completely the entire network of primary and secondary schools fostered by the several secularist groups in American Jewish life" as well as institutions of higher Jewish education found in major American cities.

Point three of the Avukah program emphasizes the defeat of "anti-progressive" forces, and as such Jews should not fight for "past traditions or for 'allegiance to Judaism'" (5). According to YPZA, from this follows the idea that "there can be no such thing as Jewish unity because of the economic interests of some Jewish industrialists and financiers outweigh their special needs as Jews." This, says the critique, is a familiar argument from "anti-Zionist circles." So, "not only has Avukah placed the question of the struggle against Fascism at the head of its entire educational program, but it has also chosen to adopt a hopelessly sectarian point of view in this area. The editors and contributors to *Student Action* are opposed to Collective Security with all the intellectual vehemence which they can muster and devote a great deal of the space in *Student Action* to pleading the cause against it. What is worse is the belief in the undesirability of Collective

Security is made a criterion for a full-hearted membership in Avukah. Yet the stationary of Avukah still lists the organization as a Student Zionist Federation (6)." In fact, Avukah had taken this approach to collective security because they saw it as a euphemistic way of promoting collective war. For Avukah, Roosevelt should not be leading such a war, and, as the person who set up the embargo of arms to Spanish republicans during the Spanish civil war, could not be trusted.

As regards Palestine, the YPZA found fault in the idea of Palestine as a "non-minority" center for Jews, as opposed to a Jewish National Home, and the "extreme anti-partitionist point of view," as we have seen, and as we have heard supported by Harris but also by Einstein in his constant reiteration of the importance of not alienating the Arabs in the region. In short, the YPZA finds that Avukah has "given way to an intellectual nightmare which is filled with distortion and misstatement," and which finds Avukah's leaders "free to follow any mental aberration they desire and to organize for such purposes" (7). As such, the YPZA called for a complete revision of Avukah's program and its policies in line with their stated desire of making it more inclusive and representative of a broad Zionist youth organization.

In a January 13, 1939, letter to the then president of Avukah, Stephen S. Wise, Harris makes it clear that Avukah has prepared "a reply to the charges brought against them by the YPZA," which he was at that time reviewing. The undated and unsigned document that was the result of these efforts is, like the attacking document, a series of mimeographed sheets, in this case called "Avukah's Reply to the Memorandum of the Young Poale-Zion Alliance."[9] This unpublished document is significantly longer than the YPZA attack, and my own copy contains some handwritten corrections that seem to be in Harris's own handwriting. The tone of the Avukah reply is harsh, stating that the YPZA criticism was a "bolt from the blue," and that its tactics were with "malicious intent" and "bad taste." Nevertheless, Avukah decided to reply with the formation of a committee of Avukah officials from all across the country during a three-day period in December; it was "completed" by the central Avukah offices, which was probably when Harris had the most significant input.

The reply to YPZA is in some ways rather surprising, notably in its denial of Avukah having any kind of a Marxist character, because the Avukah-supported Kibbutz Artzi, for example, does in fact integrate some of the more positive elements of Marxism. Avukah was clearly struggling for its very existence against the more mainstream and right-wing YPZA and a ZOA, and therefore was making statements that undermined the strength of their own position. The rebuttal begins with regret that YPZA has not defined Avukah's Marxism-Trotskyism or Avukah's Marxism, evidence of which could indeed have been set out in terms of editorials, book reviews, and ideals for Palestine. In any event, the authors of the reply suggest that two paths are open to them, either "presenting a complete statement of the scientific method employed in the Avukah material and thereby pointing out its completely un-Marxian character," or "by showing that the conclusions which these programs reach have no relation whatsoever to the conclusions which Marxians reach" ("Avukah's Reply," pp. 1–2). The first approach is deemed "impossible" because "this is not a philosophic discussion." Nevertheless, they do note that "many Zionists have observed that Avukah's material does not use the usual Zionist terminology, or even presentation. But the alternative to Zionist terminology is not Marxist. And those Zionists who are familiar with Avukah's material, even those who have criticized it, have not labeled it doctrinaire of one school or another." Instead, Avukah employs "modern sociological method and terminology" from such scholars as Charles Beard, Max Weber, and Harry Elmer Barnes who "are not Marxists," (2) and this has "not detracted from any of the fundamental Zionist conclusions" (3). In matters of education, Avukah issues materials from Louis D. Brandeis, Maurice Samuel, Albert Einstein, and Max Brod, and "no Marxist ideology would recommend such writers" (4).

On the next claim, that Avukah's policies are in accord with those of Hashomer Hatzair, the reply suggests that only one member of the Central Administrative Committee is also a member of Hashomer Hatzair (it is not clear to me who this is), and, further, that Hashomer Hatzair may have materials similar to Avukah's "discussions" but, the editor who has annotated the version that I have added, "we do not know of any such material" (5). The authors also deny that Fellows spend most of their time on a Kibbutz Artzi, or that they are encouraged to embark on any specific pathway while in Palestine. Furthermore, "it is not surprising that the YPZA should select Hashomer Hatzair, of all parties, as the sinister force in Avukah. The Hashomer Hatzair is the strongest ideological opposition to the Poale Zion in Palestine. It is to be expected that the youth section of Poale Zion carry on the fight against Hashomer Hatzair here" (7). As such, it is Poale Zion that is fighting a partisan, anti left fight in Zionism, accuses Avukah. Avukah's goals, on the contrary, are described as being "not to assemble the Zionists on the campus," but rather "to convert the non and anti-Zionists to Zionism" (9).

Avukah then defends its stance promoting the improvement of Jewish education in America, and then, in a very important section on their sociological approach, discuss the "analytical method" employed in some of Avukah's writings. The details, concerning the relationship between the "Jewish problem" and "Jewish culture" are not as important, in light of our understanding of Harris, as the question of methods employed to arrive at the Avukah conclusions. "What the YPZA fail to understand, and what they characterize as 'a confused attempt to do away with positive factors within Jewish life,'" is that this is a simple presentation of scientific method, which abstractly would read (1) begin with no preconception as to the character of the material to be studied; (2) deal only with observable data; (3) draw conclusions consistent with observed data" (11). This "scientific method" will come to play an important part in Harris's own work in a range of fields to which he contributed.

Another area of interest is the Avukah reply to charges that it does not promote a "Jewish National Home," an idea they find "vague." More important, however, they also argue against nationalism. "Rightly or wrongly, the American student-body, the Jews in particular, view nationalism—or more specifically, political movements covered by nationalism—as the social weapons which sent Italy to Ethiopia, France and Mussolini to Spain, Hitler in his expansion program through Europe. Nationalism in post war times is almost synonymous with oppression, terrorism, suppression, and imperialism. Students are not prepared to endorse nationalistic movements, as yet, not even American ones" (16). As such, Zionism in "American terms" should according to Avukah be expressed in terms of minority status as opposed to nationalism, partly because "it implies no predatory designs against the Arabs," partly because it is more "expedient in propaganda work," partly because "it is a more exact statement of Jewish needs," and partly because "it implies no preconceived plan for the government of Palestine" (17). After defending its three-pronged approach to Zionism, and its antifascist pro-Zionist stance, the document then concludes with a call for criticism. "The directness—or more correctly, insolence—of the YPZA attack has forced Avukah to speak out with bluntness and perhaps with an over-bearing air of self-assured independence. This impression must be corrected. Avukah's work is open to criticism. Avukah solicits the advice and correction of Zionists. Avukah fully and openly acknowledges its responsibility to the Zionist organization of America to preserve its absolute and unswerving loyalty to Zionism. And should this sincerity and devotion ever appear to wane, Avukah invites the censure of its parent body (25).

The problem was perhaps more deeply rooted than Avukah members knew at the time. However, in private correspondence (on official letterhead) dated January 4, 1939, between Charles A. Cowen, an executive member of the Zionist Organization of America, and Dr. Solomon Goldman, of Chicago (President of the Zionist Organization of America), we learn that members of the Committee on Education of the organization hoped to meet with Goldman "for the purpose of discussing educational activities." The occasion for the discussion was that Goldman, as well as "Lipsky, and a number of others have received a communication from the Young Poale Zion protesting against Avukah and the nature of its work." Far from finding that its critique was marginal, Cowen wrote that "I am inclined to believe that during the last year or more, Avukah certainly was not entitled to represent us on the campus. Orally and in writing, I have protested to Avukah against its policy and program. About two years ago, the Committee on Education was relieved of all authority in matters of organization, etc. in connection with the youth organizations and for a considerable time there has been no proper supervision."

The time period that Cohen describes here coincides exactly with Harris's departure as president of national Avukah, and indeed Cohen writes, in a critical passage, "When Zellig Harris was heading the organization and in a position to give considerable amount of his time, Avukah was full of promise. He should either resume the leadership or steps must be taken to bring about a new state of affairs. The leadership during the last year, has not had the slightest conception of Zionism as a mass movement and in my judgment, has failed to grasp the fundamentals of Zionist aims." These criticisms are not the same as those leveled by the YPZA in that what Cohen speaks out for is a stronger engagement on the part of Avukah in educational matters and, presumably, a greater role for the Zionist Organization of America in discussing orientation. This is indeed what seems behind Cohen's suggestion that Zionist youth activities and organizations be studied, "leading to the formulation of a definite program of work." At the time of this letter, the Executive (of the ZOA) had not "gotten around to considering this resolution," which had been proposed at the last Zionist convention, but, says Cohen, "we ought to get at it as soon as possible."

Joseph Epstein, president of the Avukah chapter at the University of Chicago, added his own critique of Avukah in a letter he wrote to Rabbi Solomon Goldman, president of the Zionist Organization of America on January 9, 1939. Therein he provided a litany of complaints, suggesting that in the past few years, "the tendency in Avukah has been away from a Zionist program. A desire on the part of the leadership to change the name of the organization and the non-support of the Basle Program bears this out." Once again, of critical concern was Avukah's recent (re)statement, in a 1938 Avukah conference, that the organization supports "a non-minority center in Palestine," as opposed to a Jewish National Home. This criticism would have applied to Harris as well, which makes this critique quite different from Cohen's approach. Further, Epstein complained that members find that "Avukah is too radical, that undue emphasis is placed on political discussions and activities," and that "leaders are trying to build up some type of Marxist group and that the leaders are working behind a cover hiding their real objectives." As such, Epstein suggested that "the policy and program should be examined, the leaders should be questioned and the publications of Avukah scrutinized." This rift between the "left" and the, for lack of a better word, "center" of the Zionist movement remained, of course, and remnants of it exist even today. In the end, as the criticisms and the replies suggest, the Avukah programs were certainly scrutinized constantly, not only by Zionists but, as will be made clear further on, by the American government, which cast a cold eye on foreigners' involvement in anti–status quo politics. Harris would not be above such questioning, as would many people in his entourage, direct and indirect, particularly as the growing world war followed its early route, with grave consequences and whole new responsibilities for Harris both as a left-oriented Zionist and as a researcher.

Amid these discussions the horrors leading to the war multiplied, and the plight of the Jews, already deeply worrisome, was soon to be desperate. Avukah was still working hard to promote the idea of bringing Jews to Palestine, and their publications reflect growing urgency as the realities of the war took hold. As we have seen, Avukah was concerned about general issues which were to lead to the catastrophes of the war, notably the rise of fascism and the concomitant destruction of left-wing opposition to an increasingly divisive and unfair status quo. Peter Novick's point that "after the war began, and after the main outlines of the Holocaust had become known, it was common for Jewish writers to interpret Nazi atrocities in a universalistic fashion—stressing that Jews were far from the only victims" (38) was indeed consistent with Avukah's overall approach. Harris, and other Avukah members, pursued efforts to establish a general critique of society, fascist and otherwise, and in certain analyses we find the suggestion, historically accurate, that the opposing sides in this conflict wished for the destruction not only of their respective enemies, but of valid opposition to ruling elites. The reaction of Avukah to the events as they unfolded on the continent was more muted than one might expect, at least in hindsight, but it is clear that nobody in the movement imagined just how far, and how fast, the Germans would go.

This period was ripe with growing strife amongst Zionists, and moves were being made on several fronts to resolve critical questions. Samuel Goldman wrote to Harris on March 30, 1939, to ask that he present "a program of Zionism for Youth, to give the ideology as well as the technique of implementation" for a paper to be presented three weeks hence, at the ZOA convention. The other burning issue at this juncture was the imminent publication of the British White Paper on policy in Palestine, which led the revisionist Benjamin Akzin to write to Louis Brandeis to urge him to take drastic action, that is, to "prevent the White Paper from being published" (May 10, 1939). His proposed tactics were drastic, and thus worth citing at length.

What we really should do, is to seize the Government of Palestine before the White paper is issued; the ensuing unpleasantness would certainly change the facts of the Palestine situation sufficiently to bring about a different solution on an entirely different basis. But I am not so stupid as to ask *you* to take the initiative in such a move. What even I have the right to suggest even to you, Sir, is that you announce *publicly* your willingness to head the Zionist movement in order to lead it in its coming fight. Accompanied by a sufficiently strong wording, such a public announcement might go some way toward convincing the world and the British that we are in earnest, and it would do much to focus American public attention on our problem. And if you are willing to make such a sacrifice, for a sacrifice it is that is needed at a time like this, I hope that you will realize the importance of the time element.[10]

This was a bold suggestion, but these were heady times, and in a May 16, 1939, letter to Goldman (in the Goldman archive), Philip Moskovitz suggested that Weizman's proposal for binationalism in Palestine be rejected. These ideas, along with all other discussions about alternatives to the Jewish state in Palestine, have somehow been erased from history even despite the fact that in the 1930s the British Government's own Royal Commission (popularly known as the Peel Commission) proposed the partition of Palestine into Jewish and Arab states with certain areas remaining under British jurisdiction. In this same letter, Moskovitz also suggested that they make the appropriate moves to encourage a "mass migration" of Jews to Palestine, bring revisionists into the picture by creating a friendly relationship between them and the Histadrut, and assimilate them "back into the fold" of the ZOA, and using Louis Brandeis to contest the British plan for an Arab state in Palestine.

With the publication of the White Paper, Zionists like David Ben-Gurion followed Akzin's lead and begged for the assistance of Brandeis. In a June 6, 1939, letter, delivered secretly to avoid it being opened en route,

Ben-Gurion revealed Britain's "secret" plan to drastically limit Jewish emigration to Palestine, to under 10,000 for the period of April to September, 1939. Ben-Gurion suggested that they were thereby "entering a new phase of Zionism," which he called "Militant Zionism." The description is all the more important with the vision of hindsight. "Our position is a very unique one. We are not fighting like the Indians or the Irish for self-government and independence against foreign domination. We are not fighting for the rights of the existing Jewish community of Palestine. We are fighting on behalf of the Jewish people in its entirety and we are fighting, in particular, to keep the doors of Palestine open for Jewish immigration, and the soil of Palestine open for Jewish settlement. Such a struggle requires great courage and devotion, but it also requires great foresight."

Some of the issues raised here were discussed during the 1939 Avukah summer school. Harris had a Guggenheim Fellowship that year to work on language revivals, a project he barely started before having to return to the United States (from Europe and the Near East) on account of the war.[11] He also gave talks at the Avukah camp, and in an article summarizing his talks, in the *Avukah Student Action* of July 28, 1939 (7), we find Harris suggesting that the standard of living of ordinary Americans is "not that high" and getting lower, and that this situation is exacerbated for Jews and other minorities, on account of the nature of "modern industrialization." This is a preface to a consideration of problems facing Jewish refugees, that is, persons who have "already experienced what may come here" (to America). Speaking about German-Jewish refugees, Harris (with the collaboration of another Avukah member, Jesse Orlansky) suggested that if someone "had been a progressive in his native country, it is perfectly understandable why he should be routed from a totalitarian state. The fascist creed demands that one 'obey, follow and fight.' In practice this is possible only with subsistence levels of existence (cannons not butter), blind obedience, and anti-cultural bias." Harris suggested that "the progressive Jew and Gentile fights against this because it is unacceptable to him as a human being. If this is the issue, a conflict must follow and the loser will be the one with the inferior force, in a real political sense." But the Jews have been in a peculiar situation because "they were often accused of being the main financiers as they were accused of being radicals." Further, many of these refugees "did not even consider themselves to be Jews," but were nevertheless subjected to the "artificial decree, the Nuremberg laws." Typical of his analysis is the move to the situation in the United States, which is deemed similar, whereby Jewish bankers and radicals are attacked, which scores "real dividends to its leaders, and also for "the private sources who supply [the government] funds it pays dividends as it weakens progressive forces and lowers the wage-level." As a consequence, Harris argued that we "must help the refugees," both for their sake and for that of American Jews. Further, Americans must challenge Britain's policies regarding emigration to Palestine, the only true homeland for the millions of Jews who want to leave Europe.

Seymour Melman, and the Onset of War

In 1939, a young student by the name of Seymour Melman received an Avukah travel fellowship, which he used for travel to the World Zionist Congress in Geneva and then on to the Kibbutz Artzi near Haifa. There he met up with some of his friends, such as Sylvia Binder (who had been the secretary of Avukah in 1935), and made acquaintance with Arabs, Poles (Poland had just been overrun by the Nazis), and Palestinians. Melman became an important figure, first because of his growing involvement in Avukah, and second because he became over the years a close friend of Harris and an advocate for the work he did. Melman was often mentioned in Avukah newspapers and publications, including an article, in *Avukah Student Action* of December 2, 1940, called "Meet ... Seymour Melman." He is described therein as being "Avukah's omnipresent Field Organizer," a "legendary figure" who is "affectionately called Schmelke." He had started as an economics major at City College where, as a freshman, he "somehow strayed into Avukah and immediately invented, advertised, and reputed the now famous Pamphlet Service." Then, "triumph followed triumph, from chapter president to Palestine Fellow for 1939–40 to his present distinction of having said more to more people than can be imagined." Finally, he was described as "the most accomplished Yiddish dialectician we know" and, from a range of sources, as a very charismatic person. Indeed, he was so impressive that Nathan Glazer recalls that he joined Avukah following his having heard Melman at an Avukah talk.

The speaker was Seymour Melman, a recent graduate of City College who had just spent a year in Palestine and was reporting on his experiences. Had Avukah been simply a Jewish organization, I doubt that it would have made much impact on me. But these were *socialist Zionists*. What is more, they were *intellectual* socialist Zionists and looked down on nonintellectual socialist Zionists. Melman was a charismatic figure. . . . What led me to speak to him after his lecture I do not know.

A December 6, 1939, letter from the executive secretary of Avukah, Alfred J. Kahn, describes a trip that Seymour Melman had taken with Aryeh

Korin, and then gives details about his arrival in Palestine and the tour he made of that country. Avukah officials feared throughout the trip that "Palestine might become involved in the war," but he stayed on nevertheless, residing in several of the Kibbutzim. Upon returning to the United States in the spring of 1940, Melman, Harris, and other Avukah members wrote material that appeared in a special issue of the Avukah newspaper concerning the condition of the Yishuv (the Jewish settlement) with regard to the Arab side and the British government. Further, Melman undertook a national tour of Avukah chapters, described in an Avukah newspaper article on April 18, 1940, in part to discuss the Masada-Avukah relationship, which will be of concern in the next section.

Masada, Revisionists, and the Communist Party

One way to further clarify the nature of Avukah, and by extension the approach that Harris had to the Zionist movement and to political ideas more generally, is to look at internal documents relating to alliances and foes. On January 15, 1940, a new proposal was put forth to encourage closer relations between Masada and Avukah, the former a group that was started in 1934 because "it was realized that young men of a specific age group were not being provided for in any Zionist group" (2). The idea seems to have come from the executive board of Avukah, and Alfred Kahn, the executive secretary, circulated early versions to both Solomon Goldman, of the Zionist Organization of America, and Louis D. Brandeis. The goal was to increase the scope and effectiveness of Zionist youth work by either joining forces, or by cooperating, whichever would be deemed the most effective. On the one hand, a union would make of the resulting group a larger unit, on the other, "what is necessary in view of the crucial situation is a tremendous appeal to youth directly related to the European crisis, on a far larger scale than anything done before" (1). For the moment, however, one way of linking the groups was, according to memos, to use Masada as an endpoint for Avukah "graduates."

There has not existed, in the past, a satisfactory channel for bringing Avukah graduates into the Zionist organization. Avukah has decided in the last few months to strongly encourage the graduates to join the Z.O.A. [Zionist Organization of America], preferably in groups. Should it be found desirable, however, a mechanism could be set up to direct all Avukah graduates into Masada. In large cities, graduates could form Masada groups made up in large part of ex-Avukah members. Graduates who live in smaller cities would be educated so that they would consider it a Zionist obligation to organize Masada chapters upon graduation. (3)

The stated goal of Avukah was to promote further work and discussions regarding concerns such as the war, fascism, and threats to civil liberties, and Masada was considering similar activities.

The response from Masada was not enthusiastic, as was clear from an editorial written by Solomon Goldman of the Zionist Organization of America in the *Masada News*. "Masada committed a blunder when it agreed to enter into the proposals for the new Zionist Youth Councils without insisting that the present incomprehensible relationship of Avukah to the rest of the organized General Zionists be completely clarified." Alfred J. Kahn, in a letter to Goldman dated March 13, 1940, disputes the Masada view that the Avukah leadership is determined "to permit nothing which might interfere with the vested interests of a tight little organization which has decided to be a law unto itself." By way of rebuff, Kahn repeats the idea of maintaining two separate organizations, with the combining of efforts where it seems desirable (education, propaganda, fund-raising), and, "following a period of such cooperation administered by a joint committee, discussion as to future steps would be in order." Seymour Melman, in the course of his tour of Avukah chapters, waded into this discussion; in a letter to Leon Agriss, the Avukah Executive Secretary Meyer Rabinovitz wrote, "As you can see from the enclosed memorandum, Seymour has a good deal of valuable information concerning recent events in Palestine which should be of considerable interest to all Jewish groups. Is it possible for you to arrange meetings with various Zionist and Jewish groups at which Seymour can speak?" Rabinovitz did make the arrangements, and in a May 29, 1940, letter, Leon Agriss, of Masada, described Melman's reception among those who attended: "They were all most impressed by his knowledge of the facts concerning Palestine today and were probably as shocked as are other audiences at the revelations about the British actions. The meeting was useful also in making more firm the relationships of Masada with young Judea and Junior Hadassah here, although only a few of both groups attended." According to Agriss, Melman took up the issue of Avukah's relation to other groups, notably Masada, in discussions following his talk.

It was noted that the several endeavors to bring about a unity of Masada and Avukah were unsuccessful and, while we didn't go far into that subject, we did concern ourselves with another relationship of the two groups. Melman told us that for the most part Avukah members who leave college do not affiliate with any Zionist organization, primarily because they find themselves unable to find a fit after their experiences with Avukah. He confessed that possibly it would be best if these persons were urged to affiliate to Masada, and that is the position we take here. We are not in a position, either from experience or knowledge of the facts, to have a very definite and yet fair opinion on the question of unity, but we do feel that the men and women of Avukah, even if their training does not reach the level Melman says it had (and I hope it does), owe it to their idealism and their belief in the movement to make a place for themselves in other organizations. It is they who have much to offer Masada, and I believe Masada can offer them much. Avukah grads can give Masada chapters political direction and education, while Masada can offer them experience of learning to work with the masses of Jewish youth, for we have found that college persons in the Zionist movement generally are quite idealistic but speak and act too much from an academic point of view without the knowledge and experience of practical group work.

This letter is significant in terms of the relationship between Palestine and the United States, and Agriss's own views point to some of the problems relating to the Jews' pursuit of political idealism and sustained Zionism in the long term, through continued relations with Jewish organizations.

Why shouldn't Young Judeans who go to college, also be taught to look forward to affiliation with Avukah, and why shouldn't Avukah members look forward to activity in Masada during the remainder of their youth, and later to ZOA? If the answer is that these groups do not meet the political requirements of the college youth, all right, let them affiliate to any organization which meets their philosophy most closely. But they must be affiliated to something! But in almost every community large or small, there are found young persons who find themselves unable to fit into the existing social strata. They find small town or small city life dull, unintellectual, petty, gossipy, hypocritical, etc. and consequently remove themselves from it. Their idealism is valueless for they make no effort to apply it, and sooner or later lose it and fall subject to the very elements of society which they now detest. Even in a small city like this it is surprising how many well-to-do business men will sometimes confess to having been a Bundist, or socialist, or some sort of marxist, and yet today they exploit their workers as much as the next fellow, and belong to the temple, and country club, and play poker, and all those other matters because it is the THING to do! If youth who have idealism will go into those organized elements with which they have some minimum in common, they can and should influence them to the point that perhaps an Hadassah meeting won't just be a gathering of primped-up women, but will be a place where the adult Jewess can really realize a valuable expression of her Judaism. I know Masada, and Junior Hadassah, and Young Judea aren't the types of organizations which you and many in Avukah would like to see, and they aren't everything I'd like to see in the Youth Zionist movement. So what? Are we to sit back and do nothing? Can the two or three or even half dozen of us in all the lesser communities in America isolate ourselves because the masses of Jewish youth and Adults are unable to see our point of view? Our duty is to go out and get Zionists, make them, lead them, but without that air of superiority of not wanting to work in the type of program needed to attract the less advanced elements in Jewish youth. (Letter from Agriss, May 29, 1940)

Al Kahn of Avukah responded on June 11, 1940, picking up once again on the question of affiliations to Masada, voicing his accord with Agriss's ideas, and bemoaning the fact that Avukah wanted their graduates to go into Masada, but that Dr. Goldman had been so "concerned with their maximum demands (amalgamation of the organizations) that they allowed this very important suggestion to go by." He then gives an interesting sense of Avukah's goals during this period.

I think that your justifications of the type of activity you undertake despite realization of the failings of the group with which you have to deal are extremely well taken. What we in Avukah are trying to do, and with increasing emphasis, is to prepare people with the proper qualifications so that they may go back to their communities and build up the relationship which you call for. We don't want snobbishness. We do want people who are ideologically trained, politically aware, and with organizational experience. We insist that Avukah be of such a character that it will prepare people so that they will know what to do when they go back to the communities and will not allow the status quo to remain. In resisting the attacks we justify our program. Some people interpret that as snobbishness but it is really the only way that an organization convinced of the justification of its program can defend itself.

Interestingly enough, this amicable discussion between Kahn, of Avukah, and Agriss, of Masada, led to further efforts to link the organizations. A meeting was held at the Ninth Annual Avukah Summer School on June 17, 1940, proposing collaboration based upon meetings held between Zellig Harris's brother, Tzvee, Seymour Melman, and executives of Masada. In an article from the series "Meet . . .," from January 7, 1941, we have "Meet . . . Tzvee Harris," who later became "a distinguished med school student" who "edited the graduating class journal as an apprenticeship for his activities in [University of Pennsylvania's] Avukah chapter and for managing the old Avukah Bulletin." Tzvee Harris is indeed a very accomplished individual who completed his degree in Physics in 1933 at the University of Pennsylvania before going on to study medicine at the same institution, finishing his internship in 1938. He became an Instructor in Bacteriology at the Penn School of Medicine in 1938, an Instructor in Pediatrics in 1941, Assistant Chief of Pediatric Service in the Philadelphia General Hospital in 1943, Assistant Cardiologist to the Out-Patient Department at the Children's Hospital of Philadelphia in 1944, Associate in Pediatrics at Penn in 1945, Chief of the Rheumatic Fever Clinic at Philadelphia General in 1945, and Assistant Research Professor of Pediatrics at

Penn in 1946. He has continued a long and brilliant career, including writing a range of papers relating to infectious diseases, and in my own meeting with him in 2008, he spoke warmly of his Avukah years.

In an Avukah communiqué signed by Alfred J. Kahn, we learn that Melman and Tzvee Harris met with officers of Masada and came up with a plan for "immediate collaboration between the two groups." The links would be based upon Avukah providing free copies of Zionist publications and full participation in a new series of writings on Zionism and Palestine. They also proposed that Avukah and Masada share facilities, notably a conference room and a mimeograph machine, to be funded by the Zionist Organization of America. They suggested that Avukah alumni enter Masada, in accordance with previous suggestions made by Avukah, and finally, "several other and less important plans of collaboration have been discussed. For the time being, Avukah suggests that these proposals be carried out, and hopes that the great Zionist effort which we must all make during the coming year will not be hampered by lack of trust and cooperation." This was recalled in a July 25, 1940 letter from Kahn to Agriss, which noted that Avukah had suggested to Matthew Huttner, of Masada, that conversations be held between the two groups and that they had indeed taken place, and that proposals had been made to further cooperation between the two groups. This did not rectify matters, however, and Kahn's letter noted that "less than two weeks later, Masada's president took occasion at the ZOA executive meeting in Pittsburgh to charge that Avukah had rejected all proposals of unity and close cooperation with Masada," which led Kahn to conclude that "Avukah cannot contemplate any negotiations until Masada revises its publicly expressed attitude." Nevertheless, relations between the two groups did ultimately improve, along the lines of what had been originally proposed by Avukah, and relations with Masada's Leon Agriss, remained cordial; he was even invited to participate in the Avukah Summer School in 1941, which was to feature contributions from Abraham Revusky, Kurt Lewin, Kurt Blumenfeld, and Dwight Macdonald.

The war raged on, and so too did Avukah's work, with its numbers growing to 60 chapters and a total of 1,800 members, with new chapters in places like St. Louis, Missouri, Austin, Texas, and even Kingston, Ontario. Nevertheless, Avukah remained absent between Iowa and the Pacific Coast, with only one campus in California (UCLA) and one in the South (Tulane), and it was not drawing considerably on the estimated 100,000 Jewish university students in America. More important, Avukah newspapers were reporting the horrors of the war to a reasonably large body of American students. Novick found that "in the course of 1940, 1941, and 1942, reports of atrocities against Jews began to accumulate. But these, like the numbers cited, were often contradictory" (Novick, 22). Unlike the mainstream press to which he referred for his research, the Avukah news sources were accustomed to reporting atrocities committed against Jews, and news reports were unequivocal about what was happening, increasingly, in countries such as Germany. So Novick's point on reliability of press reports, for example, once again needs qualification as regards Avukah's news sources: "In the nature of the situation, there were no first-hand reports from Western journalists. Rather, they came from a handful of Jews who had escaped, from underground sources, from anonymous German informants, and, perhaps most unreliable of all, from the Soviet government. If, as many suspected, the Soviets were lying about the Katyn Forest massacre, why not preserve a healthy skepticism when they spoke of Nazi atrocities against Soviet Jews?" (22). This applies to the *New York Times*, the example that Novick then provides, but it is not reflected in Avukah's newspapers and pamphlets. Indeed, ambiguity about the fate of Jews and questions about the reliability of reports describing their situation were never raised in the decades during which their newspapers were circulated among its several hundred, and eventually several thousand, members. We will return to these concerns further on, as they become exacerbated during World War II.

Despite the upheaval caused by the war, the Avukah summer camps continued, and the July 22, 1940, issue carried abstracts of talks given by Zellig Harris, Joseph Israel, Aryeh Korin, Seymour Melman, Abraham Revusky, Arthur Rosenberg, Manya Schochat, and Adrian Schwartz. Zellig Harris's talk was on the familiar theme of fascism in America, the result of inequality and the absence of social justice. "Who will support these groups? Young unemployed people, who can find no place in the economy, and middle-class men who are being pushed into the lower groups. Who on the other hand, are the ones to fight Fascism? Organized labor is the strongest protection any country can have against Fascism. Not all Jews can be relied on since some follow their class interests," said Harris, and "many Jews supported Hitler." In a conclusion that once again points to his interest in the "good society," Harris said that "it is our task to see to it that Jews do not lend themselves to supporting fascist tendencies and to show how we can strengthen the groups that offer a progressive solution to economic and social problems" (2).

The 1941 camp lectures were given by Shmuel Ben-Zvi, D. Dwight Macdonald, Israel Mereminski, Alfred Kahn, Nathan Glazer, Adrien Schwartz, and Arthur Rosenberg. The students who were involved came to participate in very interesting work, including the summer school lectures of June 1941, summarized in Avukah memos (no author cited). Nathan Glazer, by then the managing editor of *Avukah Student Action*, recalls some of the activities of the organization in his article "From Socialism to Sociology."

As editor of Avukah Student Action one of my duties—as Chester Rapkin explained—was to liven up the pages with pictures and cartoons, and I could find them free at the *New Leader* by burrowing through a pile of cuts they received from unions and other sources. There I met Daniel Bell. An informal seminar took place every Friday afternoon at the *New Leader* office. I did not participate directly but listened as I looked for something we could use in *Avukah Student Action*. Seymour Martin Lipset, with whom for a while I took the subway to college, joined Avukah briefly."

Glazer gave a "history of American Zionism talk" at the summer camp that year, as did Alfred Kahn on "Politics for Zionists—Arabs and Britain" and "The Organizing of Jewish Students"; Arthur Rosenberg on "Why Jews Should Have a Political Program"; and Adrian Schwartz on "The Development of Avukah."

The Kahn talk on Arabs and Britain reiterated the point that "the interests of the Arab lower and middle classes are in complete harmony with the interests of Jews in Palestine," even though "conflict does exist between the interests of the Jews and the small effendi group which sees in Western industrialization and democracy the undermining of its social position." Kahn further insisted that Zionism had been of benefit to the Arabs, partly because of Britain's policy of "divide and rule," which pitted Muslim Arabs against Christian Arabs, Husseini against Nashashibi, Revisionists against Histadrut, and Arabs against Jews, and partly because "the British favored Husseini Arab against Nashashibi, Arab as opposed to Jew," because they "preferred feudal lords to a new capitalist ruling class." Kahn proposed fostering Arab-Jewish relations in Palestine by encouraging "joint defense activity, if it is combined with clear antifascist propaganda," the promotion of knowledge about the respective parties, economic cooperation, a "program of joint trade union activity, and the promotion of a "non-effendi Arab leadership." Kahn's other talk, on the organizing of Jewish students, was recorded in note form by Seymour Melman (dated 1941), and contains some interesting points relating to the Jewish minority position in the United States. He began the talk with some statistics about Jewish students at that time: 1/5 of Jews of college age attend college, compared with 1/12 for non-Jews, they make up 9.13 percent of the college population in 1934–1935 but only 3.5 percent of the total population of the United States, Jews attend primarily large schools, they prefer "individualist" professions in which discrimination is minimized, most Jews have roommates, and most have Jewish friends, many are not "practicing" Jews, and so forth.

Dwight Rosenberg's presence at the camp was particularly important because he served as a kind of intellectual leader, a touchstone for Avukah's program material and publications; he was the author of *The Birth of the German Republic, A History of Bolshevism, The History of the German Republic,* and *Democracy and Socialism,* and in his talk he suggested that fascism, of which "a man with a little moustache in Berlin" is but a symptom, must be countered, as must totalitarianism, which he described as "essentially the same as the Russian system today." Fascism has "brought some progress to Germany" and some security, but it "gives a very limited amount of security to the masses of people" and workers "have to work for others." Further, fascism scapegoats the Jews, while totalitarianism exploits the masses. To offer an example, Rosenberg then spoke of Palestine, which contained peoples of all political tendencies.

The democratic front is represented by labor, the Histadrut, the Kibbutz. On the other side we have a nucleus of Fascism, the Revisionists. It is not enough for Jews merely to be politically active; their politics must also be correct. It is useless to make wrong politics, politics of totalitarian nature. Therefore Revisionism is an enormously dangerous tendency. The Revisionists are an enemy among us who would undermine the democratic forces among the Jew and open the gate to the enemy whenever possible.

In short, "the task and duty of the Jew today [is] to engage in politics. First, national politics in Palestine, and secondly, world politics, to fight Fascism—because Fascism and totalitarianism are the worst enemies of human principles, especially Jewish principles." Rosenberg was immensely important to the movement, and Melman's notes include copious descriptions of this talk, and for good reason.

The analysis provided by Rosenberg in a talk called "The War Situation" is original and, moreover, it helps explain the links in Harris's own thinking about the relationship between antifascism, Zionism, and anticapitalism. In this talk, Rosenberg emphasized the heterogeneity of the Nazi Party, suggesting that it was divided on "social lines" with a right wing of Nazi conservatism and a left wing, with Hitler, Himmler, and Hess occupying the "center group." Following the "blood-purge of Nazi leaders" in 1934, the "capitalist group won a victory," leading to an important change in emphasis to the buildup of the party in the direction of a "state social commonwealth," which Rosenberg considered "nearer to Bolshevism." This proximity to the Soviet Union caused certain problems for Hitler, "who could not attack the symbol of workers' power" (the USSR) while at the same time making "grandiose promises to the workers of Germany." For this reason, he did not come out against Bolshevism, but, rather, against the Soviet Union's "secret cooperation with England." The point of all this for the Avukah talk was to suggest that the "totalitarian machine," as he described the Nazis, was not as strong as it seemed, and it would eventually "fall under the burden of its own contradictions"; but it needed a push. For this reason, Rosenberg urged that "the task and duty of the Jew today is to engage in politics," first "national politics in Palestine," and second, "world politics, to fight fascism." Most important in terms of Harris's own position is the idea, always close to Rosenberg's thinking, that "the Jew must understand that by strengthening all positive elements in society he is bettering his own position. Polite society and elegant ladies don't help anybody. It is therefore futile to judge our political activity by their standards. They will never help the Jewish people in an emergency." So we return to several key notions, present as far back as the shtetl in Balta; Jewish self-reliance and anti-fascism in the broadest sense of the term which, as we have seen, is in some ways necessarily anti-capitalist.

Aside from Paul Mattick and Arthur Rosenberg, someone whose political ideas were important to Harris, at this time and beyond, was Dwight MacDonald, who Glazer described in terms of the objectives of the Avukah movement in the aforementioned chapter on the move from socialism to sociology.

Avukah, following the pattern of other left sectarian organizations, had "study groups," in which we read not only Zionist classics but also socialist classics: Bukharin's *Historical Materialism* was particularly favored by some of our elders. But we were not Leninists. Though left, and critical of social democrats, the radical leaders of Avukah who tried to influence us were (Rosa) Luxemburgian—revolutionary but against a directing central party and for education of the working masses. It was a very congenial bent. The only issues that called for action were Zionist ones; for the rest education was sufficient. The doctrine hardly mattered, I am convinced. It is almost embarrassing to say we believed in revolution. The only way to relieve the embarrassment is to confess that we really did not. What actually mattered to us was not our doctrines but the people we met and the things we read. For example, we read *Partisan Review* and *The New International*, in which Sidney Hook, James Burnham, and Dwight Macdonald then wrote. We often invited Macdonald to our summer camps, devoted to intensive "education." He had started the journal Politics; some members of our group attended the early meetings and some wrote for it.

MacDonald was present at this particular Avukah camp to talk about "the war economy." Melman's reconstruction of MacDonald's talk makes it clear that any war economy, unless in situations of obvious production surpluses, must rely upon totalitarian control, and that the similarity of wartime situations move economies in this same direction. The alternative, for MacDonald, is to erect an economy built on socialist principles, because it is only under totalitarianism or democratic socialist planning that it will be possible to win the war. "Only by Socialism," he concludes, "can the defeat of Fascism be made a certainty. And only an uncompromising fight against capitalism—which means implacable opposition to the Roosevelt-Churchill governments—and for the democratic rights of the masses can win socialism."

Adrian Schwartz then outlined the development of Avukah, suggesting that its early period, 1925–1933, had been a Romantic one, during which time the Jewish students' main problem was "social exclusion." From 1934 to 1936 Avukah was in an "era of political awakening," marked by the depression, the rise of fascism in Germany, and the Revisionist problem. Finally, there was the "Golden Era of Ideology," "reflecting a deepening of the depression and a heightening of anti-Semitism." Schwartz described Avukah's activities during each period, and then reiterated the importance of the three-point program, suggesting that Front I and Front III needed to be bolstered through community action. In Melman's notes, we find further elaboration of these ideas, with emphasis upon some crucial issues, such as the fact that Jews must remain in the minority in Palestine: "In evaluating Avukah's Three Front Program it is necessary to realize that a Jewish student organization must deal with all the problems that confront Jewish students. These are the problems entailed by membership in a minority group within a contracting society. This requires the development of a non-minority center in Palestine, the strengthening of democracy here, and action within the American Jewish Community in the directions indicated by Fronts I and III." His final suggestion—that it is no longer necessary to "sell" anti-fascism to Jews, but, rather, Avukah must now concentrate upon "community action," and "action rather than persuasion,"—was of course crucial; but, as we know in hindsight, it was a plan that fell short.

Shmuel Ben-Zvi's talk focused upon the nature of the collectives in Palestine, emphasizing that the form they take, the kibbutzim, is not comparable to the Fourier or Owens colonies in America, which were based on the principle of "fleeing from reality"; rather, the kibbutz exists to answer the specific needs in the country: economic, military, and social. Nevertheless, this idea could be applied elsewhere, said Ben-Zvi, and this discussion helped show the links between the kibbutz movement and the council communists from which it drew some inspiration and to which Harris would return with great vigor throughout his life. The kibbutz works, just as workers councils work, because of their autonomy but also because they are federated, socially and economically, and this type of system, Ben-Zvi said, could extend beyond the agricultural setting, its original base, to urban plans, including Tel Aviv which "was built up completely by private initiative." We will see similar discussions, and strong support of principles relating to kibbutzim organization, in Harris's work on Employee Stock Ownership Plans and the transformation of capitalist society, in the last chapter.

Fighting the War

Avukah's principal concerns in this period were, of course, the war in Europe and America's involvement in it, subsequent to the attack on Pearl Harbor in December 1941. In the February 1942 issue of *Avukah Student Action*[12] a report appeared describing an Avukah conference aimed at discussing Avukah activities in the face of the war. Adrian Schwartz suggested that they "continue their activities as in peacetime," Arthur Rosenberg suggested that in the face of fascism that Zionism was the best activity for Jews, and Seymour Melman suggested that in the face of the fact that other student organizations were crumbling, Avukah had an even greater role to play for "bewildered college youth." On staff for that issue was Milton Shapiro, the author of a number of Avukah pieces, who eventually became Harris's brother-in-law (he was the brother of Tzvee Harris's wife Suzanna).

The February 1942 issue also featured an article on a new book by Erich Fromm titled *Escape From Freedom*. This is particularly significant in light of Harris's work, notably his interest in the psychological basis of fascism, the psychological obstacles that stand in the way of promoting the "good society," and other psychological issues relating to the transformation of capitalist society. The review, written by Roy Brown, assessed the book's approach to explaining fascism with reference to Freudian principles, and the idea that "fascism is an escape, in this case, an escape resorted to by individuals who are overburdened with freedom." Although Brown found the theory unoriginal, and he questioned whether there is in the human character "an innate drive toward freedom," he nevertheless found the book "well written, interesting, and, in addition, makes a valuable contribution to the understanding of Fascism." Fromm's work was of great interest to Harris, and was frequently discussed by Avukah members.

Fromm's overall hypothesis is that although freedom has brought independence and rationality, it has also made the individual "isolated and, thereby, anxious and powerless. This isolation is unbearable, and the alternatives he is confronted with are either to escape from the burden of his freedom into new dependencies and submission, or to advance to the full realization of positive freedom which is based upon the uniqueness and individuality of man" (viii).[13] Fromm cites John Dewey's *Freedom and Culture*,[14] which states that "the serious threat to our democracy is not the existence of foreign totalitarian states. It is the existence within our own personal attitudes and within our own institutions of conditions which have given a victory to external authority, discipline, uniformity and dependence upon The Leader in foreign countries. The battlefield is also accordingly here—within ourselves and our institutions." This fear of latent fascism is consistent with Avukah's sense that people need to be enlightened and educated, and that fascism must be better understood so as to be better combated, an idea that runs throughout Fromm's text. Consistent as well with Harris's approach is the idea that society must be changed, to help individuals realize their potential.

[I]f the economic, social and political conditions on which the whole process of human individuation depends, do not offer a basis for the realization of individuality in the sense just mentioned, while at the same time people have lost those ties which gave them security, this lag makes freedom an unbearable burden. It then becomes identical with doubt, with a kind of life which lacks meaning and direction. Powerful tendencies arise to escape from this kind of freedom into submission or some kind of relationship to man and the world which promises relief from uncertainty, even if it deprives the individual of his freedom. (52)

In this sense, Zionists like Harris encouraged migration to Palestine because the United States, although not fascist at that time, could nevertheless become so, since many of the conditions prerequisite to it were already in existence there. In the next issue, Avukah's Nathan Glazer reviewed the book *Toward Freedom: The Autobiography of Jawaharlal Nehru*, an example of Avukah's burgeoning interest in Indian affairs.

Fascism at home and abroad remained the central concern for Avukah in this period, led by Harris's own reflections upon the dangers of homegrown fascism. One way that this was studied was through analysis of the links between U.S. business interests and the Nazi war machine, a precursor to recent books such as *IBM and the Holocaust*[15] and *Henry Ford and the Jews*.[16] An early article on this subject is found in *Avukah Student Action*, which blares out that "Henry Ford, No. 1 Anti-Semite, Fattens on Government Contracts." The article, by Rosalind Schwartz, notes that despite a recent award of more than $100,000,000 in U.S. government contracts, Ford is "still supporting Nazi-anti-Semitic propaganda" through the "notorious forgery," *Protocols of the Elders of Zion*,[17] which has an endorsement by Ford, and *El Judio Internacional*,[18] which has Ford's name on its cover and which is "full of virulent attacks on Jews." Further, Ford "still has the medal he received on July 10, 1938, from Adolf Hitler, the Grand Cross of the German Eagle, the highest decoration to which foreigners are eligible." And the May 1942 edition of the same newspaper contains an article and a diagram indicating links between U.S. big business and the Nazi war effort, via connections, direct and indirect, between the German firms (including I. G. Farben, Krupp, Allgemeine Elektricitäts-Gesellschaft, Siemens & Halske, and Vereinigte Stahlwerke) and a whole host of American corporations (including DuPont, Standard Oil, Sterling Products, Winthrop Chemical, Central Aniline and Film Corp., Aluminum Ltd. (Canada), Alcoa, Ansco General, Aniline, Ford, National Cash Register, General Electric, Westinghouse, ITT, American Bemberg, North American Rayon, and American Rolling Mill).

Avukah adopted an "official stand" on fascism at regional conferences held in the spring of 1942. The *Avukah Student Action* reported that the Central Administrative Committee, led by Harris, had set goals for itself in light of the war and recent events, including the "Struma" incident, the drowning of 750 refugees who had been refused entrance into Palestine on account of policies of the Palestine administration and the policies of the British government relating thereto. The newspaper's leading article included the statement that "the Jewish people everywhere, as the first victims of fascism, have a special interest in its destruction and in the elimination of all abuses which lead to its development. Our part in the defeat of fascism and the liberation of the Jewish people is the support of a positive program for a true democratic victory." Furthermore, in a statement reflecting the broader aims of the group, "Avukah believes that a democratic victory must assure a world based on a new freedom within and among nations, economic security and plenty, and the liberation of all oppressed peoples." As such, the article mentions not only native fascism and anti-Semitism, but Jim Crow as well, making the link between the Black liberation movement early this century, and Jewish struggles. The efforts that were to be pursued, therefore, were outlined as follows: "As American Jews, we must cooperate with other forces in this country to win the democratic victory on the military and home front. As the largest free Jewish community in the world, we must take the leadership in the political and financial support for the Zionist program." Avukah also stressed that all forms of appeasement, toward British colonial policy regarding Palestine and India, and also American foreign policy as regards Franco Spain and Vichy France, must be countered. As regards Palestine, Avukah reiterated its support for land purchase, immigration, colonization, the Histadrut, the Palestine labor federation, cooperation with Arabs through joint economic endeavors and trade unionism, and greater independence for the Jews in Palestine.

This list of activities, planned and actual, is discussed in terms of the Jewish community, which Avukah attempted to foster through its actions. In the opinion of most commentators there was a sense that the students who were part of Avukah, despite differences in origin and geographical location, had a range of common and identifiable characteristics. Sometimes this was descriptive, sometimes it was wishful thinking, but the idea of this community was in the minds of those who worked with this organization. One ongoing activity was the much-awaited Avukah Summer School of 1942, for which Harris, in his capacity as faculty advisory committee member, was looked to for guidance and direction by Avukah groups beyond Pennsylvania. Harris gave three lectures on native fascism and on how Jews should be political. An unsigned article titled "Front I: Fascism a Real Danger; Jews Not Secure, warns Dr. Harris" in the summer 1942 *Avukah Student Action* (p. 2) features a photo with Harris, shirtless and evidently seated among a group of students, that "there can be no victory for real democracy if fascism wins out on the home front." He also emphasized that "a popular misconception . . . is that only Axis agents and fifth columnists are a menace to democracy." He then went on to show how the forces of fascism and conditions which breed it "cut across all national boundaries." In the United States, Harris described "the existence of such fascist elements as Coughlin and Dennis as well as leaders of the press, industry, and government—who play a prominent anti-liberal and anti-labor role, provides a permanent center for the forces of fascism." He also suggested that if American fascism comes, it "would differ only in form from the German example [and] would thrive primarily on the critical social and economic inequalities of our present society. These conditions make for permanent discontent and widespread insecurity, and furnish fertile soil for fascist demagogy." As we learned from the German example, fascism thrives in these situations of insecurity and discontent, aided by the propaganda of heavy-industry interests: "The fascist concoction of promises of a pseudo-socialist character, plus a hyper-nationalism and a sadistic racial doctrine served as a cover-up for the real pro–big business role of the Nazis."

For Harris, the need to stand up to the fascist challenge also grows from the fact that "fascism also won everywhere else through legal channels rather than by 'militaristic revolt.'" Further, "many South American countries so-called 'democratic' governments are actually headed by totalitarian-fascist rulers who came into power through the regular election process." The only defense involved programs of social betterment and social progress, which would both be attacked by powerful business interest. "In the fight against native fascism, Dr. Harris emphasized the need of following closely the moves of the native fascists—the Coughlinites and their allies in big business, the press and public institutions—since the fascist menace is permanent in our stage of society, regardless of the turns in the war."[19] Democracy was, therefore, a defense against fascism to the degree that "it provided wide-spread economic opportunity, social equality and political freedom." But even with strong efforts against it, fascism could, according to Harris, succeed because, the article reports,

it appeals to prevalent discontent, which might arise from discrimination, the unequal sharing of the war burden, the profits of big business. Anti-Semitism is, of course, only a scapegoat trick. Our only answer is to offer a program for domestic social progress and economic betterment, even as the war goes on. This would cut away poverty and discontent, the soil upon which fascist demagogues thrive. This is of course a difficult task. It will be opposed by the present holders of power, for although many business interests may not desire the fascist alternative, they still do not want to pay the price required if we are to avoid fascism: the reduction of profits and the subordination or elimination of business privileges.

In such reports we begin to understand the links in Harris's mind between his version of Zionism (which is largely reflected in Avukah's approach) and his approach to society, which he eventually articulated in *The Transformation of Capitalist Society.*

In his second lecture that summer, Harris followed up on some of these themes, suggesting that many of the courses of action followed by Jews reflect their "insecurity" and lack "political realism and practicality." Currently, said Harris, Jews were divided between the well-to-do, which accepts the "current order of things" and has no "particular political interests," and the intellectuals and lower-class Jews, who are either "left-assimilationists" or nationalists and Zionists who "seek certain changes in order to assure security." These groups, diverse as they may be in approach, were "incapable of acting towards fundamental improvement of the Jewish situation or thwarted other groups from doing so." What was needed, according to Harris, was an approach that does not advocate that Jews be "nice" and "submissive," or that they simply learn "positive cultural and ethical values," or that they become assimilated; instead, "Jews need a political program pointing out the need to guarantee security in this country and indicating the steps to be taken. Jews also need Palestine, for Jews who need or wish to go to a center where they will not be a minority. For many American Jews Palestine is a potential second home." The surprising element of this last suggestion is the idea that Jews should be a majority in Palestine, an approach he and other members of Avukah had previously rejected.

Right underneath the article describing Harris's contribution to the 1942 summer camp appears another long letter to the editor of *Avukah Student Action* from Bruria Kaufman. She opens by mentioning the division of Avukah's work into three fronts and suggesting that there be discussion about it because it was adopted, as a slogan, in 1937, a time when it may have been an adequate description for Avukah's work. Regrettably, says Kaufman, "people who have come into Avukah since that time have accepted three fronts without questioning them. Nevertheless, when one tries to describe Avukah's work now in terms of three fronts, one meets with considerable difficulties." For Kaufman, "slogans and symbols should be used only as long as they are practical," and people shouldn't be "attached to them" unless "they fit our work." As such, she suggests "first, to open a discussion on accepted statements in Avukah; second, to get a clearer picture of what Avukah is like." She then summarizes that "Avukah has one primary goal before it: security of Jews now in America. It makes two recommendations: work for general security in America (front 1) and work for a strong and independent Palestine (front 3). In addition to work on these two fronts, Avukah undertakes the job of educating American Jews along these two directives." The thing is, for Kaufman, the effort of educating American Jews about fronts 1 and 2 is "not on the same level as the other two fronts." In short, "Avukah does three types of work: It acts on fronts 1 and 3," and it educates the Jewish community "toward the program formulated" in fronts 1 and 3. So for Kaufman, if the 3-front slogan is to be retained, "it should be with this understanding of the difference between front 2 and the others."

This issue appeared in a very turbulent moment, of course, and Avukah members were acting on a series of initiatives. Alfred Kahn and Seymour Melman had both enlisted in the armed forces, Arthur Rosenberg, another faculty advisory committee member, provided an assessment of the Near East War, and the paper announced as well a mass demonstration, to be held in Madison Square Garden on July 21, 1942, to demonstrate against Hitler atrocities, notably "the massacre of 1,000,000 Jews in Nazi-occupied Europe." Avukah as a group reiterated its commitment to its program and also rejected an offer from Dr. Abraham Sachar, who would eventually become the first president of Brandeis University, to become the Zionist arm of Hillel. In addition, Avukah developed a growing interest in Asia, with Max Grünwald suggesting (in a summer school talk) that Avukah seek Zionist friends in India and China. It is surprising in retrospect to read that there was any news other than that of the massacre of a million Jews in Europe, for it is indeed the case that beside these news stories were more pots-and-pans discussions about Avukah activities, other affairs in the world, and the progress of the war in a broader sense. But Avukah readers were most certainly aware that the Jews were, proportionately, suffering unimaginable horrors and that everything ought to be done to get them out of Europe and, preferably, safely to Palestine.

The October issue of *Avukah Student Action* came in the wake of the battle of Stalingrad and debate about opening up a second front against the Axis powers. There was also continued interest in India, which the Avukah Clipping Bureau,[20] a new project instigated to further research in areas deemed to be of particular concern, took as its first subject for investigation, for two reasons. First: "India is the main colonial problem of the British Empire, and an understanding of the British policy there will help us understand British policy in Palestine, perhaps giving us clues on how to deal successfully with Britain"; and, second, "very little is known in America about the Indian problem. India has been given a generally inadequate and uninformed coverage in the American press, combined with unfair editorial treatment. This effort demonstrates the overall approach of Avukah, and its expanding concerns not only to fundamental issues of fascism and unequal distribution of wealth, but other concerns likely to affect Zionists such as, in this example, colonialism. Avukah's position, made clear in this article, is that the British were holding on to the colony for the purely economic interests of the upper classes, "which draws at least $250,000,000 in interest from investments in India, and the impoverished Indian people" (3).

On the internal side, Avukah reported that the Revisionists had been asked to reenter the World Zionist Organization, and that Avukah itself was still caught up in discussions concerning its potential affiliation to adult Zionist bodies. It had rejected becoming an arm of Hillel, for which it was being threatened with expulsion from the WZO, which Avukah regretted. Nevertheless, noted a front page editorial, "it demands as its right freedom of thought and action, always subject to the discipline of the World Zionist Organization, in order to carry on a vigorous and creative student Zionism."

Avukah remained committed throughout the war to new efforts aimed at
Arab-Jewish cooperation, which Zellig Harris supported on a range of
fronts. A leading article in October of 1940 reported that a new Arab-Jewish
"Unity Party" (*ichud*) had been formed, following the publication in Jeru-
salem of an article by Dr. Judah L. Magnes of the Hebrew University advo-
cating a bi-national state in Palestine. "Later in the summer," reports
Avukah Student Action, a group of prominent Palestinian Jews—Henrietta
Szold, Judah Magnes, Professor Martin Buber of the Hebrew University,
Julius Simon, President of the Palestine Economic Corporation, and Moshe
Smilansky of the Palestine Jewish Farmers League—"formed a unity asso-
ciation (Ichud) to work for the goals set forth in Dr. Magnes's article: a
bi-national state in the Palestine which would be part of Near Eastern
Federation understanding and reconciliation between the Arab and the
Anglo American worlds to be brought about by Jews, work for rapproche-
ment of Jews and Arabs in political, social and economic fields." This idea
was attacked by the Revisionists, the religious Zionist group called the
Mizrachi Organization, and the labor Zionist alliance called The Jewish
Frontier, and the Jewish agency in Palestine launched its opposition based
upon Magnes's belief that Jews must remain a minority in Palestine, limited
to 500,000 people.

Harris was sympathetic to efforts at Arab-Jewish cooperation and was
associated with a group that grew out of the left wing of Avukah, known
as the Council for Arab-Jewish Cooperation, the main activity of which was
the publication of the *Bulletin of the Council on Jewish-Arab Cooperation* from
the summer of 1944 to the summer of 1949 (which, incidentally, received
the endorsement of Hannah Arendt). This league also upheld beliefs in
Jewish-Arab working-class cooperation and anti-imperialism; its members,
like those in Avukah, were not in favor of the creation of a Jewish state.
This organization was similar in its objectives to the League of Arab-Jewish

Rapprochement, which grew out of debates in the late 1930s about the Jewish national home. "When the war broke out, a League for Jewish-Arab Rapprochement and Co-operation was founded by former members of Brit-Shalom, members of Left Po'alei-Zion, and Aliyah Hadasha [New Immigration Party], representing mainly immigrants from Central Europe. It also numbered within its ranks, on a personal basis, several prominent members of ha-Shomer ha-Tza'ir" (281).[1] The League was formed to support the idea that, in Israel Kollatt's words,[2] the "realization of the National Home would be possible only as an out-growth of agreement with the Arabs. The absence of such agreement could only lead to an undermining of the partnership with Britain as well" (639). This pitted the League against those who upheld the official Zionist line, which was that "only after certain Zionist goals were achieved . . . could the ground be prepared for a Jewish-Arab agreement that would permit full Zionist realization" (639). The League was not entirely isolated, however, since in 1942 they were joined by Hashomer Hatzair, but only after considerable disputation. "Many objected to the alliance with the Ihud, who had always been regarded as minimalist Zionists and bourgeois; some feared that bi-nationalism, as a practical political programme, would lead to collaboration with the reactionary elements in Arab society" (Gôrnî, 292). With the addition of Hashomer Hatzair, the League was thus split between members of this group and those of *Ihud*, which had been established in 1942, and "saw in Zionism the creation of an ethical Jewish society" (Kolatt 643).

The League's activities during the war were considered by Avukah to be of the upmost importance, and in *Avukah Student Action* of November 11, 1940, it was announced with great optimism that the "fear of their common Fascist and Nazi enemy" was "drawing Jews and Arabs closer together." In fact, "the League for Arab-Jewish Cooperation in its report of August 18, pointed out that a considerable part of the Arab population sympathizes with Great Britain and is afraid of German or Italian rule. This conclusion was the result of investigation among Arabs in Hifa, Nablus, Jaffa, and Nazareth, as well as among Jews who have associated with Arabs for many years." Nevertheless, as might be expected, "another part of the Arab population is influenced by Axis propaganda, some of which was being broadcast to the Moslem world" (5).

Terrorism and David Ben-Gurion's Federated Palestine

A letter from Israeli statesman David Ben-Gurion to Louis Brandeis, dated December 6, 1940, sets forth the types of proposals on the table that stood between Jews and Arabs during the war. In discussions with Arab leaders, Ben-Gurion found that "the Arab people as such, and especially those who represent the true national interests of the Arabs, would never willingly agree to hand Palestine to the Jews, or even to share it with the Jews on a basis of equality." Mussa Alami, who was once the attorney general in Palestine, suggested to Ben-Gurion that the best solution would be "economic and social cooperation with those Jews already in Palestine" rather than heavy Jewish immigration. Ben-Gurion's preferred solution, which he proposed to Arab officials, was "the idea of a federation—a federation between a Jewish Palestine and neighboring Arab states." The advantages were clear; first, "the Arabs in Palestine, with a Jewish majority, although numerically a minority, would not feel that they were in a foreign state, as they belonged together with the whole of Palestine to a larger unit which would be predominately Arab." Second, "they would have the political and economic help of the Jews in establishing Arab unity and independence in the greatest part of Arab territory." And third, "they would have the benefit of a highly developed Palestine, as a member of the larger Arab federal unit." This idea was "more popular amongst the Arabs," including Auni Abdul Hadi, the head of the Independence Party in Palestine, Readi Sulch, the leader of the National Bloc in Syria, Amir Aslan, the head of the Palestine-Syrian delegation in Geneva, and others. There was resistance even to this compromise, however, on the basis that Jewish Palestine would be independent before Arab unity could occur; Palestine "is the natural link to all the Arab countries"; and, moreover, "a highly developed Palestine, instead of being a source of strength, might become a menace to the neighboring Arab countries." These obstacles did not dissuade Ben-Gurion in his attempt to "get nearer to the Arab leaders," and indeed several leaders, notably in Syria, Lebanon, and Transjordania, were anxious to secure an agreement with the Jews as soon as possible. On the other hand, Ben-Gurion also notes that the position of Jews worsened during the war because although the Arabs didn't sympathize with Mussolini, there was "wide-spread sympathy for Hitler" because "the Arabs respect and admire strong action." Furthermore, "the Nazi philosophy, in certain respects, is not altogether strange to the philosophy of Islam," and many Arabs believed at the time that a Nazi victory would allow for the establishment of an Arab empire. Yet again, all of this seems haunting, from so many standpoints, in light of September 11, 2001, and the current state of Israel and the Palestinians.[3]

An article by Margolith Shelubsky from the April 1942 *Avukah Student Action* recalls that the League for Arab-Jewish Cooperation was founded in

1938 and "comprises Arab and Jewish individuals and groups who see the need for working for rapprochement between the two peoples. Its activities are chiefly in the economic and social fields." Cited in the article is a report written by Moshe Smilansky, which discusses the role that foreign influences played in promoting the "Arab terror" of 1936–1939 and which continued to strain relations between the two groups.

The terror was never an outbreak of basic hatred towards Jews but rather an expression of temporary anger, inspired by foreign forces. Evidence of this can be found in the fact that when the terror stopped Jews and Arabs met once again as good friends and good neighbors. Even after the long period of terror, which many feared was permanent and deep rooted, Arabs literally fell into the arms of their Jewish neighbors and asked for peace. Even during the terror, there was evidence that basic friendship and trust existed. Arabs made use of Jewish medical and social services. The hostile relations stemmed from foreign influences. Today we witness Arab-Jewish rapprochement taking place naturally, almost spontaneously in many areas. (2)

Hashomer Hatzair upheld a belief in Arab-Jewish cooperation, first in Palestine and then in Israel. An example of this kind of cooperation is described in the League for Arab-Jewish Cooperation's report and recalled in the April 1942 *Avukah Student Action*. According to the article, the Kibbutz Artzi, National federation of Hashomer Hatzair, "recently started activity which is significant in establishing contact with neighboring Arab villages. The Kibbutz Artzi has organized courses to train agents who will establish contact with Arab villages that are near Kibbutzim . . . [and who will] seek to strengthen favorable attitudes to Zionism among Arabs. Some 300 are now taking courses which teach Arabic, Arab customs, and Arab community life. It is hoped that about one-seventh of the Arab village communities will be reached by workers trained in these courses" (2).

The *Avukah Student Action* of April 1943 shed further light on this movement in the course of a discussion about Moshe Shertok, the chief of the political department of the Jewish Agency for Palestine, and his 1943 visit to the United States. Shertok's view was that "we should be for Federation but we must have a guarantee that Palestine will remain Jewish. He pointed out that if the Agency 'prematurely' provoked the British for a commitment on the future of Palestine, there would come a reaffirmation of the white paper policy restricting immigration and land purchases. This would be bad for Jews" (1). Interestingly, the Agency was discussing during this period Arab-Jewish cooperation with Syria, Egypt, and Iraq, producing the following assessment of the Arab leaders' attitudes: "We don't know if the Federation can be realized. It is impractical to favorably commit ourselves now on the question of Jewish immigration for an agreement which is still vague," and "regardless of any other factors, Jewish immigration to Palestine is out of the question." The agency's position "was to warn the Arab leaders that they could not have Palestine without Jewish consent. . . . Perhaps we are not strong enough to make Palestine what we want it to be, but we are strong enough to say what we don't want it to be. There must be a Jewish State in Palestine as part of an Arab Federation. Otherwise, we say to the Arabs, try and get Palestine." The article also referred to ongoing efforts by the League for Arab-Jewish Rapprochement to find bases for economic cooperation and joint trade unionism, although Shertok himself expressed doubt about the practicality of expanding such efforts in any significant fashion. The Avukah stance was then reiterated in this article, again, consistent with what it (and Harris) had suggested previously; cooperation is the only way for Palestine to survive peacefully and constructively, and this goes far beyond the question of practicality.

The talk of "practicality" is based on a defense of the status quo in Palestine. Who could have proven in 1920 that the kibbutz collective would prove 'practical?' In matters so complex as Palestine development, one cannot prove in advance the 'practicality' of a project. What one can do is to show that his project is in the long-range interests of the people (as the collectives proved to be). Only when a project is related to the basic needs of the people is its success feasible. This is the lesson of Zionist experiences in Palestine, and this should be the principle guiding us to a policy of cooperation in the economic, social and political spheres between the peoples of both nations in Palestine.

This editorial, signed by M. Shapiro, indicates the direction of Avukah and of Harris toward a broader and longer-range vision of the interests and needs of "the people," a project he developed in his own political work.

The People

In this same period, the early 1940s, when Harris worked in both the background and the foreground to mold Avukah policies, he was also associated with a small group called "The People," the vestige of which has seemingly dropped out of history's view. It is worth examining the manifesto I received in a package of Avukah materials given to me by a former member,[4] since it was apparently written by Harris and indeed bears the traces of many concerns he had during this period. The People, according to the first paragraph of the text, "are in various measures disturbed by the suffering, inefficiency, dishonesty, inequality, lack of freedom, bourgeois and automaton character structures, etc., which occur in this culture;

feel limited and insecure in the carrying out of their own work and career lines; believe that if anything can be done to improve things (and if so, what can be done) is determinable only by careful empirical observation and scientific analysis." Some of these people would "be prepared to change their present occupations, e.g. to enter workers' occupations," they do not (except for one or two exceptions) "intend to use their political interests in advancing their careers," they "work cooperatively, without officers or orders," and they often work in groups with "authors rarely named." These individuals "assume nothing as being true *ex cathedra*, no person as repository of authority or truth," that as far as economic and historical analysis goes "Marx fits the facts and is useful for prediction," and that the elements of this society that they consider unsatisfactory will continue to exist "as long as there is a controlling class, wages and profits, and a lack of complete freedom in the utilization of the means of production." They do not believe in reform in the framework of the capitalist society, nor that any bureaucratic structure or any other attempt to manage or lead the people "will in the long run aid in the development in the desired direction." References are made to historical-materialist works such as the histories of Arthur Rosenberg and the work of Erich Fromm (from the Frankfurt School), as well as work in American cultural anthropology, modern natural sciences, and mathematical logic. All of this points to a Harris connection, since he combined his interest in anti-Bolshevik Marxism (Rosenberg) with a commitment to Fromm's psychoanalytic/Marxist work.

The People have no dogma, Marxist or otherwise, and the members of the group work together as a "way of resisting the present social order, of helping spread the resistance to it." In this regard, they don't consider themselves leaders of the working classes, although they do agree that revolution or "collapse" are the only means of ending present power relations. And finally,

the relation of their work to social change is the compiling of such information about the economy and culture and the control methods and development of the ruling class, and about the change of technology, social relations, working-class attitudes, etc., as would be useful to the political understanding and action of an increasingly restive working-class; the reduction of the methods of science to a form that will be graspable and usable by workers in the understanding and control of their social and natural environment; the development of the theory and prediction of social change; and the dissemination and elaboration of scientifically valid social-political discussion among those who may be expected to act, in terms of their position and times, in the direction of a free, egalitarian, classless society.

Many of these links—to Fromm's work, to psychoanalytic efforts aimed at understanding attitudes, to anti-Bolshevik Marxism, and to the development of adequate theories of social change—will resurface in the story of Harris, finding their ultimate expression in his *Transformation of Capitalist Society*, half-a-century later.

In 1943, Harris was promoted to associate professor and assumed the chair of his department, which he held for the next twenty years. But this hardly slowed his work with Avukah; indeed, in 1943 Harris wrote *An Approach to Action: Facing the Social Insecurities Affecting the Jewish Position*. This fourteen-page pamphlet addresses the Jewish situation against the backdrop of the Second World War, and the problems that "victory alone cannot solve" (2). Recall that this was published amid the death and destruction of World War II, and that at this point of the war, the author assumes that two million Jews have perished in Europe and that eight million more were prisoners. On the domestic front, Harris notes that significant discrimination is directed against the Jews and "a great social distance and frequent mutual suspicion between Jews and non-Jews, which makes the Jews, whether 'Jewish financier' or 'Jewish Communist,' ideal scapegoats onto which mass resentment may be deflected" (3). There was as well the fear that not only Europe, but the United States as well, would become fascist, and the tendency appeared to be in that direction "as the society in which we live becomes more authoritarian, more intolerant of minority differences, more regimented and militarized, with the freedom of individuals more limited" (4). So, once again, the point that the Holocaust was not foremost on certain American Jews' minds clearly doesn't apply to Harris and his entourage; nevertheless, it does give pause to consider that it did not attract the attention one might have expected. For example, the November 25, 1942, report from the Polish government-in-exile that Heinrich Himmler had allegedly ordered all Polish Jews to be killed by the end of 1942 is not mentioned at all in Avukah's organs, one of many news stories that seem in retrospect to have deserved very serious consideration.

The fact is, life was going on in the United States, and people had to look ahead to the end of the war and to the defeat not only of the Nazis, but of fascism everywhere, not only of a brutal enemy incarnated in the figures of Axis soldiers and leaders, but of oppression in all its forms. Further, the Avukah goal of establishing a Jewish homeland received significant support with the realization that the Nazis had murdered millions of Jews, although certain organizations remained true to earlier statements, by Harris, Einstein and others, that Palestine should not become a Jewish state precisely because methods had to be found to avoid future bloodshed. Yôsēf Gôrnî reminds us that the Ihud leaders proposed to the UN Commission of Enquiry that there be a binational state that would represent "an 'ideal' theoretical model of equilibrium and restraint in the relations between the two peoples." The principle was based on a sense of "the historical rights of the Jews and the natural rights of the Arabs as equal under all conditions," a belief that equality should be a "numerical balance between the two peoples," and, in the constitutional sphere, "it was envisaged as equal representation of Jews and Arabs in the future Palestinian state institutions." This plan, which was rejected by the UN Commission "for practical reasons," was to establish a "federation under Western protection" to allay "the fascist tendencies of Arab nationalism and the possible Levantinization of the Palestinian state" (288).

Turning the Page

The other way in which life was going on in the United States relates to its newly entrenched status as *the* superpower, holding not only vast economic might but also the capacity to annihilate any city anywhere in the world if it deemed this necessary, as it had made clear in Hiroshima and Nagasaki. This led many Jewish scientists to address the issue of nuclear destruction, an effort that was led, predictably, by Albert Einstein. In a letter to Salo Baron, dated February 10, 1947, Einstein wrote the following, as chair of the Emergency Committee of Atomic Scientists,[5] to solicit aid:

Through the release of atomic energy, our generation has brought into the world the most revolutionary force since prehistoric man's discovery of fire. This basic power of the universe cannot be fitted into the outmoded concept of narrow nationalisms. For there is no secret and there is no defense; there is no possibility of control except through the aroused understanding and insistence of the peoples of the world.

We scientists recognize our inescapable responsibility to carry to our fellow citizens an understanding of the simple facts of atomic energy and its implications for society. In this lies our only security and our only hope—we believe that an informed citizenry will act for life and not for death.

We need $1,000,000 for this great educational task. Sustained by faith in man's ability to control his destiny through the exercise of reason, we have pledged all our strength and our knowledge to this work. I do not hesitate to call upon you for help.

Salo Baron did indeed offer assistance and support, as did many others, sometimes repeatedly.

In short, the end of World War II, the rise in status of the United States, and the promise that the international community would support the establishment of a Jewish state in Palestine, if for no other reason than to offer some form of compensation for the Holocaust, marked a period of both resignation and optimism for many persons, notably Zellig Harris, who had struggled on behalf of Palestine for most of his life. Right up until May 1947, the executive committee of the Hashomer Hatzair Workers' Party in Jerusalem was making *The Case for a Bi-National Palestine*[6] under the assumption that it was "the best manner whereby Zionist aims might be realized on a bi-national basis and on the steps necessary to secure cooperation between Jews and Arabs for the development of Palestine and the establishment of a common State while maintaining unhindered Jewish immigration" (5). Offering salient critiques of partition (of the type proposed by the British in the Royal Commission), and of the idea of establishing Swiss-style cantons, the book concludes that these "alternatives . . . are nothing less than disastrous and would inevitably end in hideous failure" (122). I cite but one of the many criticisms of such a plan.

The protagonists of the partition plan cherish the illusion that certain Jewish and Arab circles favor partition as the "lesser evil" so that their support, or at least their acquiescence, might be gained. They overlook the fact that what these Jews and Arabs respectively have in mind is a "good" partition,—"good" meaning favorable to their own point of view. But there is no partition that would be "good" for Jews and Arabs at one and the same time. If it were "good" for the Jews, it would rally *all* the Arabs against it, and *vice versa*. Most probably, it would rally both sides against it. (127)

But while Avukah-like proposals continued after the war, Avukah itself was ostensibly inactive following the national convention in the summer of 1943, and many of its ideals, of kibbutz economics and Arab-Jewish cooperation, were either quashed or forgotten soon thereafter even if they continued to burn in the minds of its members. There are, however, a few indications of continued critique and hope, in for example the Council for Jewish-Arab Cooperation, which, right up to the creation of the Jewish state, was looking for alternatives and contributing to crucial debate. In December 1946, the Council published a *Bulletin* issue (volume 3, no.3), written for the most part by Harris with the input of Seymour Melman and others, which spoke to the "menace from the right" in Palestine. This menace is in the form of a trap, which is described as two-fold. "On the one hand, the impasse in Jewish nationalist politics—evidenced by stoppage of immigration, restrictions on land purchase, colonization and economic development—has led in Palestine to a suicidal terrorism as the activist alternative to submission to the British." In the assessment, which digs far deeper, we see the other side: "this growth of terrorism, besides worsening the political situation vis-à-vis Britain, is being used to spearhead the attack by the Right upon the Jewish working class" (1). Examining the situation in Palestine pre-Israel from a class perspective allowed the authors to consider the real stakes of the contemporary debate about the future of Palestine, terrorism in the region, and the crucial issue of Arab-Jewish relations.

By analyzing the situation of Jews, in class rather than in national categories, the very real dilemmas of nationalism (in effect of the upper classes) are by-passed. That is because we now find that the nationalist programs do not exhaust the range of [possible] political actions for Jewish workers. Quite the contrary. By showing that the nationalist plans are all that is possible for the upper class *only*, we are able to open the question of Jewish-Arab cooperation for serious discussion. (13)

The conclusion is prescient.

If the Jewish workers were to concentrate now on Jewish-Arab cooperation instead of supporting the bargaining for a toy state, they would have a job no more difficult than the one they are now engaged in, far less costly, far more relevant to basic security in the long run and by strengthening Jewish workers vis-à-vis England, to immigration in the short run, far more effective towards an ultimate expulsion of the British and any other empires; and lastly, an activity which, unlike nationalist activism, cannot be led by the business classes, since Jewish-Arab cooperation can succeed only on a working class level and with anti-status-quo, egalitarian, aims. (15)

In short, it is clear from this that Harris never forgot what he learned through his association with the movement, and in the decades that follow we will see him looking for theoretical and practical backing for ambitions he developed as a young man.

Politics Post-Avukah

The State of Israel was created with the passage of UN General Assembly Resolution 181 on November 29, 1947, which called for the partition of the British-ruled Palestine Mandate into a Jewish state and an Arab state. It was approved with 33 votes in favor, 13 against, 10 abstentions, and one absent. The list of dissenting states includes Afghanistan, Cuba, Egypt, Greece, India, Iran, Iraq, Lebanon, Pakistan, Saudi Arabia, Syria, Turkey, and Yemen, and, most notably, it was rejected by Arabs in Palestine. Abstentions included a number of Latin American countries—Argentina,

Chile, Colombia, El Salvador, Honduras, Mexico—as well as China, Ethiopia, Yugoslavia, and, presumably for reasons of conflict of interest, the United Kingdom. The Declaration of the Establishment of the State of Israel occurred on May 14, 1948, the day in which the British Mandate over Palestine expired. It was recognized that night at 11:00AM Israeli time by the United States and three days later by the USSR.

In the United Nations Security Council official records, for its 2340th meeting, dated March 30,1982,[7] we find a provisional agenda that includes as item 69 the following reference to what Israel was becoming, followed by reference to a letter, signed in 1948 by Harris and others from the milieu we have described thus far.

"Professor-General Milson identified his brutal campaign as a 'kind of moral crusade'. What crusade, when even the plus sign that resembles the cross is removed from the mathematics books and replaced by an inverted 'T'. What moral values are those that fire machine-guns and tear-gas canisters at demonstrating students? What moral basis does this Milson have for ousting elected mayors and city councils and replacing them by members of his own gang? And, then, what struggle is this between Israel and the Jewish people, on the one hand, and the PLO, on the other? What Jewish people does he claim to represent? If it is Jews like Albert Einstein, Bruria Kaufman, Stefan Wolfe and Hannah Arendt, then let us listen to the following from a letter signed by them and published in *The New York Times* of 4 December 1948*." This letter is worth recalling in its entirety:

Among the most disturbing phenomena of our time is the emergence in the newly created State of Israel of the Freedom Party, a political Party closely akin in its organization, methods, political philosophy and social appeal to the Nazi and Fascist parties. It was-formed out of the membership and following of the former Irgun Zvai Leumi, a terrorist, right-wing, chauvinist organization in Palestine. The current visit of Menachem Begin, leader of this Party, to the United States, is obviously calculated to give the impression of American support for his Party in the coming Israeli elections, and to cement political ties with conservative Zionist elements in the United States. Several Americans of national repute have lent their names to welcome his visit. It is inconceivable that those who oppose fascism throughout the world, if correctly informed as to Mr. Begin's political record and perspective, could add their names and support to the movement he represents. Before irreparable damage is done by way of financial contributions, public manifestations in Begin's behalf and the creation in Palestine of the impression that a large segment of America supports fascist elements in Israel, the American public must be informed as to the record and objectives of Mr. Begin and his movement. The public avowals of Begin's Party are no guide whatever to its actual character. Today they speak of freedom, democracy and anti-imperialism, whereas recently they openly preached the doctrine of the Fascist State. It is in its actions that the terrorist Party betrays its real character: from its past actions we can judge what it may be expected to do in the future. A shocking example was their behavior in the Arab village of Deir Yassin. This village, off the main roads and surrounded by Jewish lands, had taken no part in the war and had even fought off Arab bands who wanted to use the village as their base. On 9 April [1948] terrorist bands attacked the peaceful village, which was not a military objective in the fighting, killed most of its inhabitants—240 men, women and children—and kept a few of them alive to parade as captives through the streets of Jerusalem. Most of the Jewish community was horrified at the deed, and the Jewish Agency sent a telegram of apology to King Abdullah of Trans-Jordan. But the terrorists, far from being ashamed of their act, were proud of this massacre, publicized it widely, and invited all the foreign correspondents present in the country to view the heaped corpses and general havoc at Deir Yassin. The Deir Yassin incident exemplifies the character and actions of the Freedom Party. Within the Jewish community they have preached an admixture of ultra-nationalism, religious mysticism and racial superiority. Like other fascist parties, they have been used to break strikes, and have themselves pressed for the destruction of trade unions. In their stead they have proposed corporate unions on the Italian Fascist model. During the last years of sporadic anti-British violence, the Irgun Zvai Leumi and Stern group inaugurated a reign of terror in the Palestine Jewish community. Teachers were beaten up for speaking against them; adults were shot for not letting their children join them. By gangster methods, beatings, window smashing, and widespread robberies, the terrorists intimidated the population and exacted a heavy tribute. The people of the Freedom Party had no part in the constructive achievements in Palestine. They reclaimed no land, built no settlements, and only detracted from the Jewish defense activity. Their much publicized endeavors were minute and were devoted to bringing in Fascist compatriots. The discrepancies between the bold claims now being made by Begin and his Party and their record of past performance in Palestine bear the imprints of no ordinary political party. This is the unmistakable stamp of a Fascist party for whom terrorism (against Jews, Arabs, and British alike) and misrepresentation are means and a 'leader State' is their goal. In the light of the foregoing considerations it is imperative that the truth about Mr. Begin and his movement be made known in this country. It is all the more tragic that the top leadership of American Zionists has refused to campaign against Begin's efforts or even to expose to its own constituents the dangers to Israel from the support to Begin. The undersigned therefore take this means of publicly presenting a few salient facts concerning Begin and his Party, and of urging all concerned not to support this latest manifestation of fascism.

The letter was signed by: Isidore Abromowitz, Hannah Arendt, Abraham Brock, Rabbi Jessurun Cardozo, Albert Einstein, Herman Eisen, M.D., Hayim Fineman, M. Galen, M.D., H. H. Harris, Zellig Harris, Sidney Hook, Fred Karush, Bruria Kaufman, Irma L. Lindheim, Macham Maisel, Seymour

Melman, Myer S. Mendelson, M.D., Harry Orlinsky, Samuel Pitlick, Fritz Rohrlich, Louis P. Rocker, Ruth Sager, Itzhak Sankowsky, T. J. Schoenberg, Samuel Schuman, M. Enger, Irma Wolfe, and Stefan Wolfe.

In the commentary following the letter, the speaker says that "I only wish that not just the American Zionists but the United States Administration would read this letter every morning, read it again and again, because everything that was envisaged by those respectable and noted people has come to, pass."[8]

Even Yoram Hazony's book on *The Jewish State*[9] offers an impassioned plea for Israel and provides some really salient evidence that, historically speaking, attacks from outside of Israel are generally less voracious than those who criticize from inside it. He begins by offering a sense of current and recent opposition to the Jewish state from those he calls the "culture makers."

For well over a century, Jewish intellectuals—and especially those German-Jewish academics who constituted the mainstream of Jewish philosophy in the last century—have had serious doubts concerning the legitimacy and desirability of harnessing the interests of the Jewish people to the worldly power of a political state. On the Holocaust, the most extreme demonstration of the evil of Jewish powerlessness imaginable, succeeded in turning the objections of the intellectuals to the Jewish state into an embarrassment, for the most part driving their opposition underground. Yet Jewish intellectuals, even in Israel, never became fully reconciled to the empowerment of the Jewish people entailed in the creation of a Jewish state.

The examples he provides, of Buber stating that "the belief in the efficacy of power embraced by so many Jews in his generation had been learned from Hitler" (6), of Yeshayahu Leibowitz calling the Jewish armed forces "Judeo Nazis" and suggesting that Israel "would soon be engaging in the 'mass expulsion and slaughter of the Arab population'" (6), of Jacob Talmon's statement that "there is no longer any aim or achievement that can justify . . . twentieth-century battle" (7), are powerful indeed. They are testaments as well to the Jews' proclivity to offer critiques that in many cases surpass those made by outsiders, a striking characteristic of the Israeli intellectual culture, in my opinion.

Hazony contributes in a very powerful way to this debate by assessing the vehemence and one-mindedness of this attack.

This then, is the achievement of post-Zionism in Israeli academia. A systematic struggle is being conducted by Israeli scholars against the idea of the Jewish state, its historical narrative, institution, and symbols. Of course, there are elements of truth in *some* of the claims being advanced by Israeli academics against what was once the Labor Zionist consensus on these subjects. But so overwhelming is the assault that it is unclear whether any aspect of this former consensus can remain standing and such is the state of confusion and conceptual decay among those who still feel loyal to the old ideal of the Jewish state that they themselves are often found advancing ideas that are at the heart of the post-Zionist agenda. (14)

This "post-Zionist" agenda is hardly in accord with the ambitions that Harris and Avukah had promoted; but from the perspective of a story about Zellig Harris, this is not the real point, because the very idea of Palestine was considered differently by those who saw in this region the hope of bringing a whole range of peoples together, with a common, but not statist, mission. Amos Oz suggested that "A state cannot be Jewish, just as a chair or a bus cannot be Jewish. . . . The state is no more than a tool, a tool that is efficient or a tool that is defective, a tool that is suitable or a tool that is undesirable. And this tool must belong to all its citizens—Jews, Moslems, Christians. . . . The concept of a 'Jewish state' is nothing other than a snare."[10]

The Transformation of Capitalist Society

From the outside, it would be difficult to conclude that Harris had an ongoing political agenda at this point, particularly after the demise of Palestine in 1948, when his public commentary relating to Zionism more or less ceased. There are a few signs, though, including an open letter that he and a number of U Penn professors wrote to the Senate Committee on Foreign Relations, concerning the imminent confirmation hearings of Henry Kissinger as Secretary of State. In light of Christopher Hitchens's indictment of Kissinger for war crimes,[11] it seems all the more poignant to read what Harris, as well as George Cardona, Richard S. Dunn, Murray Gerstenhaber, David R. Goddard, Henry T. Hiz, Michael H. Jameson, Richard C. Jeffrey, Adam Seybert, Charles H. Kahn, Jerre Mangione, J. Robert Schrieffer, Mary Amanda, and Bernard Wolfman were writing on September 11, 1973. Interestingly, concern is not voiced about Kissinger, or about U.S. policy, but rather about their doubt "whether it can be in the long-term interest of our country to contribute to strengthening economically, and hence militarily, a government that is prepared to crush every free voice raised in criticism of official policy." Examples are offered from Alexander Solzhenitsyn and Andrei Sakharov, as well as "the ominous tendency of the recent trial of Pyotr Yakir and Victor Krasin, which brings back the memories of the Stalinist persecutions." The letter supports protection for the two dissidents, and also the justifiable concern for "the cause of religious freedom in the Soviet Union." In the long run, "the peace of the world will depend upon a gradual liberalization of the Soviet regime," and it "cannot be in the interests of the United States to acquiesce in, and indirectly support, a policy aimed at putting out all the significant lights of freedom in the second most powerful country in the world." As such, the authors "urge that a warning be sounded" that "the continued persecution of Solzhenitsyn and Sakharov will jeopardize the policy of economic and scientific collaboration between the United States and the Soviet Union, a collaboration that could be so fruitful to both parties."

Despite the penury of published materials, Harris maintained a lifelong interest in politics, often radical politics, through his left-Zionism and through his engagement with an approach to society articulated in the "Frame of Reference" project, and in scattered texts relating to the transformation of capitalist society. He had a strong interest in the work of a range of left-leaning thinkers, and he developed his political ideas through discussions with colleagues, friends, and in his "society" courses, the informal gatherings with bright students who shared common concerns. There is no single reference for Harris's political thinking; although a number of his students became important political thinkers in their own right, Noam Chomsky and Seymour Melman in particular; it would be inappropriate to see in Harris's political ideas a single strand of influence or effect. On the other hand, for the reasons I have outlined here, there are individuals (notably Murray Eden, William Evan, Erich Fromm, Karl Korsch, Paul Mattick, Seymour Melman, Anton Pannekoek) and movements (Anarchosyndicalism, Council Communism, left Zionism) to which one would have to refer to understand Harris's ideas about how to organize society. *The Transformation of Capitalist Society*, which appeared five years after his death, must be understood in this context and is best read alongside the large "Frame of Reference" project, which outlined the general approach he developed for this work.

As we have seen, Harris shared his political ideas only with certain hand-picked students and those concerned directly with the work he was doing (and even with them he was guarded). Otherwise, for linguists at Penn he was known for his linguistics, for a wider public he was the author of works on discourse analysis and structural linguistics, for persons on the kibbutz in Israel he was known for his kibbutz work, for coworkers in Avukah he was known for his Zionism, and so on. Furthermore, with his death there seemed to be no source of his political ideas, except those memories of people with whom he had worked. In 1997 this changed with the publication of *The Transformation of Capitalist Society*. That this book ever appeared, however, is as much a tribute to Harris's efforts near the end of his life as to three of Harris's friends, Murray Eden, William M. Evan, and Seymour Melman, who "collaborated in preparing the manuscript for publication." In this posthumous work, on employee ownership and control of enterprises, Harris insists on the possibility of, and the need for, an orderly transition of both capitalist and state-run societies to participatory enterprises through the rise and eventual dominance of Employee Share Ownership Plans (ESOP).

Henry Hoenigswald suggested to me in 1997 that "as you can see from Harris's posthumous political/economic book he was not much interested in quoting authority or recognizing 'schools' or in getting lost in polemics. This was even more true of his linguistics, much to the scandal of traditional as well as fashionable scholarship." Overall, as is evident in the book, Zellig Harris had "deep interest and sympathy for anti-Bolshevik radicals. Unlike many of his political friends he had escaped the specific City College variety of that atmosphere by spending his decisive formative year(s) in Palestine (as he continued to call the country till the end of his life). He retained an active admiration for some of the kibbutzim and a good deal of contempt for the state." One would expect a flurry of interest in a book like this, particularly given how eminent Harris had been at Penn, and how many famous students and colleagues were associated with him; instead, the book produced a small amount of interest among people who knew him, and then more or less disappeared. This could perhaps have been predicted on the basis of the fact that he was referring to ideas that were little known to the public and, consistent with his linguistics, he did not engage a significant amount of contemporary theory or debates, deferring instead to some historical work that is little known except in small political circles. Furthermore, the book did not impress early readers enough to produce significant interest, even among people interested in this type of work. For example, endorsements for the book were requested from Joel Rogers (University of Wisconsin), Wolfgang Streek (Max Planck Institute, Cologne), Michael Mann (University of London), Robert Stern (Cornell University), Noam Chomsky (MIT), Alan Wolfe (Boston University), Mayer Zald (University of Michigan), Michael Buraway (University of California, Berkeley), Robert Heilbroner (The New School), Ad Teulings (University of Amsterdam), and Andrew Lamas (University of Pennsylvania), but in the end only Lamas and Teulings obliged. Despite these positive endorsements, suggesting that it is "the most important work of its kind in the 1990s" (Lamas) and that it is "a brilliant analysis" and a "major contribution," no major review appeared anywhere, in any language.

Harris's Approach

The *Transformation* book is rooted in decades of research undertaken for the "Frame of Reference for Social Change"[12] project (FoR), which was, according to the preface, "based on a stated political purpose" plus "existing, rather than new, data" aimed at bolstering the objective of eliminating class rule and "changing out of capitalism." This is, therefore, a quest to change contemporary (American) society "in the direction of having much more nearly equal allocation, efficient production, and lack of controlling and controlled behavior." It is worth considering some of the project's objectives before turning to the *Transformation* book, because FoR sets out the basic ideas that underwrite it. The Frame of Reference project draws from some standard social science investigations as well as work done outside standard frameworks, and for the most part, "the theory is generally Marxist." Nevertheless, "pure Marxist vocabulary doesn't cover many of the new problems" in society in part because it was "developed at a time when physical sciences were simply mechanistic, and are not well suited to express processes that are in constant (though uneven) change and whose interaction with each other cannot be disregarded." Current conditions are assessed from a more comprehensive standpoint, but the critique is specifically "radical"; despite the fact that many leftists had given up on radicalism in favor of "small reforms" because of a perceived "limitation of the possible," this study takes the opposite course with the assumption that contemporary methods of scientific inquiry allow for new optimism. In this sense, the project is based on similar assumptions about scientific progress as were previously described in discussions about linguistics, and upon the idea that problems need new articulation to meet the rigid scientific criteria: "Not only the temper of modern science, but also the requirement of more exact prediction, lead us to seek ways of talking that express all this better." Among the main terms employed for this work are:

treatment of the business routine as a simultaneous production-signaling and consumption-allocating system; analysis of productional (allocational) activities into signal-giving, activities necessary for the carrying out of the signaling-allocating routine; managerial and technical integration of output activities (not including business managership), and actual output (directly producing items consumed as standard of living); claims on labor hours, as an expression of the exchange features of money (but not credit, etc.) and also certain non-money relations in and out of capitalism. (preface)

This new terminology is put to the service of "extensive methodologically controlled observations and considerations" about personal ends, with the assumption that scientific and technical investigation can be put to the service of effective political action. This is not to say that individuals cannot take "effective political action by use of intuitive judgments or after trial and error," but rather that this type of inquiry can help bolster efforts aimed at effective action through interdependent consideration of intuitive and "scientific" approaches. Interestingly as regards previous discussions of Einstein's influence on social sciences and humanities is the point that a fundamental critique of current conditions is advanced through the "relativism of scientific method," which helps account for "observer bias."

Elements of the framework that underwrites portions of Harris's linguistic project are present here as well, suggesting that the link between the politics and the linguistics is a shared conception of the nature of the human mind. This is clear throughout the study and is articulated at the very outset with the rejection of the idea that people have a "fixed human nature," and the suggestion, "derived in the following chapters," that "behavior is determined by conditions" (23ba), and that people learn "patterned" (institutional) behavior, notably of how to interrelate and how to satisfy their needs, from the society in which they live.

30c) The individual learns these ranges of behavior from infancy on; he thence develops what we may call particular expectations of behavior of particular other persons or groups, and generally acts in accordance with particular expectations which particular others have of him. For the most part, he would not know how to satisfy his needs by himself, and would not have available the means to do so.

30d) These patterned ways (including avoidance) are for these persons the only utilized means of satisfying their needs (the only means that these people are "prepared" to use), so that their continuation becomes a need in itself; except to the extent that these ways are gradually changing or that they may begin to fail to satisfy needs.

Pervasive as well, even in the setting out of these categories, is the sense that the science of behavioral studies can yield information about what motivates people to act, providing some sense of how to change society in a positive direction. "Any study of this type gives the leftist some picture of his possible effectiveness, thus removing some of the uneasiness which so many leftists have felt as to their role in the course of events. For this uneasiness derives not only from the present lack of visible successes, but also from what is not yet known about the processes of social change" (22fb). This is indeed the "political purpose of the writers" of this report, who put this version of "scientific" and "empirical" operations analysis to work on issues relating to interaction among people (12b). This work requires a new type of social science research which does not suffer from the inadequacies of Marxist analysis as regards "culture and character," and which has not been developed within the "capitalist matrix," and therefore "applied for control and maintenance of class relations."

But leftists have a not unrelated question to ask; what ways are there of changing from the present power relations and business system? A good many of the investigations, data, and methods developed in answering the capitalist questions can also be used in the use of answering the leftist one (though very many are unscientific or irrelevant in their categories or problems); in some cases investigations (like psychoanalysis) develop which are only partially usable in capitalism but which leftists can develop more fruitfully. In using the data, sophistication, etc., of the social sciences in answering our own questions we have to check and modify them for our own investigations." (12ba)

A whole range of issues are discussed as a means of understanding these problems and advancing toward the stated ends. The organization of the text follows the systematic style typical of Harris and the other authors, beginning with the types of methodological foundations just described, an assessment of the relevant elements such as available technology, decision making for production and allocation, division of labor, correlations between personnel and productional functions, methods of control, and the relationship between decisions systems and social ways in the contemporary society. The manuscript then moves to consider how these elements can be changed, what relation these changes have upon social relations as a whole, alternative futures in terms of decision making and class rule, and strategies of political action appropriate for the desired ends. This is a long and complex project, difficult to summarize without reference to details discussed, but a few are worth assessing in light of *The Transformation of Capitalist Society*. Significant discussions of transitions from one power to another occur, for example, leading to reflections upon the conditions of change from business rule to some other kind of rule, or from management decision making to worker decision making:

63a) The increasing difficulties in the business patterned class rule may lead, not to modifying the ruling group and freeing it from the business pattern, but to a sharp struggle between defenders and opponents of business rule, which may end with the replacement of the business rulers by entirely new rulers. The new rulers and the reorganization would not come in with the cooperation and personal participation of part of the signaling group.

63.b) Such developments may occur when the dissatisfaction of the productional occupations is great and cannot be allayed by anything that the business signalers [decision makers] are free to do.

This transformation may not be sustainable, of course, depending upon "the form of production of technology, the division of labor that has grown around it, the kind of productional interdependence," and "the techniques of signaling production and of group interaction available to the people at the time the old ruling patterns are discarded" (63ac–ad). Much of this area of the discussion relates to workers control and worker decision making, which lead the authors to suggest that "a necessary step toward elimination of class rule would therefore be if production signaling (the real veto power in production decisions) became an automatic part of the system of production, or were democratically decided by all producers or consumers, or were carried out by an occupational group which any individual could enter or leave fairly freely" (64ba).

On the basis of the detailed assessment offered of the then-current situation, the authors present a range of possible useful social action, including:

action tending to separate the output integrators from the signalers and their managerial functionaries; action associating the output integrators . . . with other output personnel (technicians, workers) by division of labor adjustments, political collaboration, social contact, etc.; action reducing the participation of output personnel in lower reaches of business-process signaling—this participation being one of the factors in the continued acceptance by the output personnel of the inefficient and scarcity-maintaining system of signaling; action to circumvent the effect of the growing non-output occupations . . . , etc. (74fa)

These efforts should be coupled with "developing the potential advantages of non-class-rule," (74fd) developing a "strong critique of present social organization" (74fe), providing a "blueprint" for the beginning of the next society on the basis of detailed accounts of what didn't work in class society, and so forth, all of which can help guide the actions of those involved in "considered intervention," including individual or small radical groups. The criteria for effective action is to be determined on the basis of the prevailing form of social organization, developments in world politics, cultural issues, and the way that the ruling classes choose to act and to respond.

Certain situations developed by the ruling class necessitate a complete reconsideration of the possibilities for the forms of the class struggle; the development of psychological, sociological, and even medical forms of control raises the question of how counter-measures can be developed and whether the output occupations can be really checked; the development of military techniques raises the question of whether and in what form military revolts will be possible in the future, and whether political disorganization of the military will be possible; finally, the occurrence of world wars (largely at times when popular dissatisfaction due to the inefficiencies of the system is increasing) is a major complication in the class struggle. (74gb)

This is the area of the work that ties concerns with political change to elements of control and potential, that is, the "media of interaction," which is "controlled by the signalers and their supporters, who also impose upon the people participation in them (i.e., subjection to their activities): church, certain features of the family, education, media of information, amusements, political machines, commitment of the government to maintain production in terms of the signaling-allocation system" (38ec).

A society without class rule thus depends upon the creation and naming of conditions adequate for the erection of a new form of power relation in society. A range of preconditions and developments are thus set out as relating to this transformation, including inequalities of allocation, relatively high overhead for production, the availability of "plenty," continued industrialization, increasing knowledge of how humans cooperate, the division-of-labor developments, and so forth. The obstacles are vast, however, and assessed in this study in terms of material, technological, cultural, historical, and psychological factors. The latter leads the authors to discussion of "diversions" effected by the rulers, psychological impediments toward mass rebellion (including direct references to Erich Fromm's work on the escape from freedom), "Freudian mechanisms," and a host of alternate satisfactions ("circus instead of bread") (36). A particular example from this section bears mention in light of this discussion of the relation between attitudes and action.

Some . . . outlets for dissatisfaction are institutionally developed. Such as the catharsis offered by churches (especially the Catholic confession), or the release of tensions provided by various styles of popular music (martial music, jazz, jitterbugging, etc.). Note also the diverting effect of theology, exemplified by Kafka in *The Trial*. There the priest talks with K who is hounded without cause. The priest tells K a somewhat parallel story from the holy writ, and then proves, by a philological critique of the statements made in that story that the accused person in that story has no case. The priest's function here (like that of a lawyer) is to change the merits of the case from the human problems of K to the literary-criticism problems of what the particular story says and whether the accused in the story has any claims in terms of the statements made in that story. (36.6)

This section contains as well a discussion of certain psychiatric practices that allow the individual to cope with "the inadequacies of the social arrangements" on a case-by case basis, which is indeed "the effect, and often explicit intention, of most psychiatric practice" (36.24). This question of the relationship between worker attitude and avenues of social change is everywhere present, by inference and in direct ways, in Harris's discussion of the transformation of capitalist society.

Transforming Capitalist Society

The book inspired by this study begins with a preface by Wolf V. Heyderbrand, which recalls that despite the inherent problems with liberal capitalism, it has the virtue of (sometimes) promoting individualism and a dynamic growth of technology, both of which exist as well in Harris's version of the good society. More important for this book, however, is the fact that "the non-centralized and self-regulating properties of liberal capitalism permit the mechanisms of decision-making as well as actual decisions to be either delegated to democratic government or to be relinquished to employees." The crucial verb here though is "permit," since this mechanism is certainly not unconditional or automatic, but is rather "a potential that arises both from internal weaknesses and contradictions of capitalism and from legal and constitutional rights already achieved, such as political and social rights as well as employee share ownership plans (ESOP) and, generally, gradual growth of employee ownership and control" (xi–xii).

There is a range of ways in which the contents of this book are consistent with Harris's overall approach to society and to analytical models I have described. He begins with criticisms of contemporary society and possibilities for change, then moves to a description of social structures with a clear delineation of methodological considerations, and then turns to the question of decision-making in the production of goods under capitalism, including both strengths and instabilities inherent in the current system. Consistent with his interest in the evolution of (workers') attitudes, he assesses possibilities for social change, including the crucial question of what induces action, before moving on to post-capitalist directions for this change. He looks back to history to find the roots of capitalist society and then, in some very interesting sections, recalls actual alternatives to capitalist organization including collectives (like kibbutzim) and workers councils. Then, in a step which Harris and his supporters deems essential, he sets forth a description and blueprint for a post-capitalist society, turning eventually to his support for ESOPs. Finally, in sections that bring his ideas up to date, he assesses the aftermath of Soviet communism, as well as a range of strategies and issues relevant to the task of exposing and then benefiting from capitalism's weaknesses. Along the way, a few familiar signposts are indicated, including, in his chapter on the relinquishing of decision-making power under capitalism, "the development of computer-integrated design and production as well as new forms of work organization such as project teams, task forces, flexible specialization, and matrix organization" (xii).

Rather than assessing each of Harris's arguments, I focus on telling areas of this book that link this text to his past approach and therefore offer some sense of his overall approach to society. As is often the case, the details of the argument bear consideration, but the real issue here is what Harris considers possible and worth pursuing in this project. The sources of the Harris approach are consistent with much of what we have seen about him to this point. There are a few fundamental ideas that guide Harris in this book and are related to the work he did in Avukah and the ideas he worked through subsequently. He was always anti–status quo, antifascist, and for some version of society informed by democratic socialism, anarchosyndicalism, and council communism; but being a pragmatic person, he also had to consider the current state of society, if only to determine a pathway toward peaceful and sensible transformation. His starting point was that the current system is untenable in the long term, for reasons relating, first, to the immanent destruction of the environment, brought on by the systemic capitalist requirement to maximize profits. Fundamentally, there has to be a conflict of values here, because efforts aimed at protecting or conserving would, in almost any instance, reduce short-term profit. Second, societies built on capitalist principles, in whatever form, generally produce large sectors of impoverished or unemployed people, necessarily, on account of the unequal distribution of resources, the cyclical nature of capitalist economies, and the ongoing need for a surplus of readily accessible cheap labor. And third, there is the problem that any system built upon maximized profits relies upon an expanding domain of operation, which, as a result of systemic downturns and limited resources, cannot be maintained forever. If history is any indication, even brute force directed against the domestic population will not ensure that a current ruling class will be able to maintain its control over society indefinitely. There are some directions in which society might evolve, on account of the existence of cyclically recurring unemployment and destitution, and Harris tries to work out what these might be, and how they might be harnessed to effect a sane transformation of society.

This book looks ahead to a time when the decline of capitalist production in various countries, economic sectors, and companies, leaves workers without job prospects and sectors of production inadequately covered for the needs of the population. The book examines the possibility that under these conditions worker-controlled enterprises, where employees are included in sharing control, may be able to arise and to fill an economic niche, and thus to survive within a capitalist environment. The book suggests that if, and as, such enterprises become a significant part of a country's economy, they will give rise to a new social economic understanding and different political attitudes, they may pave the way for a more humane and equitable society. Indeed, politically-centered changes toward such a society may well fail—even if only after decades—unless such enterprises have become part of the economy by the time the political changes are made. (2)

This paragraph offers the gist of Harris's whole enterprise: a capitalist society necessarily operates under conditions of growth and decline; this cycle produces economic downturns that can be very severe. Under these conditions certain segments of the economy become unprofitable and are therefore abandoned by the owners in favor of other sectors; workers in the failing sectors are therefore offered the opportunity to take control of their workplaces. And finally, because the workers have a greater say and a greater stake in the success of the operation, they will operate in a more efficient and, therefore, more profitable fashion. This is relatively unproblematic and logical, and is even anticipated by the current system; but as we move into the twenty-first century, logic has it that these problems will become more severe on account of a number of factors, notably "the possible rising costs of depleted energy, raw materials, pollution reduction, and the greater profitability of producing in third world plants" (3). These are the conditions that make employee shared ownership plans viable, particularly in less profitable sectors, and, in the short term at least, noncapitalist production could survive alongside the capitalist sectors of society since competition between the two realms would be minimal.

A few points deserve mention here; first, notice that Harris looks forward to a time when the move toward workers control would emerge in a gradual fashion, and not through revolutionary upheaval, massive revolution, or a sequence of political changes. This challenges those criticisms that might suggest that Bolshevism was one such experiment, or that such ideas are out of date, because it shows, on the contrary, a way in which ongoing problems could be resolved without massive structural change. Indeed, to refer back to the key paragraph cited earlier, capitalism in some cases relies upon the growth of employee participation in workplace decisions, and, moreover, upon occasional reorientation of capital away from sectors that, although unprofitable, are nevertheless necessary.

Harris's approach is directed to analyzing "social groupings"—occupations and the "economic political 'system' that interconnects economic arrangements, political power, social institutions and cultural ways and attitudes"—rather than individuals, and avoids "purely abstract" or "hypothetical concepts," favoring instead "specifiable types or aggregates of specifiable institutions, groups and actions" (11). Among these institutions Harris includes those who control the economy, of course, but in an area of discussion that resembles Chomsky's work, he also talks about those institutions (religion, education, the press, entertainment) that "reinforce these social values and cultural attitudes through indoctrination, domestication and control" (15). Among the structural elements he considers, Harris specifies the criteria for decision making, the "specification of persons" empowered to make decisions, and the "interrelation of the decision-making status and activities with the forms of political power and of status-quo maintenance" (army, government, wealth, acceptance, and so forth). Is there a link here between this form of analysis and the types of work Harris did as a linguist? He thinks so, since in an appendix on methodological considerations he notes that just as "each organism's structure affects the kind of behavior it carries out," and just as "each language has its own structure affecting the kinds of meanings it can carry, and the way the meanings are expressed, . . . major standardized interrelations within a society delineate the social behavior of people in it, and the kind of changes that are possible in it." The study of this latter structure is important since people do not always act according to their own self-interest; indeed, "many people support existing social arrangements even when these are counter to what one would suppose to be their own self-interest." One must understand these social arrangements in order to effect fundamental transformations because, according to Harris, "the interrelation of those actions that are based on the actors' participation in particular social sub-groups constitutes a more or less stable structure of social relations, which affect or determine much of the participating individuals' behavior" (22).

Harris then outlines the way decisions are made under capitalism, notably, how business decisions regarding production are taken in capitalist society, as a way of setting out both the realities of the present system and the opportunities it affords for those interested in changing it. He returns to a discussion regarding the attitudes of people in society, mentioning such factors as conformity, institutional norms, ideology, stability, tradition, culture, and so forth. The principle concern here is, of course, the question of what leads to action for social change, which he suggests occurs when "special openings arise," notably "unbearable situations" or "special opportunities for action" (51). Then, as a means of going beyond capitalism, Harris considers, first, post-capitalist developments in society, and then, true to form, offers "a detailed analysis of structure and forces in other social situations that are sufficiently close in time or similar in conditions to the situation we are considering" (87). This section of the book suggests, implicitly and explicitly, that there are things to be learned from history, both in terms of wrong turns taken, and possibilities that existed but were never put into practice.

This to me is the most intriguing part of Harris's book, because at this point Harris recalls a gamut of radical theories, practices, and practitioners, notably classical liberalism (Mill), anarchism (Herzen, Bakunin, Proudhon, Kropotkin, Berkman, Jura watchmakers, Catalonians), syndicalism (Sorel), worker militantism, and council communism. For Harris, these forces of "opposition to the evils of the ruling system" were "given a great push from Marxism" because "Marx presented his work as a theory of capitalism together with an effort to change or replace it" (108). Having recounted the relations that Harris had to Einstein, as far as his linguistic studies went, we can now see the relation between Harris and Marx, another rational, structured, Jewish thinker, a "scientific socialist" (109) whose work was a "watershed" for those "not only in the workers' movement but also in the thinking about economy, society, and human values." This is precisely where Paul Mattick and Paul Mattick Jr. link Harris's Marxism with his later linguistics work[13], and where Arthur Rosenberg[14] returns to link Harris's Avukah days with this analysis of society. It is also where Harris tries to go beyond Marxism, suggesting that Marx's failings were partly the result of the diversity of paths taken, which "as due in part to the lack of clarity in understanding the conditions for transition and the processes involved," turn out to be Harris's advantage over Karl Marx. Harris has the obvious benefit of hindsight and of describing a very different stage of capitalism, whereas "Marx's own work was so early in the development of the workers' movement that he could not see either how workers could develop their decision potential in the workplace rather than spill over into street protest and revolutionary or parliamentary action, or how the dynamics of capitalism would take capitalist control proper ever farther away from the workplace" (109).

Kibbutzim, Collectives, and Communities

After showing how in times of economic downturn those responsible for business decisions can cede various domains of decision making to the government or to workers, Harris then turns to the ways that relinquishing powers to noncapitalist enterprises can actually take place in the current and foreseeable world. Here, he begins with a historical discussion about self-governing innovations, notably collectivist communes and cooperatives that share in profits and control their workplaces. He mentions, for example, the Hutterite communities, the Owenite colonies, and the 1960s movement of "dropping out," before turning to the "one serious success of the communes," the "Kibbutz movement in what is now Israel." By offering a long description of Kibbutzim, Harris on the one hand returns to earlier discussions from the Avukah days, while on the other he addresses the concern with finding a system for organizing society that "offers a pragmatic solution to the immediate needs of their participants" (114). His description is, predictably, very positive, and it becomes clear that his idea of workers' participation is very much founded upon the success of that experience, and upon the positive impressions he had while a resident of Mishmar Ha'Emek. But one can find as well the link that Harris makes between a good society and successful worker enterprises through his condemnation of the state, which, once established, necessarily challenged Kibbutzim identity. He recalls that the "Kibbutzim were first formed in the pioneering community of Jewish immigrants to Palestine, where the Labor Party and its umbrella trade union held the loyalty of the great bulk of the population," and "where the Kibbutz members were admired as pioneers and practicing socialists." This changed, however, in 1948.

With the establishment of the State of Israel in 1948, the bringing in of large Jewish communities that had no socialist background, the wars wit the Arabs, the rise of living standards, both in the Kibbutzim and in the country, the growing militarist, capitalist, business-minded, and religious attitudes in Israel combined to weaken the socialist ideals that were in any case declining in Europe as well, and overwhelmed the special place that the Kibbutzim had enjoyed in the country. (117)

And yet even despite this degradation in ideals and practices, the kibbutz remained for Harris, and for "many of the younger generation," a positive experience because it remained true to some of its foundational precepts: "There is no power elite or bureaucracy in the Kibbutz, and no person or group has power over the production and life of the rest of the population." For this reason, "the sense of liberation and underlying equality is palpable," and "the uncomfortable distance among people that characterizes all societies in which there are major differences in income or in power is not felt in the Kibbutz" (117). So even though it has lost its explicit political ideology, and many of "the political and social values of the original socialist belief," the kibbutz nevertheless offers an egalitarianism and a model of self-governance that Harris still finds pertinent.

The other examples of working models for worker participation to which Harris refers are cooperatives, notably producer cooperatives, including the Owenite examples (based on the utopian socialist philosophy of Robert Owen), the Rochdale movement (based on cooperative efforts of the Rochdale Society of Equitable Pioneers, the anarchist collectives in Catalonia (based on principles of anarchosyndicalism), the Shanghai workers movement of the 1920s (that involved the worker takeover of factories and other cooperative efforts), the small-scale workers collectives in France, Italy, India and El Salvador, and, of course, the Mondragon Cooperative Group in the Basque area of Spain, (which began in 1956 through the initiative of Father José Maria Arismendi-Arrieta). Returning to areas of common interest between Harris and Erich Fromm (who for some reason is not mentioned), Harris talks about the psychological effects of encouraging workers to become responsible and active participants in work (subjects of Fromm's 1959 "Freedom in the Work Situation,"[15] and *The Sane Society*[16]). With reference to his friend Paul Mattick, Harris also discusses workers' councils, those examples of "self-governed industrial production" that "fitted closely with those trends in European radicalism (such as anti-Bolshevik Marxists, e.g., Rosa Luxemburg and Karl Liebknecht, with antecedents in the syndicalism of Georges Sorel) that framed the issues in terms of the ongoing interests and potentialities of industrial workers beyond the single goal of seizing political power, in particular by means of a party," the Bolsheviks, "speaking in the name of a generalized proletariat but in actuality ruling over it" (124–125). These councils, deemed "soviets," were crushed by the USSR, just as the workers councils (Arbetarräte) were eventually disbanded in Hamburg. These efforts closely mirror Harris's own vision and serve as historical precursors for his support for ESOPs, and Harris, like Anton Pannekoek before him, is the scientist who recalls and supports such popular endeavors.

In the wake of this and of kindred trends, there was a movement for legal and public recognition of such workers' councils (expounded by Karl Korsch and others) and considerable discussion such as in the work of Anton Pannekoek (the Dutch astronomer who together with Rosa Luxemburg rejected Lenin's 1915 Bolshevik program that was later to become the Communist Third International) and of the Council Communist movement (as in the work of Paul Mattick and his journals *Living Marxism* and *New Essays*). (125)

But even with the interest that Harris had in these efforts, which promoted egalitarian democratic participation of workers and a decision structure "that is free of outside control except for the productionally necessary considerations of materials, technology, consumers, and adequate but not maximal profitability," there are nevertheless limitations to this approach. "Important as this subject is for long-term analysis of possible arrangements of self-governed production, it is not discussed here because there are not enough ongoing processes or pressures, even in local special conditions, to offer any insight at present into how such arrangements may come to be" (126).

The subsequent discussion of self-governed production, with the long overview of ESOPs, updates the visions provided by these historical examples by trying to adapt them to current business practices while attempting to account for obstacles to the transformation of capitalist society. The principle question here relates to how workers' attitudes might change to favor democratic participation, in the face of the economic and political power of the employer class, something that Harris had been interested in since the 1940s (Noam Chomsky discusses these efforts, and explains his own relationship to this work in an interview I conducted with him in May 2009 that appears in the appendix).

This issue of changing workers' attitudes is never satisfactorily addressed in Harris's book, though, because even if Harris is right—that employees involved in such plans have less grounds to oppose decisions that affect them personally and therefore a greater stake in the enterprise—there is still the problem that such experiments tend to remain short term. So while Pride Bakery, Weirton Steel, and Republic Engineered Steels offer some concrete examples of how such efforts have functioned in the past (Harris offers up these examples of companies that were bought out and then run by employees), there is no clear indication that they can be sustained in the long term. Harris is wise to such obstacles, however, describing the challenges as "vast"; but he holds that there is enough historical and contemporary data to suggest possible success and that such efforts are worthwhile in light of the failings, and the "evils," of contemporary capitalism.

We have seen small ongoing pressures toward increased work-place decision-making by workers, and larger pressures toward workers' partial or complete ownership of their workplace. All these developments are taking place within the business world, mostly with no post-capitalist intent. In particular, employee ownership does not in itself encourage leftist attitudes, and may even encourage the worker-owners' hiring of additional non-owning owners [something we see today on kibbutzim]. However, what is important here is not the immediate attitude or political stance, but the long-range interests and power that are bred by the new decision-making and ownership statuses. (171)

In the end, he says, "the methods and strategies have to be tried out in real cases within the present society, and not just thought out in theory while waiting for political change" (170–171). This is the challenge that Harris left, and which a society of alienated workers and disenfranchised individuals were to follow up on, in their own interest and in the interest of preserving the planet's resources.

Reviewing Transformation

In spite of the challenge posed and the needs described, Harris's political book passed with nary a recognition in the period of its publication. Aside from a few references to the book on, for example, Internet sites, there are two short notices, by John P. Burke in *Philosophy in Review*,[17] and by Sally Lerner for *Alternatives Journal: Environmental Thought, Policy and Action*,[18] where it is given short shrift alongside another book on experiments in community economic development, and there is one substantial review by Bruce Nevin for the March 11, 1997, Linguist List (8.350–351). Burke describes in not very glowing terms Harris's attempt to grapple with the nonrevolutionary move to a "more humane, democratic" postcapitalist society from a "left-libertarian perspective that succumbs to utopianism." Consistent with several reviews of Harris's later linguistic work, Burke describes the book as "curious," filled with "anomalies" and "ambiva-lence," a work whose ambition is "fulfilled neither by a convincing empiri-cal case or a persuasive normative theory." Burke is surprised that Harris invokes Marx but disavows revolutionary change, and that he "pecks at capitalist reformism as utopian" but casts "its own normative prescriptions for post-capitalist society . . . in utopian terms of 'may' and 'maybe'." I myself am unsure as to why "may" is utopian (the stock market may after all rise tomorrow, or may not), since what Burke is criticizing is Harris's uncertainty, that cooperatives and collectives "may prove feasible again," but only if certain conditions are fulfilled, which seems obvious. But once again, this review relays the impression, not necessarily negative but gener-ally deemed so, that despite "some insightful observations and suggestive chapters" (264) Harris's work hearkens from and speaks to another era, possibly rather far from our own.

Sally Lerner's review, appropriately treating both Harris's book and also Greg MacLeod's *From Mondragon to America: Experiments in Community Economic Development*,[19] is much more hands-on and far less equivocal, finding that both books "offer compelling arguments for pursuing a posi-tive future of work for Canada. Well-designed non-profit and for-profit

community co-ops and corporations clearly offer alternatives to unemployment and the insecurity of contract-based 'just-in-time' jobs, and that both
Harris and MacLeod show us some paths less traveled that could prove
invaluable over the next decades" (35). This last point is well taken, and
indeed could serve as the leitmotif for much of Harris's work, for he did
follow "paths less traveled" in his work, and along the way, society itself
moved askance of where he wanted to be, in terms of Palestine, the organization of workers, and even linguistic research. To rethink cooperatives
and ESOPs from this standpoint is to consider an alternative to profit-
driven forces whose actions frequently result in human misery, the destruction of creativity, and the annihilation of the environment.

Nevin's laudatory review begins with some general statements about
Harris's approach: "The ability to step aside from the way things 'naturally'
are, to perceive that their basis is in conventional expectations, and to
recognize the seeds of a successor 'social reality', is a rare gift indeed. This
is the gift that Harris presents to us in this posthumous book." He describes
Harris as "one of the great figures of American linguistics," and "the origi-
nator of transformational grammar," and the person responsible for "fostering the work and early career of his most famous student, Noam
Chomsky." Nevin points to "Chomsky's comment that he was first attracted
to Harris because of his political views" as a starting point of a discussion
of "what those views were."

Harris had a profound understanding of history, economics, sociology, and anthropology. In this, he had much in common with Edward Sapir, who it is said regarded
him as his intellectual heir; in particular in his sensitivity to the inadequacies of
established social arrangements (inadequacies made especially obvious in the Great
Depression) and in his interest in the possible shapes of alternatives. He was always
an originative thinker. Before undertaking this book, he read and re-read widely,
because he did not want to re-do what someone else had already adequately done.
Harris does not decry the worth of capitalism, as far as it goes, nor deny the great
benefits that it has brought. It is obvious that there have been great advances in
culture and in the material standard of living of most people, even in the last 100
or 50 years. Rather, he asks "whether, in spite of its success, the capitalist system will
end or change substantially in the foreseeable future. If so, what are the possibilities
that the change will foster more equitable socio-economic conditions?" (2).

Nevin provides an outline of Harris's ideas and concludes that "the book
is well reasoned and its generalizations, methods, and conclusions are supported throughout by evidence, much of it familiar but perhaps cast in a
somewhat new light by Harris's treatment"; this type of unequivocal and
clear statement has certainly helped with the success of this book in certain

Notes

Preface

1. Bruce E. Nevin and Stephen B. Johnson, eds., *The Legacy of Zellig Harris: Language and Information into the 21st Century*. Amsterdam: John Benjamins Publishing Company, 2002.

2. Michael Stanislawski, *Zionism and the Fin de Siècle: Cosmopolitanism and Nationalism from Nordau to Jabotinsky* (Berkeley: University of California Press, 2001), p. 16.

Chapter 1

1. Cited in the manuscript of Thomas Ryckman's "Zellig Harris' Methodology of Language and Information," October 8, 1991, p. 4 [unpublished].

2. See, most notably, Pannekoek's *Workers' Councils,* edited and with comments by Robert Barsky, containing interviews with Noam Chomsky, Ken Coates, and Peter Hitchcock, and a republication of a seminal piece by Paul Mattick (London: AK Press, 2002).

3. Much of the details about Balta come from the remarkable International Jewish Cemeteries Project, http://www.jewishgen.org/cemetery.

4. Irving Howe with Kenneth Libo, *World of Our Fathers* (New York: Galahad Books, 1994).

5. Seymour Martin Lipset, "Steady Work: An Academic Memoir," *American Sociologist* 34, nos. 1–2 (March 2003).

6. Cambridge University Press, 1981.

7. Chimen Abramsky, "Nationalism and Universalism—the Unresolved Dilemma," *Soviet Jewish Affairs* 13, no. 1 (1983): 57–66, p. 61.

8. Cited in Michael Aronson, *Troubled Waters: The Origins of the 1881 Anti-Jewish Pogroms in Russia* (Pittsburgh: University of Pittsburgh Press, 12).

9. Benjamin Harshov, *Language in Time of Revolution* (Berkeley: University of California Press, 1993).

10. Ibid., 203.

11. Ibid., 41.

12. Ibid., 203.

13. Stephen M. Berk, *Year of Crisis, Year of Hope: Russian Jewry and the Pogroms of 1881–1882* (Westport, CT: Greenwood Press, 1985), 80.

14. Ibid., 65.

15. Mary Antin, who emigrated in 1891, cited in Howe, 27.

16. Zachary Lockman, *Comrades and Enemies: Arab and Jewish Workers in Palestine, 1906–1948* (Berkeley: University of California Press, 1996), 25.

17. See Robert F. Barsky, *Arguing and Justifying: Assessing the Convention Refugee Choice of Moment, Motive and Host Country* (Aldershot, UK: Ashgate Press, 2000).

18. Stuart E. Knee, "The Diplomacy of Neutrality: Theodore Roosevelt and the Russian Pogroms of 1903–1906," *Presidential Studies Quarterly* 19 no. 1 (1989): 71–72.

19. The all-Ukrainian Central Committee of Assistance to Victims of Military Actions was comprised of: L. Ye. Mandelberg, Chairman of the Committee; N. Yu. Gergel, P. G. Dubinsky, Kh. Fialkov, N. I. Shtif, and others; see O. V. Kozerod, S.Ya. Briman, "A.I. Denikin's Regime and the Jewish Population of Ukraine in 1919–1920," at the Jewish Heritage Organization site, http://www.jewish-heritage.org/prep53.htm.

20. One petition that was published in the *New York Times.* (December 2, 1948) aimed to publicly present "a few salient facts concerning Begin and his party; and of urging all concerned not to support this latest manifestation of fascism." It was signed by: Isidore Abramowitz, Hannah Arendt, Abraham Brick, Rabbi Jessurun Cardozo, Albert Einstein, Herman Eisen, M.D., Hayim Fineman, M. Gallen, M.D., H. H. Harris, Zellig S. Harris, Sidney Hook, Fred Karush, Bruria Kaufman, Irma L. Lindheim, Nachman Majsel, Seymour Melman, Myer D. Mendelson, M.D., Harry M. Orlinsky, Samuel Pitlick, Fritz Rohrlich, Louis P. Rocker, Ruth Sager, Itzhak Sankowsky, I. J. Shoenberg, Samuel Shuman, M. Singer, Irma Wolpe, Stefan Wolpe. New York, Dec. 2, 1948.

21. Enya Harris (later Enya Live), Cooperative Enterprise in Palestine (Zionist education series), Education Department, Zionist Organization of America, 1937. She also translated a text into English, Meir Yaari's *Analysis of Zionism*. This article appeared in Hebrew in Sefer ha-shomrim, published by Hashomer Hatzair, Warsaw 1934, pp. 377–387, and was translated for this series by Enya Harris. Originally written in 1929; (see p. 13. microfiche, Zug, Switzerland: Inter Documentation Co., 1975). Of note as well is Shoshanna Harris Sankowsky's book *Short History of Zionism* (London:

Federation of Zionist Youth) (originally published by American Student Zionist Federation) circa 1936.

Chapter 2

1. Bennett M. Berger, ed., *Authors of their Own Lives: Intellectual Autobiographies by Twenty American Sociologists* (Berkeley: University of California Press, 1990), 194.

2. Irene Schumer remembers the claim that they were represented by upward of 2,000 members, in colleges from the Midwest to the East Coast, with a small contingency in New Orleans.

3. *The Emblem*, Chicago Normal College, 1934, accessed at http://www.archive.org/stream/emblem1__1934chic/emblem1__1934chic_djvu.txt

4. On Thomas, see, for example, Harry Fleischmann', *Norman Thomas: A Biography* (New York: Norton & Co., 1964); Robert Hyfler, *Prophets of the Left: American Socialist Thought in the Twentieth Century* (Westport, CT: Greenwood Press, 1984); Bernard Johnpoll, *Pacifists Progress: Norman Thomas and the Decline of American Socialism* (Chicago: Quadrangle Books, 1970); Murray B. Seidler, *Norman Thomas: Respectable Rebel* (Binghamton, NY: Syracuse University Press, 1967, second edition); W. A. Swanberg, *Norman Thomas: The Last Idealist* (New York: Charles Scribner and Sons, 1976).

5. http://jwa.org/encyclopedia/article/hunter-college.

6. http://www.pbs.org/arguing/nyintellectuals_krystol_2.html.

7. Described in a January 2, 1940, article in the journal called *The Mirror* "as the most brazen supporter of Communism among American youth is the American Student Union, which claimed in 1940 to have 30,000 members in 150 U. S. schools and colleges. . . . Formed in 1935, when the Socialist Student League for Industrial Democracy joined hands with the Communistic National Student League, the American Student Union has since been the tell-tale weathervane in the wind blowing from Moscow. Make 'The Campus a Fortress of Democracy', as its letterhead read, was the slogan of the ASU for popular consumption." http://newdeal.feri.org/students/tc.htm.

8. *Methods in Structural Linguistics* (Chicago: University of Chicago Press, 1951, xvi).

9. Lanham, MD: Roman and Littlefield, 1997.

10. E. F. K. Koerner, "Zellig Sabbettai Harris: A comprehensive bibliography of his writings, 1932-1991" *Historiographia Linguistica* 20, nos. 2/3: 509–522.

11. Personal correspondence, November 27, 1997.

12. NewYork: Holt, 1994 (first published in 1941).

13. Jean Cantineau, in his "Review of Methods in Structural Linguistics, by Zellig Harris," described him as a "good Semiticist," and there are regular mentions of his

having made important contributions to that field. *Bulletin de la Société de Linguistique de Paris* 50, no. 2 (1954):4–9.

14. The core of this text was published in the *Journal of the American Oriental Society* in 1933, a "coup" of sorts for master's level work, according to Bruce Nevin.

15. Zellig Harris, "Acrophony and Vowellessness in the Creation of the Alphabet," *Journal of the American Oriental Society* 53 (1933): 387.

16. Henry Hiz, "Zellig Harris," *Proceedings of the American Philosophical Society* 138, no.4 (1994): 519.

17. *Language*, originally published by the University of Chicago Press in 1933, is an introduction to linguistics but has been described as being the single most influential work of general linguistics published in this century, and it has become the major text of the American descriptivist school.

18. Peter Matthews, "Obituary: Zellig Sabbettai Harris," *Language: Journal of the Linguistic Society of America* 75, no. 1 (March 1999): 112.

19. Personal correspondence, September 27, 1997.

20. Samuel Hughes, "Speech!" *The Pennsylvania Gazette*, The Alumni Magazine of the University of Pennsylvania, July/August, 2001. http://www.upenn.edu/gazette/0701/hughes.html.

21. Noam Chomsky, *The Logical Structure of Linguistic Theory* (New York: Springer, 1975).

22. The results of this study were published as part of Harris, "From Phoneme to Morpheme," *Language* 31 (1955): 181–122.

Chapter 3

1. Available in Special Collections, Columbia University.

2. Zellig Harris, *The Transformation of Capitalist Society* (Philadelphia: Roman and Littlefield, 1997).

3. Ber Borochov, *The National Question and the Class Struggle* (1905). Available online at: http://www.zionism-israel.com/hdoc/ber_borochov_national_question.htm.

4. This objective was central to Avukah, but it had corollary approaches in some other organizations, such as Brit Shalom, for instance, which aimed to create a binational state in Palestine. Brit Shalom supporters and founders included Martin Buber, Hugo Bergmann, Arthur Ruppin, Gershom Scholem, and Henrietta Szold as well as luminaries such as Albert Einstein and Judah Leon Magnes who supported its views. The organization was formed in 1925, and announced in its 1927 program that its objectives were to create a binational state of Palestinians and Jews who

would enjoy equal rights no matter what the population makeup. Although it never affirmed it as a minority principle, it was nonetheless the position of the organization that Jews would remain a minority in Palestine, limited to 500,000 (http://histmove.ouvaton.org/pag/chr/pag_004/fr/pag.htm#_ednref11).

5. Alexander Mitchell Palmer became attorney general in 1919, and he narrowly escaped an attack on his person by anarchist groups on two occasions. Convinced that the menace posed by anarchists and the radical left was real, and armed with a clear mandate for action from President Wilson, Palmer became a zealous opponent of anarchist communists, insurrectionary anarchists, and other radicals who advocated revolution and/or the violent overthrow of the federal government of the United States.

6. Incidentally, Lipset's aforementioned "Steady Work: An Academic Memoir," in *Annual Review of Sociology* 22 (1996), that recalls his background at City College, his affiliation to the Trotskyites and radical politics, and his early training, never mentions Avukah. Nor does Marshall Sklare recall in any of his writings his work in Avukah.

7. British policy outlined in White Papers prior to the creation of the state of Israel.

8. Clement Greenberg and Dwight Macdonald, "10 Propositions on the War," *Partisan Review* 8 (July-Aug. 1941), 271–278.

9. Michael Stanislawski, *Zionism and the fin de siècle: Cosmopolitanism and Nationalism from Nordeau to Jabotinsky.* Berkeley, CA: University of California Press, 2001.

10. Pieter A. M. Seuren, *Western Linguistics: An Historical Introduction* (Hoboken, NJ: Wiley-Blackwell, 1998).

11. Gerald Holton, *The Advancement of Science, and Its Burdens* (Cambridge: Harvard University Press, 1998 [1986], 290).

12. W. C. Watt. "Zellig Harris, 1909–1992. *Biographical Memoirs*, volume 87. Washington DC: The National Academies Press, 2005.

13. http://www.dmi.columbia.edu/zellig/watt.pdf.

14. http://www.dmi.columbia.edu/zellig/watt.pdf.

15. http://linguistlist.org/issues/3/3-445.html.

16. Bruce E. Nevin, and Stephen B. Johnson, eds., *The Legacy of Zellig Harris: Language and information into the 21st century,* 2 Volumes, (Amsterdam: John Benjamins, 2002).

Chapter 4

1. Edited by Bruce E. Nevin and Stephen M. Johnson. *The Legacy of Zellig Harris: Language and Information into the 21st Century.* Volume 2, *Computability of Language*

and Computer Applications (Philadelphia: John Benjamins, 2002). I have benefited enormously from Nevin's many comments on Harris's work and legacy.

2. http://www.dmi.columbia.edu/zellig/Symposium.htm.

3. "Acrophony and Vowellessness in the Creation of the Alphabet" *Journal of American Oriental Society* 53 (1934): 387.

4. See Jean Cantineau, "Review of *Methods in Structural Linguistics*," *Bulletin de la Société de Linguistique de Paris* 50, no. 2 (1954): 4–9.

5. Zellig S. Harris, "The Structure of Ras Shamra C," *Journal of the American Oriental Society* no. 54 (1934): 80–83.

6. Zellig S. Harris, with James A. Montgomery. *The Ras Shamra Mythological Texts* (NewYork: American Oriental Society, 1935).

7. Review of James A. Montgomery and Zellig S. Harris, *The Ras Shamra Mythological Texts*, in *Language* 13 (1937): 326–331.

8. *Proceedings of the American Philosophical Society* 138, no. 4, (1994), available online at http://www.dmi.columbia.edu/zellig/obit-Hiz.htm.

9. William Chomsky review of *Grammaire de l'Hébreu Biblique* by P. Paul Joüon, in *The Jewish Quarterly Review*, New Series 25, no. 3 (Jan. 1935): 311–315.

10. *Language* 15 (1939): 60–65.

11. *Archiv Orientàlnì* 11 (1939): 177–178.

12. *Revue des Études Sémitiques* (1940): 94–96.

13. *Wissenschaftliche Zeitschrift für die Kunde des Morgenlandes* 48 (1941): 153.

14. *Journal of the American Oriental Society* 54 (1934): 93–95.

15. Volume 11 (pp. 262–263).

16. Volume 56 (1936): 410.

17. Translated by Hans-Jakob Wilhelm.

18. Chicago: University of Chicago Press, 1951.

19. *The Jewish Quarterly Review* 27 no. 3 (1936–37): 261–264.

20. For a discussion of the importance of the Linguistics Institute, see Dell Hymes and John Fought, *American Structuralism* (The Hague: Mouton, 1981).

21. From Joos's obituary of Bloch in *Language* 43 (1967): 3–19.

22. "A Conditioned Sound Change in Ras Shamra," *Journal of the American Oriental Society* 57 (1937): 151–157.

23. "Expression of the Causative in Ugaritic," *Journal of the American Oriental Society* 58 (1937): 103–111.

24. See note 7.

25. In volume 29, pp. 191–193. This is a review of Charles Virolleaud's *La légende de Daniel* and *La légende de Keret, roi des Sidoniens*, edited by Claude F.-A. Schaeffer.

26. *Journal of the American Oriental Society* 60 (1940): 414–422.

27. *Kirjath Sepher* 17 (1940): 370–381.

28. *Bulletin de la Société de Linguistique de Paris* 123 (1940–41): 162.

29. *Syria: Revue d'art oriental et d'archéologie* 21 (1940): 228–230.

30. *Journal of Biblical Literature* 59 (1940): 546–551.

31. *Language* 17 (1941): 167–170.

32. *Journal of the Royal Asiatic Society of Great Britain and Ireland* series 64, no. 17 (1941): 167–170.

33. *Orientalia* 11 (1942): 179–185.

34. *Le Muséon* 53 (1940): 135.

35. *Vivre et Penser* (1941): 157–159.

36. *Journal of the Palestine Oriental Society* 19 (1941): 329–330.

37. *Journal of Near Eastern Studies* 1 (1942): 378–380.

38. Antoine Meillet was "the best-known scholar of the so-called Paris school of Linguistics in the first quarter of the century." He was a personal friend of Ferdinand de Saussure, who famously described *Cours de Linguistique générale* as a fraud because it foregrounded "synchrony and system over diachrony and society. In particular, the main line of the book, according to which 'the study of linguistics is the study of language in and for itself' . . . was totally opposite to the general orientation of Meillet's school and was perceived as a clear and direct polemical attack on a linguistic tradition dear to Saussure and Meillet," which was "based on historical and comparative philology." Lawrence D. Kritzman, ed, *The Columbia History of Twentieth-Century French Thought* (New York: Columbia University Press, 2006), 426.

39. Marcel Cohen, *Bulletin de la Société Linguistique de Paris* 40–41 (1939): 62.

40. *Journal of the American Oriental Society* 59 (1939): 409–410.

41. In *Journal of the American Oriental Society* 59 (1939): 1–4.

42. Indianapolis, Indiana Historical Society, 1939 (Reprinted by AMS Press, New York, 1975).

43. From the Goldman archives.

44. Cited in Jamie Sayen's *Einstein in America* (NewYork: Random House, 1990).

45. Recipient's name is illegible in the original.

46. New York, Macmillan for the journal *Language* 16, no. 3 (1939): 216–231.

47. Zellig S. Harris, "The Background of Transformational and Metalanguage Analysis," in Bruce Nevin, ed., *The Legacy of Zellig Harris: Language and Information into the 21st Century*, vol. I (Philadelphia: John Benjamins, 2002).

48. Peter Seuren, *Western Linguistics: An Historical Introduction*. Oxford: Blackwell, 1998, 62.

49. William Chomsky, "The History of our Vowel-System in Hebrew," *Jewish Quarterly Review* 32, no. 1 (1941): 27–46.

50. Zellig S. Harris, "Linguistic Structure of Hebrew," for the *Journal of the American Oriental Society*" 61 (1941):143–167, also published as the *Publications of the American Oriental Society*, offprint series 14.

51. Nikolaj Sergeevic Trubetzkoy, *Grundzüge der Phonologi* (Prague: Cercle Linguistique de Prague, 1939).

52. Zellig S. Harris, "Review," *Language* 17 (1941): 345–349.

53. Zellig S. Harris, "Cherokee Materials." Manuscript 30 (I2.4). Typed D. and A.D. 620L., 575 slips, 10 discs (Philadelphia: American Philosophical Society Library).

54. Zellig S. Harris, "Morpheme Alternants in Linguistic Analysis," *Language* 18, no. 3 (1942): 169–180.

55. Zellig S. Harris, "Phonologies of African Languages: The Phonemes of Moroccan Arabic," *Journal of the American Oriental Society* 62, no. 4 (1942): 309–318. This work was critiqued by Jean Cantineau in "Réflexions sur la phonologie de l'arabe marocain," *Hesperis* 37 (1951): 193–207.

56. "Linguistic Structure of Hebrew," *Journal of the American Oriental Society* 61 (1941):143–167.

57. "Phonologies of African Languages: The Phonemes of Moroccan Arabic," *Journal of the American Oriental Society* 62, no. 4 (1942): 309–318.

58. Zellig S. Harris and William E. Welmers, "The Phonemes of Fanti," *Journal of the American Oriental Society* 62 (1942): 318–333.

59. Zellig S. Harris and Fred Lukoff, "The Phonemes of Kingwa Swahili," *Journal of the American Oriental Society* 62 (1942): 309–318 and "The Phonemes of Moroccan Arabic," *Journal of the American Oriental Society* 62 (1942): 333–338.

60. John Goldsmith postulates in personal correspondence dated April 28, 2009, that "the circumpolar problems might well refer to the relationship between Siberian languages and those of the New World, especially the Athabaskan and Eskimo languages spoken in Canada."

61. Personal correspondence, April 28, 2009.

62. Albert Einstein, *Ideas and Opinions of Albert Einstein*. London: Crown Publishers, 1962. This essay is based on a talk that was originally broadcast on September 28, 1941. This speech, titled "The Common Language of Science," was addressed to a meeting of the British Association for the Advancement of Science. For a brief discussion about this text, see *Selected Writings: Contributions to Comparative Mythology; Studies in Linguistics and Philology*, 1972–1982, by Roman Jakobson, Stephen Rudy, and Linda R. Waugh (Berlin: Walter de Gruyter, 1985).

63. Cited in the aforementioned *Ideas and Opinions of Albert Einstein*.

64. This is a contentious area. Michael Holquist notes in personal correspondence (August 11, 2009) that "Whitney was deeply committed to the idea that more work needed to be done in Indo European before plunging into languages outside this well studied but still developing tradition, where real breakthroughs might be expected soon. He loved (critically) von Humboldt, but was dubious about his work in North American native languages and Basque. But at core he believed in a general theory of language, so was not as opposed to study of indigenous languages as some accounts suggest—it's also true that Whitney was a genius who was followed by a lot of American non-geniuses (Boaz had critics in Germany from the same tradition). I'm convinced that what inspired Boaz was his conversion experience from seeking to scientize Kant to linguistics on his first trip to North American wilderness."

65. Susan Krook, "Clio's Fancy: Documents to Pique the Historical Imagination." Franz Boas (a.k.a. Boaz) and the F.B.I.," American Philosophical Society, Chicago 1989, a file contained in the APS depository of Boas documents. http://opac.amphilsoc.org/cgi-bin/koha/opac-ISBDdetail.pl?biblionumber=42233

66. Herbert Mitgang, "Annals of Government: Policing America's Writers," *New Yorker* October 5, 1987, 47–90.

67. This list of organizations is interesting, containing progressive groups as well as Russian creations, like the League Against Fascism. John Goldsmith notes, in personal correspondence, that "I probably feel much the same way you do about Hoover and the FBI, but from the point of view of evil, the Comintern and the groups it sponsored in the West were no better. There's a lot of literature now on the hypocritical ways in which Western intellectuals were exploited for Russian aims."

68. Franz Boas "The Myth of Racial Excellence," *New Masses* 40, no. 5 (1942): 6.

69. Other committee members included Manuel J. Andrade, Jaime de Angulo, Roland B. Dixon, Pliny E. Goddard, Bernard Haile, John P. Harrington, Harry Hoijer,

Melville Jacobs, Diamond Jenness, Alfred V. Kidder, Alfred L. Kroeber, Truman Michelson, Frans M. Olbrechts, Gladys A. Reichard, Frank G. Speck, Edgar H. Sturtevant, Morris Swadesh, and John R. Swanton.

70. In *Language* (21, no. 3, supplement).

71. Vol. 14 no. 3 (1948): 209–211.

72. The American Philological Society, Library Bulletin (1947): 80–97.

73. "How the Study of Hebrew Grammar Began and Developed," *The Jewish Quarterly Review* 35 (1944–45): 281–301.

74. *The Jewish Quarterly Review* 38, no. 4 (April 1948): 407–412.

75. *Transactions of the American Philosophical Society*, new series vol. 37, part 3 (1947): 201–377.

76. *Journal of American Folklore* 61 (1948) 414–415.

77. In *Word* 4 (1948): 58–63.

78. Note as well Boas's censure by the American Anthropological Association during World War I as "pro-German."

79. *American Anthropologist* 49, no. 4 (1947): 588–600.

80. A contrasting assessment of this work was offered years later by Noam Chomsky in his book *Language and Mind*: "The belief that anthropological linguistics has demolished the assumptions of universal grammar seems to me to be quite false in two important respects. First, it misinterprets the views of classical rationalist grammar, which held that languages are similar only at the deeper level, the level at which grammatical relations are expressed and at which·the processes that provide for the creative aspect of language use are to be found. Second, this belief seriously misinterprets the findings of anthropological linguistics, which has, in fact, restricted itself almost completely to fairly superficial aspects of language structure. This is not to criticize anthropological linguistics, a field that is faced with compelling problems of its own—in particular, the problem of obtaining at least some record of the rapidly vanishing languages of the primitive world. Nevertheless, it is important to bear in mind this fundamental limitation on its achievements in considering the light it can shed on the theses of universal grammar. Anthropological studies (like structural linguistic studies in general) do not attempt to reveal the underlying core of generative processes in language—that is, the processes that determine the deeper levels of structure and that constitute the systematic means for creating ever novel sentence types" (77–78).

81. Zellig S. Harris, Review of David G. Mandelbaum, ed., *Edward Sapir: Selected Writings in Language, Culture and Personality: Essays in Memory of Edward Sapir, Language* 27, no. 3 (1951): 288–333.

82. *The Collected Works of Edward Sapir*, edited by Edward Sapir, Regna Darnell, Judith T. Irvine, William Bright, Philip Sapir, Victor Golla, Pierre Swiggers (Berlin: Walter de Gruyter, 1994).

Chapter 5

Some of this material overlaps with the discussion on precursors to Chomsky's approach in my 2007 book, *The Chomsky Effect: A Radical Works Beyond the Ivory Tower* (MIT Press), and in my 1997 biography, *Noam Chomsky: A Life of Dissent* (MIT Press). It bears recollection, however, in the context of fully documenting Harris's work and relation to his famous student, and for the purposes of this discussion, I have emphasized Harris's perspective.

1. http://www.upenn.edu/gazette/0701/hughes.html, *The Pennsylvania Gazette*, The Alumni Magazine of the University of Pennsylvania, July/August 2001.

2. Ibid.

3. Noam Chomsky, *Language and Mind* (New York: Houghton-Mifflin, 1972), 3–4.

4. Probably around 1945 or early 1946.

5. Noam Chomsky, *The Logical Structure of Linguistic Theory* (New York: Springer, 1975).

6. Given the chronology, this must in fact have been a draft rather than proofs.

7. Wentian Li's Web site at Rockefeller University notes that: "Zipf's law, named after the Harvard linguistic professor George Kingsley Zipf (1902–1950), is the observation that frequency of occurrence of some event (P), as a function of the rank (i) when the rank is determined by the above frequency of occurrence, is a power-law function $P_i \sim 1/i^a$ with the exponent a close to unity" (http://linkage.rockefeller.edu/wli/zipf/).

8. According to Goldsmith, this is a reference to Joos, on the basis of the following: "There is more to this story. Zipf couldn't stand linguistics (so he called what he did philology, and deplored the term linguistics) and Joos was by some accounts possessed of a mean streak—so I've heard. I read Zipf's book a few years ago and found it brilliant if dated" (personal correspondence August 7, 2009).

9. For a discussion on Sapir's relations to psychoanalysis, see Regna Darnell's biography of Sapir titled *Edward Sapir: Linguist, Anthropologist, Humanist* (Berkeley: University of California Press, 1989). It's notable that this link is explored later on as well, by Roman Jakobson. In the May 11, 1964, minutes of the study group in linguistics and psychoanalysis of the New York Psychoanalytic Institute, Jakobson "recalled his regular meetings with Drs. Lowenstein, Spitz, de Saussure, and others (including the anthropologist Lévi-Strauss)" and he "expressed his long-standing belief in the relevance of linguistics for psychoanalysis." This was not solely on the basis of "vulgar behaviorisms," which Jakobson mentioned in the meeting as being

"rejected by most linguists," but more on the basis of how "our expressive (emotive) modes" are coded.

10. http://www.upenn.edu/gazette/0701/hughes.html, *The Pennsylvania Gazette*, The Alumni Magazine of the University of Pennsylvania, July/August 2001; this must be the MA, though, not the PhD.

11. Noam Chomsky, *Morphophonemics of Modern Hebrew* (New York: Taylor and Francis, 1979).

12. Noam Chomsky, "Systems of Syntactic Analysis," *Journal of Symbolic Logic* 18, no. 3 (September 1953): 242–256.

13. Noam Chomsky, *Language and Responsibility*, based on conversations with Mitsou Ronat, translated from the French by John Viertel (Hassocks: Harvester Press, 1979).

14. Noam Chomsky. *Knowledge of Language: Its Nature, Origin, and Use* (New York: Prager, 1986).

15. *An Integrated Theory of Linguistic Ability* (New York: Crowell, 1976), edited by Jerrold J. Katz, Thomas G. Bever, and Terence Langendoen.

16. Vol. 5 (1986): 721.

17. Robert A. Hall, Jr., *A Life for Language: A Biographical Memoir of Leonard Bloomfield* (Philadelphia: John Benjamins, 1990).

18. Bruce E. Nevin and Stephen B. Johnson, eds., *The Legacy of Zellig Harris: Language and Information into the 21st Century,* vols. 1 and 2 (Philadelphia: John Benjamins, 2002), 109.

19. T. A. Ryckman, "Method and Theory in Harris's Grammar of Information," in Nevin and Johnson (2002).

20. In Nevin and Johnson (2002).

21. Pieter Seuren, *Western Linguistics: An Historical Introduction* (Malden, MA: Blackwell, 1998).

22. Quoted in Bruce Nevin's review of *A Grammar of English on Mathematical Principles, Computational Linguistics* 10, nos. 3–4 (1984): 203.

23. *American Anthropologist* 54, no. 3 (1951): 404–405.

24. "Reviews and Letters: A New Study of Fundamentals," *American Speech* 27, no. 1 (1952): 117–121.

25. It is valuable to consult the aforementioned volume 2 of *The Legacy of Zellig Harris* to survey where sophisticated computers have led researchers in the areas of language and information.

26. Noam Chomsky, *Language and Mind.* (Cambridge: Cambridge University Press, 1996).

27. *American Anthropologist* 54 (1954): 404–405.

28. *American Oriental Society* 72 (1952): 113–115.

29. *Chronique des livres,* vol. 7 (1952): 272–284.

30. *International Journal of American Linguistics* 18, no. 4 (1952): 260–68.

31. *International Journal of American Linguistics* 18, no. 3 (1952): 257–260.

32. *Language* 28, no. 4 (1952): 495–504.

33. It is notable that the single main focus of Goldsmith's (computational) work over the last decade or more has been, in his words, "working out this idea of Harris's; developing software that can take a large sample of a language as its input, and give as its output the morphemes of the language, plus the principle of how those morphemes may be combined" (personal correspondence August 7, 2009). See his PowerPoint presentation "Analogy in Morphology: Only a Beginning" http://hum .uchicago.edu/~jagoldsm/Powerpoint/2006LeipzigAnalogy.ppt.

34. *Journal de Psychologie normale et pathologique* 47th–51st years, nos. 1–2 (1954): 637–639.

35. *The Legacy of Zellig Harris* 1, p. 167.

36. In, for example, a review of I. J. Gelb's *A Study of Writing,* published in the *Jewish Quarterly Review* 45, no. 1 (July 1954): 82–85.

37. One case is particularly humorous, however, in which the University of Michigan linguist John M. Swales draws parallels between various key figures in linguistics, including the Bakhtin brothers, Ludwig Wittgenstein, Zellig Harris, and Noam Chomsky, in *Moments in the Modern History of the Language Sciences, Written Communication* 16, no. 4 (1999): 526–529.

A thoughtful Zellig Harris hustled across the University of Pennsylvania campus one bright if windy morning in late March. He was on his way to a meeting with his brilliant young student, Noam Chomsky, who had just finished his master's thesis on the morphophonemics of modern Hebrew. He was wondering what Chomsky would say about possible dissertation topics and about the carbon copy of a small monograph—apparently to be published later in the year by Oxford— that had been smuggled out of the Soviet Union and sent to him by Rupert Firth. He also sincerely hoped that the wretched Senator Joseph McCarthy would never get wind of the treatise.

"Morphophonemics, schmorphophonemics" announced Chomsky, "this is stunning stuff, and casts your article in Language on discourse analysis in a new light. Bakhtin is correct that all utterances are in some way dialogic, and the future of linguistics depends on all of us recognizing this, including you, sir." Harris nodded curtly and then said mildly, "In my defense, let me quote my distinguished colleague at the University of Michigan, Ken Pike: 'Linguists are rarely wrong about what they say, but mostly wrong about what they don't say,' and in that sense, I had insufficiently recognized to see discourse as response to prior texts."

"So what should I do?" asked Chomsky.

"Given your new enthusiasm, there's nothing much for you on the East Coast," was the reply. "Go west, go to sunny California, go to Garfinkel."

And the rest, as they say, is history.

Afterword

That history, as I said at the outset of this small reminiscence, does not now need to be retold in any detail. But perhaps I should remind anybody who might read these few pages of just a few facts. Bakhtin's *The Problem of Speech Genres*, as it was finally called, was published in the same year and by the same press as Ludwig Wittgenstein's Philosophical Investigations, and these two seminal works have been linked in the thoughts of the world's intelligentsia ever since. They remain, despite the academic industries that have grown up around them, tantalizingly similar and tantalizingly different. However, language sciences really shot to its current preeminence with the appearance in 1964 [wrong date] of *Aspects of a Theory of Language* [wrong title] and *Social Life* by Noam Chomsky (!) and Erving Goffman. Within the space of 10 years, a Nobel Prize in language sciences had been established, and fittingly, the first laureate was Mikhail Bakhtin, although he was too frail to travel to Stockholm to receive it. Instead, it was presented to him at his retirement home on Klimovsk, where he made his last public utterance, this time about dialogism and religious practice. Later laureates were, of course, Chomsky and then Halliday, the latter for his masterpiece *Context in Text and Text in Context*. There is doubtless more to say, but the hour grows late and the cat is scratching at the door.

Chapter 6

1. *The Private Lives of Albert Einstein* (London: Faber and Faber, 1993).

2. Cited in Ronald W. Clark, *Einstein: The Life and Times* (New York: World Publishing Company, 1971), 614.

3. *A Bushman Dictionary*. American Oriental Series, vol. 41 (New Haven, CT: American Oriental Society, 1956).

4. Senta Plötz, ed., *Transformationelle Analyse: Die Transformationstheorie von Zellig Harris und ihre Entwicklung / Transformational Analysis: The transformational theory of Zellig Harris and its development* (Frankfurt/Main: Athenäum-Verlag, 1972).

5. "Gatekeepers and the Chomskian Revolution," *Journal of the History of Behavioral Sciences* 16, no. 1 (1980): 73–88.

6. Plötz, Senta, ed., *Transformational Analysis: The Transformational Theory of Zellig Harris and its Development* (Frankfurt/Main: Athenäum-Verlag, 1972).

7. Konrad Koerner, "The Anatomy of a Revolution in the Social Sciences: Chomsky in 1962," *Dhumbadjil, History of Language* 1, no. 4 (1994): 3–17.

8. Robert F. Barsky, *Noam Chomsky: A Life of Dissent* (Cambridge: MIT Press, 1997).

9. Bruce E. Nevin and Stephen B. Johnson, *The Legacy of Zellig Harris: Language and Information into the Twenty-First Century* (Philadelphia: John Benjamins, 2002).

10. Bloch papers, Yale University.

11. Bloch papers.

12. See note 1.

13. Zellig Harris, *Discourse Analysis Reprints* (The Hague: Mouton, 1963).

14. Irene Rima Makaryk, ed., *Encyclopedia of Contemporary Literary Theory: Approaches, Scholars, Terms* (Toronto: University of Toronto Press, 1993), 35.

15. Zellig Harris, "Discourse Analysis" *Language* 28, no. 1 (1952): 1–30.

16. Not everyone I have interviewed agrees with this perspective, and even from this chapter it is clear that Harris had some disciples who would receive considerable attention for a period of time, and would then be dropped. It may also be fair to say that this happened in the politics as well, since Harris's line was quite rigid and, as we'll see in the next chapter, he did not readily bear dissent in situations such as Avukah or with close coworkers.

17. This program was presented in TDAP and included TDAP (Transformations and Discourse Analysis Project) 19, "Higher-order Substrings and Well-formedness" and TDAP 20, "Iterative Computation of String Nesting (Fortran Code)," both by Bruria Kaufman.

18. Noam Chomsky, *Language and Mind* (New York: Harcourt, Brace, Jovanovich, 1968).

19. Goldsmith suggested in personal correspondence (8/7/09) that what is being studied is not the "output," but rather the "less rich thing that it has excreted."

20. N. R. Cattell, "The Syntactic Procedures of Zellig Harris,"*Language and Speech* 5, no. 1 (1962): 159–170, p. 159.

21. Zellig Harris, *String Analysis of Sentence Structure*. The Hague: Mouton & Co., 1962, reviewed by László Antal in *Linguistics* 1 (1963): 97–104.

22. Murray Fowler, review of Zellig Harris's *String Analysis of Sentence Structure* in *Word* 19 (1963): 245–247.

23. Harris's 1968 book on *Mathematical Structures of Language* discusses the specific properties of language that make it amenable to mathematical analysis, and chapter 20 of his *Methods* book discusses the open-endedness of natural language.

24. *International Journal of American Linguistics* 30, no. 4 (1964): 415–420, p. 415.

25. Ibid., p. 420. In personal correspondence (August 7, 2009), John Goldsmith takes issue with this comment. "Even if those guys manage to do something impressive

with a computer program, it's never going to be of interest to me and mine for reasons that I'm sure of now, even before I've seen their work; that's what Lees was saying, and there were a good number of such closed-minded people, both then and, alas, now."

26. N. Sager and N. T. Nhàn, "The computability of strings, transformations, and sublanguage." In *The Legacy of Zellig Harris: Language and Information into the Twenty-First Century,* Bruce E. Nevin and Stephen M. Johnson, eds., vol. 2 (Philadelphia: John Benjamins Publishing Co., 2002), 79–120.

27. Aravind K. Joshi, 2002. "Hierarchical structure and sentence description." In *The Legacy of Zellig Harris: Language and Information into the Twenty-First Century,* Bruce E. Nevin and Stephen M. Johnson, eds., vol. 2 (Philadelphia: John Benjamins Publishing Co., 2002), 121–141.

28. Henry Hiz, ed., *Papers on Syntax* (Dordrecht, Holland: D. Reidel, 1981), v.

29. Frederick Chen Chung Peng, in *Lingua* 16, no. 1 (1966): 325–330.

30. Vol. 18 (1968): 233–235, p. 233.

31. *Language* 46, no. 3 (1970): 754–764, pp. 757–758.

32. Jonathan Culler, *Structuralist Poetics* (Cornell: Cornell University Press, 1978).

33. I have found no reason for this in any material in the archive.

34. Maurice Gross, review article in *Semiotica* 2, no. 4 (1970): 380–390.

35. Furthermore, as Lucia Vaina-Puscă notes (in *Revue romaine de linguistique* 16 (1971): 369–371), there is the question of the relationship between the detection of grammatical elements and their mathematical arrangement: "the set of elements and operations (the grammar) must be detected empirically and only thereafter it may be schematized into an abstract form having common traits with mathematical structures" (370).

36. Yves Gentilhomme, in *Bulletin de la Société linguistique de Paris* 69, no. 2 (1974): 37–53.

37. Zellig Harris, *Structures mathématiques du langage,* trans. C. Fuchs (Paris: Dunod, 1971).

38. 37–38, my translation.

39. Zellig S. Harris, *Notes du cours de syntaxe.* trans. Maurice Gross (Paris: Seuil, 1976).

40. Jean-Pierre Déscles, "Un modèle mathématiques d'analyse transformationelle selon Z. S. Harris," in Antonio Zampolli and N. Calzolari, eds., *Computational and Mathematical Linguistics* (Florence: Olschi, 1973), 23–37.

41. Danielle Leeman, "Distributionnalisme et structuralisme," *Langages* 29 (1973): 6–42.

42. Philadelphia: John Benjamins Publishing Co.

43. C. Fuchs, and P. Le Goffic, *Les linguistiques contemporaines: Repères théoriques* (Paris: Hachette, 1992).

44. Ferenc Kiefer in *Linguistics* 7 (1971): 60–63.

45. David Cohen in *L'Année sociologique* 21 (1970): 507–510.

46. Michael B. Kac in *Language* 49, no. 2 (1973): 466–473.

47. Eric S. Wheeler in *Computers in the Humanities* 17, no. 3 (1983): 88–92.

48. Bruce Nevin in *Computational Linguistics* 10, nos. 3–4 (July–December 1984): 203–211, available on-line at: http://io.cpmc.columbia.edu/zellig/gemp.html.

49. Frank Heny in *Journal of Linguistics* 20, no. 1 (1984): 181–188.

50. Cf. William Frawley's short review in *Language* 60, no. 1 (1984): 150–153.

51. This review is available on-line at http://io.cpmc.columbia.edu/zellig/gemp .html.

52. Terence Langendoen in vol. 70, no. 3 (1994): 585–588.

53. In correspondence with me (8/7/2009), John Goldsmith adds that "it's notable there that there is no "old" or "new" sign language, and the sign language of the deaf are not based in any significant way on spoken languages, or knowledge of spoken language."

54. Funded by a twelve-month grant, IST-8544976, for $197,055, provided to Charles Parsons and Isaac Levi, Columbia University, for "The Structure of Information in Science: Fact Formulas and Discussion Structures in Related Subsciences."

55. *Annals of the American Academy of Political and Social Science* 495 (January 1988): 73–83.

56. Henry Hiz, "Zellig S. Harris (23 October 1909–22 May 1992)," *Proceedings of the American Philosophical Society* 138, no. 4 (December 1994): 518–527.

Chapter 7

1. Seymour Melman, Zellig Harris's close friend and collaborator, has generously donated hundreds of pages and documents to the University of Pennsylvania archives, as well as the archives of the New York Public Library and Columbia University, in the interest of promoting increased interest in, and understanding of, Zellig Harris's work. I have drawn liberally upon these references.

2. See http://www.jewishvirtuallibrary.org/jsource/judaica/ejud_0002_0018_0_18421 .html

3. Isaak Landman, *The Universal Jewish Encyclopedia*, Volume 1 (New York: Varda Books, 2009), p. 650.

4. Cited in Stern, 239.

5. From an unsigned editorial in the same issue.

6. See *Jewry and the Zionist Project* (Cambridge: Cambridge University Press, 1997), 168 ff.

7. *Avukah Bulletin,* May 1930, p. 2.

8. The October 1931 *Avukah Bulletin* recalls the August 1929 events that led to the setting up of this fund: "At Huldah a band of twenty-three Chalutzim, led by Ephraim Chizik, held off a mob of fanatical Arabs for hours in their attempt to save the colony from destruction. Our great loss in that battle was not the burned fields, the ruined homes and barns, but the loss of the courageous leader—Ephraim Chizik. Ephraim Chizik—his life and death are an inspiring example to all Zionists of the greatness of Palestine. From the time when he was only eight, when he was taken to Palestine by his family, he gave his entire life to Eretz Israel, its development and its defense" (2).

9. Along with Joseph Goldenberg, Sarah Finkelstein, Leonard Finkelstein, Tzvee Harris, Shoshanna Harris, and Simon Greenberg.

10. Einstein to Pëtr P. Lazarev, May 16, 1914, *CPAE* 8A: 18.

11. Einstein to Paul Epstein, October 5, 1919, cited in Stern, 136.

12. Haber was a Nobel laureate who had led a world famous laboratory and had discovered the means of fixing nitrogen from the air (and poison gas warfare).

13. Haber to Einstein, March 9, 1921, cited in *Einstein's German World*, 137.

14. From the Jewish National and University Library in Jerusalem.

15. Einstein to Haber, March 9, 1921, cited in Stern 138.

16. Stern, 138.

17. Alice Calaprice, ed., *The Quotable Einstein* (Princeton: Princeton University Press, 1996), 95.

18. Amsterdam: Querido Verlag, 1934.

19. "Addresses on Reconstruction in Palestine," in *Ideas and Opinions by Albert Einstein,* based on *Mein Weltbild,* ed. Carl Seelig, and other sources, new translations and revisions Sonja Bargmann (New York: Wings Books, 1954), 179.

20. The March 1931 *Avukah Bulletin* noted that The National Office eventually obtained a "talking motion picture" portraying Professor Einstein's talk, translated by James Waterman Wise.

21. Letter dated November 29, 1929, cited in Stern, 246.

22. *The Quotable Einstein*, p. 98.

23. The details of this are complex, and very ably treated in Zachary Lockman's excellent book on the subject.

24. Albert Einstein, *About Zionism. Speeches and Letters* (London: Soncino, 1930). Translated and edited with an introduction by Leon Simon. It is also notable that Einstein authored *Cosmic Religion*, with other opinions and aphorisms (New York: Covici Friede, 1931), which includes the chapter on "The Jews: The Jewish Homeland" (pp. 71–93).

25. Seymour Melman has placed over a thousand pages of typewritten manuscript in the University of Pennsylvania library as a resource for those interested in this project.

26. The First Report on Agricultural Development and Land Settlement in Palestine, by Lewis French (Director of Development), was submitted to the Palestine Government on December 23, 1931. A "Supplementary Report on Agricultural Development and Land Settlement in Palestine," was submitted April 20, 1932.

27. Boston: Houghton Mifflin, 1999.

28. This is discussed in the November 1934 issue of *The Torch* in terms of both pros and contras for this effort.

29. Einstein's letters, with the exception of this one, quoted from the *Avukah* Bulletin, were translated by Dr. Hans-Jakob Wilhelm.

Chapter 8

1. Hashomer Hatzair, the socialist youth movement, had links to Avukah because they had tried to bring American members to rural settings in order to prepare them for life in Palestine. Grand recalls that "Hashomer Hatzair, with its meager financial resources, could neither purchase nor rent a farm with the necessary installations and equipment. It took a scholarly Zionist farmer as idealistic as the *shomrim* [volunteer civilian patrols] themselves to take in these pre-*halutzim* [Jewish pioneers] and to help them learn farming the hard way. Z. Roochwarg, a retired pharmacist, was persuaded by Judah Lapson, one of the founders of Avukah and a long-standing friend of Zionist youth, to convert a part of his farm to a *hakhsharah* [training to become a halutzim] training center for the shomrim" (13).

2. Zellig S. Harris, *The Transformation of Capitalist Society* (Philadelphia: Roman and Littlefield, 1997).

3. May 29, 1936, p. 1.

4. The Stratford Company, Boston, Massachusetts. There is some confusion in this volume, since it is specifically called the 1936 volume (the year of Brandeis's 80th birthday), but many of the essays make reference to it being the 1932 volume, and

much of the historical information mentioned refers to 1932. What matters here though is the role that Brandeis played in Avukah, as spiritual leader and guide, and the relations that thus existed between Zellig Harris and Brandeis through the Avukah organization.

5. Peter Novick, *The Holocaust in American Life* (New York: Houghton Mifflin, 2000).

6. "In April 1936, William B. Redmond of Nashville challenged, through counsel, the right of the officials of the University of Tennessee College of Pharmacy to deny him admission to this school. Counsel for Redmond contended that the law establishing the old Tennessee Agricultural College, predecessor of the State University, gives him the right to enter the university and it is up to the university to provide separate accommodations for him." A section of the state constitution which says, "no school established or aided under this section shall allow white and Negro children to be received as scholars together in the same school," was cited by President James D. Hoskins as the reason for forbidding Negroes from entering the University of Tennessee. "None of us has any choice in the matter," President Hoskins explained. In August 1936, the attorney general of the state, after insistent demands, finally gave Redmond's attorneys the right to inspect the minutes of the Board of Trustees of the university. The Attorney General's office asked Redmond's attorneys to submit a memorandum on points they wanted to clear up so that the "proper sections" of the minutes could be opened to them. The two attorneys refused to accept any limitation upon their inspection and insisted upon perusing the minutes thoroughly. The formal trial of Redmond's suit was held in Memphis, March 29, 1937. On April 16, 1937, the court denied Redmond's application." Monroe N. Work, ed., *Negro Year Book, Annual Encyclopedia of the Negro* (Tuskegee, Alabama: Tuskegee Institute,1937), 136–137.

7. Translation of Einstein's words by Hans-Jakob Wilhelm.

8. Bennett M. Berger, ed., *Authors of Their Own Lives: Intellectual Autobiographies by Twenty American Sociologists* (Berkeley: University of California Press, 1990).

9. This document was eventually published in the official organ of the YPZA (the Young Poale Zion Alliance).

10. Personal correspondence between Benjamin Akzin and Louis Brandeis, May 10, 1939.

11. Harris suggested relaunching that project in a letter to Bernard Berelson, the director of the Ford Foundation's Behavioral Sciences project, dated January 23, 1957.

12. Nathan Glazer, managing editor, Rosalind Schwartz, Margolit Shelubsky, Milton Shapiro, Bernard Mandelbaum, staff.

13. Erich Fromm, *Escape from Freedom* (New York: Avon Books, 1969 [1941]).

14. *Freedom and Culture* (New York: Putnam, 1939; London: Allen & Unwin, 1940).

15. Edwin Black, *IBM and the Holocaust: The Strategic Alliance between Nazi Germany and America's Most Powerful Corporation* (New York: Crown Publishing, 2001).

16. *Henry Ford and the Jews: The Mass Production of Hate* (New York: Public Affairs, 2002).

17. The notorious anti-Semitic hoax and forgery that was first published, privately in 1897 in Russia and was reproduced in different languages subsequently.

18. The reference here is to *The International Jew: The World's Foremost Problem* (Dearborn MI: The Dearborn Publishing Co., 1920), the reprint of a series of articles published by the *Dearborn Independent* from May 22 to October 2, 1920.

19. "Front I: Fascism a Real Danger; Jews Not Secure, warns Dr. Harris," *Avukah Student Action* (summer 1942): 2.

20. This bureau took clippings from major news sources of the period, including, for this story, the *New York Times*, the *New York Post*, *Time*, *Current History*, *Asia*, *Foreign Policy Bulletin*, *The Nation*, and the *New Republic*.

Chapter 9

1. Yôsēf Gôrnî, *Zionism and the Arabs 1882–1948: A Study of Ideology* (Oxford: Clarendon Press, 1987), 281.

2. Israel Kolatt, "The Zionist Movement and the Arabs," in Anita Shapir, author, and Jehuda Reinharz, ed., *Essential Papers on Zionism* (New York: New York University Press, 1995).

3. Letters from the Jacob Rader Marcus center, part of the American Jewish Archives, Cincinnati, Ohio.

4. My thanks to Norman Epstein for this document. Here, as elsewhere in the book, I recall discussions from my two earlier MIT Press books that related to these issues, *Noam Chomsky: A Life of Dissent* (1997) and *The Chomsky Effect: A Radical Works Beyond the Ivory Tower* (2007) in order to document the full story relating to Zellig Harris and Avukah.

5. Other members listed on the letterhead include Harold C. Urey, vice-Chairman, and Hans A. Bethe, T. R. Hogness, Philip M. Morse, Linus Pauling, Leo Szilard, and V. F. Weisskopf, members.

6. New York: Shulenger Bros Publishing Co.

7. http://domino.un.org/UNISPAL.NSF/be65b75f931fa995052567270057d45e/81e4fdf0922c597605256802005c4668!OpenDocument

8. This document is available online at: http://unispal.un.org/UNISPAL.NSF/0/81E4FDF0922C597605256802005C4668.

9. New York: Basic Books, 2000.

10. "A Laden Wagon on an Empty Wagon? Reflections on the Culture of Israel," *Free Judaism*, (October 1977): 5.

11. Christopher Hitchens, *The Trial of Henry Kissinger* (New York: Verso, 2001).

12. This is an unpublished, unsigned, and undated manuscript that was presumably worked on for many years, beginning sometime in the 1940s, and that was deposited in the Penn library archives by Seymour Melman. The manuscript has no page numbers, but it is divided up with an odd number-letter system that I will use in order to help guide the reader who might wish to return to the original document for further study.

13. Zellig Harris mentions Paul Matticks's book *Marxism, Last Refuge of the Bourgeoisie* (New York: Sharpe, 1983), as well as Karl Korsch, about whom Mattick wrote.

14. Zellig Harris recalls Arthur Rosenberg's *The Birth of the German Republic, 1871–1918* (London: Russell & Russell, 1962) as a source for some of his ideas.

15. Introduction to Michael Harrington and Paul Jacobs, eds., *Labor in a Free Society* (Berkeley: University of California Press), 1–16.

16. New York: Holt, Rinehart and Winston, 1955.

17. Vol. 18 (August 1998): 263–264.

18. Vol. 24, no. 4 (fall 1998): 33–35.

19. Sydney, Nova Scotia: University College of Cape Breton Press, 1997.

20. Seymour Melman, *After Capitalism: From Managerialism to Workplace Democracy* (New York: Knopf, 2001).

Interview with Noam Chomsky, May 2009

Robert Barsky: In the context of many interviews I've been doing about Zellig Harris, his milieu, and about Avukah, I've also been undertaking interviews in the hope of preserving the important stories about that world. I in particular wanted to do the first interview with you because twelve or so years ago we sat in your old office in Building 20 at MIT, and you suggested that I write about Harris and about Avukah.

Noam Chomsky: The timing is perfect; in a couple more years, everyone will be gone. So you just caught it. And you did speak to Seymour Melman?

RB: I did.

NC: He was the most important person, the one who kept it alive.

RB: I remember us speaking together in your old office, all those years ago, and you suggested that I be concerned with, and write about, both Zellig Harris and Avukah. Why?

NC: Well as you know, I came onto the scene when Avukah was already over, but the aura of it was still around, and it was clear that the Frame of Reference project had grown out of it. The people in that milieu were interesting—particularly Harris—but others too. For instance, I got to know Seymour Melman very well at that time, and I could just see that there was something pretty exciting going on. And in fact, as far as I know, a substantial number of young Jewish left intellectuals did pass through Avukah, in all kinds of ways, from Nathan Glazer, who went way off to the right, to Seymour Melman, who kept pretty true to the general picture. And then of course most of the people just dropped out. But Avukah was clearly a formative experience that had a big effect on anybody who went through it. For example, I met Glazer in the 1960s, and after I'd spoken to him for around two minutes, I asked him if he'd ever known Zellig Harris, and he said "Ya, how did you know?" I didn't tell him, but he imitated every one of Zellig Harris's mannerisms, his hair style, his motions, everything was characteristic of Zellig. Zellig had clearly left an imprint.

RB: Avukah got started in the late 1920s, but it's in the 1930s that it takes on such importance. One of the people with whom I've had long discussions is Irene Schumer, and she said that a lot of the people who originally gravitated toward the organization thought of it as a Jewish social group. They were interested in Zionism, they were interested in ideas that were floating around that regarded Palestine, but then there came an added urgency to their work, that grew year by year, with the election of Hitler and then the war.

NC: It was not just Zionism, it was worker self-management and the critique of the Russian Revolution. The thirties was a period that featured very lively debates about all kinds of social issues, and therein Avukah took an interesting position. It was like the work of Paul Mattick, a Marxist critic of Bolshevism from the Left, strongly critical from the Left, something that existed, but Avukah had a unique role in this.

RB: When you met Zellig Harris and began to work with him, did he mention to you the work that had been done under the auspices of Avukah?

NC: I certainly knew about it very quickly. For one thing, in the background there was this group that became the Frame of Reference group, and they kept circulating materials. I wasn't part of it, but the materials would come in, we would read them and talk about them. And it was clearly an offshoot of Avukah.

RB: The Framework project produced reams and reams of unsigned documents.

NC: How do they read after sixty years?

RB: Most of it is incomprehensible without the context. There are many discussions about workers' attitudes, and attitudes more generally, and there are occasional references to people, like Erich Fromm, as well discussions about production and surplus and so forth, that all seem to have been informed by readings and discussions of Marx, but there are few references to actual events. So it's often hard to construct retroactively the overall conception.

NC: I knew there were a lot of discussions about social psychology because Zellig had his students, me and others, read social psychology research on attitude-shifting and its effects. There was some big study that I remember on attitudes of couples, union couples, and the result was supposed to have been that the husband who was a union member would be more committed to, say, workers' self-management than the wife, but if they weren't union members, it was the opposite. The theory was supposed to have something to do with point of production. If you are close to the point of production, you want to control it. On the other hand, if the worker is not a union member he's probably remote from the point of production, so he doesn't want anything to do with it, and his wife doesn't care either. Studies like that. It had to do with ideas they were playing around with at the time, on how to change attitudes.

RB: That aspect does come out in Harris's political book, *The Transformation of Capitalist Society*, this question of how to modify attitudes based on whether or not the person in question is close to the point of production, and whether or not they feel a sense of ownership over the means of production. Does that reflect the kinds of things that were talked about, all those years earlier?

NC: Indeed, and that reminds me that there was a guy named Joe Blasi who wrote a book about ESOPs [Employee Share Ownership Plans], a way to move toward worker ownership or management, and I think he came out of the group and went in to these kinds of topics.

RB: Did you have a sense of the overall intentions of those involved in the Framework project and what motivated them? Was this a modern revolutionary group?

NC: They had revolutionary intentions; they wanted to change the economy, which in those days was not all that utopian. If you look at polls back in the late 1940s, a lot of working people weren't thinking about worker self-management, but they were receptive to the ideas. A lot of people thought, for example, that the government ought to own the factories. This was worldwide, in part because the Depression and the Second War had a really radicalizing effect upon people. And in fact the first commitment of the victorious western allies, which started at the end of the war already, in 1943, 1944, and into the postwar period, was to undermine this radicalism. The United States, and the UK as their lackey, had as one of their first tasks to destroy the radical democracy concepts that had developed all over the world. So when the British and American troops came up through Italy, a lot of the country had been liberated by the partisans, so they had to overthrow the partisans, restore the traditional, profascist structure, especially when they got to the north. This was the British Labor Party. They were appalled that factories had been taken over by working people, and the rights of management weren't being preserved. So by force they had to dismantle this and restore the old order. They pretty much did the same things in Japan. It was kind of interesting how it was done. As long as Japan and Germany were under military rule, they didn't care that much, they kind of believed what they learned in 8th-grade civics classes about shared democracies. But when the liberals in

Washington found out about it, they were furious, and they instituted what they called the "reverse course," to get rid of worker-owned factories, to undermine unions, and to bring back the old order. There's a fair amount of research on this. There was less research on Germany, but France was the same, and it's why the CIA got involved in breaking up the unions, reestablishing the mafia, and so on. In fact, in country after country, that was the first thing to happen after the war. And it happened at home too. So you get the immediate reaction against labor organizations, working-class independence, radical ideas, national health care, and so forth. It has been pretty well studied in the United States, there's good scholarship on it. The scale is just shocking, and that's what people like Alex Carey and Elizabeth Fones-Wolf, and others were working on. Anyhow, this went on in the late forties, right in the middle of the radical democracy period. There's a pretty interesting book by Basil Davidson, known now as an Africanist historian, but during the Second World War he was a British officer who was seconded to the Partisans, I think in Yugoslavia. He has a book called *Scenes from the Anti-Fascist War*, where he describes the mood that was coming out of the anti-fascist war, and the resistance. A lot of it was communist, but a lot of it was just radical democracy, and it was just quashed by the occupations. That's a worldwide phenomenon that here is called McCarthyism.

RB: So is the image one of brutal force that puts down individuals who have, through their work and understanding, come to a completely different attitude about how society ought to be organized?

NC: Yes, under the occupation there was a lot of brute force, but in the home countries, say, here, it was things like the Taft-Hartley Act, huge propaganda programs, Americanism, captive audiences in factories to teach the American way of life. It was enormous and very coordinated and very class conscious. They took over churches, schools, sports leagues—everything was deluged with propaganda. You can even see it in the cinema. Take, say, films like "On the Waterfront" and "Salt of the Earth." Both films came out around 1953. "Salt of the Earth" was made by a tiny studio with few resources, but it was a terrific film, far better than "On the Waterfront." But it disappeared, because it was about a successful strike, also feminist and anti-racist. "On the Waterfront" was a huge hit because it was anti-union. It had this nice pairing,—which is standard right-wing propaganda—of the workers against the unions. So the workers, led by Marlon Brando, are fighting against the corrupt union boss, and it ends up with Brando throwing him in the water, or something like that. That's the idea: "'We, the right wing, are supporters of the working class, and they—the outsiders, the unions—they are trying to impose this union on us people who are living in harmony." There is pretty good scholarship on this, and it's kind of striking, because the director of "On the Waterfront" was on the Hollywood list, but it doesn't matter. So at the time of the Frame of Reference stuff, it was not so unrealistic to think of a large-scale moves toward industrial democracy. In fact, Dewey was writing about it at the time, it really wasn't far from the mainstream.

RB: Was the language work that Harris was doing at that time directed to these efforts?

NC: This never went into print. If you look into his discourse analysis papers, in the early fifties, they are all about chemical abstracting and stuff like that. But that's not what we were doing in Harris's seminars in discourse analysis. What we were doing was political analysis.

RB: Of political speeches?

NC: Yes, things like that. I remember a project that I was assigned to and worked on, in which I was to take Sydney Hook's writings during the transition period from the time he was a communist to when he became strongly anti-communist. I was to do discourse analysis, to tease out the changes that were going on, using the kind of linguistic-style analysis that Harris was experimenting with. That was most of the work. There was very little on things like chemical abstracting. I think that Harris was very cautious about getting any of his political notions public, as you know.

RB: It's really striking, the degree of concern he had for this.

NC: And it got particularly striking in the sixties when things were really getting heated up. I don't know if you're aware, but Bruria Kaufman (later Harris) and I used to be very close friends. But we couldn't talk to each other about these things in the sixties.

RB: Was she particularly concerned because of the types of involvement she had with Einstein?

NC: She was an anarchist. A committed anarchist. Very anti-Zionist. By the late sixties it all changed. I probably still have some letters from her when she was furious about what I was doing. And we had been very close friends. Same with Henry Hiz. He had been in the Polish resistance and was kind of a leftist activist, but by the mid-sixties he went far to the right.

RB: So were Bruria's politics different from Zellig's?

NC: As far as I was aware, she didn't think about it too much, she kind of tagged along. My impression was that she was sympathetic, but not really active. And her views, as far as I could tell, from personal conversations, were basically anarchist. She would probably deny it now.

RB: Was it informed by a particular set of experiences or writings?

NC: It was just intuitive. That's the way the world ought to be! [laughter]

RB: Was there any relation between the work your father was doing, and the work of Zellig Harris? Were there common threads of interest, either political or linguistic?

NC: There was a certain similarity. My father was doing historical linguistics, and so was Zellig, with his history of Canaanite dialects, and so on. I knew my father's work from childhood, and when I met Harris and read his history of the Canaanite dialects, it was recognizable to me. As a matter of fact, it was more sophisticated in many ways, but it had a similar thread to it.

RB: But the overlap is strictly in the language work.

NC: Strictly language work, yes; there's no politics overlap.

RB: Do you feel as though the idea of revitalizing the history of Avukah and Harris's work at that moment would serve any purpose for contemporary debates about what was lost, or where we could go from here?

NC: I think so, because the basic motivating concepts, the kinds of things that Seymour Melman later wrote about, are very apposite today. Out of this came Seymour's work, and he had a pretty incisive critique of modern industrial society that is very much to the point. One of the things he was pointing out, back in the sixties, was—and he was in a school of industrial management studying management—he was pointing out then already that the managerial classes, General Motors management and those guys, are moving further and further away from point of production and toward finance. In the 1970s and 1980s, that became overwhelming, and that's the very seed of the crisis. If you go back further, to, say, Alfred Sloan, he came out of the school of industrial engineering here at MIT, and his background was engineering. The guys who were running the plants back then, and managing the company, had a production background, so they were thinking of production. By the time you get to the seventies and eighties, they have a finance background and were coming out of the Harvard Business School with MBAs. You see it happening, just as Seymour was predicting in the early stages, with this shift toward the financialization of the economy, in which the production system is shifted abroad. The kinds of things he was talking about are very appropriate today. He was studying, for example, a city that was trying to rebuild its subways, and to do so officials had to go to Hungary or somewhere because nobody in the United States knows how to make anything. And meanwhile he started working with the engineering groups in the maintenance systems for the New York subways, and those guys all knew how to do this kind of stuff. But there's no infrastructure for it. Take right now; they are closing down auto plants all over the place, and they desperately need high-speed trains, so they're going to Spain. It's in the *Wall Street Journal*, an article about how French and Spanish companies are all getting in line to pick up the stimulus money. So here's the stimulus money coming in from the American taxpayer, to build high-speed rail lines in California, and here's GM and Chrysler shutting down, with work required that working people here are perfectly capable of doing.

RB: And there's no call for retooling, as Seymour Melman had suggested in his work on the military-industrial complex.

NC: Yes, it's not on the agenda. It's a profit-finance-oriented economy, not a production-oriented economy. And these ideas, starting with workers' self-management and so on, these are the kinds of things that ought to be in the center of discussions right now. Even in a straight reformist sense, it's a fantastic indictment of the economy that you're closing factories and kicking out workers and what you need, what you agree that you need, is production. But you can't put those two ideas together, because nobody makes enough profit out of them.

RB: Not only can you look to Japan or Germany or Hungary, but I've just been back to Montréal, home to Bombardier, the company that builds subway trains and airplanes and other kinds of vehicles. Their perspective on the crisis is different from the U.S.'s because Quebec, and Quebec companies, have become production hubs for all things transportation related. It's fascinating to see how this is affecting a company that is based five hours from Boston. It's a completely different mentality up there. Each year I bring students there from Vanderbilt University to show them how such a system can work, including the very successful healthcare system that the U.S. manages to denounce at every turn on the basis of false information.

NC: There's an interesting cultural difference that I think led to that. Back around forty or fifty years ago, Canada and the U.S. were pretty similar on health care. In both countries the unions led reforms, but with a different emphasis. In Canada unions called for national health care, and in the U.S. the unions worked for their own health care. So the UAW made a good deal with car companies, so those guys have good health care. Of course the moment the companies break out of the bargain, there it goes. But this sense of social solidarity is just driven out of people's minds here in the U.S. You can see it in the anti-tax movements. Why are people opposed to taxes? April 15th should be a day of celebration, and in a democracy it would be. We are getting together, we're working to implement programs we're all in favor of, and so forth. Here, it's that alien force from Mars that's coming in to steal your hard-earned money. That's the intuition that people have, and it's not by accident. There were massive propaganda campaigns, from the 1940s, that try to drive those concepts into people's heads.

RB: But in reading Zellig Harris's *Transformation of Capitalist Society,* one is led to imagine that if a capitalist society moves in the direction of the kinds of ESOPs you described before, then that type of worker solidarity would come to be a part of people's lives, and therefore come to be ingrained into their experience. Instead it seems that it happens, and then the workers make money and retire.

NC: What happens is that our managers who run our enterprises will hire their managers to run the place where we work. That's happening right now. The United Auto Workers union theoretically owns a fairly large piece of General Motors, but they aren't going to have any role in running the company. In fact, the taxpayer is probably going to end up owning 60 percent of GM. But nobody is going to be talking about keeping the factories functioning to produce high-speed rail lines, because that's inconsistent with the ideology.

RB: There's this contrast between what is clearly good for the individual in this country versus what benefits some distant powerful organization from which that individual derives no benefit; and often, as you say, it's the latter interests that prevail. It's counterintuitive.

NC: It's counterintuitive that a majority of the population wants a Canadian-style health care that is not even on the agenda. People have such a feeling of helplessness that they don't even know what to do about it. This is a very atomized society, and I think that the suburbanization of it had something to do with it. After all, this process was the product of social engineering, an effort to scatter around social units so that people won't interact with one another. If you live out in the suburbs, you don't know anybody.

RB: Is it appropriate now to work toward returning to the local? Given corporate homogenization—not only on a social level but environmentally—would an emphasis upon creating local diversity be the next best struggle in which to engage? It has become the case that the most depressing magazine in the world is *National Geographic,* which so often talks about the elimination of the varieties of life across the globe, from the microscopic organisms all the way up the animal kingdom. There is this horrifying homogenization, speeded along by corporations, that is killing everything.

NC: It's all true, and of humans as well. The United Nations came out with a report yesterday estimating the impact of global warming upon different parts of the world. It shows that 90 percent of this impact will be on poorer countries, one of the reasons why they don't care about it here. If global warming was shifting the gulf stream to the south, meaning that Europe might turn into the North Pole, then there would be worry. You can read articles in the *Wall Street Journal* that suggest that global warming isn't such a big deal, since we'll have better farming here, better weather, and so forth.

RB: You can from what you're suggesting link up what is going on in the environment to trends in social movements.

NC: It has to happen. The environmental crisis is becoming really, really serious. MIT just came out with a big study done by climatologists who have created sophisticated models predicting global warming, and they suggest that it's much worse than the international scientific organizations have been predicting, and that's bad enough. There's a lot of talk about technical fixes, like carbon taxes and so on, but the real problem, which is a major social problem, is how do you overcome the structures of life that have been constructed around wasteful energy? How do you get around urbanization, which cannot survive in the contemporary model? That's a huge project that involves large-scale social movements. Markets are virtually useless, even in principle. The market doesn't give you the option of building a subway system, that's a democratic option, not a market choice. And that's the kind of thing that is needed everywhere.

RB: Individual decision making on the basis of rationally determined need and cooperation among the different individual decisions makers would seem to offer some hope, but how do we bring such efforts, like the ESOPs you mentioned earlier and that were of interest to Zellig Harris and Seymour Melman, to fruition in the face of massive resistance from corporate power?

NC: We happen to be at a turning point, and if there was a functioning democratic society, working people would not be taking their pink slips, they'd be taking over the factories. And there have been a couple of attempts to try to do so. The Youngstown Steel case, for instance, around 1980. U.S. Steel was closing down its Youngstown plant, and there was an organized effort to do something about it, with Staughton Lynd as one of the leading organizers. He's the son of the famous Lynd family in Middletown, and is a radical American historian and civil rights activist. He was kicked out of Spellman College at the same time Howard Zinn was for supporting Black students, and he went to law school and became a labor lawyer. He took part in organizing an effort to get the community and workforce to take over the Youngstown steel plants. He made a case, that went to the courts, that said that there is no reason why a corporation cannot be owned by stakeholders—workforce and community. They lost in the courts, of course, but with enough popular support, it could have gone through. And that's the kind of thing that could be happening right now, in the rust belt, and for very good reasons: there's a social need for it, there are the facilities for it, but what is blocking it is archaic social structures. It's kind of like how feudalism blocked the early rise of capitalism.

RB: These archaic social structures were kept in place, in part, by a common discourse about what was possible.

NC: Yes, a discourse that is in your head. A discourse in your head that says that you have to do things for yourself. That explains the popularity of Ayn Rand, or Eric Hoffer, or those kinds of people. The hero is the one who does things for himself, and kicks everybody else in the face. That is what lies behind this crazed form of libertarianism that flourishes in the U.S., but not in more civilized societies. It shows up a lot, and taxes is a striking example, but take for another example, Social Security. Why is the right wing so intent upon destroying Social Security? Not just the right wing, the *Washington Post*, the *New York Times*. Every time you read about the entitlement problem, it's Social Security and health. In fact, Social Security contributes essentially nothing to it, it's all the privatized health system. But they want to kill Social Security, and I think that there's an ideological motivation for this, more than anything else. Social Security is based on solidarity, and that is just a dangerous idea. They want everyone to look out for themselves, except of course the business class, which is "socialist." It works together and expects to be cared for by the nanny state.

RB: This tendency you are describing is once again counterintuitive, and it goes against what we experience day to day in, say, the corporatized food industry. All we have to do is look around us at people who aren't ten pounds overweight but rather are one hundred pounds overweight, and these people are all over the place. Twenty-five years ago people didn't look like that, and if we are trying to look for trends, well there is a clear trend, and one might imagine a society in which people would look at that evolution, link it to the food industry, and clearly state that this system of food production is not working out!

NC: Yes, but within the individual self-satisfaction model you cannot think that. There is of course a health-fad industry, but it's not about that; it's about how you yourself should improve things. The thinking is that you yourself should stop going to McDonald's, rather than the idea that there should be some other way of organizing food production.

RB: A lot of the things we are talking about resonate with things that were happening when Harris was working. It's not that there have been dramatic changes since the period when he was working, but rather the problems he described have grown in amplitude.

NC: Yes, which is why I would suggest that the work that was being done in the context of the Frame of Reference project is very apposite to the current situation.

RB: And yet, he didn't seem to have had the desire to diffuse his work, or the work undertaken in that context.

NC: This is part of his self-abnegation. I remember someone who knew Zellig well who said that he had a fear of his own power. He was conscious of his own power to influence, and he was afraid of it. I was much younger of course than he was, but people who knew him had that feeling. I don't know if you have encountered this in your interviews with people from his milieus.

RB: There have been some inklings of this suggested by people who were somewhat away from the New York or Philadelphia centers in which he worked, people like William Schumer, from Detroit, and the Midwestern group of Avukah, who exhibited a degree of animosity toward Harris. He had the sense that Harris was very dogmatic, and that even in the face of facts to the contrary, that he was going to drive on with his own mission. Did you ever sense this?

NC: He perhaps did this, but in a way I never found offensive. For example in my own work, he had absolutely no interest, and I thought: 'Okay, why should he?'

RB: [laughter] That may be, but . . .

NC: [laughter] I mean, I was a student after all. And students expect faculty to be helpful.

RB: Was it different on the social side?

NC: He was twenty years older than I was; we occupied different worlds. For an eighteen-year-old kid, twenty years is a long time. But I remember when Carol and I got married, and we were pretty young, I was kind of reluctant to tell Harris, although I'm not exactly sure why. I finally did tell him and he said, "Okay, what is your new address?"

RB: That is shocking! [laughter]

NC: [laughter] I didn't find it shocking, I found it natural.

RB: Murray Eden told me that he was present on only one occasion when Harris exhibited strong emotion.

NC: When was this?

RB: On the news that Edward Sapir had died. And that was the one time when he really saw an outpouring of emotion from Harris. And in fact, everyone I've interviewed to date, perhaps with the exception of Melman, has mentioned Harris's coldness, his lack of *entre-gens*, the ability to get into close contact with people around him.

NC: What you are saying is very interesting, in part because he never had us read Sapir. I was surprised to see this review you mentioned in your manuscript, this long article that served as a memorial to Sapir. I was surprised because as students we never heard from Harris about Sapir. I knew he was there, but we never read him.

RB: Aren't their respective programs very different? That he would take Sapir as his leading light would seem to me at least to be somewhat surprising, since there were significant differences in the approach they took to the study of linguistics.

NC: I don't think that Harris's work had anything to do with Sapir's. Maybe somewhere in the background. We didn't read much at all with Harris, and in particular, we didn't read Sapir.

RB: Boas?

NC: No. We read descriptive linguistics.

RB: Murray Eden also said something that I found very enlightening about Harris's work, and I wanted to ask you about it. He mentioned in regards to Harris that there was an engineering side to him.

NC: I think physicist. For example, I was his undergraduate student, so I did everything he told me to do, and he at one point suggested that I read Georg Joos's *Theoretical Physics*. You should take a look at it sometime, it's a very advanced theoretical text of physics that was this thick [Chomsky indicates a large-size book]. Why? Because that was real intellectual content for him.

RB: So did physics represent the paradigm that contained the weighty work he was looking for?

NC: I think that he thought that the discourse analysis was somehow going to contribute to science in some fashion. In a way it's quite similar to Rudolf Carnap's work. I don't think that they knew each other, but Carnap's conception of logical syntax was that it would make a contribution to physics. But of course he was a physicist, who came from a physics background. And a real intellectual contribution for him would be something that advances physics. I'm pretty sure Harris felt the same way. It was partly just his milieu, and in that milieu, advanced intellectual work was done in physics. And that's what he really respected, more than engineering.

RB: So is it fair to say that he looked to these kinds of scientific paradigms in thinking about the social world?

NC: Yes, except as far as I know, for that realm it was social psychology, which was considered scientific, like the attitude formation material we talked about earlier on. He was also close to David Rappaport.

RB: I did speak about this with Harris's brother, Tzvee, and his wife Soshanna, and she told me that Harris was very taken by Freud per se, and that he was an avid reader of Freud's writings, which surprised me since I don't see it in his work.

NC: I'm not surprised. He didn't have us read Freud, but it was in the background. As you mentioned, though, he did have us look at Erich Fromm.

RB: The one place I do find mention of Freud is in Harris's letters, those I cite in the manuscript, in which he makes reference to a whole series of Freudian stages and motivations, and he does so very directly, using the terminology employed by Freud. But it's not present in the formal writings, including the Framework of Reference materials, where I would have thought that he might use some of the Freudian categories or approaches to study attitudes.

NC: I'm sure, without remembering anything specific, that he was pretty immersed in Freud.

RB: That seems surprising to me, given his work; is it?

NC: Not for that time. This was a way of breaking with tradition, ideology, it took a revolutionary perspective on the way that people are understood and comprehended. It was not the way it is considered now. And Harry Stack Sullivan was another person who was important to him.

RB: But again, he is not mentioned in Harris's writings.

NC: I had heard him mentioned enough times to start reading it.

RB: From my understanding, though, you found little in that psychological work that was of value for your own project.

NC: To me that work seemed kind of vacuous. I would pick up hints about it from Harris. A guy you respect talks about something, so you pick it up and follow it, but after that you need to use your own judgment. That's what I did.

RB: I am so grateful for this Noam, thank you.

Bibliography of Zellig Harris's Work

1932. "Origin of the Alphabet." Unpublished MA thesis, University of Pennsylvania, Philadelphia.

1933. "Acrophony and Vowellessness in the Creation of the Alphabet." *Journal of American Oriental Society* 53:387. [Summary of 1932 thesis.]

1934a. "The Structure of Ras Shamra C." *Journal of the American Oriental Society* 54:80–83.

1934b. "The Sealand of Ancient Arabia." *Journal of the American Oriental Society* 5493–95.

1935a. "Joint Expedition [of the American School of Oriental Research in Baghdad] with the Iraq Museum of Nuzi." Review of Edward Chiera. *Language* 11, vols. 4–5 (1933–1934): 262–263.

1935b. "A Hurrian Affricate or Sibilant in Ras Shamra." *Journal of the American Oriental Society* 55: 95–100.

1936a. *The Ras Shamra Mythological Texts*. Together with James A[lan] Montgomery. Philadelphia: American Philosophical Society, 1935.

Reviewed by:

Edward Sapir. "Review of James A. Montgomery and Zeillig S. Harris, 'The Ras Shamra Mythological Texts'." *Language* 13 (1937): 326–331.

1936b. *A Grammar of the Phoenician Language*. PhD dissertation, University of Pennsylvania, Philadelphia. American Oriental Series 8. New Haven: American Oriental Society, 1934.

Reviewed by:

Maria Höfner. *Wissenschaftliche Zeitschrift für die Kunde des Morgenlandes* 48 (1941): 153.

Charles François Jean. *Revue des Études Sémitiques* (1940): 94–96.

Vojtěch Šanda. *Archiv Orientální* 11 (1939): 177–178.

Edward Sapir. *Language* 15 (1939): 60–65.

1936c. "Back Formation of *itn* in Phoenician and Ras Shamra." Abstract. *Journal of the American Oriental Society* 56:410.

1937. "A Conditioned Sound Change in Ras Shamra." *Journal of the American Oriental Society* 57:151–157.

1938a. "Expression of the Causative in Ugaritic." *Journal of the American Oriental Society* 58:103–111.

1938b. "Ras Shamra: Canaanite Civilization and Language." *Annual Report of the Smithsonian Institution* (1937): 479–502.

1939a. *Development of the Canaanite Dialects: An Investigation in Linguistic History.* American Oriental Series 16. New Haven: American Oriental Society, 1939.

Reviewed by:

William F. Albright. *Journal of the American Oriental Society* 60 (1940): 414–422.

Max M. Bravmann. *Kirjath Sepher* 17 (1940): 370–381.

Marcel Cohen. *Bulletin de la Société de Linguistique de Paris* 123 (1940): 62.

René Dussard. *Syria: Revue d'Art Oriental et d'Archéologie* (1940): 228–230.

Harold Louis Ginsberg. *Journal of Biblical Literature* 59 (1940): 546–551.

Albrecht Goetze. *Language* 17 (1941): 167–170.

Alexander M. Honeyman. *Journal of the Royal Asiatic Society of Great Britain and Ireland* 17 (1941): 167–170.

Franz Rosenthal. *Orientalia* 11 (1942): 179–185.

Gonzague Ryckmans. *Le Muséon* 53 (1940): 135.

Raphaël Savignac. *Vivre et Penser* (1941): 157–159.

Bernard Baron Carra de Vaux. *Journal of the Palestine Oriental Society* 19 (1941): 329–330.

Ronald J. Williams. *Journal of Near Eastern Studies* 1 (1942): 378–380.

1939b. "Development of the West Semitic Aspect System." Abstract. *Journal of the American Oriental Society* 59:409–410.

1939c. Lowie, Robert H. *Hidatsa Texts.* With grammatical notes and phonograph transcriptions by Zellig Harris and C. F. Voegelin. Indiana Historical Society, 1939.

1940. "Gray's 'Foundations of Language'." Review of *Foundations of Language* by Louis H. Gray. *Language* 16 (1939): 216–231. Reprint, 1970.

1941a. "Linguistic Structure of Hebrew." *Journal of the American Oriental Society* 61:143–167. Also published as "Publications of the American Oriental Society" Offprint Series, no.14.

1941b. Review of *Grundzüge der Phonologie* by N. S. Trubetzkoy. *Language* 17:345–349. Reprinted, Lake Bluff, IL: Jupiter Press, 1978.

1941–46. Cherokee Materials. American Philosophical Society Library, Philadelphia.

1942a. "Morpheme Alternants in Linguistic Analysis." *Language* 18.3: 169–180. Reprinted in 1970: 78–90, and in 1981: 23–35.[1]

1942b. "Phonologies of African Languages: The Phonemes of Moroccan Arabic." *Journal of the American Oriental Society* 62.4:309–318. Reprinted under the title of "The Phonemes of Moroccan Arabic," in 1970: 161–176. [Read at the Centennial Meeting of the Society, Boston 1942. Cf. the critique by Jean Cantineau, "Reflexions sur la phonologie de l'arabe marocain," *Hespéris* 37:193–207.]

1942c. Review of *Language, Culture, and Personality: Essays in Memory of Edward Sapir.* Edited by Leslie Spier, A[lfred] Irving Hallowell and Stanley S[tewart] Newman. *Language* 18:238–245.

1942d. "The Phonemes of Fanti." Together with William Everett Welmers in *Journal of the American Oriental Society*, 62:318–333.

1942e. "The Phonemes of Kingwana-Swahili." Together with Fred Lukoff in *Journal of the American Oriental Society* 62:333–338.

1944a. "Yokuts Structure and [Stanley] Newman's Grammar." *International Journal of Linguistics* 10.4:196–211. Reprinted in 1970: 188–208.

1944b. "Simultaneous Components in Phonology." *Language* 20:181–205. Reprinted in 1970:3-31, and in *Phonological Theory: Evolution and Current Practice*. Edited by Valerie Becker Makkai, New York: Holt, Rinehart & Winston, 1972:115–133. Reprinted, Lake Bluff, IL: Jupiter Press, 1978.

1945a. "Navaho Phonology and Harry Hoijer's Analysis." *International Journal of Linguistics* 11.4: 239–246. Reprinted in 1970: 177–187.

1945b. "Discontinuous Morphemes." *Language* 21.2: 121–127. Reprinted in 1970: 91–99, and in 1981: 36–44.

1945c. "American Indian Linguistic Work and the Boas Collection." *Library Bulletin of the American Philosophical Society* (1945): 57–61.

Reviewed by Thomas A[lbert] Sebeok in International Journal of Linguistics 13 (1947): 126.

1945d. "Index to the Franz Boas Collection of Materials for American Linguistics." Together with Charles F. Voegelin. *Language* 21.3, *Language Monograph: Index to the*

Franz Boas Collection of Materials for American Linguistics 22 (Jul.– Sep., 1945): 1–3. Reprinted, New York: Kraus, 1974.

1945e. "Linguistics in Ethnology." Together with Charles F. Voegelin. *Southwestern Journal of Anthropology* 1:455–465.

1945f. Review of *Kota Texts*, vol. I by Murray B[arnson] Emeneau. *Language* 21: 283–289. Reprinted under the title "Emeneau's Kota Texts," in 1970: 209–216.

1946a. "From Morpheme to Utterance." *Language* 22.3:161–183. Reprinted in 1970: 100–125, and in 1981: 45–70.

1946b. "The Phonemes of North Carolina Cherokee." Together with Ernest Bender. *International Journal of Linguistics* 12:14–21.

1947a. "Developments in American Indian Linguistics." *Library Bulletin of the American Philosophical Society* (1946): 84–97.

   Review note by Thomas A[lbert] Sebeok in International Journal of Linguistics 14 (1948): 209.

1947b. "Structural Restatements I: Swadesh's Eskimo; Newman's Yawelmani." *International Journal of Language* 13 no. 1: 47–58. Reprinted in 1970: 217–234, and in 1981: 71–88. ["Attempt to restate in summary fashion the grammatical structures of a number of American Indian languages. The languages to be treated are those presented in H. Hoijer and others, *Linguistic Structures of Native America*, New York, 1946."On Morris Swadesh's account of Eskimo and Stanley S. Newman's of Yawelmani Yokuts].

1947c. "Structural Restatements II: Voegelin's Delaware." *International Journal of Linguistics* 13, no.3: 175–186. Reprinted in 1970: 235–250, and 1981: 89–104.

1947d. "The Scope of Linguistics." Together with Charles F. Voegelin. *American Anthropologist* 49:588–600.

1947e. Associate Editor with Helen Boas-Yampolsky of Kwakiutl Grammar (With Glossary of the Suffixes) by Franz Boas. Transactions of the American Philosophical Society 37:199–377.

   Reviewed by:

   Morris Swadesh in Word 4 (1948): 58–63.

   Charles F. Voegelin in *Journal of American Folklore* 61 (1948): 414–415.

1948. "Componential Analysis of a [Modern] Hebrew Paradigm." *Language* 24, no.1: 87–91. Reprinted-with "Hebrew" in the title dropped-in 1970: 126–130.

1951a. *Methods in Structural Linguistics*. University of Chicago Press, xvi, 384 pp. Reprinted under the title *Structural Linguistics*, as "Phoenix Books" P 52, 1960; 7th impression, 1966; 1984. [Preface signed "Philadelphia, January 1947."]

Reviewed by:

K[enneth] R. Brooks in *Modern Language Review* 48 (1953): 496.

Jean Cantineau in *Bulletin de la Société de Linguistique de Paris* 50, no.2 (1954): 4–9.

Eugene Dorfman in *Modern Language Journal* 38 (1954): 159–160.

Murray Fowler in *Language* 28 (1952): 504–509.

Paul L[ucian] Garvin in *Romance Philology* 9 (1955–1956): 38–41.

Charles F[rancis] Hockett in *American Speech* 27 (1952): 117–121.

Harry Hoijer in *Romance Philology* 9 (1955–1956): 32–38.

Fred W[alter] Householder in *International Journal of Linguistics* 18 (1952): 260–268.

Milka Ivić,in Južnoslovanski *Filolog* 20 (1953-1954): 474–478.

Norman A[nthony] McQuown in *Language* 28 (1952): 495–504. Margaret Mead in *International Journal of Linguistics* 18 (1952): 257–260.

Fernand Mossé in *Études Germaniques* 7 (1952): 274.

Stanley S[tewart] Newman in *American Anthropologist* 54 (1952): 404–405.

Walburga von Raffler[-Engel] in *Paideia* 8 (1953): 229–230.

Knud Togeby in *Modern Language Notes* 68 (1954): 19–194.

C[harles] F[rederick] Voegelin in *Journal of the American Oriental Society* 72, no. 1 (1952): 13–14.

Robert Léon Wagner in *Journal de Psychologie* 47 (1954): 537–539.

1951b. "Methods for Determining Intelligibility Among Dialects of Natural Languages." Together with Charles F. Voegelin in *Proceedings of the American Philosophical Society* 95:322–329.

1951c. Review of *Selected Writings of Edward Sapir in Language, Culture, and Personality* by David G. Mandelbaum. *Language* 27, no.3: 288–333. Reprinted in 1970: 712–764, and in *Edward Sapir: Appraisals of His Life and Work*, edited by Konrad Koerner. Philadelphia: John Benjamins, 1984, 69–114.

1952a. "Culture and Style in Extended Discourse." *Selected Papers from the 29th International Congress of Americanists* (New York, 1949), vol.III: *Indian Tribes of Aboriginal America*, edited by Sol Tax and Melville J[oyce] Herskovits, 210–215. New York: Square Publishers. Reprinted, New York: Cooper Press, 1967. Paper Reprinted in 1970: 373–389. [Proposes a method for analyzing extended discourse, with sample analyses from Hidatsa, a Siouan language spoken in North Dakota.]

1952b. "Discourse Analysis." *Language* 28, no.1:1–30. Reprinted in *The Structure of Language: Readings in the Philosophy of Language*, edited by Jerry A[lan] Fodor and Jerrold J[acob] Katz, 355–383. Englewood Cliffs, N.J.: Prentice-Hall, 1964, and also in Harris 1970: 313–348 as well as in 1981: 107–142.

1952c. "Discourse Analysis: A sample text." *Language* 28, no.4: 474–494. Reprinted in 1970: 349–379.

1952d. "Training in Anthropological Linguistics." Together with Charles F. Voegelin in *American Anthropologist* 54: 322–327.

1953. "Eliciting in Linguistics." Together with Charles F. Voegelin in *Southwestern Journal of Anthropology* 9, no.1:59–75. Reprinted in 1970: 769–774.

1954a. "Transfer Grammar." *International Journal of Linguistics* 20, no.4: 259–270. Reprinted in 1970: 139–157.

1954b. "Distributional Structure." *Word* 10, nos.2-3: 146–162. Also in *Linguistics Today: Published on the Occasion of the Columbia University Bicentennial*. Edited by Andre Martinet and Uriel Weinreich. Linguistic Circle of New York, 1954. Reprinted in *The Structure of Language: Readings in the Philosophy of Language*. Edited by Jerry A[lan] Fodor and Jerrold J[acob] Katz, 33–49. Englewood Cliffs, N.J.: Prentice-Hall, 1964, and also in Harris 1970: 775–794, and in 1981: 3–22.

1955a. "From Phoneme to Morpheme." *Language* 31, no.2: 190–222. Reprinted in 1970: 32–67.

1955b. "American Indian Work and the Boas Collection." *Library Bulletin of the American Philosophical Society* (1955): 57–61.

1956a. "A Bushman Dictionary" edited by Dorothea F[rances] Bleek. *American Oriental Series* 41. New Haven: American Oriental Society.

Reviewed by:

Henri Peter Blok in *Neophilologus*. 41 (1957): 232–234.

A. J. C[oetzee] in *Tydskrif vir Volkskunde en Volkstaal* 14 (1957): 29–30.

Louis Deroy in *Revue des Langues Vivantes* 23 (1957): 174–175.

C[lement] M[artyn] Doke in *African Studies* 16 (1957): 124–125.

Joseph H[arold] Greenberg in *Language* 33 (1957): 495–497.

Otto Köhler in *Afrika und Übersee* 43 (1959): 133–138.

E. O. J. Westphal in *Africa* 27 (1957): 203–204.

1956b. "Introduction to Transformations." *Transformations and Discourse Analysis Papers* 2. Philadelphia: University of Pennsylvania. Reprinted in 1970a: 383–389.

1957a. "Co-Occurrence and Transformation in Linguistic Structure." *Language* 33:283–340. Reprinted in *The Structure of Language: Readings in the Philosophy of Language*, edited by Jerry A[lan] Fodor and Jerrold J[acob] Katz, 155–210. Englewood Cliffs, N.J.: Prentice-Hall 1964. Also reprinted in Harris 1970: 390–457, 1972: 78–104 [in parts], and 1981: 143–210. Also anthologized in *Syntactic Theory 1: Structuralist; selected readings*, edited by Fred W. Householder, 151–185. Harmondsworth, Middlesex: Penguin Books. 1972.

1957b. "Canonical Form of a Text." *Transformations and Discourse Analysis Papers* no.3b. Philadelphia: University of Pennsylvania.

1959a. "The Transformational Model of Language Structure." *Anthropological Linguistics* 1:27–29.

1959b. "Computable Syntactic Analysis." *Transformations and Discourse Analysis Papers* 15. Philadelphia: University of Pennsylvania. Revised version published as entry 1962a; excerpted, with the added subtitle "The 1959 computer sentence-analyzer" in 1970a: 253–277.

1959c. "Linguistic Transformations for Information Retrieval". *Interscience Tracts in Pure and Applied Mathematics* 2 (1958). Washington, D.C.: National Academy of Sciences-National Research Council. Reprinted in 1970a: 458–471.

1960a. "Structural Linguistics." Chicago: University of Chicago Press, xvi. Reprinted in1984. [Reprint of entry 1951, with a supplementary preface, vi–vii.]

Reviewed by:

Simeon Potter in *Modern Language Review* 57 (1962): 139.

1960b. "English Transformation List." *Transformations and Discourse Analysis Papers* 30. Philadelphia: University of Pennsylvania.

1961. "Strings and Transformations in Language Description." MS, Department of Linguistics, University of Pennsylvania. Published under the title "Introduction to String Analysis" in 1970a: 278–285.

1962a. "String Analysis of Sentence Structure." *Papers on Formal Linguistics* 1. The Hague: Mouton, 70 pp. 2nd ed., 1964, Reprinted in 1965. [Revised version of entry 1959b.]

Reviewed by:

László Antal in *Linguistics* 1 (1963): 97–104.

Klaus Baumgärtner in *Germanistik* 4 (1963): 194.

Robert E[dmondson] Longacre in *Language* 39 (1963): 473–478.

Murray Fowler in *Word* 19 (1963): 245–247.

Robert B[enjamin] Lees in *International Journal of American Linguistics* 30 (1964): 415–420.

Karel Pala in *Sborník Prací Filolofické Fakulty Brněnské University* 13 (1964): 238–241.

Karel Pala in *Slovo a Slovesnost* 26 (1965): 78–80.

G. G. Pocekov in *Voprosy Jazykoznania* 13 (1965): 123–128.

Kazimierz Polański in *Biuletyn Fonegraficzne* 8 (1967): 139–143.

1962b. "Sovmestnaja vstreöaemost' i *transformacija v jazykovoj* strukture," edited by V. A. Zvegincev. *Novoe v lingvistike*, volume II: 528–636. Moscow: Izddatel'stvo Innostr. Literatury. Translation by T(atjana) N. Mološaja of entry 1957a, with an introduction by Sebastian Šaumjan.

1962c. "A Language for International Cooperation." *Preventing World War III: Some proposals*, edited by Quincy Wright, William M. Evan, and Monon Deutsch, 299–309. New York: Simon & Schuster. Reprinted in 1970a: 795–805.

1963a. "Discourse Analysis Reprints." *Papers on Formal Linguistics* 2. The Hague: Mouton, 73 pp. [See comment in entry 1957b.]

Reviewed by:

Klaus Baumgärtner in *Germanistik* 5 (1964): 412.

Manfred Bierwisch in *Linguistics* 13 (1965): 61–73.

György Hell in *Acta Linguistica Academiae Scientarum Hungaricae* 18 (1968): 233–235.

Tae-Yong Pak in *Language* 46 (1970): 754–764.

Fred[erick] C[hen] C[hung] Peng in *Lingua* 16 (1966): 325–330.

1963b. "Immediate-Constituent Formulation of English Syntax." *Transformations and Discourse Analysis Papers*, no.45. Philadelphia: University Of Pennsylvania. Reprinted in 1970a: 131–138.

1964a. "Transformations in Linguistic Structure." *Proceedings of the American Philosophical Society* 108:418–422. Reprinted in 1970a: 472–481.

1964b. "The Elementary Transformations." *Transformations and Discourse Analysis Papers* 54. Philadelphia: University of Pennsylvania. Excerpted in 1970a: 482–532; 1972: 57–75; and in abbreviated form in 1981: 211–235.

1965. "Transformational Theory." *Language* 41:363–401. Reprinted in 1970a: 533–577, 1972: 108–154, and 1981: 236–280.

1966a. "Algebraic Operations in Linguistic Structure." Paper read at the International Congress of Mathematicians, Moscow. 1966. Published in 1970a: 603–611.

1966b. "A Cyclic-Cancellation Automation for Sentence Well-Formedness." *International Computation Centre Bulletin* 5:69–94. Reprinted in 1970a: 286–309.

1967a. "Decomposition Lattices." *Transformations and Discourse Analysis Papers* 70. Philadelphia: University of Pennsylvania. Reprinted in 1970a: 578–602. Excerpted in 1981: 281–290.

1967b. "Morpheme Boundaries within Words: Report on a computer test." *Transformations and Discourse Analysis Papers* 73. Philadelphia: University of Pennsylvania. Reprinted in 1970a: 68–77.

1968a. Mathematical Structures of Language. *Interscience Tracts in Pure and Applied Mathematics* 21. New York: Interscience Publishers, John Wiley & Sons.

Reviewed by:

Maurice Gross in *Semiotica* 2 (1970): 380–390. Reprinted in entry 1972: 314–324 with an introduction in German by Senta Plötz [p.313] and an English abstract by the author [p.314].

Maurice Gross and Marcel-Paul Schützenberger in *The American Scientist* 58 (1970). Reprinted in entry 1972: 308–312 with summaries in German and English by Senta Plötz [p.307].

Petr Pitha in *Slovo a Slovesnost* 32 (1971): 59–65.

Wojciech Skalmowski in *ITL: Tidschrift van het Instituut voor Toegepaste Linguïstiek* 4 (1969): 56–61.

Lucia Vaina-Pusca in *Revue Roumaine de Linguistique* 16 (1971): 369–371.

1968b. "Edward Sapir: Contributions to linguistics" edited by David L. Sills. *International Encyclopedia of the Social Sciences* 14: 13–14. New York: Macmillan. Reprinted in longer form in 1970a: 765–768.

1968c. "Du morpheme a l'expression." *Langages* 9:23–50. Translation of entry 1946b.

1969a. "The Two Systems of Grammar: Report and paraphrase." *Transformations and Discourse Analysis Papers* 79. Philadelphia: University of Pennsylvania. Reprinted in 1970a: 612–692, 1972: 158–240 (revised), and in 1981: 293–351 (shortened).

1969b. "Analyse du discours." *Langages* 13:8–45. French translation of entry 1952b.

1970a. *Papers in Structural and Transformational Linguistics.* Dordrecht, Holland: D. Reidel., x, 850 pp. [Collection of 37 papers originally published between 1940–1969. These are organized under the following headings: I, "Structural Linguistics, 1: Methods"; 2, "Structural Linguistics, 2: Linguistic structures"; 3, "String Analysis and Computation"; 4, "Discourse Analysis"; 5, "Transformations," and 6, "About Linguistics." "Preface" (v–vii).]

Reviewed by:

Michael B[enedict] Kac in *Language* 49 (1973): 466–473.

Ferenc Kiefer in *Statistical Methods in Linguistics* 7 (1971): 60–62.

1970b. "La structure distributionnelle: Analyse distributionnelle et structurale" Edited by Jean Dubois and Françoise Dubois-Charlier. *Langages* 20: 14-34. Paris: Didier / Larousse. Translation of entry 1954b.

1970c. "New Views of Language." MS. Published in 1972: 242–248, with an introduction in German by the editor.

1971. *Structures mathématiques du langage*. Translated into French by Catherine Fuchs. *Monographies de Linguistique mathématique*, no.3. Paris: Dunod, 248 pp. Translation of entry 1968a.

Reviewed by:

Yves Gentilhomme in *Bulletin de la Société de Linguistique de Paris* 69 (1974): 37–S3.

1972. *Transformationelle Analyse: Die Transformationstheorie von Zellig Harris und ihre Entwicklung / Transformational Analysis: The transformational theory of Zellig Harris and its development*, edited by Senta Plötz. *Linguistische Forschungen*, no.8. Frankfurt: Athenäum-Verlag, 511 pp. [Reprint of entries 1964b (57–75), 1957 (78–104), 1965 (108- 154), 1969a (158–240)—revised by the author in 1972, and 1970c (242–248), each introduced, in German, by the editor 55–57, 76–78, 105–108, 155–157, and 241–242, respectively.]

1973a. "Les deux systèmes de grammaire: Prédicat et paraphrase." *Langages* 29:55–81. Partial translation by Danielle Leeman of entry 1969a.

1973b. Review of Charles F. Hockett, editor. *A Leonard Bloomfield Anthology*. Bloomington, IN.: Indiana University Press.1970. *International Journal of American Linguistics* 39:252–255.

1976a. "A Theory of Language Structure." *American Philosophical Quarterly* 13:237–255. Reprinted in 1981: 352–376 as "Theory of the structure and information of sentences."

1976b. "On a Theory of Language." *Journal of Philosophy* 73: 253–276. Excerpted in 1981: 377–391.

1976c. *Notes du cours de syntaxe*, translated and presented by Maurice Gross. Paris: Éditions du Seuil. [Translation of lectures on English syntax given at the Département de Linguistique, University de Paris-Vincennes, 1973–1974.]

Reviewed by:

Riccardo Ambrosini in *Studi e Saggi Linguistici* 17 (1977): 309–340.

Claude Hagège in *Bulletin de la Société de Linguistique de Paris* 72 (1974): 35–37.

G. L[urquin] in *Le Langage et l'Homme* 31 (1976): 114–115.

1976d. "Morphemalternanten in der linguistischen Analyse." *Beschreibungsmethoden des amerikanischen Strakturalismus,* edited by Elisabeth Bense, Peter Eisenberg and Hartmut Haberland, 129–143. München: Max Hueber. [Translation by Elisabeth Bense of entry 1942a.]

1976e. "Vom Morphem zur Äußerung." Ibid., 181–210. [Translation by Dietmar Rösler of entry 1946b.]

1976f. "Textanalyse." Ibid., 261–298. [Translation by Peter Eisenberg of entry 1952b.]

1978a. "Grammar on Mathematical Principles." *Journal of Linguistics* 14:120. Reprinted in 1981:392–411. [Given as a lecture in Somerville College, Oxford, March 16, 1977.]

1978b. "Operator-Grammar of English." *Lingvisticae Investigationes* 2:55–92. Excerpted in 1981: 412–435.

1978c. "The Interrogative in a Syntactic Framework." *Questions,* edited by Henry Hiz. Dordrecht, Holland: D. Reidel, 1–35.

1979a. "Zadżodżenia metodologiczne jezykoznawstwa strukturalnego [The methodological basis of structural linguistics]." Językoznawstwo *strukturalne: Wybór tekstów,* edited by Halina Kurkowska and Adam Weinsberg, 158–174. Warsaw: Pań Stwowe Wydawnictwo Naukowe, 274 pp. [Polish translation by the first editor of Harris, 1951a: 4–24, "Methodological Preliminaries."]

1979b. "Mathematical Analysis of Language." Unpublished paper delivered to the 6th International Congress on Logic, Methodology, and the Philosophy of Science, Hanover, Germany, August, 1979.

1981. *Papers on Syntax,* edited by Henry Hiz. Dordrecht, Holland: D. Reidel, vii. [Collection of sixteen previously published papers, organized under three sections: I, "Structural Analysis," II, "Transformational Analysis," and III, "Operator Grammar." Index (437–479)]

1982a. *A Grammar of English on Mathematical Principles.* New York: John Wiley & Sons, xvi, 429 pp.

Reviewed by:

William Frawley in *Language* 60 (1984): 15–152.

Frank Heny in *Journal of Linguistics* 20 (1984): 181–188.

Bruce E. Nevin in *Computational Linguistics* 10 (1984): 203–211.

Eric S. Wheeler in *Computers in the Humanities* 7(1984): 88–92.

1982b. "Discourse and Sublanguage." *Sublanguage: Studies of language in restricted semantic domains*, edited by Richard Kittredge and John Lehrberger, 231–236. Berlin: Walter de Gruyter.

1985. "On Grammars of Science." *Linguistics and Philosophy: Essays in Honor of Rulon S. Wells*, edited by Adam Makkai and Alan K. Melby. Philadelphia: John Benjamins. Also in *Current Issues in Linguistic Theory* 42:139–148.

1987. "The Structure of Science Information." [Paper submitted to the magazine *Science*, but rejected by the editor, allegedly because the author had declined to refer to Chomsky. Unpublished.]

1988a. *Language and Information*. New York: Columbia University Press. [Revised version of lectures given at Columbia University in October 1986: "A Formal Theory of Syntax"; "Scientific Sub-Languages"; "Information," and "The Nature of Language."]

1988b. "Scientific Sublanguages and the Prospects for a Global Language of Science" together with Paul Mattick, Jr. *Annals of the American Association of Philosophy and Social Sciences* 495: 73–83.

1989. *The Form of Information in Science: Analysis of an immunology sublanguage*, together with Michael Gottfried, Thomas Ryckman, Paul Mattick, Jr., Anne Daladier, Tzvee N. Harris, and Suzanna Harris. Preface by Hilary Putnam. Boston: Kluwer Academic Publishers, xvii, 590 pp.

1990. "La genèse de l'analyse des transformations et de la métalangue." *Langages* 99 (1990): 9–19.

1991. *A Theory of Language and Information: A mathematical approach*. Oxford: Clarendon Press.

1997. *The Transformation of Capitalist Society*. Baltimore: Rowman and Littlefield. Published posthumously.

Appendix: Appraisals of Zellig S. Harris, 1962–1993[2]

Anders Georg. 1984. "Feiert Chomsky, aber vergesst Harris nicht: Zur Entwicklung eines Abschnittes der neueren Sprachwissenschaftsgeschichte." *Grazer Linguistische Studien* 21:5–16. Graz/Austria.

Bar-Hillel, Yehoshua. 1964. *Language and Information*. Reading, MA.: Addison-Wesley Publishing Company.

Bar-Hillel, Yehoshua. 1970. *Aspects of Language*. Jerusalem: The Magnes Press.

Brykczyński, Piotr. 1989. "On Some Grammatical Ideas of Zellig S. Harris." *Studies in Logic, Grammar and Rhetoric*, vol. VIII: 97–123, edited by Halina Święczkowska. Bialystok: Warsaw University, Humanities Section 14: Logic, 159 pp. [Apropos of Harris (1982).]

Catell, N. R. 1962. "The Syntactic Procedures of Z. S. Harris." *Language and Speech* 5:159–169.

Corcoran, John. 1972. "Harris on the Structure of Language" edited by Plötz, (1972): 275–292.

Daladier, Anne. 1980. "Quelques hypotheses 'explicatives' chez Harris et chez Chomsky." *Langue Française* 46:58–72.

Daladier, Anne. 1990a. "Aspects constructifs des grammaires de Harris." *Langages* 99 (1990): 57–84.

Daladier, Anne. 1990b. "Une représentation applicative des enoncés et de leurs dérivations." Ibid., 92–127.

Déscles, Jean-Pierre. 1977. "Un modèle mathématique d'analyse transformationnelle selon Z. S. Harris." *Computational and Mathematical Linguistics: Proceedings of the International Conference on Computational Linguistics* (Pisa 1973), edited by Antonio Zampolli and N. Calzolari, 23–27. Florence: Olschi.

Dominicy, Marc. 1978. "Deux théories convergentes des propositions relatives: Port-Royal et Z. S. Harris." *Linguistics in Belgium / Linguistiek in Belgë / Linguistique en Belgique,* edited by Sera de Vriendt and Christian Peeters, vol. II:44–64. Brussels: V.U.B./Didier.

Dougherty, Ray C[roll]. 1975. "Harris and Chomsky at the Syntax-Semantics Boundary." *Contemporary Research in Philosophical Logic and Linguistic Semantics: Proceedings of a conference held at the University of Western Ontario, London, Canada* [in 1973], edited by D[onald] J[ames] Hockney, William Harper and (Robert) B[ruce] Freed, 137–193. Dordrecht/Holland: D. Reidel.

Eytan, Michel. 1988[1987]. "Ambiguity and Paraphrase in Harris's Theory via a Formal Model." *L'Ambiguïté et la paraphrase: Opérations linguistiques, processus cognitifs, traitements automatisés: Actes du Colloque de Caen,* 9–11 avril [1987], publié sous la direction de Catherine Fuchs, 199–203. Caen: University de Caen. [French summary.]

Fuchs, Catherine. 1986. "Z. Harris, ou l'énonciation esquivée." *Histoire-Épistémologie-Langage* 8, no.2: 221–231. [With French and English summaries.]

Fuchs, Catherine and Pierre Le Goffic. 1992. "Du distributionalisme au transformationnalisme: Harris et Gross." *Les Linguistiques contemporaines: Repères théoriques,* edited by C. Fuchs and P. Le Goffic 53–69. Paris: Hachette.

Gross, Maurice. 1990. "Sur la notion harrissienne de transformation et son application au français": *Langages* 99 (1990): 39–56.

Hymes, Dell, and Fought, John. 1981. *American Structuralism.* The Hague: Mouton Publishers.

Ihwe, Jens F. 1981. "Textanalyse und Textgrammatik: Der Beitrag von Zellig S. Harris." *Text vs. Sentence: Continued,* edited by János Pesöfi, 127–133. Hamburg: Helmut Buske.

Itkonen, Esa. 1978. "Grammatical Theory and Metascience: A Critical Investigation into the Methodological and Philosophical Implications of 'Autonomous' Linguistics," In *Current Issues in Linguistic Theory* vol. 5. Amsterdam: John Benjamins.

Kuroda, S. 1989. *Derivational and geometric conceptions of grammar: Reflections on Harris and Chomsky.* Unpublished manuscript.

Leeman, Danielle. 1973. "Distributionnalisme et structuralisme." *Langages* 29:6–42. [Presentation of Harris's procedures, notably as stated in Harris (1973a).]

Lentin, André. 1990a. "Quelques réflexions sur les references mathématiques dans l'œuvre de Zellig Harris." *Langages* 99 (1990): 85–91.

Martin, Richard M. 1976. "On Harris' Systems of Report and Paraphrase." *Language in Focus: Foundations, methods, and systems. Essays in memory of Yehoshua Bar-Hillel,* edited by Asa Kasher, 541–568. Dordrecht/Holland: D. Reidel. [On Harris (1969a).]

Matthews, P.H. 1986. *Grammatical Theory in the United States from Bloomfield to Chomsky.* Cambridge: Cambridge University Press. Munz, James. 1972. "Reflections on the Development of Transformational Theories." Plötz, editor, (1972): 251–274.

Nevin, Bruce E. 1993a. "A Minimalist Program for Linguistics: The work of Zellig Harris on meaning and information." *Historiographia Linguistica,* 20:2–3, 355–398.

Nevin, Bruce E. 1993b. "Does Harris assume the tradition?" *CWSL*10:31–32.

Nevin, Bruce E. 1993c. "What Harris assumes." *CWSL* 10:34–34.

Newmeyer, Frederick J. 1980. *Linguistic Theory in America: The first quarter-century of transformational generative grammar.* New York: Academic Press.

Paillet, Jean-Pierre. 1972. "Structural Linguistics and the Notion of Transformatton." Plötz, editor: 293–306. [On the development of Harris' theory of an 'operator-syntax'.]

Parret, Herman. 1974. *Discussing Language.* Mouton: The Hague.

[Tröml-]Plötz, Senta. 1972. "Einführung in die Transformationstheorie von Zellig Harris / Introduction to the Transformational Theory of Zellig Harris." Plötz, editor: 1–52. [Bilingual text on facing pages, with German text on verso; bib. (p.51).]

Tröml-]Plötz, Senta, Editor, 1972. *Transformationelle Analyse: Die*

Transformationstheorie von Zellig Harris und ihre Entwicklung/ Transformational Analysis. The transformational theory of Zellig Harris and its development. Frankfurt: Athenäum-Verlag. [Collection of (at times previously published) articles, especially by Harris himself and by reviewers of his work, but also containing original contributions such as those by Corcoran, Munz, and others, each preceded by a bilingual introduction written by the editor]

Putnam, Hilary. 1975. *Mind, Language and Reality, Philosophical Papers, Volume 2.* Cambridge: Cambridge University Press.

Ryckman, Thomas Alan. 1986. *Grammar and Information: An*

Investigation in Linguistic Metatheory. Unpublished Ph.D. dissertation, Columbia University, New York, [Codirector: Zellig S. Harris.]

Ryckman, Thomas (Alan). 1990. "De la structure d'une langue aux structures de l'information dans le discours et dans les sous-langages scientifiques." *Langages* 99 (1990): 21–38.

Ryckman, Thomas Alan. 1991. *Zellig Harris' Methodology of Language and Information.* Lecture, Boston Colloquium for the Philosophy of Science, October 8, 1991.

Wunderlich, Dieter. 1979. *Foundations of Linguistics.* Cambridge University Press. Cambridge.

Yngve, Victor H. 1993a. "Bloomfield, Harris, and the phonetic-phonological distinction." *CWSL* 10:32–34.

Yngve, Victor H. 1993b. "Harris, Bloomfield, and the Tradition." *CWSL* 10:34–36.

Notes

For information on a variety of details, the compiler is obliged to Fedor M. Berezin (Moscow), Gregory M. Eramian (London, Ont.), Michael Gottfried (St. Louis, Mo.), Henry Hiz (Philadelphia), Bruce E. Nevin (Boston), and Zsigmond Telegdi (Budapest). Several pre-1939 entries are due to the kind offices of Henry M. Hoenigswald (Philadelphia), who sent me a copy of his list of Harris' publications which he had compiled for *Language.*

1. Also reprinted in *Readings in Linguistics* [1]: *The development of descriptive linguistics in America since 1925* [in later editions: 1925–56], edited by Martin Joos (Washington, D.C.: American Council of Learned Societies, 1957, 4th ed., Chicago: University of Chicago Press, 1966), pp.109–115. In this volume are reprinted three more papers by Harris on pp.124–138 (1944b), 142–153 (1946a), and 272–274 (1948). Each paper has a postscript by Joos added.

2. The journal *Langages* (Paris) published as late as September 1990, as its number 99, an issue titled "Les grammaires de Harris et leurs questions," containing the following articles (listed below)—in addition to Harris (1990)—which are of relevance here: Daladier (1990a, b), Gross (1990), Lentin (1990), Ryckman (1990). The present list is a rather restricted one focusing on publications with direct reference

to Harris; however, for a more adequate picture of Harris's direct influence on twentieth-century linguistic thought, the work of not only Noam Chomsky but also that of many other scholars should be consulted, such as Henry Hiz, Aravind K. Joshi, Ellen Prince, and others associated with the University of Pennsylvania, as well as Ralph Grishmann, Richard Kittredge, Naomi Sager, along with many others who came under his influence during Harris's years at Columbia University in New York from around 1980 onward. A list of Harris's former MA (e.g., John Robert Ross in 1964) and PhD (e.g., Noam Chomsky in 1955) students would perhaps be helpful, too, for historiography of North American linguistics in the mid-twentieth century.

Index